Plant Bacterial Diseases

sponsored by:
AUSTRALASIAN PLANT PATHOLOGY SOCIETY

Plant Bacterial Diseases
A Diagnostic Guide

Edited by

P. C. Fahy

Biological and Chemical Research Institute
Department of Agriculture New South Wales

G. J. Persley

Australian Centre for International Agricultural Research

ACADEMIC PRESS

A Subsidiary of Harcourt Brace Jovanovich, Publishers

Sydney   New York   London
Paris   San Diego   San Francisco   São Paulo   Tokyo   Toronto
1983

ACADEMIC PRESS AUSTRALIA
Centrecourt, 25–27 Paul Street North
North Ryde, N.S.W. 2113

United States Edition published by
ACADEMIC PRESS INC.
111 Fifth Avenue
New York, New York 10003

United Kingdom Edition published by
ACADEMIC PRESS, INC. (LONDON) LTD.
24/28 Oval Road, London NW1 7DX

Printed in Australia

National Library of Australia Cataloguing-in-Publication Data

Plant bacterial diseases.

  Bibliography.
  Includes index.
  ISBN 0 12 247660 3.

  1. Bacterial diseases of plants. I. Fahy, P. C.
  (Peter Christopher). II. Persley, G. J. (Gabrielle
  Josephine).

581.2'3

Library of Congress Catalog Card Number: 83-70713

Academic Press Rapid Manuscript Reproduction

Contents

List of Contributors   xi

Foreword   xiii

Preface   xv

Acknowledgements   xvii

1   Preliminary Diagnosis of Plant Diseases Caused by Bacteria   1

A. C. Hayward

    1.   Introduction   1
    II.   Symptoms and Collection of Diseased Material   3
    III.   Microscopic Examination   4
    IV.   General Isolation Procedures   5
    V.   Selective Culture Media   7
    VI.   Plant Inoculation Tests   10
      References   11

2   Primary Differentiation of the Genera of Plant Pathogenic Bacteria   13

A. C. Hayward

    I.   Introduction   13
    II.   Colony Characteristics and Pigments   14
    III.   Gram Reaction   15
    IV.   Motility and Flagellation   18
    V.   Initial Screening of Yellow-pigmented Bacteria   20
    VI.   Differentiation of Genera Associated with Soft Rot in Plants   21
    VII.   Key Characteristics Used in Generic Differentiation   24
      References   25

3 *Agrobacterium*   27
  A. Kerr and P. G. Brisbane

    I.   Introduction   27
    II. Crown Gall   28
    III. Hairy Root   39
         References   41

4 *Corynebacterium*   45
  M. L. Moffett, P. C. Fahy and D. Cartwright

    I.   Introduction   45
    II. *Corynebacterium michiganense* subsp. *michiganense*: Bacterial
         Canker of Tomato and Capsicum   46
    III. *Corynebacterium michiganense* subsp. *insidiosum*: Bacterial
         Wilt of Lucerne   51
    IV. *Corynebacterium michiganense* subsp. *sepedonicum*: Ring Rot
         of Potato   54
    V.   *Corynebacterium flaccumfaciens* subsp. *flaccumfaciens*:
         Bacterial Wilt of Bean   55
    VI. *Corynebacterium* sp. Causing Annual Ryegrass Toxicity   57
         References   61

5 *Erwinia*: The "Amylovora" and "Herbicola" Groups   67
  D. W. Dye

    I.   Introduction   67
    II. Isolation   68
    III. Identification   69
    IV. The "Amylovora" Group   75
    V.   The "Herbicola" Group   80
         References   83

6 *Erwinia*: The "Carotovora" Group   87
  E. J. Cother and K. Sivasithamparam

    I.   Introduction   87
    II. Isolation   89
    III. Identification   93
    IV. Bacterial Soft Rot of Potato   95
         References   101

7   *Pseudomonas*: The Non-Fluorescent Pseudomonads   107

A. C. Hayward

    I.   Introduction   108
    II.   *Pseudomonas amygdali*: Hyperplastic Bacterial Canker of Almond   109
    III.   *Pseudomonas andropogonis*: Leaf Spot of Clover and Velvet Bean and Bacterial Stripe of Sorghum   113
    IV.   *Pseudomonas avenae*: Leaf Blight of Cereals   118
    V.   *Pseudomonas caryophylli*: Bacterial Wilt of Carnation   119
    VI.   *Pseudomonas cattleyae*: Brown Spot of Orchids   119
    VII.   *Pseudomonas cepacia*: Sour Skin of Onion   120
    VIII.   *Pseudomonas cissicola*: Bacterial Leaf Spot of *Cayratia japonica*   121
    IX.   *Pseudomonas corrugata*: Tomato Pith Necrosis   121
    X.   *Pseudomonas gladioli*: Leaf Spot and Corm Scab of Gladiolus and Soft Rot of Onion   122
    XI.   *Pseudomonas maltophilia*: Saprophyte   123
    XII.   *Pseudomonas mesophilica*: Saprophyte   123
    XIII.   *Pseudomonas paucimobilis*: Saprophyte   124
    XIV.   *Pseudomonas pseudoalcaligenes* subsp. *citrulli*: Bacterial Spot of Watermelon   124
    XV.   *Pseudomonas rubrilineans*: Red Stripe and Top Rot of Sugarcane   124
    XVI.   *Pseudomonas rubrisubalbicans*: Mottled Stripe of Sugarcane and Leaf Stripe of Sorghum   127
    XVII.   *Pseudomonas setariae* (inv.): Bacterial Stripe of Rice   128
    XVIII.   *Pseudomonas solanacearum*: Bacterial Wilt and Moko Disease   129
      References   135

8   *Pseudomonas*: The Fluorescent Pseudomonads   141

P. C. Fahy and A. B. Lloyd

    I.   Introduction   141
    II.   LOPAT Grouping and Identification   142
    III.   Group I Pathogens: The *Pseudomonas syringae* Pathovars   142
    IV.   Group II Pathogens   169
    V.   Group III Pathogens   171
    VI.   Group IV Pathogens   173
    VII.   Group V Pathogens   174
    VIII.   Ungrouped Pathogenic Species   176
      References   178

9 *Xanthomonas*   189
   M. J. Moffett and B. J. Croft
       I. Introduction   189
      II. Isolation and Identification   190
     III. *Xanthomonas campestris* Pathovars   192
      IV. *Xanthomonas albilineans*: Leaf Scald of Sugarcane   217
       V. *Xanthomonas ampelina*: Bacterial Blight of Grapevine   220
      VI. *Xanthomonas axonopodis*: Gummosis of Imperial Pasture
           Grass   220
     VII. *Xanthomonas fragariae*: Angular Leaf Spot of Strawberry 221
    VIII. *Xanthomonas populi* (inv.): Bacterial Canker of Poplar   222
           References   222

10 Mollicutes and Rickettsia-like Bacteria in Plants   229
    G. M. Behncken
       I. Introduction   229
      II. Discovery of MLO and RLO as Plant Pathogens   230
     III. Taxonomy of Plant MLO and RLO   231
      IV. Diagnostic Characteristics   232
       V. Control   242
           References   243

11 The Sugarcane Ratoon Stunting Disease Bacterium   247
    D. S. Teakle
       I. Introduction   247
      II. Symptoms   248
     III. Host Range   248
      IV. Geographical Distribution and Importance   250
       V. Diagnosis   250
      VI. Isolation   251
     VII. Characteristics of the Bacterium   252
    VIII. Control Measures   254
           References   255

12 Bacteriophages for the Identification of Plant
    Pathogenic Bacteria   259
    G. J. Persley
        I.   Introduction   259
        II. Specificity of Bacteriophages   260
        III. Methodology   261
        IV. Diagnostic Use of Bacteriophages   265
        V.   Detection of Plant Pathogenic Bacteria   268
        VI. Conclusion   269
             References   270

13 Preservation of Microbial Cultures   275
    L. I. Sly
        I.   Introduction   275
        II.   Choice of Method   276
        III. Periodic Subculture   277
        IV.   Preservation by Freeze-Drying   277
        V.   Preservation by Liquid Drying   283
        VI.   Cryogenic Storage   284
        VII. Storage under Mineral Oil   287
        VIII. Preservation in Sterile Soil   289
        IX.   Storage in Sterile Distilled Water   290
        X.   Preservation on Porcelain Beads   291
        XI.   Preservation in Gelatin Discs   292
        XII. Preservation over Phosphorus Pentoxide *in vacuo* 293
        XIII. Conclusion: The Role of Culture Collections   294
              References   295

14 Valid Names of Plant Pathogenic Bacteria   299
    Compiled by M. L. Moffett and D. W. Dye
        I.   Introduction   299
        II. *Agrobacterium*   301
        III. *Corynebacterium*   301
        IV. *Erwinia*   302
        V.   *Pseudomonas*   302
        VI. *Xanthomonas*   302
             References   314

15 Bacterial Plant Pathogens Recorded in Australia 317
Compiled by M. L. Moffett

    I. Introduction 317
    II. Explanation of Text Symbols 318
    III. *Agrobacterium* 319
    IV. *Corynebacterium* 320
    V. *Erwinia* 321
    VI. *Pseudomonas* 323
    VII. *Streptomyces* 330
    VIII. *Xanthomonas* 330
    IX. Undetermined Bacterial Pathogens 334
    X. Organisms Currently Unnamed 334
    References 336

16 Media and Methods for Isolation and Diagnostic Tests 337
Compiled by P. C. Fahy and A. C. Hayward

    I. Introduction 337
    II. General Test Procedures 338
    III. Morphological Features 338
    IV. The Gram Reaction 341
    V. Non-selective Isolation Media 344
    VI. General Growth and Maintenance Media 345
    VII. Selective Isolation Media 347
    VIII. Utilization and Decomposition of Carbon Compounds 350
    IX. Decomposition of Nitrogenous Compounds 355
    X. Decomposition of Macromolecules 358
    XI. Other Physiological and Biochemical Tests 360
    XII. Toxin Bioassays 363
    XIII. Hypersensitivity in Tobacco 366
    XIV. Diagnostic Tests Using Excised Plant Tissues 368
    XV. Pathogenicity Tests 371
    References 374

Index of Bacteria 379

Subject Index 385

Contributors

Numbers in parentheses indicate the pages on which the authors' contributions begin.

G. M. Behncken (229), Plant Pathology Branch, Department of Primary Industries Queensland, Meirs Road, Indooroopilly, Queensland 4068, Australia

P. G. Brisbane (27), Department of Plant Pathology, Waite Agricultural Research Institute, University of Adelaide, Glen Osmond, South Australia 5064, Australia

D. Cartwright (45), Plant Pathology Unit, Department of Agriculture South Australia, GPO Box 1671, Adelaide, South Australia 5001, Australia

E. J. Cother (87), Department of Agriculture New South Wales, Yanco Agricultural Centre, Private Mail Bag, Yanco, New South Wales 2703, Australia

B. J. Croft (189), Bureau of Sugar Experiment Stations, Tully, Queensland 4854, Australia

D. W. Dye (67, 299), Plant Diseases Division, Department of Scientific and Industrial Research, Private Bag, Auckland, New Zealand

P. C. Fahy (45, 141, 337), Department of Agriculture New South Wales, Biological and Chemical Research Institute, Rydalmere, New South Wales 2116, Australia

A. C. Hayward (1, 13, 107, 337), Department of Microbiology, University of Queensland, St Lucia, Queensland 4067, Australia

A. Kerr (27), Department of Plant Pathology, Waite Agricultural Research Institute, University of Adelaide, Glen Osmond, South Australia 5064, Australia

A. B. Lloyd (141), Department of Microbiology, The University of New England, Armidale, New South Wales 2305, Australia

M. L. Moffett (45, 189, 299, 317), Plant Pathology Branch, Department of Primary Industries Queensland, Meirs Road, Indooroopilly, Queensland 4068, Australia

G. J. Persley (259), Australian Centre for International Agricultural Research, P.O. Box 1571, Canberra, Australian Capital Territory 2601, Australia

K. Sivasithamparam (87), Department of Soil Science, University of Western Australia, Nedlands, Western Australia 6009, Australia

L. I. Sly (275), Department of Microbiology, University of Queensland, St Lucia, Queensland 4067, Australia

D. S. Teakle (247), Department of Microbiology, University of Queensland, St Lucia, Queensland 4067, Australia

Foreword

This book deals primarily with the isolation and identification of bacterial plant pathogens and with descriptions of the diseases they cause. The two most recent books on these topics are *Bacterial Plant Pathogens* by C. Stapp and *Plant Diseases Due to Bacteria* by W. J. Dowson, published in 1961 and 1957 respectively. Since then much new knowledge has accumulated and the classification and nomenclature of plant pathogenic bacteria have been changed radically. Clearly, there is great need for a new book. This one should prove useful to any persons, be they extension workers, professional plant pathologists, students, lecturers or research workers, who have dealings with plant diseases caused by bacteria.

All the authors live in Australia or New Zealand and, inevitably, bacterial pathogens which occur in these countries are treated in more detail than those few which have not yet reached here. I trust you will find that no important disease, wherever it occurs, has been omitted.

The 4th International Congress of Plant Pathology held in Melbourne in August 1983 was an important incentive to proceed with the book, for it seemed appropriate that a book by Australian and New Zealand plant pathologists should be launched at an international congress held in Australia. It certainly influenced the decision of the executive of the Australasian Plant Pathology Society to sponsor the book. As President of that Society, I have much pleasure in introducing you to *Plant Bacterial Diseases: A Diagnostic Guide*. I am confident it will fill a major gap in the plant pathology literature.

A. Kerr, F.A.A.
PROFESSOR OF PLANT PATHOLOGY

Preface

The Australasian Plant Pathology Society Workshop "Detection and Diagnosis of Bacterial Plant Pathogens", held in Brisbane in 1982, was the catalyst for the production of this book. The organizing committee suggested that a guide to diagnosis was needed and that the participants' experience in bacterial plant pathology could provide the basis for this book. Inevitably the undertaking was far more complicated than anticipated and the editors thank the authors for their contributions to this practical diagnostic guide.

The first chapter introduces the reader to the rationale and basic techniques for diagnosing plant bacterial diseases. Chapter 2 describes how the major groups of pathogens are differentiated and each group is treated in detail in Chapters 3–11. Each chapter is well illustrated and describes the symptoms, host range, identification, importance and distribution of the major bacterial diseases. Chapters 10 and 11 discuss the difficult to culture, or yet uncultured, prokaryotes.

Later chapters deal with methods for the identification and preservation of bacterial pathogens, including the use of bacteriophages for identification (Chapter 12) and short-term and long-term preservation of microorganisms (Chapter 13). Chapter 16 is a compilation of media and methods used in this book for the isolation and identification of bacterial plant pathogens.

The nomenclature of bacterial pathogens is discussed and all currently valid names are listed (Chapter 14). Major synonyms are listed where necessary in the text and are included in the "Index of Bacteria". Chapter 15 details a host/pathogen index for Australia that includes distribution of each pathogen, presence of herbarium specimens and cultures and notes on the accuracy of some published records.

Scientific and common names used in this text are from W. Hartley, *A Checklist of Economic Plants in Australia* (Melbourne: C.S.I.R.O., 1979) or from *Hortus Third* (New York: Macmillan, 1976).

Preface

Acknowledgements

The editors thank the following: D. W. Dye, A. C. Hayward and A. Kerr for their assistance in reading many of the chapters and for their helpful suggestions; S. Navaratnam who provided much useful information on plant diseases of quarantine significance in Australia; R. Ikin, J. Cahill and J. Bradley for assistance in preparation of the manuscript.

Some illustrations are acknowledged in the text. The following illustrations were provided by: Department of Agriculture New South Wales (Figs 2.4, 4.1, 4.2, 6.2(a), 6.3, 6.4(a), 7.1(b), 7.2(b), 7.5(b), 8.1(b), 8.2(b), 8.3(a), 8.4, 8.5, 8.6(b), 8.7, 8.8(b), 8.9(b), 8.10, 8.11(b), 9.1, 9.2, 9.4, 9.5, 9.6(a), 9.10, 9.11, 9.14); Department of Primary Industries Queensland (6.1(b), 7.1(a), 7.2(a), 8.2(a), 8.3(b), 8.6(a), 8.9(a), 8.11(a), 9.3, 9.6(b), 9.9, 9.12, 10.1, 10.2, 10.3, 10.5, 10.6); University of Queensland (7.3, 7.4, 7.5(a), 11.1(a)); Bureau of Sugar Experiment Stations, Queensland (6.2(b), 9.13, 11.1(b)); Victorian Department of Agriculture (6.1(a), 8.1(a), 8.8(a)); New Zealand Department of Scientific and Industrial Research (5.1, 5.2); University of Adelaide (3.1, 3.2, 3.3); South Australian Department of Agriculture (4.4); Western Australian Department of Agriculture (6.4(b)); Department of Primary Production Northern Territory (9.8); G. Persley (9.7). Mr Max Hill, Department of Agriculture New South Wales prepared the jacket illustration and many of the illustrations and reproductions in the text. His assistance is greatly acknowledged.

1

Preliminary Diagnosis of Plant Diseases
Caused by Bacteria
A. C. Hayward

I.	Introduction	1
II.	Symptoms and Collection of Diseased Material	3
III.	Microscopic Examination	4
IV.	General Isolation Procedures	5
V.	Selective Culture Media	7
VI.	Plant Inoculation Tests	10
	References	11

I. Introduction

The rationale for diagnosis is that a plant abnormality cannot always be diagnosed solely on symptoms. Similar pathological conditions may be caused by quite different agents. There are bacterial soft rots and fungal soft rots, insect galls and bacterial galls, fungal wilts and bacterial wilts. Bacterial soft rots may be primarily associated with species of either <u>Pseudomonas</u> or <u>Erwinia.</u> There are several examples of plant hosts affected by different bacterial diseases, which are not invariably distinct and differentiable on the basis of symptoms alone. There are, for example, various bean blights, leaf and fruit spots of tomato, and stripes or streaks of sugar cane, maize, sorghum and rice which require isolation and identification of the pathogen for correct diagnosis.

Time and resource factors will limit the amount of diagnostic work that can be undertaken. A distinction can be made between the requirements for a rapid presumptive diagnosis and the requirements for a confirmatory diagnosis. In the plant disease clinic, the needs of the horticulturist or farmer are paramount, and a rapid presumptive diagnosis

PLANT BACTERIAL DISEASES
ISBN 0 12 247660 3

is required.   Those observations should be made which can provide a correct presumptive diagnosis so that appropriate control methods can be recommended.   A further set of observations may be required to achieve a confirmatory diagnosis, particularly in situations were there is a new host or pathogen.   In these instances accuracy of diagnosis is essential for purposes of disease lists and distribution maps, as well as quarantine and other regulatory aspects of plant disease control. The requirements are most demanding of all where a new disease and new pathogen are described. At this level the requirements of adequate description and characterization are those of the taxonomist, and the resources required are beyond the scope of most diagnostic laboratories.   Although there are not yet international standards for the characterization of a new species, there are such standards for the naming of pathovars of phytopathogenic bacteria (Dye et al., 1980).

Viewed in this light, diagnosis is a three stage process in which first stage criteria satisfy the requirements of preliminary, presumptive diagnosis and the immediate needs of the grower; second stage criteria satisfy the requirement for accurate identification and the long term need for accuracy in disease lists, for example; and third stage criteria are needed for the description of new diseases and pathogens in order to satisfy the requirements and standards of the scientific community.

There is no clear cut distinction between the criteria at the different levels of investigation; the amount that can be done will depend on the circumstances of the individual worker or laboratory.   Accurate diagnosis is essential if the grower is to be helped effectively, and without accurate second and third level work there will be, in the long term, confusion, errors, loss and waste. Many disease lists are based on observations of symptoms alone, and are not supported by isolation and characterization studies.   In some cases it will be necessary to collaborate with workers specializing in taxonomic work on the disease-causing organisms themselves in order to achieve correct identification.

This chapter is concerned with diagnosis of bacterial diseases of plants in which there are leaf spots, stripes or blights, gall formations, soft rots or vascular wilts, caused by readily cultivable bacteria of the genera <u>Pseudomonas</u>, <u>Xanthomonas</u>, <u>Agrobacterium</u>, <u>Erwinia</u> or <u>Corynebacterium</u>. Diagnosis of conditions caused by the so-called new agents of plant disease, including the bacterium associated with ratoon stunting disease of sugar cane, the mycoplasma-like organisms associated with yellows disease conditions, Spiroplasma, and the bacterium associated with Pierce's disease of grapevines, and similar agents, are dealt with elsewhere in this volume.

II. Symptoms and Collection of Diseased Material

A full record of disease symptoms is the starting point of correct diagnosis. Accurate identification of the host is also essential. Certain well known text books (Smith, 1920; Elliott, 1951; Dowson, 1957; and Stapp, 1961) and numerous original papers will give a lead as to which pathogens are most likely to be involved in particular disease conditions. Photographs and/or herbarium specimens are often worthwhile for future reference.

Disease specimens are rarely examined immediately after collection in the field. The condition in which they are stored and transported may affect the success of isolation. Specimens of most diseased material intended for laboratory diagnosis should be placed in polythene bags without delay. However, material stored in polythene should be kept in a cool container which is not exposed to direct sunlight. Polythene creates a humid environment in which overheating may occur if exposure to strong sunlight is prolonged, accompanied by multiplication of unwanted saprophytes in surface films of moisture. Material should be partially dried rather than wet.

The collections of the diseased material should be representative of all the signs and symptoms of a disease, whether involving stems, roots, flowers or fruit. In the case of root-invading pathogens, part of the collection of stems and roots should be washed free from soil and excess moisture removed before dispatch; a second portion of root material should be kept separate with adhering soil attached in case isolations are to be made from soil. A polythene bag should be tied firmly round the base of the stem to prevent soiling of the rest of the plant. The earliest stages of the disease should always be included where they are present in the crop because the pathogen is usually isolated more readily from such plant material. In the case of diseases affecting the foliage this means lesions which are still water-soaked in appearance and which appear translucent when held to the light, rather than lesions which are brown and necrotic. Material of cankers and shoot die-back should always include the edge of the lesion and a few cm of the healthy tissue beyond it.

Pressed and dried specimens of leaf spots and blights should always be retained for use as herbarium material and also as a reference source.   Many bacterial pathogens survive for periods of months to many years in dried material stored at room temperature and such collections can serve as a future source of isolates of bacterial pathogens. In certain cases pressed, dried material is an alternative to such other methods as freeze-drying for preservation of bacterial pathogens.   Most xanthomonads (e.g. Xanthomonas campestris pv. malvacearum, from cotton and X. campestris pv. manihotis, from cassava) retain viability in dried material for periods greater than one year.

III.   Microscopic Examination

Before any attempt at isolation is made, the specimens should be examined for gross signs of bacterial infection. Dried exudation scales of bacterial ooze may be found on the undersurface of leaf lesions or on the surface of stems and petioles.   If the freshly infected material is incubated in a moist specimen dish for several days, drops of bacterial ooze may be observed on lesions. Freshly dug potato tubers affected by bacterial wilt caused by Pseudomonas solanacearum should be examined for the presence of soil adhering to the eyes from which bacterial ooze has emerged. On standing, ooze is frequently observed at the stolon end of the tuber.

In the case of leaf spots or stripes, small portions (3-4mm) of material should be cut out from the boundary between diseased and healthy tissue and mounted in a little water under a coverslip on a microscope slide. The cut edge of the leaf lesion should be examined at X100 and X400 magnification, ideally under phase, but ordinary 4 and 16 mm objectives can be used if the aperture is stopped down. In fresh, undried material bacterial ooze will flow freely and immediately, whereas in old or dried material ooze will be slow to egress from the cut edge. Almost all bacterial pathogens are motile with flagella and in fresh material, bacteria in the ooze may be observed to be actively motile.

Bacterial oozes differ in character with different pathogens. It is usually observed that the bacterial masses from tissues invaded by a xanthomonad are more tightly coherent than those in which pseudomonads are involved, even in freshly collected material. However, there are pseudomonads which give oozes of comparable integrity on suspension in water.

In bacterial diseases of plants (except those caused by agrobacteria) there is almost invariably ooze or streaming of bacterial masses from cut lesions; more rarely the ooze may be sparse and indistinct. The absence of demonstrable ooze suggests that bacteria are not involved, but this is not a completely reliable criterion. If a fungus is involved, fructifications may be observed under the microscope or with a hand lens.

Under the microscope, great care must be taken not to confuse other particulate material such as latex, plastids or starch granules with bacteria. Usually there are consistent differences in size, morphology or refractility under phase contrast which prevent confusion. However, bacteria from lesions may be smaller and of more irregular morphology than those observed in culture.

IV. General Isolation Procedures

When the presence of bacterial ooze has been confirmed, a second portion of diseased material is cut from the specimen using sterile implements and suspended in 2-3 ml of sterile distilled water, phosphate buffered saline or a dilute nutrient medium. The portions of diseased material are allowed to diffuse at room temperature for 30-60 min and loopfuls of the resulting suspension then streaked on a suitable agar medium.

It is essential for the surface of the medium to be dry, otherwise motile bacteria will swim in the surface moisture and a carpet of mixed growth will result instead of discrete, well-separated colonies. If the medium is cooled to about 45C before pouring and the set plates kept at an even room temperature, their surfaces usually dry in 24-48 h. Open plates may also be dried by placing them for 15-20 min in an incubator at 37-40C with the agar facing down on to the inverted lid. Open plates left in a laminar flow apparatus will dry in about 15 min.

After streaking, the plates should be incubated at a temperature of 25-30C for all the plant pathogens except the corynebacteria. Most corynebacteria have a slightly lower optimum temperature and 23-25C is more suitable. The plates should be examined daily for the appearance of bacterial colonies. There are some marked differences in growth rates amongst the different bacteria present in plants, which serve as a guide in diagnosis. Almost invariably the common saprophytes grow faster than the plant pathogens. In most cases bacteria which produce clearly macroscopic colonies after 24-36 h at 25-28C should be disregarded as they are likely to be saprophytes.

There are also differences in growth rate amongst the plant pathogens. Most pseudomonads and xanthomonads produce macroscopic colonies within 36-72 h at optimum temperature, the exceptions being the slow-growing xanthomonads, X. albilineans, X. ampelina and X. fragariae, which require 4-14 days at optimum temperature before isolated macroscopic colonies are visible. If any such pathogens are suspected, the plates should be examined daily under a dissecting microscope at a magnification of x 15-30 for the presence of slow growing colonies between the larger colonies of the common saprophytes, in the pool of inoculum and along the streak marks. If the material from which the suspension was prepared was fresh and in good condition, colonies of the pathogen will predominate on the isolation plate.

Older, diseased plant material is commonly invaded by a succession of saprophytic fungi and bacteria including the ubiquitous Erwinia herbicola and sometimes fluorescent pseudomonads. E. herbicola usually produces a slimy mucoid growth with a yellow or orange non-diffusible pigment; these are features which have frequently led in inexperienced hands to confusion with xanthomonads. Several diseases have been erroneously attributed to E. herbicola.

Material which has been left in a wet condition after collection may carry numerous saprophytes which are likely to overgrow slower growing pathogenic bacteria. In such cases it may be necessary to use a selective medium, or to prepare several dilutions from the original suspension, so that both pathogens and saprophytes are less numerous and therefore more readily separated by streaking on isolation plates. Densely opaque suspensions should be diluted to 1:100 or 1:1000 in fresh quantities of sterile suspending medium or simply by transferring a 3 mm diameter loopful of the original suspension to fresh medium.

An alternative method, which is more economical in the use of glassware, is somewhat similar to the method used by mycologists to isolate plant pathogenic fungi. A small portion of plant tissue is placed on an agar plate near the edge. A drop of sterile water is added and allowed to stand for 15-30 min. The liquid is then streaked over the agar surface to separate the bacteria in the drop on the plate.

The objective of suspending diseased material in a suitable liquid prior to streaking is to allow the bacteria to separate from the dead plant cells among which they are embedded. This process may be enhanced by teasing apart the tissue in a little sterile suspending medium in a petri dish with sterile needles, or by grinding the tissue into small fragments with a sterile pestle and mortar.

Surface sterilization is only practised rarely in the isolation of bacterial plant pathogens, unless the surface is water repellent as in the case of leaves of sugar cane, because the chemicals used in sterilization may be rapidly absorbed by the plant tissue and be lethal to bacteria contained within it. The material may be immersed in 0.5% sodium hypochlorite solution for 2 min and then rinsed in sterile water. However, it is usually better to wash leaf surfaces in running tap water prior to excision of infected tissue rather than to use surface sterilization procedures.

Goth (1965) has also described a needle-puncture method for bean pathogens which may have wider application. A sterile needle is pushed through the margin of a young leaf lesion on to a suitable agar medium, the needle being forced through the lesion and then onward to make a stab into the agar. For isolations from thick pods and mature stems, the needle is used to pierce the lesion, withdrawn and then pricked into the agar. Drops of sterile water may then be added to the stab marks prior to streaking on the plates.

V. Selective Culture Media

The isolation of plant pathogenic bacteria from soil, decomposing plant material or advanced lesions is usually difficult because of the presence of a mixed population of saprophytic bacteria. Saprophytes usually grow faster than phytopathogenic bacteria and may create an unfavourable environment for plant pathogens in isolation media through competition for nutrients, production of an adverse pH or exertion of an antibiotic effect. These problems can be overcome through selective media, which exclude unwanted saprophytes while permitting the growth of the pathogen. Their effectiveness depends on the percentage recovery of low populations of the pathogen mixed with a greatly predominant soil microflora.

TABLE 1.1   *Non-Selective Media Recommended for Isolation of Plant Pathogenic Bacteria*

Species	Media[a]	References
Agrobacterium tumefaciens	Difco nutrient agar plus yeast extract; Yeast mannitol agar	Vincent (1970)
Corynebacterium spp.	GYCA[b]	Dye (1962)
Erwinia spp.	SPA[c]; GYCA[b]	Hayward (1960)
Pseudomonas solanacearum and other non-fluorescent pseudomonads	SPA[c]; Kelman's tetrazolium medium	Kelman (1954)
P. syringae and other fluorescent pseudomonads	KBA[d]	King et al. (1954)
Xanthomonas campestris X. fragariae, X. albilineans	SPA[c]	Hayward (1960)
X. populi	glucose - peptone yeast extract agar	Burdekin (1972)

[a]*Media recipes given in Chapter 16 of this volume.*
[b]*GYCA, Glucose-yeast extract-calcium carbonate agar.*
[c]*SPA, Sucrose peptone agar.*
[d]*KBA, Medium B of King et al. (1954)*

TABLE 1.2   *Selective Media Recommended for Isolation of Plant Pathogenic Bacteria*

Species	Media[a]	References
Agrobacterium tumefaciens	Various media (see Chapter 3)	Schroth et al. (1965) New & Kerr (1971)
Erwinia amylovora	High sucrose medium MS medium	Crosse & Goodman (1973) Miller & Schroth (1972)
Erwinia carotovora	Crystal violet pectate medium and others (see Chapter 6)	Cuppels & Kelman (1974)
Pseudomonas spp. (fluorescent)	KBA[b] plus antibiotics	Sands & Rovira (1970) Simon et al. (1973) Simon & Ridge (1974)
	Proline medium	Moustafa et al. (1970)
Pseudomonas spp. (fluorescent, pectolytic)	KBA[b] plus antibiotics & pectin	Sands et al. (1972)
Streptomyces scabies	Tyrosine casein nitrate agar	Menzies & Dade (1959)
Xanthomonas campestris (some pathovars)	Soluble starch plus cyclohex- imide agar	Schaad & White (1974) Schaad (1980)
X. albilineans	SPA[c] plus penicillin and cycloheximide	Persley (1972)

[a] Media recipes given in Chapter 16 of this volume.
[c] SPA, sucrose peptone agar.
[b] KBA, Medium B of King et al. (1954).

There are certain pitfalls in the use of selective media. Apart from the fact that they are usually complex and/or expensive to prepare, they may give unrealistic measurements of population size, because selective media are rarely without some inhibitory effect on the bacteria for which they select. For most routine purposes a few non-selective media are perfectly adequate (Table 1.1).

Selective media have been useful for many quantitative population studies on the survival of pathogens in soil as saprophytes, in the rhizosphere or phyllosphere, on seed, or in moribund plant material. They have also been important in gaining understanding of cycles of infection and in recognising the existence of reservoirs of infection in the field. Selectivity is usually achieved by the introduction of specific carbon sources into defined or complex media, or by the inclusion of dyes, antibiotics or other inhibitors which favour the pathogen. Some examples of selective media and their applications are given in Table 1.2.

VI. Plant Inoculation Tests

When isolations of pure cultures of bacteria from infected plant tissues have been achieved, the next stage in diagnosis is to conduct pathogenicity tests in order to fulfil the requirements of Koch's postulates of patho-genicity. Some methods involved detached fruits or even tissue slices and are not strictly pathogenicity tests. Nevertheless these procedures have their place in diagnosis and often serve to select probable pathogens from among a collection of isolates obtained from material which is secondarily invaded by saprophytic bacteria.

The commonly used plant inoculation tests are the production of a hypersensitive reaction in tobacco leaves, bean pod inoculations for bean pathogens, detached fruit inoculation methods for pathogens of stone and pome fruits, leaf infiltration and atomisation tests for pathogens producing foliar symptoms, and stem and root inoculations for bacterial wilt pathogens such as _Pseudomonas solanacearum_. Inoculation of potato slices is a useful method for recognition of species such as _Erwinia carotovora_ which produce a soft rot. The details of these methods are given in Chapter 16.

References

Burdekin, D.A. (1972). Bacterial canker of poplar. Annals of Applied Biology 72, 295-299.

Crosse, J.E. & Goodman, R.N. (1973). A selective medium for and a definitive colony characteristic of Erwinia amylovora. Phytopathology 63, 1425-1426.

Cuppels, D. & Kelman, A. (1974). Evaluation of selective media for isolation of soft-rot bacteria from soil and plant tissue. Phytopathology 64, 468-475.

Dowson, W.J. (1957). "Plant Diseases Due to Bacteria". Cambridge University Press. 232pp.

Dye, D.W. (1962). The inadequacy of the usual determinative tests for the identification of Xanthomonas spp. New Zealand Journal of Science 5, 393-416.

Dye, D.W., Bradbury, J.F., Goto, M., Hayward, A.C., Lelliott, R.A. & Schroth, M.N. (1980). International standards for naming pathovars of phytopathogenic bacteria and a list of pathovar names and pathotype strains. Review of Plant Pathology 59, 153-168.

Elliott, C. (1951). "Manual of Bacterial Plant Pathogens" 2nd. edition. Waltham, Massachusetts: Chronica Botanica. 186pp.

Goth, R.W. (1965). Puncture method for isolating bacterial blights of beans. Phytopathology 55, 930-931.

Hayward, A.C. (1960). A method for characterizing Pseudomonas solanacearum. Nature, London 186, 405-406.

Kelman, A. (1954). The relationship of pathogenicity in Pseudomonas solanacearum to colony appearance on tetrazolium medium. Phytopathology 44, 693-695.

King, E.O., Ward, M.K. & Raney, D.E. (1954). Two simple media for the demonstration of pyocyanin and fluorescein. Journal of Laboratory and Clinical Medicine 44, 301-307.

Menzies, J.D. & Dade, C.C., (1959). A selective indicator medium for isolating Streptomyces scabies from potato tubers or soil. Phytopathology 49, 457-458.

Miller, T.D. & Schroth, M.N. (1972). Monitoring the epiphytic population of Erwinia amylovora in pears with a selective medium. Phytopathology 62, 1175-1182.

Moustafa, F.A., Clark, G.A. & Whittenbury, R. (1970). Two partially selective media; one for Pseudomonas morsprunorum, Ps. syringae, Ps. phaseolicola and Ps. tabaci, and one for Agrobacteria. Phytopathologische Zeitschrift 67, 342-344.

New, P.B. & Kerr, A. (1971).   A selective medium for Agrobacterium radiobacter biotype 2.   Journal of Applied Bacteriology 34, 233-236.

Persley, G.J. (1972).   Isolation methods for the causal agent of leaf scald disease. Sugarcane Pathologists Newsletter 8, 24.

Sands, D.C. & Rovira, A.D. (1970). Isolation of fluorescent pseudomonads with a selective medium. Applied Microbiology 20, 513-514.

Sands, D.C., Hankin, L. & Zucker, M. (1972). A selective medium for pectolytic fluorescent pseudomonads. Phytopathology 62, 998-1000.

Schaad, N.W. (Ed). (1980).   "Laboratory Guide for Identification of Plant Pathogenic Bacteria".   St. Paul, Minnesota: American Phytopathological Society. 72 pp.

Schaad, N.W. & White, W.C. (1974). A selective medium for soil isolation and enumeration of Xanthomonas campestris. Phytopathology 64, 876-880

Schroth, M.N., Thompson, J.P. & Hildebrand, D.C. (1965). Isolation of Agrobacterium tumefaciens - A. radiobacter group from the soil. Phytopathology 55, 645-647.

Simon, A. & Ridge, E.M. (1974). The use of ampicillin in a simplified selective medium for the isolation of fluorescent pseudomonads. Journal of Applied Bacteriology 37, 459-460.

Simon, A., Rovira, A.D. & Sands, D.C. (1973). An improved selective medium for isolating fluorescent pseudomonads. Journal of Applied Bacteriology 36, 141-146.

Smith, E.F. (1920). "An Introduction to Bacterial Diseases of Plants". Philadelphia and London: W.B. Saunders.

Stapp, C. (1961). "Bacterial Plant Pathogens". Oxford University Press. 292 pp.

Vincent, J.M. (1970). "Root-Nodule Bacteria." IBP Handbook No. 15. Oxford: Blackwell Scientific Publications.

Primary Differentiation of the Genera
of Plant Pathogenic Bacteria
A. C. Hayward

I.	Introduction	13
II.	Colony Characteristics and Pigments	14
III.	Gram Reaction	15
IV.	Motility and Flagellation	18
V.	Initial Screening of Yellow-pigmented Bacteria	20
VI.	Differentiation of Genera Associated with Soft Rot in Plants	21
VII.	Key Characteristics Used in Generic Differentiation	24
	References	25

I. Introduction

When isolations are made from diseased plant material on agar media it is a common experience to obtain a mixture of different bacterial colony types. In the case of leaf spot infections, if isolations are made from the margin of young, water-soaked lesions, the bacterium which causes the lesion should be greatly predominant over secondary invaders of the infected plant tissue and aerial contaminants or epiphytic bacteria adhering to the leaf. In such cases the most numerous colonies are likely to be those of the pathogen. In practice, however, diagnosis is complicated by the appearance of less numerous but faster growing secondary invaders. It is almost always the case that saprophytes are faster growing than pathogens and it can never be assumed that the colonies first to appear are those most likely to be the pathogen.

The appearance of bacterial colonies on a variety of different isolation media, and their rate of growth, provide the first clues to generic identity. Observations should always be made on pure cultures on well-dried agar media, and of discrete, well-separated colonies. Some pathogens produce fluorescent pigments on iron-deficient medium, such as the medium B of King et al. (1954); others such as Erwinia amylovora and Pseudomonas syringae produce characteristic domed, mucoid colonies on a medium containing 5% sucrose. Details of these and other media and methods described in this Chapter are given in Chapter 16 of this volume.

It is always advisable to establish pathogenicity first before carrying out cultural and physiological tests which provide a pointer to generic identity. A provisional determination of identity can be made using the following key observations: colony characteristics and diffusible pigments; Gram reaction and cell morphology; motility and flagellation; oxidase test; and oxidation and/or fermentation of carbohydrates, using the Hugh and Leifson test (Table 2.1). The value of these characteristics in the differentiation of the various genera of plant pathogenic bacteria is discussed below.

II.   Colony Characteristics and Pigments

Plant pathogenic bacteria produce a variety of pigments, some of which are manifest only on media of special composition. The yellow pigments of Xanthomonas campestris consist of a unique family of brominated aryl octanes, which have been called xanthomonadins (Starr et al., 1977). They are not carotenoids as was once thought. Pigmentation in Corynebacterium is extremely variable with age of culture and nutritional status, particularly the vitamin content of culture media. Yellow or pink carotenoid pigments are frequently encountered. Yellow or orange carotenoid pigments are also a feature of the saprophyte, Erwinia herbicola.

Erwinia chrysanthemi strains usually produce traces of indigoidine, a blue extracellular, water-insoluble pigment on glucose-yeast extract medium (GYCA) containing finely divided calcium carbonate (Dye, 1962) but the amounts produced are small, and considerably less than produced by Corynebacterium insidiosum. A pink diffusible pigment is produced optimally by Erwinia rubrifaciens on GYCA medium and by E. rhapontici on sucrose peptone agar (SPA).

In Pseudomonas, several different kinds of pigments are
encountered of which the most important diagnostically are
the green, water-soluble, fluorescent pigments, which have
been called bacterial fluorescein, but which are better
termed pyoverdines (Leisinger & Margraff, 1979). These
pigments fluoresce most strongly under ultra-violet light of
long wavelength (365 nm). Some strains of P. cepacia, P.
gladioli and P. caryophylli produce traces of yellow-green
diffusible pigments which can be distinguished from pyoverdines by their lack of fluorescence under short
wavelength (254 nm) ultraviolet light (Palleroni &
Doudoroff, 1972). Phenazine pigments are produced by other
species, e.g. pyocyanine by P.aeruginosa. P. cepacia also
produces yellow, green or purple phenazine pigments. Some
strains of P. solanacearum and P. gladioli produce a dark
brown, diffusible pigment on media containing tyrosine;
these pigments are possibly melanins.

III. Gram Reaction

A most important first step in the identification of an
unknown bacterial isolate is application of the Gram
staining procedure to smears prepared from young cultures
(16 - 24 h). This method provides useful information about
the shape and size of the cells and distinguishes between
Gram-positive and Gram-negative species. The result of this
staining reaction is essential for the decision as to which
criteria should be used in the further identification of the
strain. The Gram reaction is one of the most essential of
the 'first stage criteria' of Cowan (1974).

In most cases the interpretation of a Gram-stained smear
is done without any problems, but certain Gram-positive
species, particularly members of the genus Bacillus and some
coryneform bacteria, appear Gram-negative when they have
reached a certain age, varying from a few hours to a few
days (Cowan, 1974). Certain Gram-negative genera tend to
resist decolourization with ethanol. Such bacteria are
regarded as being Gram-variable.

Two rapid methods have recently been described which
assist in the differentiation between Gram-negative and
Gram-positive bacteria. The method of Cerny (1976, 1978) is
dependent on a colour reaction for demonstration of an
aminopeptidase mainly found in Gram-negative bacteria. The
method is rapid (10-15 min) but not entirely specific in the

TABLE 2.1 *Differentiation of the Genera of Plant Pathogenic Bacteria*

Character	Corynebacterium	Erwinia	Pseudomonas	Xanthomonas	Agrobacterium
Disease symptoms	Gumming of inflorescences. Wilts and/or leaf spots	Vascular wilts. Dry necroses. Leaf spots Soft rots	Leaf spots. Vascular wilts.[a] Soft rots.	Leaf spots. Vascular wilts.[a] Stem cankers.	Crown gall. Hairy root formation.[a] Soil saprophytes.[b]
Gram reaction	+	-	-	-	-
Motility	v[c]	+	+	+	+
Flagellation	Few polar or lateral	Peritrichous	One or several polar	One polar	Sparse lateral
Colony colour	Variable; orange, yellow or blue	White or yellow	White or yellow	Yellow (rarely white)	White (rarely yellow)
Diffusible pigments	Usually absent	Usually absent. Pink or blue in some species.	Fluorescent or phenazine or absent.	Usually[d] absent.	Usually[d] absent
Poly-β-hydroxybutyrate inclusions	-	-	v	-	v[e]
Kovacs' oxidase	-	-	v	- or weak +	+

Table 2.1 Cont'd. Differentiation of the Genera of Plant Pathogenic Bacteria

	Weak ox[f] or inert	F	Ox	Ox	Ox
Glucose metabolism					
Starch hydrolysis	v[g]	–	v[h]	v[h]	–
Nitrite from nitrate	–[g]	v[i]	v	–	v[j]
3-Keto lactose	–	–	–	–	v[k]
% guanine + cytosine in the DNA	65–75	50–58	58–70	63–69[l]	59–63

a Symptoms produced by *Pseudomonas* spp. also include stem cankers, blossom and twig blights, tumours or galls and mushroom blights.
b Holmes & Roberts (1981) use the terms tumourigenic state, rhizogenic state and saprophytic state to describe the phytopathogenic potential of different agrobacteria.
c v, indicates some species in the genus possess the property and others do not.
d Some produce browning in medium surrounding growth on tyrosine agar.
e According to Holmes & Roberts (1981) present only in *Agrobacterium rhizogenes*.
f Ox, oxidative; F, fermentative.
g Based on Dye & Kemp (1977).
h Starch hydrolysis is rare in *Pseudomonas* and unknown in *P. syringae* and other fluorescent pseudomonads, whereas most pathovars of *Xanthomonas campestris* hydrolyse starch.
i *Erwinia carotovora* and other soft-rotting species reduce nitrate; most other *Erwinia* spp. do not.
j According to Holmes & Roberts (1981) *Agrobacterium rhizogenes* and *A. rubi* do not reduce nitrate; the property is variable in *A. tumefaciens*.
k *Agrobacterium tumefaciens* +; other species - (Holmes & Roberts, 1981).
l Results for *Xanthomonas campestris* only.

case of the genus <u>Bacillus</u>. The other method (Gregersen, 1978) is based on the greater resistance of the cell walls of the Gram-positive bacteria to treatment with potassium hydroxide solution (3% KOH). In most cases, Gram-negative bacteria do not possess walls which resist solubilization in potassium hydroxide solution. These methods are described in Chapter 16. Their use is recommended when in doubt.

IV.   Motility and Flagellation

Most plant pathogenic bacteria which grow readily in culture are motile with flagella. Among motile, rod-shaped bacteria, the number of flagella per cell and their points of origin on the cell (polar versus peritrichous) are primary taxonomic criteria of considerable diagnostic significance. The type of flagellation can readily be ascertained by electron microscopy, but this technique is frequently not available for routine use. Numerous flagellar staining procedures for light microscopy are available but consistent results are not easily obtained (Leifson, 1960).

Examination of motile bacteria in hanging drop preparations under the light microscope shows that a rapid, darting motility is characteristic of polarly flagellate bacteria, whereas peritrichously flagellate bacteria terminate a period of relatively slow translational movement by chaotic tumbling. Polarly flagellate bacteria (e.g. Fig. 2.1) undergo abrupt double reversals, (i.e. they briefly reverse direction before returning along approximately the same path). This abrupt cell reversal does not appear with peritrichously flagellated cells; although some may fortuitously travel back along their path after tumbling, usually the path of motility in peritrichously flagellate bacteria involves many irregular changes in direction to give what has been termed the "random walk". These important differences in motility pattern have been well described by MacNab (1976), using the technique of high intensity, dark field illumination and time lapse photography. However, the gross differences in motility pattern can be determined using ordinary microscopy and hanging drop preparations. MacNab (1976) showed that the mean velocity of two pseudomonad species was about 50-60 μm/s whereas <u>Salmonella typhimurium</u>, which is peritrichously flagellate, had a mean velocity of about 30 μm/s.

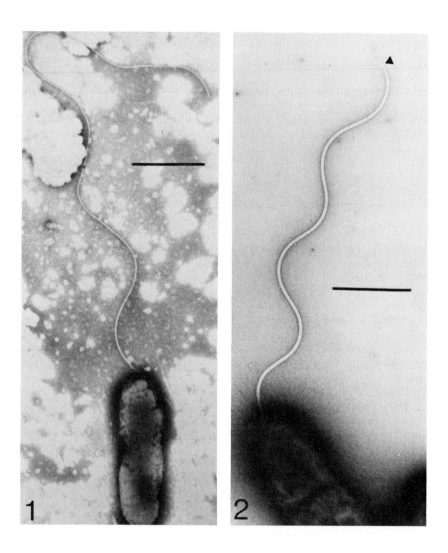

Figure 2.1 <u>Xanthomonas albilineans</u> showing a single, long polar flagellum. Scale bar 1µm. (Photo courtesy G. J. Persley).

Figure 2.2 <u>Pseudomonas andropogonis</u> showing single, polar, sheathed flagellum and portion (arrowed) of empty sheath. Scale bar 1µm. (Photo courtesy J.A. Fuerst).

In polarly flagellate bacteria the number of flagella per cell is of diagnostic significance. In xanthomonads a single flagellum is present which may be several times the length of the cell from which it arises e.g. Xanthomonas albilineans (Fig. 2.1). With pseudomonads the cells usually have one to several flagella at one or both poles of the cell. Some pseudomonad species have one flagellum only, for example, P. andropogonis, which is also notable for the fact that it is the only pseudomonad known to possess a sheathed flagellum (Fig. 2.2). This property can be readily observed by negative stain electron microscopy (Fuerst & Hayward, 1969).

V.   Initial Screening of Yellow-pigmented Bacteria

Colony colour is a useful though sometimes misleading guide to identity. For example, there are many different kinds of aerobic or facultatively anaerobic bacteria which produce yellow or orange pigments and some of these may be confused with xanthomonads, which usually also produce yellow colonies. The yellow Gram-negative rod which is most commonly confused with xanthomonads, because of frequency of occurrence on moribund plant material, is Erwinia herbicola, which has a faster growth rate than xanthomonads and has a fermentative rather than an oxidative metabolism of carbohydrates.

Infected plant material which has become invaded by secondary organisms, and particularly plant material such as roots or stems which is heavily contaminated with soil, presents most difficulty in achieving successful isolation. This is due to the greater diversity of bacteria present. Under these conditions it is most necessary to recognise the colony characteristics of the genera of yellow bacteria. These yellow saprophytes are likely to include Cytophaga, Flavobacterium, and certain yellow pigmented pseudomonads such as Pseudomonas paucimobilis and P. maltophilia, as well as pigmented coryneform bacteria (Fig 2.3). Cytophaga produces spreading colonies on isolation plates, in which the margin of the colony consists of a monolayer of cells. The margin of Cytophaga colonies appears transparent at the periphery. Generic differentiation of the yellow or orange bacteria can be made by careful observation of colony characteristics coupled with the application of relatively few cultural and physiological tests as shown in Fig. 2.3.

VI. Differentiation of Genera Associated with Soft Rot in Plants

The isolation and differentiation of soft-rotting bacteria from soil or from stems, roots and tubers often presents difficulty. Soft rots of storage organs such as potato rapidly become secondarily invaded with a variety of saprophytic bacteria. Many kinds of bacteria are pectolytic and capable of macerating parenchymatous tissue, but they are of unequal significance in relation to plant disease. The soft-rotting erwinia group are discussed in more detail in Chapter 6.

The nature of the material from which soft-rotting bacteria are isolated usually determines that they are obtained on isolation plates as members of a grossly mixed population. In order to overcome these problems various selective or enrichment procedures have been developed. For example, soil samples can be incubated anaerobically in a pectate based salt solution (Meneley & Stanghellini, 1976) in order to enrich the population of pectolytic bacteria, and then plated out on pectate based selective media such as the CVP medium of Cuppels & Kelman (1974).

An alternative to the use of selective or enrichment media is direct plating of a suspension of source material on a non-selective medium. Each distinct colony type on isolation media is then restreaked and tested for ability to produce a soft rot in potato slices. Those which macerate the slice are examined in a few key tests to determine their generic identity (e.g. Gram reaction, oxidase, fluorescent pigment production, glucose metabolism). A key for the identification of bacteria from soft-rotting tissue is given in Table 6.2 (see Chapter 6).

In potato tubers, for example, the most important soft-rotting bacteria are Erwinia carotovora pv. carotovora, E. carotovora pv. atroseptica, and E. chrysanthemi, and also Clostridium spp. which can be isolated by anaerobic incubation methods (Lund, 1972). The soft-rotting Erwinia spp. can be readily differentiated from Pseudomonas marginalis on the basis of differences in pigmentation, oxidase activity, and ability to ferment or oxidise glucose; however, in the differentiation of the Erwinia spp. from soft-rotting Bacillus spp. care must be taken to avoid confusion with B. polymyxa and B. macerans. The latter are often Gram-negative, and active glucose fermenters which do not sporulate readily.

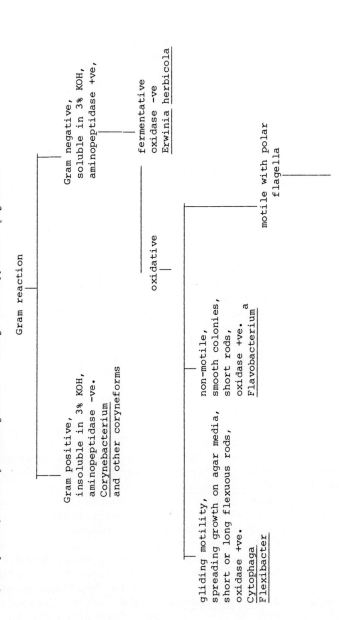

FIGURE 2.3 Primary differentiation of aerobic or facultatively anaerobic, rod-shaped bacteria from plants, which produce yellow or orange non-diffusible pigments.

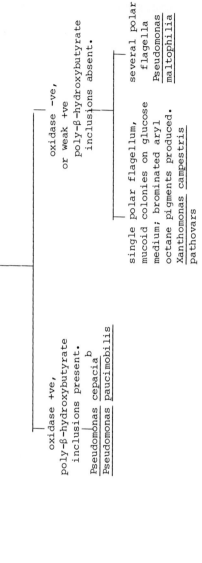

FIGURE 2.3 Cont'd. *Primary differentiation of aerobic or facultatively anaerobic, rod-shaped bacteria from plants, which produce yellow or orange non-diffusible pigments.*

[a]*Flavobacteria with peritrichous flagella have been recorded but appear to be rare (Hayes et al., 1979)*

[b]*P. cepacia often non-pigmented; diffusible pigments may be present.*

Figure 2.4 Common scab lesion on potato, caused by Streptomyces scabies.

VII. Key Characteristics Used in Generic Differentiation

Some of the major properties of the five genera of plant pathogenic bacteria which can be grown readily on artificial media are given in Table 2.1. It is evident that many properties are shared and few properties are unique to a genus, including the symptoms of the diseases caused in plants. Successful diagnosis and identification must depend on the recognition of multiple correlated features. The more information that is obtained the more likely it is that accurate identification has been made. The characteristics of the major genera which contain plant pathogenic bacteria (Agrobacterium, Corynebacterium, Erwinia, Pseudomonas and Xanthomonas) are discussed in more detail in later chapters of this volume.

Apart from the five main genera, a wider range of genera or groups including Streptomyces, Clostridium, Bacillus and methanogenic bacteria (wetwood of timber) contain some species which may be pathogenic under specific conditions or are at least associated with pathogenic disorders. Starr (1981) lists 28 genera or groups containing harmful or possibly harmful plant-associated bacteria. Some of the more important members of these groups are discussed elsewhere in this volume, including mycoplasma and rickettsia-like organisms (Chapter 10) and sugarcane ratoon stunting disease organism (Chapter 11).

One major genus not discussed elsewhere is Streptomyces which contains only a few species of plant pathogens but includes Streptomyces scabies, the cause of common scab of potato (Solanum tuberosum), which occurs worldwide and may occasionally cause severe losses in neutral to alkaline soils (Lapwood, 1973). There is some confusion over identity of the pathogen but the disease is readily diagnosed on symptoms (Fig. 2.4). Another species, S. ipomoeae, causes soil rot and pit of sweet potato (Ipomoea batatas) which may occasionally result in severe losses in the U.S.A. (Bradbury, 1981).

References

Bradbury, J.F. (1981). Streptomyces ipomoeae. CMI Descriptions of Pathogenic Fungi and Bacteria No 697. Kew: Commonwealth Mycological Institute.

Cerny, G. (1976). Method for the distinction of Gram-negative from Gram-positive bacteria. European Journal of Applied Microbiology 3, 223-225.

Cerny, G. (1978). Studies on the aminopeptidase test for the distinction of Gram-negative from Gram-positive bacteria. European Journal of Applied Microbiology and Biotechnology 5, 113-122.

Cowan, S.T. (1974). "Cowan and Steel's Manual for the Identification of Medical Bacteria". 2nd edition. Cambridge University Press.

Cuppels, D. & Kelman, A. (1974). Evaluation of selective media for isolation of soft-rot bacteria from soil and plant tissue. Phytopathology 64, 468-475.

Dye, D.W. (1962). The inadequacy of the usual determinative tests for Xanthomonas spp. New Zealand Journal of Science 5, 393-416.

Dye, D.W. & Kemp, W.J. (1977). A taxonomic study of plant pathogenic Corynebacterium species. New Zealand Journal of Agricultural Research 20, 563-582.

Fuerst, J.A. & Hayward, A.C. (1969). The sheathed flagellum of Pseudomonas stizolobii. Journal of General Microbiology 58, 239-245.

Gregersen, T. (1978). Rapid method for distinction of Gram-negative from Gram-positive bacteria. European Journal of Applied Microbiology and Biotechnology 5, 123-127.

Hayes, P.R., McMeekin, T.A. & Shewan, J.M. (1979). The identification of Gram-negative, yellow pigmented rods. In "Identification Methods for Microbiologists." 2nd edition. (Ed. F.A. Skinner & D.W. Lovelock). London: Academic Press.

Holmes, B. & Roberts, P. (1981). The classification, identification and nomenclature of agrobacteria, incorporating revised descriptions for each of Agrobacterium tumefaciens (Smith & Townsend) Conn 1942, Agrobacterium rhizogenes (Riker et al.) Conn 1942, and Agrobacterium rubi (Hildebrand) Starr & Weiss 1943. Journal of Applied Bacteriology 50, 443-467.

King, E.O., Ward, M.K. & Raney, D.E. (1954). Two simple media for the demonstration of pyocyanin and fluorescein. Journal of Laboratory and Clinical Medicine 44, 301-307.

Lapwood, D.H. (1973). Streptomyces scabies and potato scab disease. In "Actinomycetales", pp. 253-260. (Ed. G. Sykes & F.A. Skinner). London: Academic Press.

Leifson, E. (1960). "Atlas of Bacterial Flagellation". London: Academic Press.

Leisinger, T. & Margraff, R. (1979). Secondary metabolites of the fluorescent pseudomonads. Microbiological Reviews 43, 422-442.

Lund, B.M. (1972). Isolation of pectolytic clostridia from potatoes. Journal of Applied Bacteriology 35, 609-614.

MacNab, R.M. (1976). Examination of bacterial flagellation by dark-field microscopy. Journal of Clinical Microbiology 4, 258-265.

Meneley, J.C. & Stanghellini, M.E. (1976). Isolation of soft-rot Erwinia spp. from agricultural soils using an enrichment technique. Phytopathology 66, 367-370.

Palleroni, N.J. & Doudoroff, M. (1972). Some properties and taxonomic subdivisions of the genus Pseudomonas. Annual Review of Phytopathology 10, 73-100.

Starr, M.P. (1981). Prokaryotes as plant pathogens. In "The Prokaryotes" Vol. 1, pp. 123-134 (Ed. M.P. Starr, H. Stolp, H.G. Truper, A. Balows & H.G. Schlegel). Berlin: Springer-Verlag.

Starr, M.P., Jenkins, C.L., Bussey, L.B. & Andrewes, A.G. (1977). Chemotaxonomic significance of the xanthomonadins, novel brominated aryl-polyene pigments produced by bacteria of the genus Xanthomonas. Archives of Microbiology 113, 1-9.

Agrobacterium
A. Kerr and P. G. Brisbane

I.	Introduction	27
II.	Crown Gall	28
III.	Hairy Root	39
	References	41

I. Introduction

Four species of Agrobacterium are listed in the Eighth Edition of Bergey's Manual (Allen & Holding, 1974): A. tumefaciens, A. radiobacter, A. rhizogenes and A. rubi. It has been established that A. radiobacter and A. tumefaciens are synonymous (Keane et al., 1970; White, 1972; Kersters et al., 1973; Holmes & Roberts, 1981). As A. tumefaciens is the type species, it must be retained and A. radiobacter rejected (Holmes & Roberts, 1981).

Although the nomenclature of Agrobacterium is confused, the classification is clear. The confusion arises because the nomenclature has been based on pathogenicity, and the genes for pathogenicity are located on a large plasmid (c.120 x 10^6 daltons) which can be transferred from one bacterial cell to another. Such plasmids are called Ti (tumour-inducing) or Ri (root-inducing) plasmids. Hence, if Bergey's classification is accepted, one species can be changed into another by transfer of a plasmid, hardly a stable basis for classification.

The characteristics of the genus Agrobacterium are: single-celled, non-sporing rods; motile by means of reduced peritrichous flagella (Fig. 3.1); gram negative; oxidase positive; oxidative. The genus is closely related to the fast-growing strains of Rhizobium (White, 1972).

PLANT BACTERIAL DISEASES
ISBN 0 12 247660 3

27

There are three basic chromosomal forms of Agrobacterium which may be allocated the rank of species (Holmes & Roberts, 1981) or biovar (Kerr & Panagopoulos, 1977). The former is preferable, although there is still some doubt about the third species, A. rubi; the other two species, A. tumefaciens and A. rhizogenes are well defined. Revised descriptions of the three species are given by Holmes & Roberts (1981). Tests to distinguish the species are given in Table 3.1.

Two diseases are caused by strains of Agrobacterium: namely crown gall and hairy root. All three species, A. tumefaciens, A. rhizogenes and A. rubi can cause crown gall if they contain a tumour-inducing (Ti) plasmid; two species, A. tumefaciens and A. rhizogenes can cause hairy root if they contain a root-inducing (Ri) plasmid. There is no reason to believe that A. rubi is unable to induce hairy root if it harbours a Ri plasmid. However, no such strain has been described.

It will be realised that a tumourigenic strain need not therefore be designated A. tumefaciens nor a root-inducing (rhizogenic) strain A. rhizogenes. The specific epithet is just a name and it does not describe a property. Holmes & Roberts (1981) recommend that the pathogenic characteristic of a strain of Agrobacterium be designated by state, a tumourigenic, rhizogenic or saprophytic state. A more satisfactory alternative would be to indicate the plasmid complement of each strain.

II. Crown Gall

A. *Symptoms*

Crown gall results from the uncontrolled division of plant cells. In nature, the galls usually develop where a lateral root is attached to the main root, and frequently arise from root lenticels. Most occur just below the soil surface, at the crown of the plant (Fig. 3.2) and hence the name. However, the galls can develop wherever plant tissue is wounded and sometimes, particularly with grapevine (Vitis vinifera) and Rubus spp., aerial galls are formed. There is some evidence that with these hosts the bacteria can move through the vascular system and that gall formation is associated with frost damage to the stems or canes.

TABLE 3.1   *Differentiating Characteristics of Agrobacterium*
tumefaciens, A. rhizogenes and A. rubi.

Character	A.tumefaciens (biovar 1)	A.rhizogenes (biovar 2)	A.rubi (biovar 3)
3-ketolactose production	+	−	−
Acid from:			
Erythritol	−	+	−
Melezitose	+	−	−
Dulcitol	+	+	−
Ethanol	+	−	−
Alkali from:			
L-tartrate	−	+	+
Propionate	+	−	−
Oxidase production[a]	+	−	+
Poly-β-hydroxybutyrate inclusion granules	−	+	−
Growth on 2% NaCl	+	−	+

[a]*This is a false oxidase reaction because 1% glucose is
added to Difco nutrient agar. If glucose is omitted,
all species produce oxidase.*

B.   Geographic Distribution and Importance

In Australia, crown gall probably causes an annual loss
of about A\$1.5 million (Kerr, unpublished data). Economic
damage is largely confined to stone-fruit (Prunus spp.),
rose (Rosa spp.) and beetroot (Beta vulgaris ssp. vulgaris)
although the disease also occurs on grapevine. Amongst
stone-fruit crops, almond (Prunus dulcis), peach (P.
persica) and plum (P. domestica) are most seriously
affected. The disease occurs wherever these crops are grown
and infection generally occurs in nurseries. In Australia,
the three species have a marked difference in host
distribution. A. tumefaciens may be isolated from crown
galls on any plant but isolates are usually non-pathogenic.
A. rhizogenes is generally isolated from galls on stone-
fruit and rose while A. rubi is confined to grapevine.

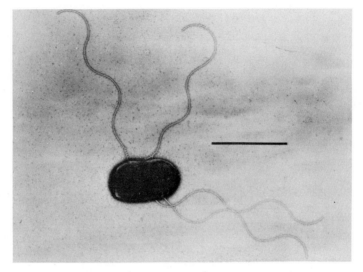

FIGURE 3.1 *Agrobacterium tumefaciens*. *Scale bar 1μm.*

C. Host Range

Six hundred and forty three plant species have been recorded as susceptible to crown gall (De Cleene & De Ley, 1976) when artificially inoculated with pathogenic bacteria. However, not all strains of Agrobacterium affect all hosts (Anderson & Moore, 1979). Many fewer hosts are naturally infected. In addition to stone-fruit, beetroot and rose, which are commonly affected in Australia, significant economic damage to apple (Malus domestica), chestnut (Castanea sativa), chrysanthemum (Chrysanthemum spp.), grapevine (Vitis vinifera), walnut (Juglans regia), Euonymus spp. and Rubus spp. has been reported elsewhere.

D. The Nature of Crown Gall

It is important to understand the nature of crown gall before some of the practical problems can be described. The molecular biology of the disease has been described by Kahl & Schell (1982).   Although crown gall is caused by three species of Agrobacterium, the presence of living bacteria is necessary for only about three days. During this period, part of the Ti plasmid, known as T-DNA, is transferred from bacterium to plant cell. The T-DNA becomes integrated into

FIGURE 3.2   *Crown Gall on Peach.*

the plant nuclear DNA and directs the plant cell to (a) grow
and divide out of control and (b) synthesize crown gall
specific chemicals called "opines" which can be catabolised
only by bacteria harbouring a Ti plasmid. As far as we know
this is a unique parasitic system and has been called
"genetic colonization" (Schell et al., 1979). The parasite
colonises the host with a piece of DNA which redirects the
metabolic activities of the host to benefit the parasite .

E. Diagnosis

Crown gall tissue is relatively soft, even when formed
on woody hosts and is not difficult to distinguish from hard
burrs. However in some situations (e.g. on cuttings), it is
impossible visually to distinguish crown gall tissue from
callus tissue. There are only three methods of doing so,
(a) by isolating pathogenic bacteria, (b) by identifying in
the putative gall a specific opine and (c) by using T-DNA as
a probe. These are described below (Sections F-H).

F. Isolation

All strains of agrobacteria grow readily in culture. For isolation, selective or non-selective media can be used. In our laboratory we have developed three selective media for the three species (Tables 3.2 - 3.4). All are based on the nutritional characteristics of the organisms with relatively few antibiotics added to inhibit other soil organisms. The selective medium for A. rubi has not yet been adequately tested in the field and further evidence is required before it can be recommended unreservedly.

Alternative selective media which we have found satisfactory are those described by Schroth et al. (1965) for A. tumefaciens (omit the streptomycin) and by New & Kerr (1971) for A. rhizogenes. The dangers of using selective media have already been emphasized in Chapter 1 of this volume. Many selective media are useful for experimental purposes, when dealing with known species or strains. In other instances, a non-selective medium is preferable. Difco nutrient agar containing 0.01% yeast extract is satisfactory. This has a low carbohydrate content and does not, therefore, promote excessive formation of extracellular polysaccharide slime. When a non-selective medium is used, most of the contaminating bacteria on the gall surface should be removed by washing.

Galls in the field are usually composed of young, white, actively growing tissue and also of moribund or decomposing tissue. Choose the former. Cut out small pieces (c.1.0mm^3) of gall tissue and macerate them in about 0.1 ml of sterile water or buffered saline. Leave for 30 min to allow the bacteria to move into the liquid and then streak on plates in the normal way. In contrast to most plant diseases caused by bacteria, infected crown gall tissue does not contain masses of bacteria and a milky suspension of bacteria never develops.

Gall tissue may be devoid of agrobacteria. Once the T-DNA is transferred from bacterium to plant cell, living bacteria are no longer required. The cells still grow and divide out of control and opines are synthesized. They diffuse to the surface of the gall where they provide agrobacteria living there with a source of carbon and nitrogen reserved for them. So genetic colonisation does not require bacterial colonisation and this explains a lack of pathogenic agrobacteria in some crown galls. Galls in stone-fruit trees usually yield pathogenic agrobacteria. In contrast, galls on Rubus spp., rose and grapevine have proved difficult on occasion. When this occurs, pathogenic

agrobacteria may be easier to isolate from the gall surface
or the adhering soil, rather than from the gall itself.
Selective media are required (Tables 3.2 - 3.4). Experience
will usually indicate which one to use; if in doubt, use all
three.

Even when selective media are used, many colonies on the
isolation plates will not be agrobacteria. Fortunately, it
is relatively easy to distinguish colonies of Agrobacterium
spp. from those of most other bacteria (Tables 3.2 - 3.4).

G. *Pathogenicity*

Not all agrobacteria are pathogenic. Pathogenic and
non-pathogenic agrobacteria cannot be distinguished by cell
or colony morphology.   Ideally, the host from which the
agrobacteria were isolated should be used to establish
pathogenicity but this is not always convenient. Almond,
grapevine, raspberry (Rubus idaeus) etc. are not always
readily available in the glasshouse. Tomato (Lycopersicon
esculentum), sunflower (Helianthus annuus) and Datura spp.
are suitable alternatives, as most strains will infect at
least one of these (Anderson & Moore, 1979). Other useful
hosts are Kalanchoe daigremontiana and Nicotiana glutinosa.
Strains of A. rubi are the main problem. So far, these
have been isolated only from chrysanthemum, Rubus spp. and
grapevine.   Some strains have quite a wide host range but
others are very restricted, frequently to their natural
host.   The reason for this is not known, but it is a
characteristic of the Ti plasmid (Loper & Kado, 1979;
Thomashow et al., 1980).   With such strains, the natural
host must be used for testing pathogenicity.

The actual testing is simple. A heavy suspension of
bacteria in water or buffered saline is transferred to the
plant and a sterile needle jabbed several times through the
suspension into the plant. In most cases the younger the
tissue, the more rapidly does the gall develop and young
stem tissue is usually inoculated. Galls develop within one
to three weeks on most hosts. Leaf, root and tuber tissue
are also susceptible and quantitative assays for virulence
sometimes use tobacco (Nicotiana tabacum) leaves (Lippincott
& Heberlein, 1965) or discs of carrot (Daucus carota) roots
(Klein & Tenebaum, 1955) and potato (Solanum tuberosum)
tubers (Anand & Heberlein, 1977). A quantitative bioassay
using young pea (Pisum sativum) seedlings has also been
described (Kurkdjian et al., 1969).

Table 3.2   Selective   Medium   for Agrobacterium tumefaciens
(biovar 1)[a]

L(-) Arabitol[b]	(20 mM)	3.04 g/l
NH_4NO_3	(2 mM)	0.16
KH_2PO_4	(4 mM)	0.54
K_2HPO_4	(6 mM)	1.04
$MgSO_4.7H_2O$	(1 mM)	0.25
Sodium taurocholate	(0.5 mM)	0.29
Crystal violet	(0.1% soln)	2.00 ml
Agar		15.00 g
Autoclave in 100 ml lots and before pouring plates add, per 100 ml:		
Actidione	(2% soln)	1.00 ml
$Na_2SeO_3.5H_2O$	(1% soln)	1.00 ml

[a]*After 4 days incubation at 28C colonies are white, circular, raised, glistening and more than 2 mm in diameter. They become more mucoid with incubation.*

[b]*A cheaper but slightly less effective alternative to L(-) Arabitol is Dulcitol (15 mM) + NaCl (150 mM).*

H. Alternatives to Pathogenicity Testing

Sometimes hundreds of colonies are isolated from a gall or from soil and many have to be tested for pathogenicity. It is sometimes simpler to screen for other characteristics coded for by the Ti plasmids. These include ability to catabolise opines and sensitivity to agrocin 84. The choice of opine is important because different strains can catabolise different opines. The appropriate opine can be selected by identifying the opines present in the gall tissue (see below).   The common opines are octopine, nopaline, agropine and mannopine, all of which can serve as a sole source of carbon and nitrogen for bacteria harbouring the appropriate Ti or Ri plasmid. Strains can be rapidly screened on a basal medium lacking C & N but containing the appropriate opine.   Unfortunately, of the opines, only

TABLE 3.3   Selective   Medium   for   Agrobacterium   rhizogenes
(biovar 2)[a]

Erythritol	(25 mM)	3.05 g/l
NH_4NO_3	(2 mM)	0.16
KH_2PO_4	(4 mM)	0.54
K_2HPO_4	(6 mM)	1.04
$MgSO_4 \cdot 7H_2O$	(1 mM)	0.25
Sodium taurocholate	(0.5 mM)	0.29
Yeast extract	(1% soln)	1.00 ml
Malachite Green	(0.1% soln)	5.00 ml
Agar		15.00 g

Autoclave in 100 ml lots and before pouring plates add, per 100 ml

Actidione	(2% soln)	1.00 ml
$Na_2SeO_3.5H_2O$	(1% soln)	1.00 ml

[a]*After 4 days incubation at 28C colonies are white circular, raised, glistening and more than 1 mm in diameter. They enlarge and may turn brown with further incubation.*

octopine is commercially available. The chemical synthesis of nopaline and agropine is described by Cooper & Firmin (1977) and by Tate et al. (1982), respectively.

Strains can also be rapidly screened for sensitivity to agrocin 84, a bacteriocin produced by strain 84 of A. rhizogenes, the strain used in the biological control of crown gall on stone fruit and rose (Kerr & Htay, 1974). The genes for sensitivity to agrocin 84 are located on a Ti plasmid and there is, therefore, a close correlation between agrocin sensitivity and virulence. However, not all Ti plasmids code for agrocin 84 sensitivity. Fortunately, the important "nopaline" strains that cause crown gall on stone fruit are sensitive and can be screened by this method.

Identification of Opines. In the plant kingdom opines are known only from galls or roots induced by agrobacteria. It follows that if they are detected in tissue, that tissue must have resulted from infection by agrobacteria. The simplest method of detection is by high voltage paper

Table 3.4   Selective   Medium   for   Agrobacterium rubi
(biovar 3)[a]

[A]	Water		500 ml
	Sodium tartrate $.2H_2O$	(25 mM)	5.75 g
	D-Glutamic acid		15.00 ml
	(4% solution; pH 7.0)		
	$NaH_2PO_4 \cdot 2H_2O$	(40 mM)	6.25 g
	Na_2HPO_4	(30 mM)	4.26 g
	NaCl	(100 mM)	5.84 g
	$MgSO_4 \cdot 7H_2O$	(1 mM)	0.25 g
	Sodium taurocholate	(0.5 mM)	0.29 g
	Yeast extract	(1% soln)	1.00 ml
	Congo Red	(1% soln)	2.50 ml
[B]	Water		500 ml
	$MnSO_4 \cdot 4H_2O$	(5 mM)	1.12 g
	Agar		15.0 g

Autoclave in 50 ml lots and before pouring add to 50 ml [B],

Actidione	(2% soln)	1.00 ml
$Na_2SeO_3.5H_2O$	(1% soln)	0.50 ml

Then add 50 ml [A] to 50 ml [B].

[a]*After 5 days incubation at 28C, colonies are white, circular, raised and about 2 mm diameter. Some A. tumefaciens strains can utilize tartrate and can grow on this medium. They can be distinguished from A. rubi because they form larger colonies.*

electrophoresis (HVPE) followed by appropriate staining. Although not many plant pathological laboratories have facilities for HVPE, research on (as distinct from casual involvement with) crown gall requires them. Details of a suitable apparatus are given by Tate (1968). The known major opines, along with some of their characteristics are given in Table 3.5. A procedure for their detection is:

1. Weigh 50-100mg gall tissue in disposable Eppendorf tubes.
2. Add absolute ethanol at 2 μl per mg of tissue.
3. Homogenise in tube using a glass rod with the tip drawn out.
4. Centrifuge for 1 min in Eppendorf centrifuge.
5. Spot 10 μl for electrophoresis on No 1 paper. (Spot up to 30 μl for electrophoresis on 3 MM paper).

T-DNA as a Probe.   If a gall has been induced by a species of Agrobacterium, it will contain T-DNA which can be detected by using (^{32}P)-labelled T-DNA as a probe (Denhardt, 1976).   Total DNA is extracted from the gall, cleaved with a restriction enzyme and subjected to agarose gel electrophoresis to separate the DNA fragments. The DNA is denatured by exposing it to high pH and then transferred to a nitrocellulose filter (Southern, 1975). T-DNA which has been cloned in E. coli is labelled with (^{32}P) by nick translation (Rigby et al., 1977) and used as the probe by appplying it to the nitrocellulose filter. If T-DNA was present in the gall tissue, it will bind to the probe which can then be detected by autoradiography, after excess probe has been removed by washing (Thomashow et al., 1980).

I. Biological Control

Since 1973, commercial stone fruit and rose growers in Australia have protected their crops from crown gall by dipping their planting material in a suspension of cells of strain K84, a non-pathogenic strain of A. rhizogenes (Kerr, 1980).   Nearly complete control of the disease is achieved (Table 3.6) and the method is now practised commercially in many other countries, including Italy, New Zealand, South Africa and the U.S.A. Cultures of strain K84 are supplied either in peat or on agar and the suspension prepared by growers should contain between 10^7 and 10^8 cells/ml.
Because the control method involves a living organism, some precautions are necessary to ensure effective treatment. The K84 bacteria should not be suspended in chlorinated water, exposed to high temperatures nor to direct sunlight.   Seeds, cuttings or roots of young plants are dipped in the bacterial suspension and sown or planted immediately.   The method protects plants from infection, it does not cure infected plants. As infection occurs through

TABLE 3.5   Major Opines in Crown Galls and Hairy Roots

Opine	Tissues in which it is a major opine	Method of detection	$M_{O.G.}$[a]
Agropine [N^2-(1'-deoxy - D-manno-hexitol-1'-yl)-L-glutamine, 1,2'-lactone]	1)Galls induced by octopine strains. 2)Roots induced by some rhizogenic strains.	Alkaline silver nitrate (Trevelyan et al., 1950)	-0.46
Mannopine [N^2-(1'-deoxy-D-manno-hexitol-1'-yl)-L-glutamine]	Roots induced by some rhizogenic strains.	As above	-0.26
Nopaline [N^2-(1,3-dicarboxy propyl)-L-arginine]	Galls induced by nopaline strains.	Modified phen-anthrenequinone reagent (Yamada & Itano 1966)	-0.45
Octopine [N^2-D-1-carboxyethyl)-L-arginine]	Many galls on grapevine induced by A.rubi.	As above	-0.54

[a]$M_{O.G}$ = *Relative mobility to Orange G in 1.0 M acetic, 0.75 M formic acid pH 1.7 (Tate et al., 1982).*

TABLE 3.6 Biological Control of Crown Gall in Naturally Infested Soil

Treatment	Mean dry weight of gall tissue per plant[a] (g)	Control[b] %
None	11.64	–
Seed inoculation with strain K84	2.50	78.5
Root inoculation with strain K84	0.59	94.9
Seed and root inoculation with strain K84	0.14	98.8

[a]*Least significant difference of mean dry weight, 0.97 (P = 0.05)*

[b] *Percentage control is the difference between the weight of gall tissue on inoculated and uninoculated plants expressed as a percentage of the gall weight on uninoculated plants.*

wounds, it is important to treat plants no more than 2h after lifting, preparatory to transplanting. Alternatively, damaged roots can be pruned just before treatment.

The mechanism of control has been elucidated. Strain K84 produces an unusual kind of antibiotic that selectively inhibits most pathogenic agrobacteria that cause crown gall on stone fruit and rose (Kerr & Htay, 1974). The antibiotic is called agrocin 84 and belongs to a new group of highly specific antibiotics known as nucleotide bacteriocins (Roberts et al., 1977). Not all pathogenic agrobacteria (e.g. those that cause crown gall on grapevines) are sensitive to agrocin 84. Unless sensitivity has been demonstrated, biological control should not be recommended.

III. Hairy Root

Hairy root looks very different from crown gall. As the name suggests, massive root proliferation occurs; so much so that the roots almost look like hairs (Fig. 3.3). The disease has not been recorded in Australia. Although crown

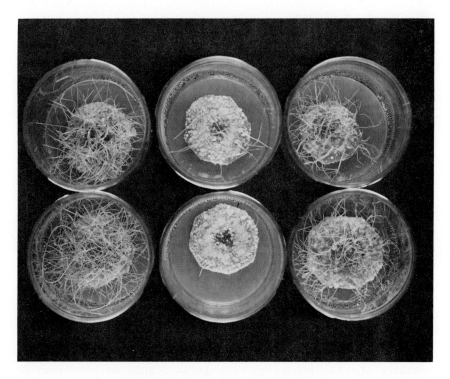

FIGURE 3.3 Hairy root on carrot

gall and hairy root look different, basically they are
nearly identical. However, instead of a Ti plasmid
determining virulence, there is a Ri (root inducing) plasmid
of approximately the same size. Both diseases involve the
transfer of T-DNA from bacterium to plant cell and this
causes cell proliferation and opine synthesis (Chilton et
al., 1982). The plant cell proliferation induced by hairy
root strains leads to excessive root formation rather than
to gall formation, although small galls are frequently
formed from which the roots develop. The difference appears
to be related to the balance of auxin and cytokinin
production. Most of the details of isolation, pathogenicity
testing, opine metabolism and detection given for crown gall
apply equally to hairy root.

The hairy root pathogens have a more restricted host
range than do those causing crown gall (De Cleene & De Ley,
1981). Natural infection has been recorded on apple,
cucumber (<u>Cucumis</u> <u>sativus</u>), rose and <u>Spiraea</u> spp. Thirty-
seven plants out of 202 inoculated were shown to be

susceptible; thirty-three of the thirty-seven belonged to the sub-classes Asteridea and Rosidea. Discs of carrot or parsnip (Pastinaca sativa) roots are also useful for pathogenicity testing (Ark & Thompson, 1961).

References

Allen, O.N. & Holding, A.J. (1974). Genus II. Agrobacterium. In "Bergey's Manual of Determinative Bacteriology" 8th edition, pp. 264-267. (Ed. R.E. Buchanan & N.E. Gibbons). Baltimore: Williams & Wilkins.

Anand, V.K. & Heberlein, G.T. (1977). Crown gall tumorigenesis in potato tuber tissue. American Journal of Botany 64, 153-158.

Anderson, A.R. & Moore L.W. (1979). Host specificity in the genus Agrobacterium. Phytopathology 69, 320-323.

Ark, P.A. & Thompson, J.P. (1961). Detection of hairy root pathogen, Agrobacterium rhizogenes by the use of fleshy roots. Phytopathology 51, 69-71.

Chilton, M.D., Tepfer, D.A., Petit, A., David, C., Casse-Delbart, F. & Tempe, J. (1982). Agrobacterium rhizogenes inserts T-DNA into the genomes of the host plant root cells. Nature, London 295, 432-434.

Cooper, D. & Firmin, J.L. (1977). Synthesis of nopaline [N-2 -(1,3 dicarboxypropyl) arginine] and isonopaline. Organic Preparations and Procedures International 9, 99-101.

De Cleene, M. & De Ley, J. (1976). The host range of crown gall. Botanical Review 42, 389-466.

De Cleene, M. & De Ley, J. (1981). The host range of infectious hairy root. Botanical Review 47, 147-194.

Denhardt, D. (1976). A membrane-filter technique for the detection of complementary DNA. Biochemical and Biophysical Research Communications 23, 641-646.

Holmes, B. & Roberts, P. (1981). The classification, identification and nomenclature of agrobacteria, incorporating revised descriptions for each of Agrobacterium tumefaciens (Smith & Townsend) Conn 1942, Agrobacterium rhizogenes (Riker et al.) Conn 1942 and Agrobacterium rubi (Hildebrand) Starr & Weiss 1943. Journal of Applied Bacteriology 50, 443-468.

Kahl, G. & Schell, J. (Eds.) (1982). "The Molecular Biology of Plant Tumors". New York: Academic Press.

Keane, P.J., Kerr, A. & New, P.B. (1970). Crown gall of stone fruit. II. Identification and nomenclature of Agrobacterium isolates. Australian Journal of Biological Science 23, 585-595.

Kerr, A. (1980). Biological control of crown gall through production of agrocin 84. Plant Disease 64, 24-30.

Kerr, A. & Htay, K. (1974). Biological control of crown gall through bacteriocin production. Physiological Plant Pathology 4, 37-44.

Kerr, A. & Panagopoulos, C.G. (1977). Biotypes of Agrobacterium radiobacter var. tumefaciens and their biological control. Phytopathologische Zeitschrift 90, 172-179.

Kersters, K., De Ley, J., Sneath, P.H.A. & Sackin, M. (1973). Numerical taxonomic analysis of Agrobacterium. Journal of General Microbiology 78, 227-239.

Klein, R.M. & Tenebaum, I.L. (1955). A quantitative bio-assay for crown gall tumor formation. American Journal of Botany 42, 709-712.

Kurkdjian, A., Manigault, P. & Beardsley, R. (1969). Crown Gall: effect of temperature on tumorigenesis in pea seedlings. Canadian Journal of Botany 47, 803-808.

Lippincott, J.A. & Heberlein, G.T. (1965). The quantitative determination of the infectivity of Agrobacterium tumefaciens. American Journal of Botany 52, 856-863.

Loper, J.E. & Kado, C.I. (1979). Host range conferred by the virulence specifying plasmid of Agrobacterium tumefaciens. Journal of Bacteriology 139, 591-596.

New, P.B. & Kerr, A. (1971). A selective medium for Agrobacterium radiobacter biotype 2. Journal of Applied Bacteriology 34, 233-236.

Rigby, P.W.J., Dieckmann, M., Rhodes, C. & Berg, P. (1977). Labelling deoxyribonucleic acid to high specificity in vitro by nick translation with DNA polymerase I. Journal of Molecular Biology 113, 237-251.

Roberts, W.P., Tate, M.E. & Kerr, A. (1977). Agrocin 84 is a 6-N- phosphoramidate of an adenine nucleotide analogue. Nature, London 265, 379-380.

Schell, J., van Montague, M., De Beuckeler, M., De Block, M., Depicker, A., De Wilde, M., Engeler, G., Genetello, C., Hernalsteens, J.P., Holsters, M., Seurinck, J., Silva, B., van Vliet, F. & Villarroel, R. (1979). Interactions and DNA transfer between Agrobacterium tumefaciens, the Ti plasmid and the host plant. Proceedings of the Royal Society, London, Series B.204, 251-266.

Schroth, M.N., Thompson, J.P. & Hildebrand, D.C. (1965).
Isolation of Agrobacterium tumefaciens - A. radiobacter
group from soil. Phytopathology 55, 645-647.

Southern, E.M. (1975). Detection of specific sequences among
DNA fragments separated by gel electrophoresis. Journal
of Molecular Biology 98, 503-517.

Tate, M.E. (1968). Separation of myoinositol pentaphos-
phates by moving paper electrophoresis (MPE).
Analytical Biochemistry 23, 141-149.

Tate, M.E., Ellis, J.G., Kerr, A., Tempe, J., Murray, K.E.
& Shaw, K.J. (1982). Agropine : a revised structure.
Carbohydrate Research 104, 105-120.

Thomashow, M.F., Nutter, R., Montoya, A., Gordon, M.P. &
Nester, E.W. (1980). Integration and organization of Ti
plasmid sequences in crown gall tumors. Cell 19, 729-
739.

Thomashow, M.F., Panagopoulos, C.G., Gordon, M.P. & Nester,
E.W. (1980). Host range of Agrobacterium tumefaciens is
determined by the Ti plasmid. Nature, London 283, 794-
796.

Trevelyan, W.E., Proctor, D.P. & Harrison, J.S. (1950).
Detection of sugars on paper chromatograms. Nature,
London 166, 444-445.

White, L.O. (1972). The taxonomy of the crown-gall organism
Agrobacterium tumefaciens and its relationship to
rhizobia and other agrobacteria. Journal of General
Microbiology 72, 565-574.

Yamada, S. & Itano, H.A. (1966). Phenanthrenequinone as an
analytical reagent for arginine and other mono-
substituted guanidines. Biochimica et Biophysica Acta
130, 538-540.

Corynebacterium

M. L. Moffett, P. C. Fahy and D. Cartwright

I.	Introduction	45
II.	*Corynebacterium michiganense* subsp. *michiganense*: Bacterial Canker of Tomato and Capsicum	46
III.	*Corynebacterium michiganense* subsp. *insidiosum*: Bacterial Wilt of Lucerne	51
IV.	*Corynebacterium michiganense* subsp. *sepedonicum*: Ring Rot of Potato	54
V.	*Corynebacterium flaccumfaciens* subsp. *flaccumfaciens*: Bacterial Wilt of Bean	55
VI.	*Corynebacterium* sp. Causing Annual Ryegrass Toxicity	57
	References	61

I. Introduction

The symptoms of the plant diseases caused by members of the genus Corynebacterium include wilt, cankers, pustules, galls and gummosis. Members of this genus can be identified tentatively by their pleomorphic morphology, particularly when observed under an electron microscope. Individual cells are short, straight or curved pleomorphic rods, often with one club-shaped end. Metachromatic granules are often present. The bacteria are non-spore forming.

The plant pathogenic Corynebacterium species have the following characteristics common to the genus (Cummins et al., 1974): colonies are semi-fluid, dark cream to yellow, and pinpoint in size in 2-5 days on a medium such as glucose yeast extract calcium carbonate agar (GYCA) (Dye, 1962) and enlarging to form round to oval colonies, 1-2 mm in diameter. Cells are usually Gram positive, non motile, single, coccoid or club shaped rods 0.4-.5 x 0.7-1.0 μm, often in a pallisade or an angular shaped arrangement indicative of snapping division. Although most members of the genus are Gram positive, frequently isolates are Gram variable. For this reason, Gram stains should always be made on 24-28 h cultures and controls used. The Gram reaction can be checked using the KOH test (Gregersen, 1978).

Carlson & Vidaver (1982a) group the plant pathogenic corynebacteria in seven species based on electrophoretic protein patterns (Table 4.1). Dye & Kemp (1977), using numerical analysis, grouped the pathogens into only four species, combining C. iranicum, C. tritici and C. rathayi as pathovars of C. michiganense. The nomenclature of Carlson & Vidaver (1982a) has been adopted in this text. The phytopathogenic coryneform bacteria have recently been reviewed by Vidaver & Starr (1981).

C. flaccumfaciens subspecies are the only group containing motile strains (Lelliott, 1966; Dye & Kemp, 1977; Carlson & Vidaver, 1982a). They are also faster growing, colonies developing to >1mm within three days at optimal temperatures. All other corynebacteria take three or more days to develop visible colonies on isolation media.

Diagnosis of the corynebacteria is relatively simple, based on cell morphology, Gram reaction, colony morphology, pigmentation, growth rate and motility. Colony pigmentation is a useful aid, although rare non-pigmented strains occur. C. michiganense subsp. insidiosum generally produces characteristic blue to violet granules of indigoidine within cream colonies on GYCA. Other species are usually cream to bright orange, although other pigments have been reported. Diagnoses are generally confirmed by pathogenicity tests. Details of diagnostic media and tests discussed below are given in Chapter 16.

The diseases caused by Corynebacterium spp. recorded for Australia are described here, together with ring rot of potato, a major disease of potato not present in Australia. All described species of Corynebacterium are listed in Table 4.1, together with their major hosts and symptoms.

II. *Corynebacterium michiganense* subsp. *michiganense*: Bacterial Canker of Tomato and Capsicum

A. *Symptoms on Tomato*

Wilting of leaflets occurs along one side of the leaf prior to its collapse (Fig. 4.1a). Leaves on one or both sides of the plant are affected. In advanced stages of the

(a)   (b)

FIGURE 4.1   Bacterial canker on tomato caused by Corynebacterium michiganense subsp. michiganense. (a) one-sided leaf collapse and (b) "bird's eye spot" on tomato fruit.

disease, the whole plant wilts and collapses (Strider, 1969; Vock, 1978).   Light brown cankers develop on the stem and petioles. The vascular tissue is discoloured dark brown and cavities develop in the pith. The affected vascular tissue tends to separate from the bark tissue as the disease progresses. On fruit, white circular spots develop up to 3 mm in width with a raised brown central area. The centre of the spots collapse, giving a ragged appearance known as "bird's eye spot" (Fig. 4.1b).

B.   *Symptoms on Capsicum*

Pale green, raised areas appear on leaves, which develop into irregular, corky pustules with a brown centre.

TABLE 4.1 *Plant Pathogenic Species of* Corynebacterium

Species/Subspecies[a]	Major Symptoms and Hosts	References
C. michiganense		
subsp. michiganense (Smith 1910) Jensen 1934	Canker of tomato (Lycopersicon esculentum) and capsicum (Capsicum annuum)	See text (II)
subsp. insidiosum (McCulloch 1925) Carlson & Vidaver 1982	Wilt of lucerne (Medicago sativa)	See text (III)
subsp. sepedonicum (Spieckermann & Kotthoff 1914) Dye & Kemp 1977	Ring rot of potato (Solanum tuberosum)	See text (IV)
subsp. nebraskense (Schuster, Hoff, Mandel & Lazar (1973) Carlson & Vidaver 1982	Wilt of maize (Zea mays)	Anon. (1980)
subsp. tessellarius Carlson & Vidaver 1982	Mosaic of wheat (Triticum aestivum)	Carlson & Vidaver (1982a, b)
C. flaccumfaciens		
subsp. flaccumfaciens (Hedges 1922) Dowson 1942	Wilt of bean (Phaseolus vulgaris)	See Text (V)
subsp. betae (Keyworth, Howell & Dowson 1956) Carlson & Vidaver 1982	Wilt and leaf spot of red beet (Beta vulgaris)	Bradbury (1973a)

Table 4.1 (Cont'd) Plant Pathogenic Species of Corynebacterium

subsp. oortii (Saaltink & Maas Geesteranus 1969) Carlson & Vidaver 1982	Spot of tulip leaves and bulbs (Tulipa spp.)	Bradbury (1973b)
subsp. poinsettiae (Starr & Pirone 1942) Carlson & Vidaver 1982	Stem canker and leaf spot of poinsettia (Euphorbia pulcherrima)	Starr & Pirone (1942)
C. fascians (Tilford 1936) Dowson 1942	Fasciation on a wide range of plants	Bradbury (1967)
C. ilicis Mandel, Guba & Litsky 1961	Blight of American holly (Ilex opaca)	Mandel et al. (1961)
C. iranicum (Scharif 1961) Carlson & Vidaver 1982	Gummosis of wheat heads	Scharif (1961)
C. tritici (Hutchinson 1917) Carlson & Vidaver 1982	Yellow slime of wheat heads	Bradbury (1973d)
C. rathayi (Smith 1913) Dowson 1942	Gummosis of cocksfoot heads (Dactylis glomerata)	Bradbury (1973c)
Corynebacterium sp.	Gummosis of annual ryegrass heads (Lolium rigidum)	See Text (VI)

[a] *Nomenclature of Carlson & Vidaver (1982a)*

Pustules   tend to collapse, leaving an irregular brown spot.
Leaf   fall   is common.   Vascular discolouration has not been
observed   in   the field in infected plants (Volcani et al.
1970;   Vock,   1978).   "Bird's   eye   spots" develop on fruit,
similar to those on tomato fruit (Fig. 4.1b).

C. Geographical Distribution and Importance

Bacterial   canker   occurs   in   Australia,   New   Zealand,
Africa,   North and South America, Asia and Europe (Hayward &
Waterston, 1964a).   In Australia, the disease is wide spread
throughout   tomato   growing areas.   The severity varies from
season   to   season but canker is one of the most destructive
diseases   of tomato.   Its occurrence on capsicum is increasing   in   Queensland and it has been recorded where capsicums
are   grown   in   conjunction   with   tomatoes, particularly in
southern Queensland.

D. Host Range

Tomato   (Lycopersicon   esculentum);   capsicum   (Capsicum
annuum); and Solanum nigrum (Ark & Thompson, 1960).

E. Isolation and Identification

Isolation.   C. michiganense subsp. michiganense is not
consistently isolated from the vascular tissue of tomato
plants nor from cankers on leaf petioles.   More consistent
results   are   obtained   when   isolations are made from fruit
spots   and   discoloured vascular tissue within the fruit.
There   is   usually   no   difficulty in isolating the pathogen
from leaf and fruit spots on capsicum.

A   section   of   the discoloured vascular tissue or fruit
spot is suspended in 9 ml of sterile distilled water for 30
min   or macerated in a few drops of sterile distilled water.
A   loopful   of   the   liquid   is   spread over a plate of agar
medium.   GYCA (Dye, 1962) is the recommended medium for isolation.   Despite the opacity of the medium, the colony type
is easily recognisable.

Identification.   After incubation for 48-72 h at 25-28C,
pinpoint   yellow   colonies   appear   on the isolation plates.
Semi-fluid,   oval   to round, raised yellow colonies, 1 mm in

diameter are present in 96 h. Proof of pathogenicity to tomato and/or capsicum is necessary to confirm the identity of suspected isolates of the pathogen.

F. *Pathogenicity*

Inoculum is prepared by suspending growth from a 48 h culture on GYCA in sterile distilled water and adjusting the turbidity to give a concentration of 10^8 cells/ml. Inoculum is prepared from a plate culture in preference to using a broth culture as described by Vidaver (1980) because of the dangers of contamination of the latter.

Inoculation of Tomato.   Plants at the second or third true leaf stage are suitable for inoculation. Older plants can be inoculated with success, but young plants are most suitable for a quick result in glasshouse tests. A sterile scalpel is dipped in the inoculum and the cotyledon is excised at the node. Application of more inoculum to the cut face is not usually necessary. The inoculated plant is left on a glasshouse bench. Early symptoms such as a one-sided wilt of the leaflets on the inoculated side of the plant appear within 14 days.

Inoculation of Capsicum.   Plants at the second or third true leaf stage are spray inoculated, using a hand atomiser attached to a pressure pump maintained at 34.5 kilopascals. Both surfaces of the leaves are sprayed to run off without infiltration.   The plants are placed in a cabinet held at about 100% r.h. or covered with a moistened plastic bag and kept out of the direct sunlight for 18-48 h. They are then placed uncovered on a glasshouse bench and symptoms appear within 14 days.

III.   *Corynebacterium michiganense* subsp. *insidiosum*: Bacterial Wilt of Lucerne

A. *Symptoms*

Symptoms on lucerne are most obvious during autumn after hay has been cut and regrowth is only 5-10 cm high. The first symptoms are pale stunted plants, often in clumps and particularly in low lying sections of the field. A gradation of mild to severe symptoms is often apparent within the clumps. Symptoms range from slight stunting and a general paleness to severely stunted plants with small puckered leaves, often with upward curling of the margins (Fig. 4.2). Stem proliferation may occur, giving a witches broom effect (Close & Mulcock, 1972; Fahy 1974).

Plants with moderate to severe symptoms frequently wilt and die during winter and the disease is less obvious by spring. Indeed, symptoms may not be evident during spring or summer. The disease is most readily detected in stands 2-4 yr old. The incidence of the disease is generally quite low in younger stands and in older stands the least tolerant plants have died, leaving only 'carrier' plants exhibiting mild or no symptoms. The disease is also present, but more difficult to detect in wilt-tolerant cultivars.

B. *Host Range*

The disease is economically important only on lucerne (Medicago sativa). It has also been recorded on other Medicago spp. and Melilotus alba (Renfro & Sprague, 1959).

C. *Geographical Distribution and Importance*

Australia; New Zealand (Hale & Close, 1974); USA, Canada, Mexico, Europe (Hayward & Waterston, 1964c). Bacterial wilt of lucerne is widespread in Australia, particularly in New South Wales, Victoria and parts of South Australia. It is a cool climate disease, active every season in stands from autumn to spring. It is a serious factor in stand decline in irrigated lucerne, especially in the higher rainfall regions from central New South Wales to southern Victoria. It is rarely important in dryland stands (Smith & Taylor, 1967).

D. *Isolation and Identification*

Isolation.   C. michiganense subsp. insidiosum is extremely difficult to isolate unless the disease is active. Hence time of year and plant and tissue selection are critical. Isolations should be attempted from young, white shoots developing from the crown or petioles and leaves of young shoots rather than from roots or stems. Active ooze is often apparent in young tissue but is difficult to detect in root tissue or when the disease is not active.

FIGURE 4.2 Bacterial wilt of lucerne caused by Coryne-
bacterium michiganense subsp. insidiosum with diseased
plant (right) showing pale, stunted regrowth and
small leaves.

If ooze is present, isolation is not difficult and
special media are not required. Both GYCA and sucrose
peptone agar (SPA) (Hayward, 1960) will provide good growth
and pigment development. Addition of "Actidione" (cycloheximide) at 250 ppm to the media is of benefit when clear
symptoms are not apparent. The success rate in these cases
is low and a minimum of ten plates per plant should be
streaked as the pathogen is readily swamped by faster
growing bacteria.

Identification.   Initial diagnosis is based on colony
morphology, cell morphology and Gram reaction. On GYCA and
SPA at 25C, colonies are visible by 5 days but after 7-10
days they are clearly distinguishable as off-white to pale
yellow shiny, mucoid and slightly raised colonies.
Irregular streaks and swirls of blue to purple pigment
usually develop within some colonies by 10-14 days. Non-
pigmented isolates can occur.

E. Pathogenicity

Identity is best confirmed by pathogenicity tests at
temperatures between 18-20C. The roots of young seedlings
are cut and the plants dipped in a suspension of about

10^7 cells/ml and transplanted. After 14 days the tips can be cut back and the regrowth frequently shows disease symptoms within a further 14-28 days.

IV.   *Corynebacterium michiganense* subsp. *sepedonicum*: Ring Rot of Potato

A. *Symptoms*

External symptoms usually appear late in the season. The leaves turn slightly yellow and tend to roll up around the midrib.   Wilting may occur in one or more stems and vascular discolouration is limited or does not occur (Dowson, 1957; Stapp, 1961; Hayward & Waterston, 1964b). Tubers develop a zone of creamy-yellow or light brown putrified tissue with a cheesy consistency in the vicinity of the vascular tissue (Fig. 4.3).   In advanced stages, gaps in the diseased tissue form between the cortex and the pith. The cheesy nature and colour of the exudate squeezed from the vascular ring of a cut tuber differs from the white milky exudate produced by <u>Pseudomonas</u> <u>solanacearum</u>, the cause of bacterial wilt on potatoes.

B. *Host Range.* Potato (<u>Solanum</u> <u>tuberosum</u>).

C. *Geographical Distribution and Importance*

North America, Europe (Hayward & Waterston, 1964b). Ring rot is not present in Australia. As it is one of the most important diseases of potato, Australia prohibits the import of potatoes from countries where this disease occurs.

D. *Isolation and Identification*

Isolation.   <u>C</u>. <u>michiganense</u> subsp. <u>sepedonicum</u> is isolated from tubers (Snieszko & Bonde, 1943) onto GYCA and incubated at 22-25C for at least five days, using common isolation procedures (see Chapter 1).

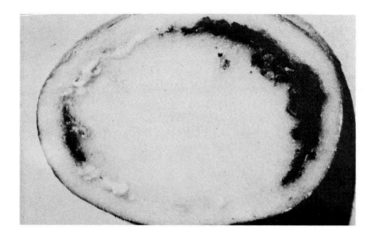

FIGURE 4.3. Ring Rot of potato caused by Corynebacterium michiganense subsp. sepedonicum, tuber symptoms. (British Crown copyright)

Identification. Initial diagnosis is based on plant and
tuber symptoms, colony and cell morphology, and Gram
reaction of isolates. Growth on isolation medium is slow
and colonies may take from five to seven days to develop.
The white or cream to pale yellow colonies, semi-fluidal
when freshly isolated, become butyrous with prolonged
culturing. Cells are pleomorphic, predominantly single with
pallisade arrangements. As with the other coryneform
bacteria, they are relatively inactive biochemically. They
differ in pathogenicity and pigmentation from other
Corynebacterium species.

V. *Corynebacterium flaccumfaciens* subsp. *flaccumfaciens*: Bacterial Wilt of Bean

A. Symptoms

C. flaccumfaciens subsp. flaccumfaciens causes a vascular wilt disease. The bacteria invade the xylem and
frequently kill or stunt young bean seedlings. In older
plants, leaves and stems lose turgidity, eventually drying
out and taking on a shrivelled appearance. Sometimes
lesions develop as irregularly shaped, necrotic areas
between the main veins and may be confused with common
blight caused by Xanthomonas campestris pv. phaseoli. Often

only   one   or two laterals may be affected and may be hidden
by healthy foliage.   The stems of infected plants may break
readily in the wind (Hedges, 1926; Dinensen, 1980).

Pod symptoms are often inconspicuous but the vascular
tissue of the sutures may be darkened. Seeds are infected
and may be discoloured yellow. Orange and purple staining
variants have been reported from the U.S.A. (Schuster &
Christiansen, 1957; Schuster & Sayne, 1967).

Field spread is generally slow (Richard & Walker, 1965),
but the disease may attain major importance if high levels
of seed borne infection occur. The disease is satisfactorily controlled by the use of disease-free seed schemes
and crop rotation.

B. Host Range

French and navy beans (Phaseolus vulgaris), mung bean or
green gram (Vigna radiata); P. lunatus, P. angularis, and P.
coccineus (Hedges, 1926; Zaumeyer & Thomas, 1957; Dye &
Kemp, 1977).

A Corynebacterium sp. similar to C. flaccumfaciens
subsp. flaccumfaciens causes a wilt disease of soybean
(Glycine max) in the U.S.A. (Dunleavy, 1963). The disease
is of infrequent occurrence (Kennedy & Tachibana, 1973). C.
flaccumfaciens subsp. flaccumfaciens also infects soybean on
artificial inoculation (Hedges, 1926; Schuster & Sayre,
1967).   However, no direct comparison of the bean and
soybean pathogens has been made.

C. Geographical Distribution and Importance

Australia, Europe, North America (Hayward & Waterston,
1965).   In Australia bacterial wilt has been recorded in
Victoria (Adams & Pugsley, 1934) and New South Wales (Anon.,
1950) on French and Navy beans and in South Australia in
1969 on French beans (Kerr, pers. comm.). The pathogen was
probably introduced on infested seed and caused little
economic loss.   Use of disease-free seed has apparently
eliminated the pathogen from Australian bean crops.

D. *Isolation and Identification*

Isolation. The pathogen is readily isolated from infected petioles, stems, leaf blades and seed on non-selective media, such as GYCA, SPA or potato dextrose agar (PDA) (Riker & Riker, 1936). It is preferable not to surface sterilize the test material. Freshly infected material should be washed thoroughly in tap water and blotted dry. Samples (1 cm^2) should be macerated in sterile distilled water, using the general isolation techniques for plant pathogenic bacteria (see Chapter 1).

Identification. On GYCA, SPA or PDA, visible colonies develop in 48 h, becoming yellow with age. Colonies are smooth, glistening and low convex. Initial diagnosis is based on plant symptoms, colony and cell morphology and Gram reaction of the bacteria isolated from infected material. The identity of the pathogen is confirmed by its reaction in pathogenicity tests and in biochemical and physiological tests. Detailed descriptions of C. flaccumfaciens subsp. flaccumfaciens are provided by Hayward & Waterston (1965) and Dye & Kemp (1977).

VI. *Corynebacterium* sp. Causing Annual Ryegrass Toxicity

A. *Disease Complex.*

Annual ryegrass toxicity is a disease of grazing animals caused by the ingestion of toxins produced in annual (Wimmera) ryegrass plants by an Anguina/Corynebacterium disease complex. The bacterial toxins cause neurological disorders in stock resulting in loss of co-ordination, nervous spasms, convulsions and death.

The nematode, Anguina agrostis (Steinbuch 1799) Filipjev 1936 (syn. A. funesta Price, Fisher & Kerr 1979) acts as the vector of a coryneform bacterium. The bacteria are carried into the plant adhering to the cuticle of the second stage juveniles of the nematode (Price, 1973; Bird & Stynes, 1977; Stynes & Bird, 1980). The larvae survive desiccation in the mature seed galls and, following microbial degradation of the galls, migrate after spring rains.

Price (1973) found that after the spring rains in southern Australia, second stage larvae emerge from galls and migrate to young ryegrass plants. The nematodes move up the stems and first formed leaves and down to the growing points of the plants. The larvae enter newly initiated ovaries and induce the formation of galls. The nematodes feed in the gall and rapidly moult through third and fourth larval stages to become adult. The adult nematodes mate and lay eggs within the gall. The eggs hatch to give second stage larvae which are resistant to desiccation and act as inoculum for the next season. Only one generation of the nematode is completed annually.

Under certain circumstances the galls are taken over by the bacteria. The bacteria produce a yellow slime which may sometimes be seen on infected ryegrass heads in the field (Fig. 4.4a). The slime may crystallize to a yellow/orange colour when dry or may be washed from the heads. The presence of slime is most easily detected when the heads emerge from the boot. The heads may occasionally show degrees of distortion (McKay et al., 1981b).

The bacteria in the galls produce a number of "corynetoxins" which, when ingested in sufficient quantity, result in the neurological disorders seen in stock. The corynetoxins closely resemble tunicamycin, a highly toxic antibiotic, the only difference being in the length of the long-chain fatty acid component (Vogel et al., 1981; Edgar et al., 1982).

B.   *Host Range*

The disease is economically significant only on annual ryegrass (Lolium rigidum) but may also be associated with other grasses (Bird, 1981). The bacterial slime occurs also on Lolium multiflorum, and Phalaris aquatica, P. minor, P. paradoxa, and Avena fatua (Chatel et al., 1979) which are present in annual ryegrass pastures. The host range of the bacterium may be limited by the specificity of the vector as the disease can be induced in a wider range of grasses after bacterial inoculation (Price, 1973).

C.   *Geographical Distribution and Importance*

Australia (South Australia, Western Australia); South Africa (Schneider pers. comm.). In Australia, annual ryegrass toxicity occurs in the wheat/sheep belt of South Australia and the south-west of Western Australia where annual ryegrass is a major component of the pastures.

(a)   (b)

*FIGURE   4.4   Annual ryegrass toxicity: (a) infected
ryegrass   heads   with   bacterial   slime;   (b) threshed
ryegrass   seed showing healthy seed (top), nematode gall
(centre) and bacterial gall (bottom).*

Annual   ryegrass   toxicity was   first   recorded   in the mid-
north   region of South Australia in 1956 and has since shown
an   apparently   slow   spread   to   other   areas   of   the   wheat/sheep
belt   within   the   State.   Fisher et al. (1979) found that
there   was   a   ten   to   fifteen   year   time   lag between the
introduction   of the nematode vector and the increase of the
disease   to   detectable   levels   within a new area.   Grazing
stock   losses   can be sudden and almost total (McKay et al.,
1981b).

D. *Isolation and Identification*

Isolation.   The   pathogen may be readily isolated from
infected   galls   on   a   sucrose-casein   hydrolysate   medium
(Price,   1973).   This   is   a   modification   of   medium D2

described by Kado & Heskett (1970).   Price (1973) found that bacteria were present in much of the above ground parts of heavily infected plants and could be readily isolated from within the lower nodes and leaves.

Identification.   Yellow, glistening colonies develop after incubation for 4 days at 25C.   The bacterium involved in the annual ryegrass toxicity complex is a Gram positive, non-motile bacterium of coryneform morphology.   Price (1973) suggested that the bacterium was closely related to C. rathayi and C. tritici (Table 4.1).   These species, as well as C. iranicum and the pathogen on annual ryegrass are associated with nematodes of the genus Anguina, and cause similar diseases on Gramineae (Bird, 1981).   However, no direct comparison of the Corynebacterium sp. from annual ryegrass has been made with the above species to establish if the bacterium is C. rathayi or a related species.

E. *Diagnosis*

The presence of the disease complex is most readily detected in the laboratory.   Field detection is dependent upon the presence of a yellow slime, which is not always produced, or the presence of nematode or bacterial galls which may be difficult to find.

Two methods are presently used in the laboratory (Stynes & Wise, 1980).   The first involves an examination in a light box of samples of threshed ryegrass heads, collected from a suspected toxic pasture (Fig. 4.4b).   Nematode galls are seen as dark brown and flask-shaped when compared to the dark brown but round-topped ryegrass seed.   Bacterial galls are similarly flask-shaped but yellow to orange in colour. The second technique involves mixing threshed samples with alcohol.   The healthy ryegrass seeds sink while the lighter nematode and bacterial galls float.   Samples are then washed, dried and viewed, using a light box.

F. *Control*

Control measures are based upon breaking the annual lifecycle of the nematode by the use of herbicides in crops to reduce ryegrass populations; the use of desiccant herbicides in pastures to prevent seed set and gall development; hard grazing of ryegrass while heads are emerging; burning of toxic or suspected toxic pastures; and fallowing (Price, 1973; McKay et al., 1981b).

McKay et al. (1981a) found that mowing or topping ryegrass pastures, as the heads emerged but before flowering, was successful in reducing nematode populations. Similarly, increasing the legume component of pastures, combined with mowing or hard grazing, was found to increase the effectiveness of these techniques. McKay et al. (1981a) also found that the presence of the plant parasitic fungus, Dilophospora alopecuri, markedly reduced the number of galls and nematodes by killng the tissues on which the nematodes feed.

References

Adams, D.B. & Pugsley, A.T. (1934). Bacterial plant diseases in Victoria. Journal of Agriculture, Victoria 32, 304-323.

Anon. (1950). New South Wales Department of Agriculture, Biology Branch Plant Disease Survey, 1949-50.

Anon. (1980). Goss' bacterial wilt and blight. In "Compendium of Corn Diseases" 2nd edition, pp. 7-8. (Ed. M.C. Shurtleff). St Paul, Minnesota: American Phytopathological Society.

Ark, P.A. & Thompson, J.P. (1960). Additional hosts for tomato canker organism Corynebacterium michiganense. Plant Disease Reporter 44, 98-99.

Bird, A.F. (1981). The Anguina–Corynebacterium association. In "Plant Parasitic Nematodes" Vol. III, pp. 303-323. (Ed. B.M. Zuckerman & R.A. Rohde). New York: Academic Press. 508 pp.

Bird, A.F. & Stynes, B.A. (1977). The morphology of a Corynebacterium sp. parasitic on annual rye grass. Phytopathology 67, 828-830.

Bradbury, J.F. (1967). Corynebacterium fascians. CMI Descriptions of Pathogenic Fungi and Bacteria No. 121. Kew: Commonwealth Mycological Institute.

Bradbury, J.F. (1973a). Corynebacterium betae. CMI Descriptions of Pathogenic Fungi and Bacteria No. 374. Kew: Commonwealth Mycological Institute.

Bradbury, J.F. (1973b). Corynebacterium oortii. CMI Descriptions of Pathogenic Fungi and Bacteria No. 375. Kew: Commonwealth Mycological Institute.

Bradbury, J.F. (1973c). Corynebacterium rathayi. CMI Descriptions of Pathogenic Fungi and Bacteria No. 376. Kew: Commonwealth Mycological Institute.

Bradbury, J.F. (1973d). Corynebacterium tritici. CMI Descriptions of Pathogenic Fungi and Bacteria No. 377. Kew: Commonwealth Mycological Institute.

Carlson, R.R. & Vidaver, A.K. (1982a). Taxonomy of Corynebacterium plant pathogens, including a new pathogen of wheat, based on polyacrylamide gel electrophoresis of cellular protein. International Journal of Systematic Bacteriology 32, 315-326.

Carlson, R.R. & Vidaver, A.K. (1982b). Bacterial mosaic, a new corynebacterial disease of wheat. Plant Disease 66, 76-79.

Chatel, D.L., Wise, J.L. & Marfleet, A.G. (1979). Ryegrass toxicity organism found on other grasses. Western Australian Journal of Agriculture No. 3, 89.

Close, R. & Mulcock, A.P. (1972). Bacterial wilt, Corynebacterium insidiosum (McCulloch, 1925) Jensen 1934 of lucerne in New Zealand. New Zealand Journal of Agricultural Research 15, 141-148.

Cummins, C.S., Lelliott, R.A. & Rogosa, M. (1974). Corynebacterium Lehmann & Neumann 1896. In "Bergey's Manual of Determinative Bacteriology" 8th edition, pp. 602-617. (Ed. R.E. Buchanan & N.E. Gibbons). Baltimore: Williams & Wilkins.

Dinensen, I.G.(1980). Bacterial wilt of beans. Danish Journal of Plant and Soil Science 84, 361-370.

Dowson, W.J. (1957). Gram-positive bacterial plant pathogens: Corynebacterium. In "Plant Diseases Due to Bacteria" 2nd edition, pp. 79-98. Cambridge University Press.

Dunleavy, J. (1963). A vascular disease of soybeans caused by Corynebacterium sp. Plant Disease Reporter 47, 612-613.

Dye, D.W. (1962). The inadequacy of the usual determinative tests for the identification of Xanthomonas spp. New Zealand Journal of Science 5, 393-416.

Dye, D.W. & Kemp, W.J. (1977). A taxonomic study of plant pathogenic Corynebacterium species. New Zealand Journal of Agricultural Research 20, 563-582.

Edgar, J.A., Frahn, J.L., Cockrum, P.A., Anderton, N., Jago, M.V. & Culvenor, C.J. Jones, A.L., Murray, K. & Shaw, K.J. (1982). Corynetoxins, causative agents of annual ryegrass toxicity; their identification as tunicamycin group antibiotics. Chemical Communications No. 4, 222-224.

Fahy, P.C. (1974). Lucerne bacterial wilt. Agricultural Gazette of New South Wales No. 5, 38-39.

Fisher, J.M., Dube, A.J. & Watson, C.M. (1979). Distribution in South Australia of Anguina funesta, the nematode associated with annual ryegrass toxicity. Australian Journal of Experimental Agriculture and Animal Husbandry 19, 48-52.

Gregersen, T. (1978). Rapid method for distinction of Gram negative from Gram positive bacteria. European Journal of Applied Microbiology and Biotechnology 5, 123-127.

Hale, C.N. & Close, R.C. (1974). A survey of the occurrence of bacterial wilt of lucerne in New Zealand. New Zealand Journal of Experimental Agriculture 2, 75-77.

Hayward, A.C. (1960). A method for characterizing Pseudomonas solanacearum. Nature (London) 186, 405-406.

Hayward, A.C. & Waterston, J.M. (1964a). Corynebacterium michiganense. CMI Description of Pathogenic Fungi and Bacteria No. 19. Kew: Commonwealth Mycological Institute

Hayward, A.C. & Waterston, J.M. (1964b). Corynebacterium sepedonicum. CMI Descriptions of Pathogenic Fungi and Bacteria No. 14. Kew: Commonwealth Mycological Institute.

Hayward, A.C. & Watertson, J.M. (1964c). Corynebacterium insidiosum. CMI Descriptions of Pathogenic Fungi and Bacteria No. 13. Kew: Commonwealth Mycological Institute.

Hayward, A.C. & Waterston, J.M. (1965). Corynebacterium flaccumfaciens. CMI Descriptions of Pathogenic Fungi and Bacteria No. 43. Kew: Commonwealth Mycological Institute.

Hedges, F. (1926). Bacterial wilt of beans (Bacterium flaccumfaciens Hedges), including comparisons with Bacterium phaseoli. Phytopathology 16, 1-22.

Kado, C.I. & Heskett, M.G. (1970). Selective media for isolation of Agrobacterium, Corynebacterium, Erwinia, Pseudomonas and Xanthomonas. Phytopathology 60, 969-976.

Kennedy, B.W. & Tachibana, H. (1973). Bacterial diseases. In "Soybeans: Improvement. Production and Uses". (Ed. B.E. Caldwell). Madison, Wisconsin: American Society of Agronomy.

Lelliott, R.A. (1966). The plant pathogenic coryneform bacteria. Journal of Appplied Bacteriology 29, 114-118.

McKay, A.C., Fisher, J.M. & Dube, A.J. (1981a). Ecological field studies of Anguina funesta, the vector in annual ryegrass toxicity. Australian Journal of Agricultural Research 32, 917-926.

McKay, A., Michelmore, A. & Mackie, D. (1981b). Annual ryegrass toxicity. South Australian Department of Agriculture Fact Sheet No. 91/77.

Mandel, M., Guba, E.F. & Litsky, W. (1961). The causal agent of bacterial blight of American holly. Bacteriological Proceedings 1961, 61.

Price, P.C. (1973). Investigation of a nematode-bacterium disease complex affecting Wimmera ryegrass. Ph.D. Thesis, University of Adelaide, Australia.

Renfro, B.L. & Sprague, E.W. (1959). Reaction of Medicago species to eight Alfalfa pathogens. Agronomy Journal 51, 481-483.

Rickard, S.F. & Walker, J.C. (1965). Mode of inoculation and host nutrition in relation to bacterial wilt of bean. Phytopathology 55, 174-178.

Riker A.J. & Riker, R.S. (1936). Culture media. In "Introduction to Research on Plant Diseases", pp. 26-35. St Louis: John S. Swift.

Scharif, G. (1961). Corynebacterium iranicum sp. nov. on wheat (Triticum vulgare L.) in Iran and a comparative study of it with C. tritici and C. rathayi. Entomologie et Phytopathologie Appliquees 19, 1-24.

Schuster, M.L. (1975). Leaf freckle and wilt of corn incited by Corynebacterium nebraskense Schuster, Hoff, Mandel & Lazar 1972. Research Bulletin 270. The Agricultural Experiment Station, University of Nebraska, Lincoln, Nebraska.

Schuster, M.L. & Christiansen, D.W. (1957). An orange colored strain of Corynebacterium flaccumfaciens causing bean wilt. Phytopathology 47, 51-53.

Schuster, M.L. & Sayre, R.M. (1967). A coryneform bacterium induces purple-colored seed and leaf hypertrophy of Phaseolus vulgaris and other Leguminosae. Phytopathology 57, 1064-1066.

Smith, P.R. & Taylor, R.H. (1967). The occurrence of Corynebacterium insidiosum (McCulloch) Jensen in Victoria. Australian Journal of Experimental Agriculture and Animal Husbandry 7, 190-192.

Snieszko, S.F. & Bonde, R. (1943). Studies on the morphology, physiology, serology, longevity, and pathogenicity of Corynebacterium sepedonicum. Phytopathology 33, 1032-1044.

Stapp, C. (1961). II. Special part. Corynebacterium sepedonicum (Spieckermann et Kotthoff) Skaptason et Burkholder. In "Bacterial Plant Pathogens", pp. 119-130. Oxford University Press.

Starr, M.P. & Pirone, P.P. (1942). Phytomonas poinsettiae n. sp., the cause of a bacterial disease of pointsettia. Phytopathology 32, 1076-1081.

Strider, D.L. (1969). Bacterial canker of tomato caused by Corynebacterium michiganense. North Carolina Agricultural Experiment Station Technical Bulletin No. 193.

Stynes, B.A. & Bird, A.F. (1980). Anguina agrostis, the vector of annual ryegrass toxicity in Australia. Nematologica 26, 475-490.

Stynes, B.A. & Wise, J.L. (1980). Distribution and importance of annual ryegrass toxicity in Western Australia and its occurrence in relation to cropping rotations and cultural practices. Australian Journal of Agricultural Research 31, 557-569.

Vidaver, A.K. (1980). Corynebacterium. In "Laboratory Guide for Identification of Plant Pathogenic Bacteria", pp. 12-16. (Ed. N.W. Schaad). St Paul, Minnesota: American Phytopathological Society.

Vidaver, A.K. & Starr, M.P. (1981). Phytopathogenic Coryneform and Related Bacteria. In "The Prokaryotes", Vol. I. pp. 1879-1887. (Ed. M.P. Starr, H. Stolp, H.G. Truper, A. Balows & H.G. Schlegel). Berlin: Springer-Verlag.

Vock, N.T. (1978). "A Handbook of Plant Diseases". Vol. 1 & 2. Brisbane: Queensland Department of Primary Industries.

Vogel, P., Petterson, D.S., Berry, P.H., Frahn, J.L., Anderton, N., Cockrum, P.A., Edgar, J.A., Jago, M.V., Lanigan, G.W., Payne, A.L. & Culveor, C.C.J. (1981). Isolation of a group of glycolipid toxins from seedheads of annual ryegrass (Lolium rigidum Gaud.) infected by Corynebacterium rathayi. Australian Journal of Experimental Biology and Medical Science 59, 455-467.

Volcani, Z., Zutia, D. & Cohn, R. (1970). A new leaf and fruit spot disease of pepper caused by Corynebacterium michiganense. Plant Disease Reporter 54, 804-806.

Zaumeyer, W.J. & Thomas, H.R. (1957). A monographic study of bean diseases and methods for their control. Technical Bulletin U.S. Department of Agriculture No. 868, 255 pp.

5

Erwinia:
The "Amylovora" and "Herbicola" Groups
D. W. Dye

I. Introduction   67
II. Isolation   68
III. Identification   69
IV. The "Amylovora" Group   75
V. The "Herbicola" Group   80
References   83

I. Introduction

Erwinia species cause a wide range of plant diseases with symptoms which include wilts, blights, cankers, dieback, leaf spots, fruit spots, soft rots and discoloration of woody tissue. The pathogen usually gains entry to the plant through wounds or natural openings. One nomenspecies (E. uredovora = E. ananas pv. uredovora) is a parasite of rust fungi and then multiplies in plant tissue killed by the rust fungus (Hevesi & Mashaal, 1975). Most species overwinter in or on plant tissue, but two species (Erwinia tracheiphila and E. stewartii) are also able to overwinter in the bodies of beetles (Leach, 1964; Pepper, 1967). E. herbicola is a common epiphyte on many plants, though instances have been reported in which it has produced disease symptoms in plants, possibly in association with other phytopathogenic bacteria (Gibbins, 1978). It has also been isolated from man and animals (Muraschi et al., 1965). The taxonomy of the genus and designation of nomenspecies in Erwinia have been complicated by the heterogeneity of the strains included in the taxon (Starr, 1981). This concept is supported also by studies of selected strains by DNA/DNA homology (Gardner & Kado, 1972),

PLANT BACTERIAL DISEASES
ISBN 0 12 247660 3

DNA relatedness (Brenner et al., 1974), and DNA/DNA segmental homology (Murata & Starr, 1974). However, there is no generally accepted proposal and the nomenspecies included in Erwinia remain unchanged at present. At the species level, Dye (1981) proposed changes following a numerical taxonomic study, and the nomenclature used here follows those proposals.

Dye (1968, 1969 a,b,c) suggested four groups amongst the Erwinia nomenspecies associated with plants:

(1) the "amylovora" group, comprising plant pathogens which cause dry-necrotic or wilt symptoms and which do not form pectic enzymes nor yellow pigments;

(2) the "carotovora" group, comprising Erwinia spp. with strong pectolytic ability, able to cause soft rots in plants;

(3) the "herbicola" group, which produce a yellow water-insoluble pigment, and which are either opportunistic pathogens of plants, animals or man, or are non-pathogenic plant epiphytes;

(4) the atypical erwinias, a group of miscellaneous species, whose taxonomic position is doubtful (Dye, 1969c). The group does not include any plant pathogens.

Although numerical analysis (Dye, 1981) has shown that these groups are not taxonomically valid, they are used here for convenience. The "amylovora" and "herbicola" groups are discussed below, and descriptions given of the plant diseases caused by members of the groups. The "carotovora" or soft-rot group is discussed in Chapter 6 of this volume.

II.   Isolation

Most Erwinia spp. are readily isolated on glucose yeast extract calcium carbonate agar (GYCA) (Dye, 1962). They will also grow readily on medium B of King et al. (1954) and sucrose peptone agar (SPA) (Hayward, 1960).

Members of the "herbicola" group are usually isolated from plants by selecting yellow-pigmented colonies on non-selective media. These often occur during attempts to isolate plant pathogenic bacteria (see Chapters 1 and 2)

Several selective or semi-selective media have been described for the isolation of the plant pathogens belonging to the "amylovora" group. E. amylovora, the cause of fire blight of pome fruit, can be isolated on MS medium (Miller & Schroth, 1972), the selective medium of Crosse & Goodman (1973), and medium D3 of Kado & Heskett (1970).

The MS medium is also valuable in isolating other members of the "amylovora" group, e.g. E. nigrifluens, E. quercina pv. quercina and pv. rubrifaciens (Schroth & Hildebrand 1981). E.q. pv. rubrifaciens is also readily detected on GYCA by the production of a red diffusible pigment. Schaad & Wilson (1970) described a selective medium for the isolation of E. quercina pv.rubrifaciens, the cause of bacterial phloem canker of Persian walnut.

III. Identification

Members of the genus Erwinia are straight rods 0.5-1.0 by 1.0-3.0 μm, occurring singly, in pairs or occasionally in short chains. They are Gram negative, motile (with mainly peritrichous flagella), and facultatively anaerobic although anaerobic growth by some species is weak. The optimum growth temperature is 27-30C, but the maximum varies from 32C to over 40C. They are oxidase negative and catalase positive. Acid is also produced from fructose, galactose, glucose, sucrose and α-methyl glucoside. They utilize as carbon and energy sources acetate, fumarate, gluconate, malate and succinate, but not benzoate, oxalate nor propionate. The mol % G+C of the DNA is 50-58.

Acid is usually produced from mannitol, mannose, ribose and sorbitol but rarely from adonitol, dextrin, dulcitol or melezitose. Decarboxylases for arginine, lysine or ornithine cannot be detected in members of the "amylovora" and "herbicola" groups (although they can be detected in a few strains of E. carotovora and E. chrysanthemi). Glutamic acid is not decarboxylated; urease and lipases are produced rarely. Additional characters of the species and pathovars are given in Tables 5.1-5.3. The type species is E. amylovora.

Presumptive diagnoses of Erwinia spp. is based primarily on disease symptoms, colony morphology on specific media and a few key tests to place the suspect pathogen into the Enterobacteriaceae. A rod-shaped bacterial isolate which conforms in colony morphology and colour to the suspected Erwinia pathogen and which ferments glucose within 24-48 h, is Gram negative, oxidase negative and catalase positive should be investigated further to determine if it conforms to the genus description.

TABLE 5.1   Cultural, Physiological and Biochemical Characters of Some Erwinia Species[a]

Character[b]	"amylovora" group							"herbicola" group				
	amylovora	mallotivora	nigrifluens	quercina pv. quercina	quercina pv. rubrifaciens	salicis	tracheiphila	ananas pv. ananas	ananas pv. uredovora	herbicola pv. herbicola	herbicola pv. milletiae	stewartii
Motility	+	+	+	+	+	+	+	+	+	+	+	-
Anaerobic growth	w	+	+	+	+	w	w	+	+	+	+	+
Mucoid growth	+	+	-	+	+	+	-	+	-	d	+	+
Growth at 36C	-	-	+	+	+	-	-	+	+	+	+	d
Growth in 5% NaCl	+	+	+	+	+	+	-	+	+	+	+	+
Growth factors required	+	+	-	-	-	-	+	-	-	-	-	-
H₂S from cysteine	-	-	+	+	+	+	+	d	-	+	+	-
Reducing substances from sucrose	+	+	-	+	-	+	d	+	+	d	-	d
Acetoin production	+	+	+	+	-	+	d	+	+	+	+	-
Nitrate reduction	-	-	-	-	-	-	-	-	+	+	+	-
Gelatin liquefaction	-	-	-	-	-	-	-	+	+	+	+	-
Indole production	-	-	+	-	-	-	-	+	+	-	+	-
Phenylalanine deaminase	-	-	-	-	-	-	-	-	-	+	+	-
Urease production	-	-	-	-	-	-	-	-	-	-	-	-
Yellow pigment	-	-	-	-	+	-	-	+	+	+	+	+
Pink diffusible pigment	-	-	-	-	+	-	-	-	-	-	-	-

TABLE 5.1 (Cont'd) Cultural, Physiological and Biochemical Characters of Some Erwinia Species

[a] Data mostly from Dye (1968, 1969) with additional data from Goto (1976), Goto et al. (1980), Sellwood & Lelliott (1978).

[b] The more important diagnostic tests are nitrate reduction, reaction in purple milk, growth factors required, growth at 36C, gelatin liquefaction, acetoin production, reducing substances from sucrose, presence of yellow water-insoluble pigment, and acid production from arabinose, rhamnose, xylose, lactose, trehalose, melibiose, sorbitol, inositol, α-methyl glucoside.

+ 80% or more strains positive;

[d] 21-79% strains positive;

− 20% or less strains positive;

W weak reaction

TABLE 5.2   Acid Production from Carbohydrates and Related Compounds by Some Erwinia Species

Species

Carbon Source[b]	"amylovora group"							"herbicola" group					
	amylovora	mallotivora	nigrifluens	quercina pv. quercina	quercina pv. rubrifaciens	salicis	tracheiphila	ananas pv. ananas	ananas pv. uredovora	herbicola pv. herbicola	herbicola pv. herbicola	herbicola pv. milletiae	stewartii
L+ Arabinose	d	–	+	–	+	–	–	+	+	+	+	+	+
Rhamnose	–	–	+	–	–	–	–	d	+	+	+	+	–
Xylose	–	+	+	–	–	–	–	+	+	+	+	+	+
Mannose	+	+	+	+	+	+	–	+	+	+	+	+	+
Ribose	+	+	+	+	+	+	–	+	+	d	+	+	+
Lactose	–	–	–	–	–	–	–	+	+	d	–	–	–
Maltose	–	–	+	–	–	–	–	+	+	+	+	+	+
Trehalose	+	+	+	–	+	+	–	+	+	+	+	+	+
Melibiose	–	–	–	–	–	–	–	+	+	–	+	+	+
Cellobiose	–	(+)	+	–	–	+	–	+	+	+	+	–	–
Raffinose	–	–	–	–	–	–	–	+	+	d	–	–	+
Melezitose	–	–	–	–	–	–	–	+	+	–	–	–	+
Starch	–	–	–	–	–	–	–	d	+	+	–	–	–
Inulin	–	–	–	–	–	–	–	–	–	+	–	–	–
Dextrin	–	–	+	+	d	–	–	+	+	–	–	–	d
Glycerol	–	(+)	+	–	–	d	–	+	+	–	–	–	–

Table 5.2 (Cont'd) Acid Production from Carbohydrates and Related Compounds by Some *Erwinia Species*

Adonitol	–	–	–	–	–	–	–	–
Mannitol	+	+	+	+	+	+	+	+
Sorbitol	–	d	–	d	+	+	–	+
Dulcitol	–	–	–	–	–	+	–	–
Inositol	+	+	+	–	+	+	–	–
Salicin	+	+	d	+	d	d	+	d
Aesculin	+	+	d	+	d	d	+	+
α-methyl glucoside	–	–	–	–	–	–	–	–

^{a} Data mostly from Dye (1968, 1969) with additional data from Goto (1976), Goto et al. (1980), Sellwood & Lelliott (1978).

^{b} acid produced within 7 days in 1% peptone water containing 1% organic compound plus brom-cresol purple as indicator and unshaken.

$^+$ 80% or more strains positive;

^{d} 21-79% strains positive;

$^-$ 0-20% strains positive;

(+) delayed positive reaction

TABLE 5.3 *Utilization of Organic Compounds By Some Erwinia Species*[a]

Species	citrate	formate	lactate	tartrate	galacturonate	malonate
"amylovora" group						
amylovora	+	+	+	−	−	−
mallotivora	+	−	−	−	−	−
nigrifluens	−	+	+	+	−	−
quercina pv.						
quercina	+	+	+	−	−	−
quercina pv.						
rubrifaciens	+	+	+	+	−	−
salicis	−	−	−	−	−	−
tracheiphila	d	d	−	−	−	−
"herbicola" group						
ananas pv.						
ananas	+	+	+	+	d	−
ananas pv.						
uredovora	+	+	+	+	−	−
herbicola pv.						
herbicola	+	+	+	d	−	d
herbicola pv.						
milletiae	+	+	+	−	d	+
stewartii	+	+	+	+	−	−

[a] *Data mostly from Dye (1968, 1969) with additional data from Goto (1976), Goto et al. (1980), Sellwood & Lelliott (1978).*

[b] *utilization within 21 days at 27C in OY medium (Dye, 1968).*

[+] *80% or more strains positive*

[d] *21-79% strains positive*

[−] *20% or less strains positive.*

Pathogenicity testing is normally essential for confirmatory diagnosis. Due to the considerable heterogeneity within the genus, extensive biochemical testing may be necessary to confirm identity (Tables 5.1-5.3).

IV. The "Amylovora" Group

A. *Erwinia amylovora* : *Fireblight*

Major Synonyms Micrococcus amylovorus Burrill 1882; Bacillus amylovorus (Burrill 1882) Trevisan 1889; Bacterium amylovorus (Burrill 1882) Chester 1897.

Symptoms. E. amylovora (Burrill 1882) Winslow, Broadhurst, Buchanan, Krumwiede, Rogers & Smith 1920, is the cause of "fireblight" of pomefruit. The name is descriptive of the most characteristic symptoms of disease, a blackening of twigs, flowers and leaves as though burned by fire (Figs. 5.1, 5.2).

In apple and pear the first symptoms usually appear in early spring, during warm humid weather. Blossoms appear to be water-soaked, then wilt, shrivel, and turn brownish to black. Peduncles may also appear water-soaked, become dark green, and finally turn blackish, sometimes oozing droplets of sticky bacterial exudate. Young fruitlets turn black, shrivel and remain attached to the tree. Leaves wilt and entire spurs turn brown in apples or dark brown to black in pears, but remain attached to the tree for some time. Immature fruit or, less frequently, mature fruit, can become infected, the infected part appearing oily or water-soaked, becoming brown to black in colour and often exuding droplets of bacterial ooze. Brown to black, slightly depressed cankers develop in the bark of twigs or branches. These may later become defined by cracks near the margin of diseased and healthy tissue.

Host Range. E. amylovora attacks most species of Pomoideae and some species in the sub-families of the Rosaceae. The most economically important hosts are pear (Pyrus communis) and apple (Malus domestica) while hawthorn (Crataegus spp.), pyracantha and cotoneaster are also common hosts. There is no authentic record of fireblight in Prunus spp. A forma specialis has been described from raspberry (Rubus idaeus) by Starr & Folsom (1951).

(a)   (b)

*FIGURE 5.1.   Fireblight   on   pear,   caused by Erwinia
amylovora: (a) twig blight and (b) stem canker.*

Geographical Distribution and Importance. Fireblight is
considered to be native to North America. For many years,
its occurrence elsewhere was limited to New Zealand, where
it was first detected in 1920.   In 1957, fireblight was
reported   from   England.   It has since been reported
elsewhere in Europe (CMI, 1979).   There are also several
unconfirmed reports from Asia, South America and the Middle
East (Hayward & Waterston, 1965).
     Fireblight is considered the most serious disease of
pome fruit. For example, pear growing in some States in the
U.S.A. is possible only with bactericidal sprays to control
fireblight.

Quarantine Precautions.   Fireblight does not occur in
Australia and represents a threat to the Austrlian pome
fruit industry. For many years there was a total ban on the
import into Australia of propagating material and fruit of

FIGURE 5.2. Fireblight, caused by Erwinia amylovora, on mature pear fruit.

all susceptible hosts. Since the 1950s, small quantities of new varieties of pome fruit have been imported as budsticks, subject to treatment and growth in quarantine. However, the importation of vegetative material of ornamental hosts of fireblight and apples and pears is still prohibited.

B. *Erwinia mallotivora : Leaf Spot of Mallotus japonicus.*

Symptoms. E. mallotivora Goto 1976 is the cause of bacterial leaf spot of Mallotus japonicus in Japan. The first symptoms are water-soaked, dark green spots on leaves. The spots enlarge slowly, being restricted by small veins, becoming angular in shape, dark brown in colour and surrounded by a yellow halo. With heavy infection, lesions coalesce, killing entire leaves and shoot blight may occur. Under humid conditions, an exudate of bacteria from the underside of the leaves gives lesions a shiny, oily appearance (Goto, 1976; Bradbury, 1981a).

Host Range.   <u>Mallotus</u> <u>japonicus</u> (Euphorbiaceae).

Geographical Distribution.   Japan.

C.   *Erwinia nigrifluens* : *Bark Canker of Walnut*

Major Synonym.   <u>Erwinia</u> <u>amylovora</u> var.   <u>nigrifluens</u> (Wilson et al.   1957) Dye 1968.

Symptoms.   <u>E</u>. <u>nigrifluens</u> Wilson, Starr & Berger 1957 is the cause of bark canker of walnut (<u>Juglans</u> <u>regia</u>) in California, U.S.A.   In the bark of the trunk and large branches, irregular, dark brown, necrotic areas develop, but are not always visible from the surface.   The presence of a canker is usually indicated by an exudation of dark brown liquid which stains the bark.   Lesions are usually confined to the phloem tissue (Wilson et al., 1957; Bradbury, 1981b). Bark canker is a less damaging disease than phloem canker of walnut, caused by <u>E</u>. <u>quercina</u> pv. <u>rubrifaciens</u>.

D.   *Erwinia quercina pv. quercina* : *Drippy Nut of Oak.*

Major Synonym.   <u>Erwinia</u> <u>amylovora</u> var.   <u>quercina</u> (Hildebrand & Schroth 1967) Dye 1968.

Symptoms.   <u>E</u>. <u>quercina</u> pv. <u>quercina</u> Hildebrand & Schroth 1967 is the cause of drippy nut of oak.   Infection appears first as a darkening at insect punctures in the acorns, followed by a copious ooze which is frothy and sticky in dry weather or watery in humid weather.   The acorns may show some rot around the puncture (Hildebrand & Schroth, 1967). A description of the organism was compiled by Bradbury (1981c).

Host Range.   Oak (<u>Quercus</u> <u>agrifolia</u>; <u>Q</u>. <u>wislizenii</u>).

Geographical Distribution.   U.S.A. (California).

E.   *Erwinia quercina pv. rubrifaciens:*   *Phloem Canker of Walnut.*

Major Synonym.   <u>Erwinia</u> <u>amylovora</u> var. <u>rubrifaciens</u> (Wilson et al. 1967) Dye 1968.

Symptoms.   E. quercina pv.rubrifaciens (Wilson, Zeitoun & Fredrickson, 1967) Dye 1978, is the cause of bacterial phloem canker of Persian walnut. Some dark brown to black streaks develop in the bark, though occasionally black streaks will also develop in the xylem immediately below the cambium. In more serious infections, the streaks coalesce into broad necrotic areas. The bark may be killed and split open releasing a dark slimy liquid which runs down the bark staining the surface (Wilson et al. 1967).

Bacterial phloem canker is distinguished from bark canker, caused by E. nigrifluens, by its development in the deeper layers of the bark and phloem, rather than in the outer bark, with only occasional penetration through cracks in the bark (Bradbury, 1981d).

Host Range.   Walnut (Juglans regia).

Geographical Distribution.   U.S.A. (California).

F. *Erwinia salicis:*   Watermark Disease of Willow.

Major Synonyms.   Bacterium salicis Day 1924; Phytomonas salicis (Day 1924) Magrou 1937; Pseudobacterium salicis (Day 1924) Krasil'nikov 1948; Erwinia amylovora var. salicis (Day 1924) Martinec & Kocur 1963.

Symptoms.   E. salicis (Day 1924) Chester 1939 is the cause of watermark disease of willow. The bacteria invade the wood, the vessels of which become plugged with masses of bacteria and the tissue becomes stained a blackish colour. Early symptoms are wilting of new shoots and a brown to reddish colouration of leaves. The leaves wither but often remain attached to the tree for some time. Branches die and the disease progresses each year until the tree is killed. A thin, sticky, colourless liquid exudes from insect wounds on infected trees. This exudate dries on the bark in a varnish-like layer. The diagnosis of the disease and some characteristics of E. salicis have been described by Preece et al. (1979).

Host Range.   The main hosts are Salix alba and S. fragilis. The disease is most severe on cricket bat willow (S. alba var. coerulea). Other tree willows including S. cinerea and S. viridis are infected occasionally.

Geographical Distribution and Importance. The disease is important in localized areas of south-east England where willows are grown commercially for use in the manufacture of cricket bats for world-wide distribution.

G.   *Erwinia tracheiphila: Bacterial Wilt of Cucurbits.*

Major Synonyms.   Bacillus tracheiphilus Smith 1895; Bacterium tracheiphilus (sic) (Smith 1895) Chester 1897; Erwinia amylovora var. tracheiphila (Smith 1895) Dye 1968.

Symptoms.   Erwinia tracheiphila (Smith 1895) Bergey, Harrison, Breed, Hammer & Huntoon 1923 is the cause of bacterial wilt of cucurbits.   This is a vascular wound disease, transmitted by insects, particularly cucumber beetles (Diabrotica spp.).   It is characterised by sudden wilting and shrivelling of foliage. Lesions first appear on cucurbit leaves as dull green, flaccid areas which spread rapidly.   General wilting of the leaves follows and finally drying and shrivelling of the stems. Bacteria are abundant in the vascular tissue and exude in viscid white droplets from the cut ends of vascular bundles. Partially resistant plants, which may wilt during the day and partially recover during the night, may also show excessive blossom and branching and considerable dwarfing.

Host Range.   Cucumis spp., Cucurbita spp., Citrullus spp. (Bradbury, 1970).

Geographical Distribution.   North America, Africa, China, Japan, Europe (Bradbury, 1970).

V.   The "Herbicola" Group

A.   Erwinia ananas pv. ananas: Brown Rot of Pineapple.

Major Synonyms. Bacillus ananas Serrano 1928; Bacterium ananas (Serrano 1928) Burgvits 1935; Pectobacterium ananas (Serrano 1928) Patel & Kulkarni 1951; Erwinia herbicola var. ananas (Serrano 1928) Dye 1969.

Symptoms. E. ananas pv. ananas Serrano 1928 causes a brown rot of pineapple fruitlets. Slight infection is not visible externally, but with more serious infections the fruitlets become brown to dark brown and the fruit tissue becomes hard and dry. The organism enters through floral parts, or cracks in the eye cavity, and the disease develops only during the ripening of fruit with no apparent spread after that time. The disese normally affects fruitlets of pineapple (Ananas comosus). Sugar cane (Saccharum interspecific hybrids) has also been recorded as a host (Elliott, 1951).

B. Erwinia ananas pv. uredovora.

Major Synonyms. Xanthomonas uredovora Pon et al. 1954; Erwinia uredovora (Pon et al. 1954) Dye 1963.

Disease and Other Specific Host Associations. E. ananas pv. uredovora (Pon, Townsend, Wessman, Schmitt & Kingsolver 1954) Dye 1978 is parasitic on urediniospores of wheat rust (Puccinia graminis f. sp. tritici). It will attack other cereal rusts (P. graminis f. sp. avenae and P. graminis f. sp. secalis), on artificial inoculation. It has been recorded attacking rust on broadbean (Vicia faba) (Hevesi & Mashaal, 1975). The host tissue of wheat or broadbean is not attacked until killed by the rust fungus (Pon et al., 1954).

C. Erwinia herbicola pv.herbicola.

Major Synonyms. Bacterium herbicola Löhnis 1911; Bacterium herbicola (Geilinger 1921) de Rossi 1927. (Subjective synonyms: Agrobacterium gypsophilae (Brown) Starr & Weiss 1943; Bacterium typhi flavum Smith 1948; Erwinia cassavae (Hansford) Burkholder 1948; Erwinia citrimaculans (Doidge) Magrou 1937; Erwinia lathyri (Manns & Taubenhaus) Magrou 1937; Erwinia vitivora (Baccarini) Du Plessis 1940; Flavobacterium rhenanum (Migula) Bergey & Breed 1948; Xanthomonas trifolii (Huss) James 1955).

Specific Host Associations. E. herbicola pv. herbicola (Lohnis 1911) Dye 1964 exists on plant surfaces and as a secondary organism in lesions caused by many plant pathogens. Some strains (syn.Agrobacterium gypsophilae) are reported to cause galls on Gypsophila paniculata. It has been isolated from water (syn. Flavobacterium rhenanum), leaf-hopper insects, the liver and spleen of deer, and the enteric tract of man (syn. Bacterium typhi flavum). It has also been implicated in human septicaemia, conjunctivitis, tonsilitis, abcesses and meningitis. It appears that this organism is an opportunistic pathogen in man and animals (von Graevenitz, 1977; Gibbins, 1978). While the question of its pathogenicity to plants is not completely resolved, its possible involvement in modifying the predisposition of plants to infection has been raised. There is evidence which suggests that strains of E. herbicola pv. herbicola may have the capacity to modify the virulence and activities of known overt bacterial phytopathogens (Gibbins, 1978).

D.   *Erwinia herbicola* pv. *milletiae*.

Major Synonyms. Bacillus milletiae Kawakami & Yoshida 1920; Bacterium milletiae (Kawakami & Yoshida 1920) Burgvits 1935; Erwinia milletiae (Kawakami & Yoshida 1920) Magrou 1937.

Symptoms. E. herbicola pv.milletiae (Kawakami & Yoshida 1920) Goto, Takahashi & Okajima 1980 causes galls up to 60 mm in diameter on stems of Wisteria floribunda (syn.Milletia japonica) and W. brachybotrys. In artificial inoculations galls are induced following the wounding on trunks, crowns, thick roots, leaf petioles, and midribs of leaflets.

E.   *Erwinia stewartii: Bacterial Wilt of Maize.*

Major Synonyms. Pseudomonas stewarti Smith 1898; Bacterium stewarti (Smith 1898) Smith 1911; Aplanobacter stewarti (Smith 1898) McCulloch 1918; Phytomonas stewarti (Smith 1898) Bergey, Harrison, Breed, Hammer & Huntoon 1923; Xanthomonas stewarti (Smith 1898) Dowson 1939; Pseudobacterium stewarti (Smith 1898) Krasil'nikov 1949.

Symptoms. E. stewartii (Smith 1898) Dye 1963 is the cause of Stewart's disease or bacterial wilt of maize and sweet corn. This is a vascular disease in which the xylem vessels become plugged with masses of bacteria and a bright yellow slime. If the stems are cut transversely, droplets of bacteria and slime exude from the vascular bundles and pure cultures of the organism can be isolated easily. Infected plants are stunted. The leaves have brownish or pale yellow stripes which appear water-soaked. Tassels may develop prematurely, then wilt and die before the rest of the plant. Some plants bear seed which may be infected.

The disease is spread by insects, particularly the corn flea beetle (Chaetocnema publicaria) in the U.S.A. The bacteria over-winter in the beetle and are able to infect young maize plantings in the spring.

Host Range. Maize (Zea mays) and sweet corn (Zea mays var. rugosa) are the principal hosts. Natural infections also occurs on Euchlaena mexicana and Tripsacum dactyloides (Bradbury, 1967).

Geographical Distribution. Widespread, occurring in North, Central and South America, Europe and Asia (Bradbury, 1967).

Quarantine Precautions. Imports of maize, sweet corn and popcorn seed into Australia are subject to strict quarantine. Seed is treated, grown in quarantine and inspected prior to release.

References

Bradbury, J.F. (1967). Erwinia stewartii. C.M.I. Descriptions of Pathogenic Fungi and Bacteria No. 123. Kew: Commonwealth Mycological Institute.

Bradbury, J.F. (1970). Erwinia tracheiphila. C.M.I. Descriptions of Pathogenic Fungi and Bacteria No. 233. Kew: Commonwealth Mycological Institute.

Bradbury, J.F. (1981a). Erwinia mallotivora. CMI Descriptions of Pathogenic Fungi and Bacteria No. 691. Kew: Commonwealth Mycological Institute.

Bradbury, J.F. (1981b). Erwinia nigrifluens. CMI Descriptions of Pathogenic Fungi and Bacteria No. 692. Kew: Commonwealth Mycological Institute.

Bradbury, J.F. (1981c). Erwinia quercina. CMI Descriptions of Pathogenic Fungi and Bacteria No. 693. Kew: Commonwealth Mycological Institute.

Bradbury, J.F. (1981d). Erwinia rubrifaciens. CMI Descriptions of Pathogenic Fungi and Bacteria No. 694. Kew: Commonwealth Mycological Institute.

Brenner, D.J., Fanning, G.R. & Steigerwalt, A.G. (1974). Deoxyribonucleic acid relatedness among erwiniae and other Enterobacteriaceae: the gall, wilt and dry-necrosis organisms genus Erwinia Winslow et al., sensu stricto. International Journal of Systematic Bacteriology 24, 197-204.

C.M.I. (1979). Erwinia amylovora. C.M.I. Distribution Maps of Plant Disease No.2. Kew: Commonwealth Mycological Institute.

Crosse, J.E. & Goodman, R.N. (1973). A selective medium for and definitive colony characteristics of Erwinia amylovora. Phytopathology 63, 1425-1426.

Dye, D.W. (1962). The inadequacy of the usual determinative tests for the identification of Xanthomonas spp. New Zealand Journal of Science 5, 393-416.

Dye, D.W. (1968). A taxonomic study of the genus Erwinia. I. The "amylovora" group. New Zealand Journal of Science 12, 590-607.

Dye, D.W. (1969a). A taxonomic study of the genus Erwinia. II. The "carotovora" group. New Zealand Journal of Science 12, 81-97.

Dye, D.W. (1969b). A taxonomic study of the genus Erwinia. III. The "herbicola" group. New Zealand Journal of Science 12, 223-236.

Dye, D.W. (1968c). A taxonomic study of the genus Erwinia. IV. Atypical erwinias. New Zealand Journal of Science 12, 833-839.

Dye, D.W. (1981). A numerical taxonomic study of the genus Erwinia. New Zealand Journal of Agricultural Research 24, 223-229.

Elliott, C. (1951). "Manual of Bacterial Plant Pathogens" 2nd. edit. Waltham, Massachusetts: Chronica Botanica. 186 pp.

Gardner, J.M. & Kado, C.I. (1972). Comparative base sequence homologies of deoxyribonucleic acids of Erwinia species and other Enterobacteriaceae. International Journal of Systematic Bacteriology 22, 201-209.

Gibbins, L.N. (1978). Erwinia herbicola: a review and perspective. In "Proceedings of the IVth International Conference on Plant Pathogenic Bacteria", pp. 403-431. (Ed. Station de Pathologie Vegetale et Phytobacteriologie). Angers, France: I.N.R.A.

Goto, M. (1976). Erwinia mallotivora sp. nov., the causal organism of bacterial leaf spot of Mallotus japonicus Meull. Arg. International Journal of Systematic Bacteriology 26, 467-473.

Goto, M., Takahashi, T. & Okajima, T. (1980). A comparative study of Erwinia milletiae and Erwinia herbicola. Annals of the Phytopathological Society of Japan 46, 185–192.

Hayward, A.C. (1960). A method for characterizing Pseudomonas solanacearum. Nature, London 186, 405–406.

Hayward, A.C. & Waterson, J.M. (1965). Erwinia amylovora. C.M.I. Descriptions of Pathogenic Fungi and Bacteria No. 2. Kew: Commonwealth Mycological Institute.

Hevesi, M. & Mashaal, S.F. (1975). Contributions to the mechanism of infections of Erwinia uredovora, a parasite of rust fungi. Acta Phytopathologica Academiae Scientiarum Hungaricae 10, 275–280

Hildebrand, D.C. & Schroth, M.N. (1967). A new species of Erwinia causing the drippy nut disease of live oak. Phytopathology 57, 250–253.

Kado, C.I. & Heskett, M.G. (1970). Selective media for isolation of Agrobacterium, Corynebacterium, Erwinia, Pseudomonas, and Xanthomonas. Phytopathology 60, 969–976.

King, E.O., Ward, M.K. & Raney, D.E. (1954). Two simple media for the demonstration of pyocyanin and fluorescein. Journal of Laboratory and Clinical Medicine 44, 301–307.

Leach, J.G. (1964). Observations on cucumber beetles as vectors of cucurbit wilt. Phytopathology 54, 606–607.

Miller, T.D. & Schroth, M.N. (1972). Monitoring the epiphytic population of Erwinia amylovora on pear with a selective medium. Phytopathology 66, 367–370.

Muraschi, T.F., Friend, M. & Bolles, D. (1965). Erwinia-like micro-organisms isolated from animal and human hosts. Applied Microbiology 13, 128–131.

Murata, N. & Starr, M.P. (1974). Intrageneric clustering and divergence of Erwinia strains from plants and man in the light of deoxyribonucleic acid and segmental homology. Canadian Journal of Microbiology 20, 1545–1565.

Pepper, E.H. (1967). Stewart's wilt of corn. American Phytopathological Society Monograph No. 4. St Paul, Minnesota.

Pon, D.S., Townsend, C.E., Wessman, C.G., Schmitt, C.G. & Kingsolver, C.H. (1954). A Xanthomonas parasitic on uredia of cereal rusts. Phytopathology 44, 707–710.

Preece, T.F., Wong, W.C. & Adegeye, A.O. (1979). Diagnosis of watermark in willows and some characteristics of Erwinia salicis (Day) Chester. In "Plant Pathogens", pp. 1-17. (Ed. D.W. Lovelock). London: Academic Press.

Schaad, N.W. & Wilson, E.E. (1970). Survival of Erwinia rubrifaciens in soil. Phytopathology 60, 557-558.

Schroth, M.N. & Hildebrand, D.C. (1981). E. amylovora or 'true erwinia' group. In "Laboratory Guide for Identification of Plant Pathogenic Bacteria", pp. 26-30. (Ed. N.W. Schaad). St Paul, Minnesota: American Phytopathological Society.

Sellwood, J.E. & Lelliott, R.A. (1978). Internal browning of hyacinth caused by Erwinia rhapontici. Plant Pathology 27. 120-124.

Starr, M.P. (1981). The genus Erwinia. In "The Prokaryotes", pp. 1260-1271. (Ed. M.P. Starr, H. Stolp, H.G. Truper, A. Balows & H.G. Schlegel). Berlin: Springer-Verlag.

Starr, M.P. & Folsom, D. (1951). Bacterial fire blight of raspberry. Phytopathology 41, 915-919.

Starr, M.P. & Mandel, M. (1969). DNA base composition and taxonomy of phytopathogenic and other enterobacteria. Journal of General Microbiology 56, 113-123.

von Graevenitz, A. (1977). The role of opportunistic bacteria in human disease. Annual Review of Microbiology 31, 441-471.

White, J.N. & Starr, M.P. (1971). Glucose fermentation end products of Erwinia spp. and other Enterobacteria. Journal of Applied Bacteriology 34, 459-475.

Wilson, E.E., Starr, M.P. & Berger, J.A. (1957). Bark canker, a bacterial disease of the Persian walnut tree. Phytopathology 47, 669-673.

Wilson, E.E., Zeitoun, F.M. & Fredrickson, D.L. (1967). Bacterial phloem canker, a new disease of Persian walnut trees. Phytopathology 57, 618-621.

6

Erwinia:
The "Carotovora" Group

E. J. Cother and K. Sivasithamparam

I.	Introduction	87
II.	Isolation	89
III.	Identification	93
IV.	Bacterial Soft Rot of Potato	95
	References	101

I. Introduction

The pectolytic and other macerating enzymes produced by some *Erwinia* spp. result in a loss of structural integrity in host tissue and a characteristic soft rot. Although generally associated with vegetables, they are also naturally pathogenic to a wide range of ornamental plants and field crops such as maize (*Zea mays*), rice (*Oryza sativa*) and sugar-beet (*Beta vulgaris* spp. *vulgaris*). *Erwinia* spp. are particularly damaging in potatoes (*Solanum tuberosum*) and the diseases caused by these bacteria have been closely studied on this crop. However, the methods and rationale of approach are also applicable to other crops where the presence of *Erwinia* spp. is suspected.

The *Erwinia* species which cause soft rots in plants belong to the "carotovora" or soft-rot group as described by Dye (1969). The three most important organisms are E. carotovora pv. carotovora, (Jones 1901) Bergey et al. 1923, E. carotovora pv. atroseptica (Van Hall 1902) Dye 1969 and E. chrysanthemi Burkholder et al. 1953. E. carotovora pv. carotovora is widely distributed and is the most common soft-rot organism. In general terms, E. carotovora pv. atroseptica may be regarded as a cool temperature variant of pv. carotovora, restricted largely to potatoes.

PLANT BACTERIAL DISEASES
ISBN 0 12 247660 3

87

TABLE 6.1　Some Soft Rot Diseases Caused by Erwinia species.

Disease and Host	Causal Agent	Reference
Bacterial soft rot of Chinese cabbage (Brassica chinensis)	E. c. pv. carotovora[a]	Mew et al. (1976)
Bacterial soft rot of celery (Apium graveolens)	E. c. pv. carotovora[a]	Wimalajeewa (1976)
Barn rot of tobacco (Nicotiana tabacum)	E. c. pv. carotovora[a]	Holdeman & Burkholder (1956)
Bacterial root rot of sugar-beet (Beta vulgaris ssp. vulgaris)	E. c. pv. atroseptica[a]	De Mendonca & Stanghellini (1979)
Fruit collapse of pineapple (Ananas comosus)	E. chrysanthemi	Lim & Lowings (1978)
Foot rot of rice (Oryza sativa)	E. chrysanthemi	Goto (1979)
Stalk rot of maize (Zea mays)	E. chrysanthemi	Hoppe & Kelman (1969)
Bacterial mottle of sugarcane (Saccharum inter-specific hybrids)	E. chrysanthemi	Steindl (1969)

[a] *E. c., E. carotovora*

E. chrysanthemi has six pathovars (see Chapter 14) whose biochemical properties and serological relationships are largely correlated with their host of origin. Methods for pathovar distinction are discussed by Samson & Nassan-Agha (1978) and Dickey (1979, 1981).

Other minor plant pathogens are E. rhapontici (Millard 1924) Burkholder 1948 and E. cypripedii (Hori 1911) Bergey et al. 1953, pathogens which occur on rhubarb (Rheum rhabarbarum) and Cypripedium orchids respectively (Dickey, 1979). Descriptions of E. rhapontici and E. cypripedii are given by Bradbury (1977d, 1977e). Some soft rot diseases caused by Erwinia spp. in crops other than potatoes (which are discussed in detail below) are listed in Table 6.1 and illustrated in Figs. 6.1. and 6.2.

Several soft rot diseases in vegetables may have predisposing causes. For example, tissue death in lettuce due to frost injury, mechanical damage, salt toxicity or lettuce necrotic yellows virus may precede invasion by soft rotting Erwinia spp. and Pseudomonas spp; fungal infection by species of Sclerotinia and Rhizoctonia can predispose carrots to infection by soft rot bacteria.

A partially-annotated bibliography of studies of E. carotovora pv. carotovora and E. carotovora pv. atroseptica in potatoes from 1930 to 1975 has been published by Miska & Nelson (1975). Bacterial soft rot of potatoes and its causal agents have been reviewed more recently by Perombelon (1979), Lund (1979) and Perombelon & Kelman (1980). The diagnosis of bacterial soft rot diseases and the characteristics of the causal agents are discussed below.

II. Isolation

A. *Isolation Methods*

Erwinia spp. may be isolated from rotting stem tissue or tubers, or from apparently sound tubers. The methods described are based on our experience with soft rot and stem rot of potatoes. However, they are applicable to other hosts where the presence of soft-rotting Erwinia spp. is suspected (Table 6.1). The isolation procedures are similar to those used for other plant pathogenic bacteria. Precautions for soft-rotting Erwinia spp. are given below.

For stems, small pieces (1-2 mm) of tissue from near the margin of the rot are placed in 3 ml sterile distilled water. The tissue is teased apart with sterile needles or

(a)   (b)

FIGURE 6.1. *Erwinia* spp. *causing bacterial soft-rot*
of (a) celery and (b) cabbage.

macerated with a sterile scalpel, and allowed to stand 15
min. A loopful of the suspension is streaked onto dry
plates of nutrient agar or selective media, as described
below. Plates are incubated at 25C.

For rotting tubers, the skin of the tuber is peeled back
to expose the rotting tissue. Isolations should be
attempted from the margin between diseased and healthy
tissue. However, if no healthy tissue remains, the
isolations should be attempted from tissue in the centre of
the tuber. A small portion (1-2 mm) of tissue is removed
and suspended in 2-3 ml sterile distilled water. Isolations
are made as for stem samples.

In apparently healthy tubers, soft-rotting bacteria may
also be present on the surface or in the lenticels of
apparently healthy tubers. These bacteria will induce a rot
after incubation in a moist anaerobic environment. This
environment can be achieved by maintaining a constant film

(a)   (b)

*FIGURE 6.2.   Erwinia spp. causing (a) barn rot of
tobacco and (b) bacterial mottle of sugar cane.*

of moisture in a mist chamber (Lund & Kelman, 1977). This
is easily organized in the laboratory using plastic sheeting
as   a   "tent" with a humidifier or a commercial atomiser
connected to a source of compressed air and water. The
temperature should be kept at approximately 20C to induce
rotting by E. carotovora pv. carotovora and pv. atroseptica
or above 25C to induce rotting by E. chrysanthemi. Tubers
should be inspected daily. Lesions can often be detected as
slight bulges in the skin, which are caused by the accumulation of gas. Isolations are made from these lesions, as
described above.

    Alternatively, a suitable environment may be obtained by
washing the tubers and wrapping single tubers in moist paper
(e.g. large Whatman No.1 filter paper or chromatography
paper) and then in plastic film or small plastic bags (De
Boer & Kelman, 1975). Several tubers are placed in a larger
plastic bag, or in a container which is flushed with carbon

dioxide or nitrogen to reduce the oxygen level. Symptom development may be accelerated by puncturing lenticels with a needle prior to incubation. It is important that the wrapping paper does not contain preservatives which inhibit bacterial development. Most commercially available industrial paper products (e.g. paper towelling, tissues) are treated with bactericides. For small numbers of tubers, anaerobic jars (BBL Gaspack or Oxoid) are ideal.

The time and temperature of incubation required to induce rotting depends on the organisms present. E. chrysanthemi will cause extensive rotting after 3 days at 30C. E. carotovora pv. carotovora and pv. atroseptica may require 10 days at 20-25C.

B. *Selective Media.*

Several selective media have been developed to isolate Erwinia spp. from soil and plant tissue. The disadvantages in the use of selective media discussed in Chapter 1 of this volume apply here (e.g. complexity and cost; efficiency of recovery). The variability in some Erwinia spp. is such that some strains may not grow on media designed to select them or alternatively, they may appear on media designed to suppress them. The composition of the soil microflora and its interaction with the target organism can also influence the efficiency of recovery on a particular selective medium, and may explain different results obtained with the same medium in different laboratories. Controls involving concurrent plating on selective media of known soft-rotting isolates should be used.

The efficiency of selective media developed for Erwinia spp. have been compared by O'Neill & Logan (1975). One of the most useful is the CVP medium (Cuppels & Kelman, 1975), which is a single layer pectate medium containing crystal violet and sodium polypectate. The modification proposed by O'Neill & Logan (1975) of manganous sulphate (0.8 g/l) increases its selectivity by inhibiting the growth of pectolytic pseudomonads. The production of foam during autoclaving (not always a problem) may be overcome by the addition of an anti-foam agent (O'Neill & Logan, 1975).

The medium of Logan (1966) containing a pectate overlay is also a useful selective medium. Without the pectate overlay, it is an easily prepared medium for distinguishing E. carotovora pv. carotovora and pv. atroseptica and sometimes E. chrysanthemi.

The D3 medium of Kado & Heskett (1970) can distinguish Erwinia spp. from non-Erwinia spp., since the former develop a deep burnt-orange colour in the colonies, while the surrounding agar changes from dark green/blue to orange. The medium of Burr & Schroth (1977) is useful in isolations from soil, particularly when the broth is used to enrich pectolytic bacteria in soil samples, under anaerobic incubation.

Kelman & Dickey (1980) recommended the media of Beraha (1968) and Hildebrand (1971) to detect pectate degradation. Both have been found to be unsatisfactory in Australia, as many Australian isolates of E. carotovora pv. carotovora and pv. atroseptica do not grow on Hildebrand's medium A, nor produce pectate liquefaction in Beraha's medium; E. chrysanthemi grows so quickly on Hildebrand's medium that the plates liquefy in less than 24 h.

The composition of the above selective media and details of their preparation are given in Chapter 16. Procedures for the laboratory-scale preparation of sodium polypectate for use in selective media have been described by Cother et al. (1980). Selective media are useful but it is advisable to experiment with more than one and not to rely solely on them for identification.

III. Identification

A. *Colony Characteristics.*

The colonies of E. carotovora pv. carotovora and pv. atroseptica on most media are greyish-white to creamy white, smooth, round, glistening and slightly raised and visible on isolation plates after about 24 h (Bradbury, 1977a, 1977b).

Colonies of E. chrysanthemi on most media are greyish-white to creamy-white, smooth, round, with margins becoming undulate to feathery, butyrous, flat to slightly raised. After 3-6 days on potato dextrose agar (PDA) at pH6.5, some colonies have a "fried-egg" appearance, being umbonate with undulate margins. On the yeast extract-dextrose-calcium carbonate (YDC) medium of Dye (1968), many (but not all) isolates produce a characteristic dark blue, insoluble pigment after 5-10 days at 22-27C (Bradbury, 1977c). The colony type on PDA and the pigment production on YDC medium help to distinguish E. chrysanthemi from E. carotovora pv. carotovora and pv. atroseptica. Other differentiating tests are described below.

B.   *Physiological Characteristics.*

A key for the identification of soft-rotting species of
Erwinia is given in Table 6.2. The characteristics which
are useful in the differentiation of E. carotovora pv.
atroseptica, and pv. carotovora and E. chrysanthemi are
ability to grow at 37C; production of reducing substances
from sucrose; production of acid from maltose, α-methyl
glucoside, lactose and trehalose; growth in 5% NaCl;
production of indole, lecithinase and phosphatase; and
sensitivity to erythromycin. Physiological tests useful for
the differentiation of members of the "carotovora" group are
given in Table 6.3.
       Detailed descriptions of E. carotovora pv. atroseptica,
E. carotovora pv. carotovora and E. chrysanthemi are available (Bradbury 1977a, 1977b, 1977c). Considerable variability within the one species or pathovar has been reported
by Dye (1968, 1969), Graham (1972), Tanii & Akai (1975),
Samson & Nassan-Agha (1978), Sands & Dickey (1978), Dickey
(1979) and Thomson et al. (1981). This variability may be
partly attributed to inherent variability within the species
or pathovar in physiological characteristics. It implies
that a new isolate may differ in a few characters from the
standard description (Lelliott, 1974), but still be a valid
member of the species or pathovar.

C.   *Serology*

Serology can be useful in the identification of
pathovars in the "carotovora" group. Techniques can be
tailored to suit the amount of information required. These
range from simple immunodiffusion (Cother & Powell, 1983) to
more complex methods (Vruggink, 1978; De Boer et al., 1979).
Lazar (1972) and Schaad (1979) should also be consulted.

D.   *Pathogenicity*

There is some debate as to whether E. carotovora pv.
atroseptica and E. carotovora pv. carotovora can be
differentiated on the basis of pathogenicity tests in
potatoes. Erinle (1975) found tuber inoculation to be
reliable but this was disputed by Burr & Schroth (1977).
Although Powelson (1980) isolated pv. atroseptica from
potato stems early in the season and pv. carotovora later in
the season, when temperatures rose, Stanghellini & Meneley

(1975) produced "blackleg" symptoms with pv. caratovora at temperatures as low as 18C. Influence of soil temperature on symptom expression has been discussed by Graham & Dowson (1960) and Molina & Harrison (1977). Care must be taken in interpreting the results of pathogenicity tests.

E. chrysanthemi is pathogenic on a wide range of hosts, (Table 6.1). There is evidence of some pathogenic special-isolation for different hosts (Dickey, 1979, 1981).

IV.   Bacterial Soft Rot of Potato

A.   *Symptoms*

One of the most important diseases caused by members of the "carotovora" group is bacterial soft rot of potatoes, which affects both tubers and above-ground parts of the plant (Lund, 1979). The most common symptom is a tuber rot which progresses over several weeks. It is commonly caused by E. carotovora pv. carotovora. The tuber rot is initially white to cream coloured and watery but symptoms are quickly altered by the presence of other bacteria. Darkening of tuber tissue is sometimes noticeable at the margin between diseased and healthy tissue. The rot may extend into the stem. A rapid, smelly decay of sown seed tubers in south-western New South Wales is caused by E. chrysanthemi pv. zeae (Cother, 1980, Cother & Powell, 1983). It is distinguished from rots caused by pv. carotovora by the speed of infection and foul smell (Fig. 6.3).

Bacterial infection can also occur in potato stems, causing a variety of symptoms. The most common symptom is "blackleg", which is associated with decaying seed (Fig. 6.4). Rotting commences in the mother tuber, and progresses up one or more stems to the above-ground level. The basal stem rot infection spreads to the stolons and daughter tubers. The stems usually become dark-brown to black. Perombelon & Kelman (1980) and Sivasithamparam (1982) have suggested that while in temperate regions, soft-rot affected stems are black, in warmer regions they may also be light brown. The leaves become chlorotic and the plant may wilt in hot weather. Blackleg is more noticeable in crops during cool, wet winters than in summer-grown crops. When the blackleg-infected stem is pulled by hand, the stem slides apart near ground level, leaving 1-2 cm of stronger ("stringy") cellulosic material on the end. This end is soft and slimy, with a characteristic odour.

TABLE 6.2   *Key   for   the Identification of the Soft-Rot*
Erwinia Species[a]

Step no.	Procedures and results[b,c]

1.   Obtain   pure   cultures of test isolates on nutrient
     agar (NA)[d]

2.   Gram stain.
        If Gram-negative rods, proceed

3.   Pectolytic   ability.   Inoculate   pectate media
     (Cuppels & Kelman, 1974; O'Neill & Logan, 1975)[d]

4.   Maintenance[d].   Transfer   pectate hydrolysers to
     YDC   or   TGE   agar slopes (Dye, 1968).   Incubate at
     15C

5.   Oxidase   test[d].   Use   24h   culture from NA, NA+1%
     glucose   or   TGE agar slopes.   The addition of 0.1%
     ascorbic   acid   to   the   reagent   is recommended to
     reduce   doubtful   positive   reactions.   If oxidase
     negative, proceed.

6.   Glucose metabolism (Dye, 1968).
        If   glucose   is   fermented   in   48-72h isolate is
        likely to be an erwinia.   Proceed to 8.

7.   If   glucose   is   not   fermented   in   48-72h, streak
     isolate   onto   plates   of   medium   B of King et al.
     (1954).   If isolate produces a fluorescent pigment,
     test   maceration   of   potato   slices.   If test
     positive,   treat   isolate   as   a   fluorescent,
     pectolytic   pseudomonad (see   Chapter 8).

8.   Indole production
        pv. atroseptica, pv. carotovora   −
        E. chrysanthemi   +

9.   Reducing substances from sucrose (Dye, 1968)
        pv. atroseptica   +
        pv. carotovora   −
        E. chrysanthemi   v

10. Growth at 37C (Dye, 1968)
        pv. atroseptica   −
        pv. carotovora   +
        E. chrysanthemi   +

11. Acid   from   carbohydrates   in   7   days   (lactose,
     maltose, trehalose, and α methyl glucoside)
        pv. atroseptica: acid   from maltose, α-methyl
        glucoside and lactose
        pv. carotovora: acid from lactose, trehalose
        E. chrysanthemi: no acid from above carbo-
        hydrates in 7 days

TABLE 6.2 Key for the Identification of the Soft-Rot Erwinia species[a]

Step no.	Procedures and results[b,c]	
12.	Lecithinase and phosphatase production (Billing & Luckhurst, 1957)	
	pv. atroseptica and pv. carotovora	−
	E. chrysanthemi[e]	+
13.	Growth in 5% NaCl (Dye, 1968)	
	pv. atroseptica, pv. carotovora	+
	E. chrysanthemi	−
14.	Sensitivity to erythromycin (15 µg)	
	pv. atroseptica, pv. carotovora	R
	E. chrysanthemi	S
15.	Utilisation of sodium malonate and sodium tartrate	
	pv. atroseptica, pv. carotovora	−
	E. chrysanthemi	+
16.	Palatinose utilisation (Sands & Dickey, 1978)	
	pv. atroseptica	+
	pv. carotovora	−
	E. chrysanthemi	−

[a] E. carotovora pv. atroseptica, E. carotovora pv. carotovora, E. chrysanthemi.

[b] Details of media and methods given in Chapter 16 of this volume

[c] Results based on response of majority of isolates (80%)in each species or pathovar; +, positive; −, negative; R, resistant; S, sensitive.

[d] NA, Difco or Oxoid nutrient agar; YDC, yeast extract dextrose calcium carbonate agar; TGE, tryptone glucose beef extract agar.

[e] E. chrysanthemi isolates from sugarcane in Queensland are lecithinase negative

FIGURE 6.3.   Potato seed tuber decay caused by E. chrysanthemi (left) and E. carotovora pv. carotovora (right). Tubers incubated 4 days at 30C.

Three types of stem rots occur in Western Australia (Sivasithamparam, 1982), and these are illustrated diagramatically in Fig. 6.4b: (1) Stem rots with symptoms typical of those described originally for blackleg, arising from infected tubers (as described above); (2) stem rots arising from injury to any point in the plant top, parts of the upper canopy or the basal stem and proceeding down to the tubers. The presence of erwinias in the frequently discoloured vascular regions may be traced to the stolen ends of the daughter tubers. The rotting stem may be brown or black in colour; (3) stem rots restricted to localised lesions affecting the leaf blades, petioles or stem. The first type of stem rot is tuber-initiated. It is of low incidence in Western Australia (Sivasithamparam, 1982). The second and third types are more common and appear after injury to crops. Stem rots are more common in Western Australia during hot weather.

Stem infections by E. chrysanthemi have been recorded in Peru (De Lindo et al., 1978) and Japan (Tominga & Ogasawara, 1979) and compared in the Netherlands (Maas Geesteranus, 1980).

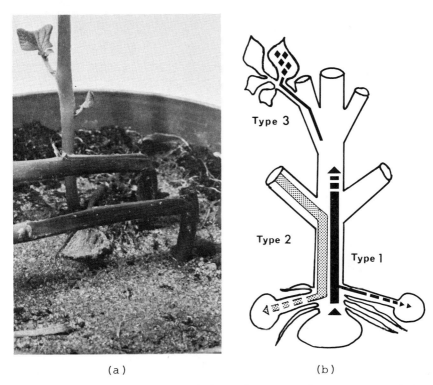

(a)   (b)

FIGURE 6.4. Bacterial soft rot of potatoes: (a) blackleg causing collapse of stems; (b) three types of stem rots (see text).

B. Causal Agents

Erwinia carotovora pv. carotovora and E. carotovora pv. atroseptica are the main causes of soft rots of potato. E. chrysanthemi is less common. The aetiology of soft rot of potatoes is complex, as similar symptoms may be caused by different bacteria.

E. carotovora pv. carotovora, E.c. pv. atroseptica or both may be isolated from infected tubers. The dominant pathovar is influenced by climatic factors. Erwinia carotovora pv. atroseptica is usually the cause of blackleg of potatoes in the field in temperate climates (Graham & Dowson, 1960). However, strains of pv. carotovora have caused blackleg in Arizona (Stanghellini & Meneley, 1975), Japan (Tanii & Akai, 1975) and Western Australia (Sivasithamparam, 1982). E. carotovora pv. carotovora

TABLE 6.3 Physiological Tests for the Differentiation of the Soft-Rot Erwinia species[a,b]

Test[c]	E. carotovora pv. atroseptica	E. carotovora pv. carotovora	E. chrysanthemi	E. rhaponticii	E. cypripedii
Production blue pigment on PDA[d]					
Growth at 37C	−	+	+	−	+
Reducing substances from[e] sucrose	+	−	v	+	−
Acid in 7 days from					
maltose	+	v	−	+	v
α-methyl glucoside	+	−	−	v	−
lactose	+	+	−	+	−
trehalose	+	+	−	+	+
dulcitol	−	−	−	+	−
Growth in 5% NaCl	+	+	+	+	+
Indole	−	−	+	−	−
Lecithinase	−	−	+	−	−
Phosphatase	−	−	+	+	−
Erythromycin sensitivity	R	R	S	S	S

[a] Descriptions based on Dye (1968) and Dickey (1979) for phosphatase only.

[b] +, 80% strains positive; −, 80% strains negative; v, results variable; R, resistant; S, susceptible.

[c] Methods as described by Dye (1968). See Chapter 16 for details.

[d] PDA, potato dextrose agar.

[e] 1% organic compound, 1% peptone water, bromcresol purple indicator, incubated unshaken (7 days, 27C). Other media may give different results.

causes rotting of stem tops in India (Shekhawat et al., 1976), Scotland (Graham et al., 1976) and Western Australia (Sivasithamparam, 1982). E. carotovora pv. carotovora is the most common cause of tuber soft rots. E. chrysanthemi causes stunting, yellowing, wilting or soft-rotting on a wide range of hosts (Bradbury, 1977c).

Bacteria from other genera are also isolated from soft-rotting potato tubers. They include starch-degrading, pectolytic clostridia, which have been isolated consistently from tubers induced to rot under anaerobic conditions (Lund & Nicholls, 1970). Methods for their isolation have been described by Lund (1972).

Other pectolytic bacteria found to be weakly pathogenic to potato tubers are Pseudomonas spp. and Flavobacterium (Sampson & Hayward, 1971), and Bacillus spp. (Jackson & Henry, 1946). The frequency of isolation of these bacteria from the margin of rotting potato tissue is relatively low compared with that of E. carotovora pathovars and pectolytic clostridia (Lund, 1979).

References

Beraha, L. (1968). A rapid method for the preparation of a semi-solid agar medium for detection of pectolytic enzyme activity in Erwinia carotovora. Plant Disease Reporter 52, 167.

Billing, E. & Luckhurst, E.R. (1957). A simplified method for the preparation of egg yolk media. Journal of Applied Bacteriology 20, 90.

Bradbury, J.F. (1977a). Erwinia carotovora var. atroseptica. CMI Descriptions of Pathogenic Fungi and Bacteria No 551. Kew: Commonwealth Mycological Institute.

Bradbury, J.F. (1977b). Erwinia carotovora var. carotovora. CMI Descriptions of Pathogenic Fungi and Bacteria No 552. Kew: Commonwealth Mycological Institute.

Bradbury, J.F. (1977c). Erwinia chrysanthemi. CMI Descriptions of Pathogenic Fungi and Bacteria No 553. Kew: Commonwealth Mycological Institute.

Bradbury, J.F. (1977d). Erwinia cypripedii. CMI Descriptions of Pathogenic Fungi and Bacteria No 554. Kew: Commonwealth Mycological Institute.

Bradbury, J.F. (1977e). Erwinia rhapontici. CMI Descriptions of Pathogenic Fungi and Bacteria No 555. Kew: Commonwealth Mycological Institute.

Burr, T.J. & Schroth, M.N. (1977). Occurrence of soft-rot Erwinia spp. in soil and plant material. Phytopathology 67, 1382-1387.

Cother, E.J. (1980). Bacterial seed tuber decay in irrigated sandy soils of New South Wales. Potato Research 23, 75-84.

Cother, E.J., Blakeney, A.B. & Lamb, S.J. (1980). Laboratory-scale preparation of sodium polypectate for use in selective media for pectolytic Erwinia spp. Plant Disease 64, 1086-1087.

Cother, E.J. & Powell, Vivienne (1983). Physiological and pathological characteristics of Erwinia chrysanthemi isolates from potato tubers. Journal of Applied Bacteriology 53 (in press).

Cuppels, D. & Kelman, A. (1974). Evaluation of selective media for isolation of soft-rot bacteria from soil and plant tissue. Phytopathology 64, 468-475.

De Boer, S.H. & Kelman, A. (1975). Evaluation of procedures for detection of pectolytic Erwinia spp. on potato tubers. American Potato Journal 52, 117-123.

De Boer, S.H., Copeman, R.J. & Vruggink, H. (1979). Serogroups of Erwinia carotovora potato strains determined by diffusible somatic antigens. Phytopathology 69, 316-319.

De Lindo, L., French, E.R. & Kelman, A. (1978). Erwinia spp. pathogenic to potatoes in Peru. American Potato Journal 55, 383 (Abstr.)

De Mendonca, M. & Stanghellini, M.E. (1979). Endemic and soil-borne nature of Erwinia carotovora var. atroseptica, a pathogen of mature sugar beets. Phytopathology 69, 1096-1099.

Dickey, R.S. (1979). Erwinia chrysanthemi: A comparative study of phenotypic properties of strains from several hosts and other Erwinia species. Phytopathology 69, 324-329.

Dickey, R.S. (1981). Erwinia chrysanthemi: Reaction of eight plant species to strains fromseveral hosts and to strains of other Erwinia species. Phytopathology 71, 23-29.

Dye, D.W. (1968). A taxonomic study of the genus Erwinia. I. The "amylovora" group. New Zealand Journal of Science 11, 590-607.

Dye, D.W. (1969). A taxonomic study of the genus Erwinia. II. The "carotovora" group. New Zealand Journal of Science 12, 81-97.

Erinle, I.D. (1975). Blackleg of potatoes: induction through tuber inoculations. Plant Pathology 24, 172-175.

Goto, M. (1979). Bacterial foot rot of rice caused by a strain of Erwinia chrysanthemi. Phytopathology 69, 213-216.

Graham, D.C. (1972). Identification of soft-rot coliform bacteria. In "Proceedings of the Third International Conference on Plant Pathogenic Bacteria", pp. 273-279. (Ed. H.P. Maas Geesteranus). Wageningen, Netherlands: Pudoc.

Graham, D.C. & Dowson, W.J. (1960). The coliform bacteria associated with potato blackleg and other soft rots. I. Their pathogenicity in relation to temperature. Annals of Applied Biology 48, 51-57.

Graham, D.C., Quinn, C.E. & Harrison, M.D. (1976). Recurrence of soft-rot coliform infections in potato stem cuttings : an epidemiological study on the central nuclear stock production farm in Scotland, 1967-74. Potato Research 19, 3-21.

Hildebrand, D.C. (1971). Pectate and pectin gels for differentiation of Pseudomonas spp. and other bacterial plant pathogens. Phytopathology 61, 1430-1436.

Holdeman, Q.L. & Burkholder, W.H. (1956). The identity of barn rots of flue-cured tobacco in South Carolina. Phytopathology 46, 69-72.

Hoppe, P.E. & Kelman, A. (1969). Bacterial top and stalk rot disease of corn in Wisconsin. Plant Disease Reporter 53, 66-70.

Jackson, A.W. & Henry, B.S. (1946). Occurrences of Bacillus polymyxa (Pnoz.) Mig. in Alberta soils with special reference to its pathogenicity in potato tubers. Canadian Journal of Research Section C. 24, 39-46.

Kado, C.I. & Heskett, M.G. (1970). Selective media for isolation of Agrobacterium, Corynebacterium, Erwinia, Pseudomonas, and Xanthomonas. Phytopathology 60, 969-976.

Kelman, A. & Dickey, R.S. (1980). Erwinia: The soft rot or "carotovora" group. In "Laboratory Guide for Identification of Plant Pathogenic Bacteria", pp. 31-35. (Ed. N.W. Schaad). St Paul, Minnesota: American Phytopathological Society.

King, E.O., Ward, M.K. & Raney, D.E. (1954). Two simple media for the demonstration of pyocyanin and fluorescein. Journal of Laboratory and Clinical Medicine. 44, 301-307.

Lazar, I. (1972). Studies on the preparation of anti-*Erwinia* sera in rabbits. In "Proceedings of the Third International Conference on Plant Pathogenic Bacteria", pp. 125-130. (Ed. H. P. Maas Geesteranus). Wageningen, Netherlands: Pudoc.

Lelliott, R.A. (1974). II. Genus XII *Erwinia* Winslow, Broadhurst, Buchanan, Krumwiede, Rogers & Smith 1920. In "Bergey's Manual of Determinative Bacteriology", 8th edition, pp. 332-339. (Ed. R.E. Buchanan & N.E. Gibbons). Baltimore: Williams & Wilkins.

Lim, W.H. & Lowings, P.H. (1978). Infection sites of pineapple fruit collapse and latency of the pathogen *Erwinia chrysanthemi* within the fruit. In "Proceedings of the IVth International Conference on Plant Pathogenic Bacteria", pp. 567-575. (Ed. Station de Pathologie Vegetable et Phytobacterologie). Angers, France: I.N.R.A.

Logan, C. (1966). Simple method of differentiating *Erwinia carotovora* variety "atroseptica" from *E. carotovora* and *E. carotovora* variety "aroideae". *Nature, London* 212, 1584-1585.

Lund, B.M. (1972). Isolation of pectolytic clostridia from potatoes. *Journal of Applied Bacteriology* 35, 609-614.

Lund, B.M. (1979). Bacterial soft-rot of potatoes. In "Plant Pathogens", pp. 19-49. (Ed. D.W. Lovelock). London: Academic Press.

Lund, B.M. & Kelman, A. (1977). Determination of the potential for development of bacterial soft rot of potatoes. *American Potato Journal* 54, 211-225.

Lund, B.M. & Nicholls, J.C. (1970). Factors influencing the soft-rotting of potatoes by bacteria. *Potato Research* 13, 210-214.

Maas Geesteranus, H.P. (1980). Differences in soft-rot symptoms on potato plants caused by various *Erwinia* strains. *Potato Research* 23, 468.

Mew, T.W., Ho, W.C. & Chu, L. (1976). Infectivity and survival of soft-rot bacteria in Chinese cabbage. *Phytopathology* 66, 1325-1327.

Miska, J.P. & Nelson, G.A. (1975). Potato seed piece decay: a bibliography 1930-1975. *Canadian Plant Disease Survey* 55, 126-146.

Molina, J.J. & Harrison, M.D. (1977). The role of *Erwinia carotovora* in the epidemiology of potato blackleg. I. The effect of soil temperatures on disease severity. *American Potato Journal* 57, 351-363.

O'Neill, R. & Logan, C. (1975). A comparison of various selective isolation media for their efficiency in the diagnosis and enumeration of soft rot coliform bacteria. Journal of Applied Bacteriology 39, 139-146.

Perombelon, M.C.M. (1979). Ecology of soft-rot erwinias in relation to potatoes. In "Report of the Planning Conference on Developments in the Control of Bacterial Diseases of Potatoes", pp. 94-119. Lima, Peru: International Potato Center.

Perombelon, M.C.M. & Kelman, A. (1980). Ecology of the soft-rot erwinias. Annual Review of Phytopathology 18, 361-387.

Powelson, M.L. (1980). Seasonal incidence and cause of black-leg and a stem soft-rot of potatoes in Oregon. American Potato Journal 57, 301-305.

Sampson, P.J. & Hayward, A.C. (1971). Some characteristics of pectolytic bacteria associated with potato in Tasmania. Australian Journal of Biological Sciences 24, 917-923.

Samson, R. & Nassan-Agha, N. (1978). Biovars and serovars among 129 strains of Erwinia chrysanthemi. In "Proceedings of the IVth International Conference on Plant Pathogenic Bacteria", pp. 547-553. (Ed. Station de Pathologie Vegetale et Phytobacteriologie). Angers, France: I.N.R.A.

Sands, D.C. & Dickey, R.S. (1978). Palatinose utilisation as a differential test for Erwinia species. In "Proceedings of the IVth International Conference on Plant Pathogenic Bacteria", pp. 555-559. (Ed. Station de Pathologie Vegetale et Phytobacteriologie). Angers, France: I.N.R.A.

Schaad, N.W. (1979). Serological identification of plant pathogenic bacteria. Annual Review of Phytopathology 17, 123-147.

Shekhawat, G.S., Nagaich, B.B., Rajpal, R. & Kishore, V. (1976). Bacterial top rot : a new disease of potato. Potato Research 19, 241-247.

Stanghellini, M.E. & Meneley, J.C. (1975). Identification of soft-rot Erwinia associated with blackleg of potato in Arizona. Phytopathology 65, 86-87.

Sivasithamparam, K. (1982). Blackleg ---- a confusing potato disease. West Australian Journal of Agriculture 11, 17-18.

Steindl, D.R.L. (1969). Lesser known diseases of sugarcane (1): Bacterial mottle. Sugarcane Pathologists Newsletter 2, 2-4.

Tanii, A. & Akai, J. (1975). Blackleg of potato plant caused by a serologically specific strain of Erwinia carotovora var. carotovora (Jones) Dye. Annals of the Phytopathological Society of Japan 41, 513-517.

Thomson, S.V., Hildebrand, D.C. & Schroth, M.N. (1981). Identification and nutritional differentiation of the Erwinia sugar beet pathogen from members of Erwinia carotovora and Erwinia chrysanthemi. Phytopathology 71, 1037-1042.

Tominaga, T. & Ogasawara, K. (1979). [Bacterial stem rot of potato caused by Erwinia chrysanthemi]. Annals of the Phytopathological Society of Japan 45, 474-477.

Vruggink, H. (1978). Enzyme-linked immunosorbent assay (ELISA) in the serodiagnosis of plant pathogenic bacteria. In "Proceedings of the IVth International Conference on Plant Pathogenic Bacteria", pp. 307-310. (Ed. Station de Pathologie Vegetale et Phytobacteriologie). Angers, France: I.N.R.A.

Wimalajeewa D.L.S. (1976). Studies on bacterial soft rot of celery in Victoria. Australian Journal of Experimental Agriculture and Animal Husbandry 16, 915-920.

Pseudomonas:
The Non-Fluorescent Pseudomonads
A. C. Hayward

I.	Introduction	108
II.	*Pseudomonas amygdali*: Hyperplastic Bacterial Canker of Almond	109
III.	*Pseudomonas andropogonis*: Leaf Spot of Clover and Velvet Bean and Bacterial Stripe of Sorghum	113
IV.	*Pseudomonas avenae*: Leaf Blight of Cereals	118
V.	*Pseudomonas caryophylli*: Bacterial Wilt of Carnation	119
VI.	*Pseudomonas cattleyae*: Brown Spot of Orchid	119
VII.	*Pseudomonas cepacia*: Sour Skin of Onion	120
VIII.	*Pseudomonas cissicola*: Bacterial Leaf Spot of *Cayratia japonica*	121
IX.	*Pseudomonas corrugata*: Tomato Pith Necrosis	121
X.	*Pseudomonas gladioli*: Leaf Spot and Corm Scab of Gladiolus and Soft Rot of Onion	122
XI.	*Pseudomonas maltophilia*: Saprophyte	123
XII.	*Pseudomonas mesophilica*: Saprophyte	123
XIII.	*Pseudomonas paucimobilis*: Saprophyte	124
XIV.	*Pseudomonas pseudoalcaligenes* subsp. *citrulli*: Bacterial Spot of Watermelon	124
XV.	*Pseudomonas rubrilineans*: Red Stripe and Top Rot of Sugarcane	124
XVI.	*Pseudomonas rubrisubalbicans*: Mottled Stripe of Sugarcane and Leaf Stripe of Sorghum	127
XVII.	*Pseudomonas setariae* (inv.): Bacterial Stripe of Rice	128
XVIII.	*Pseudomonas solanacearum*: Bacterial Wilt and Moko Disease	129
	References	135

I. Introduction

Detection of yellow-green, diffusible, fluorescent pigments on a medium of low iron content, such as medium B of King et al. (1954), is an important first step in the identification of species of the genus Pseudomonas. Plant pathogens in the fluorescent group include P. syringae, P. cichorii and P. viridiflava. The pigment is usually not produced in media of high iron content and is a property which can be lost as a result of mutation and selection in artificial medium. Occasionally, freshly isolated, non-pigmented strains of normally fluorescent species are obtained. Examples include isolates of P. syringae pv. syringae (Basit et al., 1970), pv. pisi, pv. phaseolicola and pv. morsprunorum. However, these aberrant isolates are otherwise similar to the fluorescent pseudomonads.

Apart from the occasional occurrence of non-fluorescent pathovars of P. syringae, there are species of Pseudomonas which are invariably non-fluorescent and clearly distinct in phenotype from P. syringae. Although some of these non-fluorescent pseudomonads do not produce inclusions of poly-β-hydroxybutyrate (PHB), the majority do so. PHB formation confers upon the cell the property of refractility under phase contrast microscopy and a strong affinity for the lipid stain, Sudan Black B. PHB has not been found in fluorescent pseudomonads.

The following account covers seventeen of the non-fluorescent species of Pseudomonas which are either plant pathogens or, in the case of P. paucimobilis, P. mesophilica and P. maltophilia, found in association with plants. Several non-fluorescent species such as P. stutzeri, P. acidovorans and P. testosteroni have no known plant associations and they, like P. pseudomallei and P. mallei, which are human and animal pathogens, have been excluded.

P. amygdali shows some affinity with P. syringae but is considered below because it is slower growing than P. syringae and a clearly non-fluorescent species. Further work particularly on nucleic acid hybridization is required to determine the possible relationship of P. amygdali to the fluorescent pseudomonads. However, the present placement of this species with the non-fluorescent pseudomonads is arbitrary.

Some of the key cultural and physiological properties which serve to differentiate sixteen of the species are given in Table 7.1. An additional species, P. setariae has been excluded from Table 7.1 because of insufficient information on the characteristics. The sources of the data on the physiological characteristics are given in Table 7.2. Each species is considered below in relation to symptoms, host range, and geographical distribution and importance, including quarantine significance.

II. *Pseudomonas amygdali*: Hyperplastic Bacterial Canker of Almond

A. Symptoms

P. amygdali Psallidas & Panagopoulos 1975 is the cause of hyperplastic bacterial canker of almond (Prunus dulcis). The disease is characterized by the production of extensive cankers, swollen at the periphery, on the trunk, branches, twigs and shoots (Psallidas et al., 1968; Psallidas & Panagopoulos, 1975). The perennial cankers are slow in development and active throughout the year. Affected trees show a progressive decline leading eventually to death. Infection usually occurs at leaf scars.

B. Host Range

Psallidas & Panagopoulos (1975) showed that isolates were pathogenic on inoculation only to almond. Inoculations at monthly intervals showed that infections are possible throughout the year. The bacterium does not infect leaves and artificial inoculations were successful only through shoots. All the isolates gave a positive hypersensitive response on tobacco leaves within 24-48 h. The existence of an epiphytic phase was not shown.

C. Geographical Distribution and Importance.

Hyperplastic bacterial canker of almond has been reported only from the Greek islands of Crete, Rhodes and Chios (Psallidas & Panagopoulos, 1975) and Turkey (Bradbury, 1977).

TABLE 7.1 Properties of Non-Fluorescent Pseudomonas Species Isolated From Plants[a]

Character	Species[b,c,d]															
	1	2	3	4	5	6	7	8	9	10	11	12	13	14	15	16
No. polar flagella	1-6	1[e]	1-2	>1	1-2	>1	1	>1	>1	>1	>1	1	1	1-2	>1	>1
PHB[f]	-	+	+	+	ND	+	+	+	+	-	-	+	d	+	+	+
Mol.% G + C[g]	ND	58-59	72	65-66	ND	66-68	61	ND	68-69	67	66	65	66	ND	ND	66-69
Kovacs' Oxidase	-	-	+	+	ND	+	+	+	+	d	-	+	+	+	+	+
Arginine dihydrolase	-	-	-	+	ND	-	-	-	+	-	ND	-	-	-	-	-
Growth at 4C	+	ND	+	-	ND	-	ND	ND	-	ND	-	-	-	ND	ND	ND
Growth at 41C	-	-	d	d	-	d	-	-	+	ND	-	-	+	+	+	-
Gelatin hydrolysis	-	-	d	d	ND	d	+	+	+	+	-	-	+	+	-	+
Starch hydrolysis	-	-	+	-	-	-	+	-	-	-	ND	d	-	-	-	-
Potato soft rot	-	-	-	-	ND	ND	+	-	ND	ND	ND	ND	ND	-	-	ND
Denitrification	-	-	-	+	-	-	-	-	-	d	-	-	-	-	-	d
Nitrite from nitrate	-	-	+	-	+	d	-	+	d	d	-	-	+	+	+	+
Tween 80 hydrolysis	+	-	+	d	ND	+	ND	ND	+	+	+	+	+	+	-	+
Oxidative on glucose	+	+	+	+	ND	+	+	+	+	-	-	d	-	+	+	+
Inert on glucose	-	-	-	-	ND	d	-	+	-	-	-	d	+	-	-	-
Acid from sucrose	+	-	-	+	+	d	+	+	+	d	-	+	-	-	-	+
Non-diffusible pigments[h]	-	-	-	-	-	gr,yl pl	-	-	-	yl	pk	yl	-	-	-	-
Diffusible pigments[h]	-	-	gr,yl	gr,yl	-	d	-	gr,yl	gr,yl	-	-	-	-	-	-	d(br)

TABLE 7.1 Cont'd Properties of Non-Fluorescent Pseudomonas Species Isolated From Plants

[a] *Sources of data given in Table 7.2.*

[b] *Species code: 1, P. amygdali; 2, P. andropogonis; 3, P. avenae; 4, P. caryophylli; 5, P. cattleyae; 6, P. cepacia; 7, P. cissicola; 8, P. corrugata; 9, P. gladioli; 10, P. maltophilia; 11, P. mesophilica; 12, P. paucimobilis; 13, P. pseudoalcaligenes subsp. citrulli; 14, P. rubrilineans; 15, P. rubrisubalbicans; 16, P. solanacearum.*

[c] *All are Gram negative rods, not producing endospores, or a pigment which fluoresces under long wavelength ultra-violet light (360 nm) when grown on medium B of King et al (1954).*

[d] *+, 90% or more strains positive; −, 90% or more strains negative; ND, no data available; d, 11–89% strains positive or variable results obtained by different authors.*

[e] *P. andropogonis produces an unusually thick, sheathed polar flagellum (Fuerst & Hayward, 1969) (see Fig. 2.2).*

[f] *PHB, Poly-β-hydroxybutyrate inclusions.*

[g] *Mol. % G+C, % guanine plus cytosine in DNA*

[h] *gr, green; yl, yellow; pl, purple; pk, pink; br, brown.*

TABLE 7.2   *Sources of Data on the Physiological Properties of Non-Fluorescent Pseudomonas Species Isolated from Plants[a]*

Species	References
P. amygdali	Psallidas et al. (1968); Psallidas & Panagopoulos (1975).
P. andropogonis	Allen et al. (1970); Burkholder (1957); Burkholder & Guterman (1935); Goto & Okabe (1965); Goto & Starr (1971); Hale & Wilkie (1972b); Nishiyama et al. (1979); Rothwell & Hayward (1964); Schaad et al. (1978); Tominaga (1972).
P. avenae	Goto & Starr (1971); Hale & Wilkie (1972b); Schaad et al. (1975); Schaad et al. (1978); Tominaga (1972).
P. caryophylli	Ballard et al. (1970); Lukezic (1979).
P. cattleyae	Ark & Thomas (1946).
P. cepacia	Ballard et al. (1970); Bazzi (1979); Esanu & Schubert (1973); Geftic et al. (1979); Peel et al. (1979); Holmes et al. (1977); Scarlett et al. (1978).
P. cissicola	Goto & Makino (1977).
P. corrugata	Scarlett et al. (1978); Lukezic (1979).
P. gladioli	Ballard et al. (1970); Hildebrand et al. (1973); Scarlett et al. (1978).
P. maltophilia	Gilardi (unpublished); Hugh & Ryschenkow (1961); Mandel (1966).
P. mesophilica	Austin & Goodfellow (1979).
P. paucimobilis	Holmes et al. (1977); Peel et al. (1979).
P. pseudoalcaligenes subsp. citrulli	Schaad et al. (1978).
P. rubrilineans	Christopher & Edgerton (1930); Hale & Wilkie (1972b); Hayward (1962).
P. rubrisubalbicans	Christopher & Edgerton (1930); Hale & Wilkie (1972a,b); Hayward (1962).
P. solanacearum	Harris (1972); Hayward (1964); Palleroni & Doudoroff (1971).

[a]*Data given in Table 7.1.*

III. *Pseudomonas andropogonis*: Leaf Spot of Clover and Velvet Bean and Bacterial Stripe of Sorghum

A. *Major Synonyms*

Pseudomonas stizolobii (Wolf) Stapp 1935; Pseudomonas woodsii (Smith 1911) Stevens 1925.

B. *Symptoms*

P. andropogonis (Smith 1911) Stapp 1928 primarily affects parenchymatous tissue causing leaf spots, streaks and stripes on a variety of hosts.

Symptoms on Leguminous Hosts. In black spot of clover (Trifolium spp.), the lesions are usually concentrated at the leaf margins or along the midrib and are mainly formed on leaflets but occasionally on stipules. On artificial inoculation, the disease develops as pinhead-sized spots with a water-soaked appearance. Under humid conditions, they enlarge rapidly and form dark green lesions with a water-soaked appearance, especially on the undersurface of the leaflets. The colour of the lesions becomes brown or black as the lesions become dry and necrotic. In dry weather, the lesions turn dark brown soon after disease development and enlarge slowly (Fig. 7.1a).

The spots are usually round in shape but are sometimes angular and restricted by the veins. They are usually 0.5-2.5 mm in diameter but sometimes up to 4.0 mm when lesions coalesce. Yellow halos are frequently observed around spots, which become broad as the disease advances. Occasionally, tiny droplets of bacterial ooze are noticeable on the underneath surface of the lesions. Narrow and dark brown stripes, 5-10 mm long, are sometimes observable on stipules (Goto & Okabe, 1965).

In bacterial leaf spot of velvet bean (Mucuna deeringiana), only the foliage is attacked. The disease first appears as small, pin-point, translucent areas. The centres of these areas become dark brown at an early stage and the translucent character largely disappears except at the edge. Mature lesions lack the water-soaked border which is characteristic of most bacterial leaf spots. An area near the centre of mature spots is characteristically lighter in colour than the margin. The lesions are surrounded by chlorotic zones, and this chlorosis may involve all the leaf surface not occupied by lesions.

(a)   (b)

FIGURE 7.1. Pseudomonas andropogonis on (a) white clover and (b) sorghum.

Mature spots are angular and limited by the veins except when they are so abundant as to merge into large, irregular areas. The lesions are commonly 2-3 mm across, although they vary in size from pin points to spots 8 mm wide. Severely diseased leaves may have several hundred spots on each leaflet. The symptoms on the upper and lower leaf surface are similar and no bacterial exudate is manifest (Wolf, 1920).

Symptoms on Gramineous Hosts. In bacterial stripe of sorghum (Sorghum bicolor) the infection is mainly confined to the leaf and leaf-sheath (Fig. 7.1b). The lesions are initially water-soaked, dark green specks, which gradually become reddish-brown to reddish-purple stripes. Sometimes these stripes are intermingled with light, greenish-brown stripes. The stripes are several mm wide, limited by leaf veins but they often coalesce. Their length varies from several mm to the whole length of the leaf. Bacterial

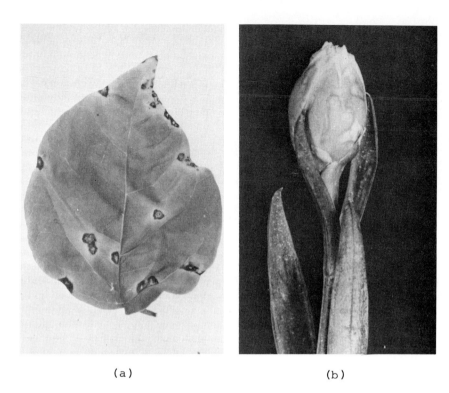

(a)   (b)

FIGURE 7.2. <u>Pseudomonas andropogonis</u> on
(a) Bougainvillea, (b) carnation.

exudate occurs on the undersurface of the leaves and after
drying appears as a light red scale (Goto & Starr, 1971).
   Two kinds of symptom have been described on maize (<u>Zea</u>
<u>mays</u>), a stripe symptom (Ullstrup, 1960) and a leaf spot
(Vidaver & Carlson, 1978). In the latter case symptoms
consist of circular to ellipsoidal, tan to brown spots, with
irregular margins, 1-4 mm in diameter, with one or more
darker brown rings within the lesion. Some spots are
surrounded by a chlorotic ring 1 mm wide, and all spots tend
to have a slightly sunken appearance. Occasionally the
spots coalesce into irregular, somewhat elongated blotches
(Vidaver & Carlson, 1978).

   Symptoms on Ornamental Hosts. On <u>Bougainvillea</u> spp.
infection first shows as small red-brown spots on the
younger leaves (Fig. 7.2a). These enlarge to irregular,
dark, necrotic lesions, delimited by the smaller veins.

During some periods of high rainfall and humidity, these lesions are almost black, and the infection of young developing growth results in puckered, distorted leaves later. This type of infection results in severe defoliation. Lesions developing more slowly are circular with a brown centre surrounded by a darker red-brown margin which in turn is bordered by a chlorotic halo running into the normal green of the leaf. Lesions are 1-6 mm wide. Under favourable conditions dark, angular lesions develop on the coloured bracts (Rothwell & Hayward 1964).

P. andropogonis is the cause of a leaf spot on carnation (Dianthus caryophyllus) (Fig. 7.2b) (Burkholder & Guterman, 1935) and also of bacterial black rot of tulip (Tulipa gesneriana). The tulip disease occurs on post-harvest bulbs; affected bulbs usually show brownish irregular spots on an outside scale, and sometimes show symptoms on the second and third inner scales without any symptoms on an outside scale. Severely infected bulbs dry and become dark brown (Nishiyama et al., 1979). The pathogen also causes a firm rot of Terete Vanda orchid (Vanda spp.) (Oshiro et al., 1964).

C. Host Range

P. andropogonis has a wider host range than indicated by the early literature. Most of the hosts fall within three groups, gramineous (sorghum and maize); leguminous including clovers, velvet bean, common vetch (Vicia sativa ssp. sativa) and chick pea (Cicer arietinum); and ornamental (Bougainvillea, certain orchids, tulip and carnation). A bacterial leaf spot leading to severe defoliation on ornamental Triplaris filipensis, and a bacterial dark spot of coffee (Coffea arabica) have also been reported in Brazil (Robbs et al., 1981).

There is some evidence of pathogenic specialization to particular hosts, suggesting that certain pathovars may be designated in the future. Goto & Starr (1971) examined the host range of seven isolates of P. andropogonis and found that all produced typical red stripes on inoculation to sorghum and all produced small brown spots on common bean (Phaseolus vulgaris). There was variation in the ability of different isolates to infect white clover (Trifolium repens). Robbs et al. (1981) found that seven strains could infect sorghum, maize and velvet bean by artificial inoculation. However, sorghum strains were not pathogenic on

Triplaris spp. or coffee. The coffee strain did not infect Triplaris spp. and vice versa. None infected Bougainvillea spp.

Nishiyama et al. (1979) have proposed that P. woodsii be reduced to synonymy with P. andropogonis on the basis of their comparative study of the host range and close similarity in cultural and physiological properties between isolates from a black rot of tulip, from sorghum and from carnation. Isolates from each of the three hosts cross infected each of the hosts with production of similar symptoms. However, none of the tulip isolates produced disease symptoms on inoculation to red clover.

D. *Geographical Distribution and Importance*

P. andropogonis is widely distributed in Africa, Asia, Australasia and Oceania, Europe, North America and South America. However, some strains of P. andropogonis which appear to be specialized to particular hosts are of limited distribution. A strain affecting Bougainvillea was first reported in Zimbabwe by Rothwell & Hayward (1964), and this remains the only published record of a bacterial disease on this host. In 1980 a disease resembling bacterial leaf spot was observed on nursery-grown Bougainvillea plants in south east Queensland (Hayward & Moffett, unpubl.). Subsequent tests have confirmed that the disease is caused by P. andropogonis. The disease is apparently confined to nurseries. Field infection has not been observed on Bougainvillea glabra nor on B. glabra cv. variegata in either Zimbabwe or Australia.

The only record of this pathogen on orchids is that of Oshiro et al. (1964) in Hawaii. There is one record of a leaf spot of chick pea caused by P. andropogonis occurring on imported seed under quarantine in Australia (Navaratnam & Hayward, 1979). An infection of velvet bean grown from imported seed from the U.S.A. observed at Grafton, New South Wales (Hynes, 1941) is probably the first record of P. andropogonis on a leguminous host in Australia. A bacterial blight of common vetch occurs in northern New South Wales (Allen et al., 1970) but has not been reported from any other country.

Black spot of red and white clover is widespread in eastern coastal areas of Australia during the summer months, with greater severity during years of high rainfall. This contrasts with the rarity of infection on either sorghum or maize.

IV.   *Pseudomonas avenae*: Leaf Blight of Cereals

A. Major Synonym

Pseudomonas alboprecipitans Rosen 1922.

B. Symptoms

P. avenae Manns 1909 is the cause of bacterial leaf blight of oats (Avena sativa), bacterial leaf blight and stalk rot of maize and teosinte (Euchlaena mexicana) and bacterial brown stripe of foxtail (Alopecurus spp.) and other grasses. Infection of leaves and sheaths results in spots and streaks. In maize the pathogen produces a stalk rot on the upper part of the stem; the top of the plant is killed and the cob rots. The pathogen causes red spots but not stripes on sorghum and in this respect is distinct from P. andropogonis.

C. Host Range

This species occurs naturally on oats, barley (Hordeum vulgare), rye (Secale cereale), slender pigeon grasses (Setaria gracilis), Italian millet (Setaria italica), Setaria lutescens, Sorghum bicolor, Sorghum sudanense, wheat (Triticum aestivum) and maize. Schaad et al. (1975) showed that one isolate was non-pathogenic for watermelon (Citrullus lanatus var. caffer), cantaloupe (Cucumis melo), squash (Cucurbita spp.), cucumber (Cucumis sativus), tomato and cowpea. There is no convincing evidence of pathogenicity to clover, although infection is reported to occur on bean.

D. Geographical Distribution and Importance.

The pathogen is known to occur in parts of the U.S.A., Brazil, Japan and the Philippines (Bradbury, 1973a), on a variety of hosts.

V. *Pseudomonas caryophylli*: Bacterial Wilt of Carnation

A. Symptoms

P. caryophylli Starr & Burkholder 1942 is the cause of bacterial wilt and bacterial stem crack of carnation. Vascular tissues are disrupted and frayed by invasion by the pathogen resulting in wilting of plants.

B. Host Range

The major host is carnation. Schaad et al (1978) found that no infection resulted on inoculation to watermelon, cantaloupe, squash, cucumber, tomato, cowpea or maize. Ballard et al (1970) found that their strains could produce a soft rot of onion bulb slices, as do some strains of P. cepacia and P. gladioli.

C. Geographical Distribution and Importance

Scattered distribution in parts of Asia, Europe, North and South America (Bradbury, 1973b). The bacterium has caused serious damage in the U.S.A. since it was first reported in 1940.

VI. *Pseudomonas cattleyae*: Brown Spot of Orchid

A. Symptoms

P. cattleyae (Pavarino 1911) Savulescu 1947 causes brown spot disease on orchids. Small, dark, water-soaked spots appear on the leaves; they increase rapidly in size, change from light-brown to dark chestnut brown with age and may coalesce to form larger areas, and kill the plant.

B. Host Range

The disease affects Phalaenopsis spp. and Cattleya spp.; several other orchids are susceptible on artificial inoculation (Ark & Thomas, 1946).

C. Geographical Distribution and Importance

The disease occurs in parts of Europe and the U.S.A. The pathogen has been recorded on Phalaenopsis spp. in Queensland, Australia (Simmonds, 1966), but little is known of its incidence or importance.

VII.   *Pseudomonas cepacia*: Sour Skin of Onion

A. Major Synonym

Pseudomonas multivorans Stanier et al. 1966.
P. cepacia Palleroni & Holmes 1981 was originally described and named by Burkholder (1950). The name was inadvertently omitted from the Approved Lists (Skerman et al., 1980) and became invalid but was later revalidated by Palleroni & Holmes (1981).

B. Symptoms

P. cepacia is the cause of a wound infection in onion (Allium cepa var. cepa) known as sour skin. Sour skin is a rot that attacks only part of the outer fleshy scales of the bulb, but not necessarily the outermost scale; the inner scales that give rise to leaves are not infected naturally or artificially (Burkholder, 1950). Infected onions may show a shrinkage of the upper portion of the bulb and in advanced stages of the disease the outer dry skin readily slips off during handling, while the portion of the bulb within the diseased slimy scales remains firm. The disease has been observed in the field and in onions held in store (Bazzi, 1979). Onion is the only recorded host.

C. Geographical Distribution and Importance

P. cepacia is a versatile microorganism which rarely occurs as an opportunist pathogen in man and in plants, and which also occurs in soil and water. The species is sometimes encountered in hospitals. The species is probably cosmopolitan in distribution; however, sour skin of onions has been recorded only in the U.S.A. and Italy (Bazzi, 1979).

VIII. *Pseudomonas cissicola*: Bacterial Leaf Spot of *Cayratia japonica*

A. Symptoms.

P. cissicola (Takimoto 1939) Burkholder 1948 causes bacterial leaf spot of Cayratia japonica. Circular or irregularly shaped, dark brown spots 3-5 mm in diameter are formed on leaves. The surface of the lesions show an oily appearance. When many spots are formed on a leaf, they coalesce to form large, reddish brown lesions which soon kill diseased leaves. Yellow halos are sometimes observed around lesions. In the later stage of the disease, the lesions turn light brown, become dry and crack in the centre (Goto & Makino, 1977). The disease has only been recorded in Japan.

B. Host Range

All isolates are pathogenic on C. japonica but not on grapevine (Vitis vinifera) or Parthenocissus tricuspidata (Goto & Makino, 1977).

IX. *Pseudomonas corrugata*: Tomato Pith Necrosis

A. Symptoms

P. corrugata Roberts & Scarlett 1978 is the cause of tomato pith necrosis. The symptoms on mature tomato plants include brown discolouration and/or necrosis and collapse of the pith. These are sometimes accompanied by vascular browning, external dark brown to black stem lesions, bacterial flux from stem wounds and adventitious root formation (Scarlett et al., 1978).

B. Host Range

Tomato is the only host in which disease symptoms appear. However, this species has been isolated in the U.S.A. from the roots of symptomless lucerne plants grown in the glasshouse but not from field-grown lucerne (Lukezic, 1979).

C. Geographical Distribution and Importance

P. corrugata has so far only been recorded in glass-houses in the United Kingdom, where occurrence of tomato pith necrosis is associated with soft growth and high humidities (Scarlett et al., 1978), and from symptomless lucerne plants in the U.S.A.

X. *Pseudomonas gladioli*: Leaf Spot and Corm Scab of Gladiolus and Soft Rot of Onion

A. Major Synonyms

Pseudomonas alliicola Starr & Burkholder 1942, Pseudomonas marginata (McCulloch) Stapp 1928.

Two pathovars of P. gladioli Severini 1913 have been designated P. gladioli pv. gladioli Severini 1913 Young et al. 1978 and P. gladioli pv. alliicola (Burkholder 1942) Young et al. 1980.

B. Symptoms

P. gladioli pv. gladioli causes a leaf spot, basal leaf rot, corm scab and soft rot of Gladiolus. The leaves begin dying at the tips, the yellowing extending along one or both margins. Leaf lesions are usually confined to the basal fleshy portion and are first visible as tiny specks of bright reddish-brown colour. These spots enlarge to circular or elongated spots, dark brown to black in colour, with a slightly elevated margin and sunken centre. Aerial parts can be easily pulled from the corm. Yellow or reddish sunken spots develop on the corm which eventually becomes flaccid. A yellow brown odourless mass can be squeezed from the corms.

P. gladioli pv. alliicola causes a soft rot of onion bulbs. In early stages the bulb may appear sound on the outside, but on being cut open one or two infected scales are revealed. The symptoms are similar to those produced by P. cepacia (see VII above). Both are reported to be wound pathogens only, capable of infecting leaves and mature bulbs, which may infect maturing onions in the field prior to harvest (Tesoriero et al., 1982)

C. Host Range

P. gladioli pv. gladioli occurs naturally on Gladiolus spp., Freesia hybrida, Crocus spp., and other members of the Iridaceae. P. gladioli pv. alliicola is primarily a pathogen of onion.

D. Geographical Distribution and Importance

P. gladioli pv. gladioli occurs in North and South America, Europe and Australasia. It is sometimes severe on gladioli in Queensland, Australia. The distribution of P. gladioli pv. alliicola appears to be more restricted. In Australia, it has been reported in New South Wales (Tesoriero et al., 1982) and Tasmania.

XI. *Pseudomonas maltophilia*: Saprophyte

P. maltophilia Hugh 1981 was originally described and named by Hugh & Ryschenkow (1961). The name was inadvertently omitted from the Approved Lists (Skerman et al., 1980) and became invalid but was later revalidated by Hugh (1981). It is commonly isolated from moribund plant material but is not known to be the primary cause of disease in plants. Some isolates show yellow but, unlike xanthomonads, never mucoid growth. The species is widespread and has been isolated from a variety of clinical materials, soil and water (Hugh & Ryschenkow, 1961).

XII. *Pseudomonas mesophilica*: Saprophyte

P. mesophilica Austin & Goodfellow 1979 has been isolated from leaf surfaces, particularly of perennial ryegrass (Lolium perenne) but is not known to be a plant pathogen (Austin & Goodfellow, 1979).

XIII.   *Pseudomonas paucimobilis*: Saprophyte

P. paucimobilis Holmes et al. 1977 is not known to be a plant pathogen but has been isolated from plant sources, and because of its yellow, water-insoluble pigment has been confused with xanthomonads. The primary source is water.

XIV.   *Pseudomonas pseudoalcaligenes* subsp. *citrulli*: Bacterial Spot of Watermelon

A. Symptoms

P. pseudoalcaligenes subsp. *citrulli* Schaad et al. 1978 is the cause of a bacterial disease of watermelons, characterized by water-soaked lesions on the cotyledons. This species was referred to as being fluorescent by Schroth et al. (1981) but this is not in accord with the description of the species by Schaad et al. (1978).

B. Host Range and Geographical Distribution

This pathogen appears to be limited to members of the Cucurbitaceae, including watermelon, cucumber and squash. The disease occurs in Georgia, U.S.A., but has not been reported elsewhere (Schaad et al., 1978).

XV.   *Pseudomonas rubrilineans*: Red Stripe and Top Rot of Sugarcane

A. Major Synonym

Xanthomonas rubrilineans (Lee et al. 1925) Starr & Burkholder 1942.

B. Symptoms

P. rubrilineans (Lee et al., 1925) Stapp 1928 is the cause of red stripe of sugarcane (Saccharum interspecific hybrids) (Fig 7.3). There are two forms of disease: leaf stripe and top rot (Martin & Wismer, 1961). These may occur

singly or together, and under field conditions are favoured
by periods of relatively high atmospheric humidity. The
leaf stripe form is characterized by the presence of long,
narrow, uniform, dark-red stripes. Young cane is more susceptible to attack than older cane. At the earliest stage
of infection, watery-green stripes appear, usually midway in
the leaf and near the midrib, but in some instances the
stripes are concentrated toward the leaf base. The stripes
spread rapidly up and down the leaf and become reddish,
later turning to dark red. The stripes are uniform,
straight and sharply delineated. The stripes vary in width
from 0.5-4 mm and in length from a few cm to the entire
length of the leaf blade. Two or more stripes frequently
coalesce to form broad bands of diseased leaf tissue. The
red stripes may also appear on the lower surface of the
midrib. Lesions on the lower surface of the leaves are
often covered with whitish flakes of dried bacterial ooze.
Red stripe occurs mostly on leaves which are young or of
intermediate age, rather than on the oldest leaves of the
plant. The disease may attack the youngest leaves which are
partially unrolled and, if sufficiently severe, cause a top
rot.

Plants affected by top rot from natural infection or
artificial inoculation develop yellowing and wilting of the
older leaves and may exhibit the typical reddish leaf
striping. Top rot may also result from stem or bud infection without manifesting leaf symptoms. Affected internodes
frequently show sunken areas which are first water-soaked
and later turn red or brown. The internal tissues are of a
similar colour and, as the rotting progresses, large
cavities are formed within the internodes. At an advanced
stage of the disease the leaf spindle is easily pulled out
of the enveloping sheaths. The rotted portion seen when the
diseased spindle is pulled out has a characteristic,
unpleasant odour, which is an important diagnostic feature
of the disease.

C. Host Range

P. rubrilineans occurs naturally on sugarcane. It is
pathogenic to maize and Sorghum spp. on inoculation. More
information is required on the possible existence of
alternative grass hosts in the field. Symptoms similar to
those caused by P. rubrilineans on sugarcane have been
observed on Sorghum stipoideum in the Ord River district of

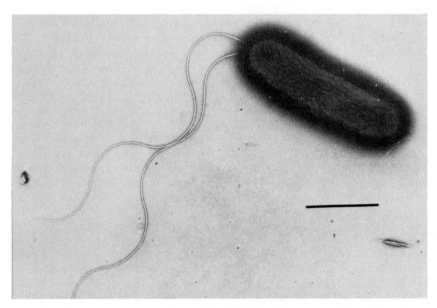

FIGURE 7.3 <u>Pseudomonas rubrilineans</u>, cause of red stripe of sugarcane, showing two polar flagella. Scale bar 1μm.

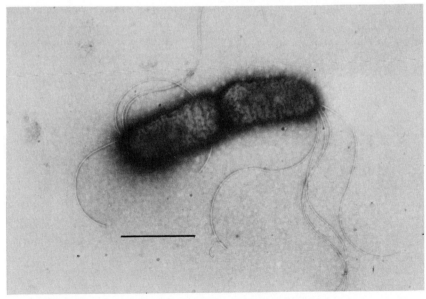

FIGURE 7.4 <u>Pseudomonas rubrisubalbicans</u>, cause of mottled stripe of sugarcane, showing tufts of polar flagella. Scale bar 1μm.

north-western Australia. It is likely that this weed is an alternative host for P. rubrilineans, which commonly occurs on sugarcane in the Ord River Irrigation Scheme (Persley, pers. comm.).

D. Geographical Distribution and Importance

Red stripe is widely distributed in areas of the world where sugarcane is grown, but is rarely of economic importance. The pathogen is found in coastal areas of Queensland, Australia and is moderately severe in restricted areas, particularly where there is a high incidence of the top rot symptom. Red stripe and top rot also occur in experimental sugarcane plantings in north western Australia (Irwin et al., 1983)

XVI. *Pseudomonas rubrisubalbicans*: Mottled Stripe of Sugarcane and Leaf Stripe of Sorghum

A. Major Synonym

Xanthomonas rubrisubalbicans (Christopher & Edgerton 1930) Savulescu 1947.

B. Symptoms

P. rubrisubalbicans (Christopher & Edgerton 1930) Krasil'nikov 1949 is the cause of mottled stripe of sugar cane and leaf stripe of sorghum (Hale & Wilkie, 1972a) (Fig. 7.4). In contrast with red stripe disease of sugarcane, mottled stripe is primarily a disease of the leaf blade. The stripes are predominantly red with white areas or white margins (Christopher & Edgerton, 1930). The stripes run parallel to the leaf veins and range in length from 1-2 cm to up to a meter or more, while the width is usually from 1-4 mm. Several stripes may occur on the same leaf. These sometimes coalesce, forming mottled red and white bands. Bacterial exudate is not observed.

Bacterial leaf stripe of sorghum has been reported in New Zealand (Hale & Wilkie, 1972a,b). Irregularly-shaped, dark red lesions are narrow and extend in streaks between the veins. Older lesions are more extensive, and may result in premature senescence of leaf tissue. Red crusts of dried exudate are abundant on the upper and lower leaf surfaces.

C. Host Range

Sorghum spp. and sugarcane.

D. Geographical Distribution and Importance

Mottled stripe of sugarcane is of general distribution and little importance in Australia and other countries where sugarcane is grown.

XVII. *Pseudomonas setariae* (inv.): Bacterial Stripe of Rice

This species is invalid because it was not included in the Approved Lists (Skerman et al., 1980). The name has not yet been revived.

A. Symptoms

P. setariae (Okabe 1934) Suvalescu 1947 is the cause of a disease known as bacterial stripe or bacterial brown stripe of rice. The pathogen only infects seedlings and young plants in the nursery, producing leaf spots. Italian and Panic millets are also attacked at all stages.

B. Host Range

The disease occurs naturally on rice (Oryza sativa), Italian millet (Setaria italica), millet (Panicum miliaceum), barley, Agropyron intermedium, A. trichophorum, Bromus catharticus, B. marginatus (Bradbury, 1970).

C. Geographical Distribution and Importance

Japan, Taiwan and the Philippines (Bradbury, 1970).

XVIII. *Pseudomonas solanacearum*: Bacterial Wilt and Moko Disease

A. Symptoms

There are numerous common names for the diseases caused by P. solanacearum (Smith 1896) Smith 1914, depending on host and locality. They include brown rot of potato (Solanum tuberosum), Moko disease of banana (Musa spp.), Granville wilt of tobacco (Nicotiana tabacum) (Kelman 1953; Buddenhagen & Kelman, 1964). The symptoms of disease on five of the major hosts (tomato, ginger (Zingiber officinale), potato, tobacco and banana) are described below.

Symptoms on Tomato. A rapid wilting of the foliage occurs which is particularly noticeable during the warmest part of the day. Stunting frequently precedes the wilting and leaflets and leaf stalks may curl downwards. Where the disease has developed slowly, large numbers of adventitious roots are produced along the stem above ground level. If the stem is cut across at ground level, a brown discolouration of the water-conducting tissues just beneath the bark will be seen. A milky exudate is also apparent if the end of the cut stem is placed in water (Fig. 7.5a) (Kelman, 1953; Vock, 1978).

Symptoms on Ginger. In bacterial wilt of ginger, wilting and yellowing of the lower leaves occurs, extending upwards until all the leaves are affected. The stem becomes water-soaked and readily breaks away from the rhizome. Water-conducting tissues in the stem darken. Affected rhizomes are generally darker than normal and have water-soaked areas with pockets of milky fluid beneath them. When rhizomes are cut and a little pressure applied, a milky exudate appears.

Symptoms on Potato. In bacterial wilt of potatoes, a sudden wilting of leaves occurs without preliminary yellowing. If the stem is cut at ground level a whitish exudate may be seen on the cut surface. On tubers a wet breakdown occurs at the point of attachment to the stolon and at the eyes. The disease may be best recognised if a tuber is cut across. In affected tubers, a light-brown breakdown of the water-conducting tissues will be seen. Milky fluid may be squeezed from this discoloured area (Fig. 7.5b).

(a)   (b)

FIGURE 7.5.   Bacterial wilt caused by Pseudomonas solanacearum (a) milky exudate from infected tomato stems after standing (from left to right) for 30 min, 30s, 30s, 10s; (b) milky exudate in infected potato tuber.

Symptoms on Tobacco. In bacterial wilt of tobacco, the symptoms are generally first noticed near the budding stage when leaves wilt and turn yellow prematurely. Sometimes only leaves on one side of the plant are affected. In many cases, only one half of a leaf may show symptoms. Roots on affected plants are discoloured and decayed with the rot commencing at the tip and progressing towards the stem. Later, dark, narrow streaks may be seen in the woody tissues beneath the bark.

Symptoms on Banana.   Moko disease is manifest as a wilt which may be confused with Fusarium wilt (Panama disease). On young, rapidly growing plants, the youngest three leaves turn pale green or yellow and collapse near the junction of the lamina and the petiole. Within 3-7 days, most leaves collapse. The most characteristic symptoms occur on young suckers that have been cut back once and begun regrowth. These are blackened, stunted and may be twisted. If sucker leaves are present, these may turn yellow or become necrotic (Fig. 7.6). Vascular discolouration in plants that have not shot fruit is concentrated near the centre of the pseudostem, becoming less apparent peripherally and centrally.

If fruit symptoms are present, it is indicative that the disease is Moko and not Panama disease. The presence of yellow fingers in an otherwise green stem will often indicate the presence of Moko disease. A firm, brown, dry rot is found within the fruit (Fig. 7.7)(Buddenhagen, 1961).

B. *Host Range*

The host range of P. solanacearum is exceptionally wide; there are many hosts of economic importance, as well as many weed hosts, representing more than 30 families of plants, including monocotyledons as well as dicotyledons. Families in which many hosts are found include Solanaceae, Musaceae, Asteraceae and Fabaceae (Kelman, 1953).

C. *Identification*

Much evidence indicates that P. solanacearum is a complex and variable species and several attempts have been made to devise special purpose classifications at the infrasubspecific level. Three races have been proposed on the basis of pathogenic specialization and certain cultural properties: Race 1 affects tobacco, tomato, many solanaceous and other weeds and certain diploid bananas; Race 2 causes bacterial wilt of triploid bananas (Moko disease) and Heliconia; Race 3 affects potato and tomato, but is not highly virulent on other solanaceous crops (Buddenhagen & Kelman, 1964). Some races and the strains of which they are comprised are catholic and others restricted in the range of plants in which they are capable of causing wilt under field conditions.

According to another system four biotypes (biovars) (I, II, III and IV), were designated on the basis of certain biochemical properties (Hayward, 1964). The two systems of classification are not easily correlated, except for the fact that Race 3, the potato race, is equivalent to Biotype II.

FIGURE 7.6 Moko disease of banana. Typical symptoms of banana infected with Pseudomonas solanacearum from roots or previously cut sucker surfaces. Note blackened, stunted, twisted suckers. (Photo courtesy I.W. Buddenhagen).

FIGURE 7.7 Fruit symptoms of Moko disease, resulting from the systemic invasion of banana fruit by the B strain of Pseudomonas solanacearum. Note characteristic firm, brown, dry rot. (Photo courtesy I.W. Buddenhagen).

D. *Geographical Distribution and Importance*

Bacterial wilt is widely distributed and damaging in the tropics, sub-tropics and warm temperate regions of the world (Kelman, 1953). It is a major limiting factor in the cultivation of potatoes and other vegetables in sub-tropical and tropical regions.

For example, the disease is the most widespread and economically the most important bacterial disease of plants in Queensland, Australia. The disease is generally found where potatoes are cultivated and is often severe. The disease on ginger is limited to the Nambour area in south east Queensland and is now uncommon. The disease is common on tomato and is usually of moderate severity, being most severe in poorly drained soils. The disease on tobacco has increased in importance in the past decade in north Queensland. Bacterial wilt is scattered on capsicum and widespread and often severe on egg fruit (Solanum melongena).

Study of the distribution of biotypes in Australia has shown that Biotype II is endemic in some potato-growing areas of Queensland and New South Wales. The same biotype has also been recorded in parts of Victoria and in south western parts of Western Australia and has recently been reported in South Australia (Akiew, 1982). There are no records of the occurrence of bacterial wilt in Tasmania. Biotypes III and IV are widely distributed in Queensland and many hosts are affected (Pegg & Moffett, 1971; Hayward, 1975). Bacterial wilt is a common disease of tomatoes in the northern coastal areas of the Northern Territory. It occurs less commonly in a number of other hosts and in isolated localities as far as 350 km from the coast. Biotypes III and IV have been recorded on tomato and on several other hosts in the Northern Territory (Pitkethley, 1981).

Moko disease of banana is much more restricted in distribution than bacterial wilt on other hosts and is therefore of considerable quarantine significance. It is one of the most serious diseases of banana and plantains, which has caused severe losses in small-farmer crops of bananas and plantains of South and Central America and the Caribbean. Crop losses in commercial plantations have been minimized by extensive control programs. The disease was for many years confined to these areas (Buddenhagen & Kelman, 1964), but there are recent reports of the disease occurring in the Philippines (Rillo, 1979) and South India

(Gnanamanickam et al., 1979). It is possible that distribution of the disease in South-East Asia is more widespread than the records indicate. There are no confirmed reports of the occurrence of Moko disease in Australia. Infected banana, plantain and Heliconia plants pose the greatest risk of introducing Moko disease to Australia. The import of Heliconia plants is prohibited but seed is permitted entry. The import of banana fruit from affected areas is prohibited and the import of banana plants is subject to strict quarantine control.

References

Akiew, S. (1982). Bacterial wilt of potato in South Australia. Australasian Plant Pathology 11,10.

Allen, R.N., Hayward, A.C., Halliday, W.J. & Fulcher, J. 1970. Bacterial blight of Vicia sativa: aetiology of the disease and identification of the pathogen. Australian Journal of Biological Sciences 23, 597-606.

Ark, P.A. & Thomas, H.E. (1946). Bacterial leaf spot and bud rot of orchids caused by Phytomonas cattleyae. Phytopathology 36, 695-698.

Austin, B. & Goodfellow, M. (1979). Pseudomonas mesophilica, a new species of pink bacteria isolated from leaf surfaces. International Journal of Systematic Bacteriology 29, 373-378.

Ballard, R.W., Palleroni, N.J., Doudoroff, M., & Stanier, R.Y. (1970). Taxonomy of the aerobic pseudomonads: Pseudomonas cepacia, P. marginata, P. alliicola and P. caryophylli. Journal of General Microbiology 60. 199-214.

Basit, A.A., Francki, R.I.B., & Kerr, A. (1970). The simultaneous transmission of a plant-pathogenic bacterium and a virus from rose by grafting and mechanical inoculation. Australian Journal of Biological Sciences 23, 493-496.

Bazzi, C. (1979). Identification of Pseudomonas cepacia on onion bulbs in Italy. Phytopathologische Zeitschrift 95, 254-258.

Bradbury, J.F. (1970). Pseudomonas setariae. C.M.I. Descriptions of Pathogenic Fungi and Bacteria No. 237. Kew: Commonwealth Mycological Institute.

Bradbury, J.F. (1973a). Pseudomonas avenae. CMI Descriptions of Pathogenic Fungi and Bacteria No. 371. Kew: Commonwealth Mycological Institute.

Bradbury, J.F. (1973b). Pseudomonas caryophylli. CMI Descriptions of Pathogenic Fungi and Bacteria No. 373. Kew: Commonwealth Mycological Institute.

Bradbury, J.F. (1977). Pseudomonas amygdali. CMI Descriptions of Pathogenic Fungi and Bacteria No. 556. Kew: Commonwealth Mycological Institute.

Buddenhagen, I.W. (1961). Bacterial wilt of bananas: history and known distribution. Tropical Agriculture (Trinidad) 38, 107-121.

Buddenhagen, I.W. & Kelman, A. (1964). Biological and physiological aspects of bacterial wilt caused by Pseudomonas solanacearum. Annual Review of Phytopathology 2, 201-230.

Burkholder, W.H. (1950). Sour skin, a bacterial rot of onion bulbs. Phytopathology 40, 115-117.

Burkholder, W.H. (1957). A bacterial disease of clover and velvet beans. Phytopathology 47, 48-50.

Burkholder, W.H. & Guterman, C.E.F. (1935). Bacterial leaf spot of carnations. Phytopathology 25, 114-120.

Christopher, W.N. & Edgerton, C.W. (1930). Bacterial stripe diseases of sugarcane in Louisiana. Journal of Agricultural Research 41, 259-267.

Esanu, J.G. & Schubert, R.H.W. (1973). Zur Taxonomie und nomenklatur von Pseudomonas cepacia. Zentralblatt fur Bakteriologie und Hygiene, I Abteilung Originale A 224, 478-483.

Fuerst, J.A. & Hayward, A.C. (1969). The sheathed flagellum of Pseudomonas stizolobii. Journal of General Microbiology 58, 239-245.

Gettic, S.G., Heymann, H. & Adair, F.W. (1979). Fourteen years survival of Pseudomonas cepacia in a salts solution preserved with benzalkonium chloride. Applied and Environmental Microbiology 37, 505-510.

Gnanamanickam, S.S., Lockeeswari, T.S. & Nandini, K.R. (1979). Bacterial wilt of banana in Southern India. Plant Disease Reporter 63, 525-528.

Goto, M. & Makino, T. (1977). Emendation of Pseudomonas cissicola, the causal organism of bacterial leaf spot of Cayratia japonica (Thunb.) Gagn, and designation of the neotype strain. Annales of the Phytopathological Society of Japan 43, 40-45.

Goto, M. & Okabe, N. (1965). Bacterial plant diseases in Japan X. Bacterial black spot disease of clover caused by a strain of Pseudomonas andropogonis. Report Faculty of Agriculture, Shizuoka University 15, 45-49.

Goto, M. & Starr, M.P. (1971). A comparative study of Pseudomonas andropogonis, P. stizolobii, and P. alboprecipitans. Annales of the Phytopathological Society of Japan 37, 233-241.

Hale, C.N. & Wilkie, J.P. (1972a). Bacterial leaf stripe of sorghum in New Zealand caused by Pseudomonas rubrisubalbicans. New Zealand Journal of Agricultural Research 15, 457-460.

Hale, C.N. & Wilkie, J.P. (1972b). A comparative study of Pseudomonas species pathogenic to sorghum. New Zealand Journal of Agricultural Research 15, 448-456.

Harris, D.C. (1972). Intra-specific variation in Pseudomonas solanacearum. In "Proceedings of the Third International Conference on Plant Pathogenic Bacteria", pp. 289-292. (Ed. H.P. Maas Geesteranus). Wageningen, Netherlands: Pudoc.

Hayward, A.C. (1962). Studies on bacterial pathogens of sugarcane. II. Differentiation, taxonomy and nomenclature of the bacteria causing red stripe and mottled stripe diseases. Mauritius Sugar Industry Research Institute Occasional Paper 13, 13-27.

Hayward, A.C. (1964). Characteristics of Pseudomonas solanacearum. Journal of Applied Bacteriology 27, 265-277.

Hayward, A.C. (1975). Biotypes of Pseudomonas solanacearum in Australia. Australian Plant Pathology Society Newsletter 4, 9-11.

Hildebrand, D.C., Palleroni, N.J. & Doudoroff, M. (1973). Synonym of Pseudomonas gladioli Severini 1913 and Pseudomonas marginata (McCulloch 1921) Stapp 1928. International Journal of Systematic Bacteriology 23, 433-437.

Holmes, B., Owen, R.J., Evans, A., Malnick, H. & Willcox, W.R. (1977). Pseudomonas paucimobilis, a new species isolated from human clinical specimens, the hospital environment, and other sources. International Journal of Systematic Bacteriology 27, 133-146.

Hugh, R. (1981). Pseudomonas maltophilia sp. nov., nom. rev. International Journal of Systematic Bacteriology 31, 195.

Hugh, R. & Ryschenkow, E. (1961). Pseudomonas maltophilia, an Alcaligenes-like species. Journal of General Microbiology 26, 123-132.

Hynes, H.J. (1941). Plant diseases recorded in New South Wales. Bulletin of the New South Wales Department of Agricultural Science No.46 Suppl. No.2.

Irwin, J.G.A., Persley, G.J., Conde, B. & Pitkethley, R.N. (1983). Research for improved crop management: Diseases. In "Proceedings of CSIRO Symposium on Agro-Research for Australia's Semi-Arid Tropics, 21-25 March, 1983" (in press).

Kelman, A. (1953). The bacterial wilt caused by Pseudomonas solanacearum. North Carolina Agricultural Experiment Station Technical Bulletin 99.

King, E.O., Ward, M.K. & Raney, D.E. (1954). Two simple media for the demonstration of pyocyanin and fluorescein. Journal of Laboratory and Clinical Medicine 44, 301-307.

Lukezic, F.L. (1979). Pseudomonas corrugata, a pathogen of tomato isolated from symptomless Alfalfa roots. Phytopathology 69, 27-31.

Mandel, M. (1966). Deoxyribonucleic acid base composition in the genus Pseudomonas. Journal of General Microbiology 43, 273-292.

Martin, J.P. & Wismer, C.A. (1961). Red stripe. In "Sugar-Cane Diseases of the World" Vol.I, 109-126. (Ed. J.P. Martin, E.V. Abbott & C.G. Hughes). Amsterdam: Elsevier.

Navaratnam, S.J. & Hayward, A.C. (1979). Bacterial blight of chick pea. Australasian Plant Pathology 8, 18.

Nishiyama, K., Kusaba, T., Ohta, K., Nahata, K. & Ezuka, A. (1979). Bacterial black rot of tulip caused by Pseudomonas andropogonis. Annales of the Phytopathological Society of Japan 45, 668-674.

Oshiro, L.S., Hine, R.E. & Goto, S. (1964). The identification of Pseudomonas andropogonis as the cause of a firm rot disease of the Terete Vanda orchid in Hawaii. Plant Disease Reporter 48, 736-740.

Palleroni, N.J. & Doudoroff, M. (1971). Phenotypic characterization and deoxyribonucleic acid homologies of Pseudomonas solanacearum. Journal of Bacteriology 107, 690-696.

Palleroni, N.J. & Holmes, B. (1981). Pseudomonas cepacia sp. nov., nom. rev. International Journal of Systematic Bacteriology 31, 479-481.

Peel, M.M., Davis, J.M., Armstrong, W.L.H., Wilson, J.R. & Holmes, B. (1979). Pseudomonas paucimobilis from a leg ulcer on a Japanese seaman. Journal of Clinical Microbiology 9, 561-564.

Pegg, K.G. & Moffett, M.L. (1971). Host range of the ginger strain of Pseudomonas solanacearum in Queensland. Australia Journal of Experimental Agriculture and Animal Husbandry 11, 696-698.

Pitkethley, R.N. (1981). Host range and biotypes of Pseudomonas solanacearum in the Northern Territory. Australasian Plant Pathology 10, 46-47.

Psallidas, P.G. & Panagopoulos, C.G. (1975). A new bacteriosis of almond caused by Pseudomonas amygdali sp. nov. Annales de L'Institut Phytopathologique Benaki New Series 11, 94-108.

Psallidas, P.G., Panagopoulos, C.G. & Malathrakis, N.E. (1968). A new bacterial disease of almond. Annales de L'Institut Phytopathologique Benaki New Series 8, 85-88.

Rillo, A.R. (1979). Bacterial wilt of banana in the Philippines. F.A.O. Plant Protection Bulletin 27, 105-108.

Robbs, C.F., Neto, J.R., Ribeiro, R. de L.D. & Kimura, O. (1981). Bacterial leaf spot of ornamental Triplaris caused by Pseudomonas andropogonis. In "Proceedings of the Fifth International Conference on Plant Pathogenic Bacteria, Cali, Colombia, 1981, 54-59". (Ed. J.C. Lozano). Cali, Colombia: Centro Internacional de Agricultura Tropical.

Rothwell, A. & Hayward, A.C. (1964). A bacterial disease of Bougainvillea. Rhodesian Journal of Agricultural Research 2, 97-99.

Scarlett, C.M., Fletcher, J.T., Roberts, P. & Lelliott, R.A. (1978). Tomato pith necrosis caused by Pseudomonas corrugata n. sp. Annals of Applied Biology 88, 105-114.

Schaad, N.W., Kado, C.I. & Sumner, D.R. (1975). Synonymy of Pseudomonas avenae Manns 1909 and Pseudomonas alboprecipitans Rosen 1922. International Journal of Systematic Bacteriology 25, 133-137.

Schaad, N.W., Sowell, G., Goth, R.W., Colwell, R.R. & Webb, R.E. (1978). Pseudomonas pseudoalcaligenes subsp. citrullis subsp. nov. International Journal of Systematic Bacteriology 28, 117-125.

Schroth, M.N., Hildebrand, D.C. & Starr, M.P. (1981). Phytopathogenic members of the genus Pseudomonas. In "The Prokaryotes", 701-718. (Ed. M.P. Starr, H. Stolp, H.G. Truper, A. Balows, H.G. Schlegel). Berlin: Springer-Verlag.

Simmonds, J.H. (1966). "Host Index of Plant Diseases in Queensland". Brisbane: Queensland Department of Primary Industries.

Skerman, V.B.D., McGowan, V. & Sneath, P.H.A. (1980). Approved lists of bacterial names. International Journal of Systematic Bacteriology 30, 255-420.

Tesoriero, L.A., Fahy, P.C. & Gunn, L.V. (1982). First record of a bacterial rot of onion in Australia caused by Pseudomonas gladioli pv. alliicola and association with internal browning caused by Pseudomonas aeruginosa. Australasian Plant Pathology 11, 56-57.

Tominaga, T. (1972). Studies on diseases of forage crops in Japan II. Etiological studies on bacterial diseases of forage crops in Japan. Review of Plant Protection Research 5, 125-130.

Ullstrup, A.J. (1960). Bacterial stripe of corn. Phytopathology 50, 906-910.

Vidaver, A.K. & Carlson, R.R. (1978). Leaf spot of field corn caused by Pseudomonas andropogonis. Plant Disease Reporter 62, 213-216.

Vock, N.T. (1978). "A Handbook of Plant Diseases" Vol. 1&2. Brisbane: Queensland Department of Primary Industries.

Wolf, F.A. (1920). A bacterial leafspot of velvet bean. Phytopathology 10, 73-80.

8

Pseudomonas:
The Fluorescent Pseudomonads

P. C. Fahy and A. B. Lloyd

I.	Introduction	141
II.	LOPAT Grouping and Identification	142
III.	Group I Pathogens: The *Pseudomonas syringae* Pathovars	142
IV.	Group II Pathogens	169
V.	Group III Pathogens	171
VI.	Group IV Pathogens	173
VII.	Group V Pathogens	174
VIII.	Ungrouped Pathogenic Species	176
	References	178

I. Introduction

Publication of the "Approved Lists of Bacterial Names" (Skerman et al., 1980) by the International Committee of Systematic Bacteriology (ICSB) has reduced the number of valid plant pathogenic species of Pseudomonas from over 100 to 23. Nine of these species are fluorescent pseudomonads. The reasons for this reduction are the recent intensive taxonomic study of this genus which has resulted in recognition of a number of synonyms and the decision by the ICSB to exclude from the Approved Lists invalid names, species not adequately described or for which no culture is available, and species which cannot be separated adequately by standard laboratory tests.

Host specificity alone is not regarded by the ICSB as sufficient reason for retaining species names. Hence most of the fluorescent pseudomonads are now classified as one species, Pseudomonas syringae. However, such a reduction to one species is unsatisfactory for plant pathologists who need to distinguish strains that are distinct because of their differences in host range and the disease symptoms they cause. For this reason the term 'pathovar' is now

PLANT BACTERIAL DISEASES
ISBN 0 12 247660 3

141

used to differentiate strains of P. syringae on the basis of pathogenic characteristics (Young et al., 1978). This species now contains approximately 40 distinct pathovars.

II.   LOPAT Grouping and Identification

Lelliott et al. (1966) published "A determinative scheme for the fluorescent plant pathogenic pseudomonads". The five key tests of the scheme are levan production, oxidase reaction, potato rot, arginine dihydrolase production and tobacco hypersensitivity; they are widely known as the LOPAT tests. Using these tests Lelliott et al. (1966) were able to distinguish pathogenic from non-pathogenic fluorescent pseudomonads and also to separate the pathogens into five groups (I-V). Subsequent taxonomic studies (Stanier et al., 1966; Misaghi & Grogan, 1969; Sands et al. 1970) supported the determinative scheme of Lelliott et al. (1966). Table 8.1 is based on this scheme and on later studies. Details of media and methods referred to in this Chapter are given in Chapter 16 of this volume.

Suspect pseudomonads (see Chapter 2) should be streaked initially on to sucrose peptone agar (SPA) and medium B of King et al. (1954) (KBA) and after incubation for 24-48h at 25C, colony size, levan production, oxidase reaction and fluorescence should be determined. Reactions are shown in Table 8.1. Group I and II pathogens are slow growing and frequently take 48h or longer to develop visible colonies in contrast to Group III, IV and V pathogens which grow much faster and generally take only 24h to develop visible colonies.

Pathogenicity testing, together with further biochemical tests (Table 8.1) are desirable as variation in strain reaction to the LOPAT tests sometimes occurs. Some "fluorescent pseudomonads" may even fail to produce a fluorescent pigment.

III.   Group I Pathogens: The *Pseudomonas syringae* Pathovars

A.   *Diagnosis*

Once the isolated bacterium has been identified by the LOPAT and supplementary tests (Table 8.1) as belonging to Group I, additional tests are necessary to determine the correct pathovar. This is necessary as each pathovar has its own host range and may cause an etiologically distinct disease. Separation of pathovars is based primarily on pathogenicity tests. Bacteriophage typing (Chapter 12) and carbon source utilization (Table 8.1) are also useful for some pathovars. Ice nucleation activity, toxin production and serology are useful for some pathovars and are discussed below.

B. *Pseudomonas syringae pv. syringae*

Major Synonyms. P. syringae van Hall 1902; P. oryzicola Klement 1955; (see Hayward & Waterston, 1965a).

Diseases. P. syringae van Hall 1902 causes many important and common diseases including bacterial canker of stone fruit; blossom blight or blast of pear; brown spot of bean; citrus blast and black pit; and blights and leaf spots of pea, cowpea and lilac. This pathovar has also been recorded as a pathogen or epiphyte on a wide range of unrelated plants (Elliott, 1951; Stapp, 1961; Hayward & Waterston, 1965a), but in many cases identity beyond P. syringae has not been clearly established. Confirmation of a P. syringae isolate as P. syringae pv. syringae must include inoculation of a range of known hosts. Carbon source utilization tests, bacteriophage reactions, ice nucleation, syringomycin production (Gross & De Vay, 1977a,b) and serological tests (Taylor, 1970a) are also of value.

Bacterial Canker of Stone Fruit Trees.

Symptoms. The bacterium infects young leaves, causing irregular, brown, necrotic leaf spots. When the dead tissue disintegrates, the leaf has a typical shot-hole appearance. Other characteristic symptoms are dieback of buds, twigs and branches from infection of woody tissue and formation of sunken cankers which frequently exude gum (Fig. 8.1).

The bacterium survives the winter in cankers and then, in spring, multiplies in the cankers and spreads by rain splashes onto the surface of leaves where large epiphytic populations develop, providing the main source of inoculum for wound and leaf scar infections during the following autumn (Crosse, 1957, 1959, 1966; Klement, 1977).

TABLE 8.1   A Determinative Scheme to Aid in the Identification of Fluorescent Plant Pathogenic Pseudomonads[a,b]

Suggested test sequence — 1: Fluorescence on KBA, Oxidase, Arginine dihydrolase, Levan; 2: Potato rot, Tobacco hypersensitivity; 3: Nitrate reduction, Gelatin hydrolysis; 4–5: Carbon source utilization tests (Glucose, β-Alanine, 2-Ketogluconate, Trehalose, Sucrose, D(−) Tartrate, m-Tartrate, Sorbitol); 6: Geraniol, Growth at 41C, Pyocyanin on KAA, Polymer granules.

Group	Species	Fluorescence on KBA[c]	Oxidase	Arginine dihydrolase	Levan	Potato rot	Tobacco hypersensitivity	Nitrate reduction	Gelatin hydrolysis	Glucose	β-Alanine	2-Ketogluconate	Trehalose	Sucrose	D(−) Tartrate	m-Tartrate	Sorbitol	Geraniol	Growth at 41C	Pyocyanin on KAA[c]	Polymer granules
Pathogens																					
I.	P. syringae pathovars[d]	+	−	−	+[e]	−	+	−	f	+	−	−	−	+[k]	f	f	f	−	−	−	−
II.	P. viridiflava	+	−	−	−	+	+	−	+	+	−	−	−	−	f	f	+	−	−	−	−
III.	P. cichorii	+	+	−	−	−	+	v	−	+	−	−	−	−	+[g]	+	+[h]	−	−	−	−
IV.	P. agarici	+	+	−	−	+	−	−	−	+	+	+	−	−	−[g]	+	−	−	−	−	−
	P. marginalis 1 (P. fluorescens biotype II)	+	+	+	+		−	+	+	+	+	+	+	+	v	−[i]	+	−	−	−	−
V.	P. tolaasii	+	+	+	−	−	−[j]	−	+	+	+	+	v	−	−	+	+	−	−	−	−

TABLE 8.1 (Continued) A Determinative Scheme to Aid in the Identification of Fluorescent Plant Pathogenic Pseudomonads[a,b]

Saprophytes														
P. fluorescens biotype I	+	+	+	+	+	+	+	+	·+	+	−	−	−	−
= " II	+	+	+	+	+	+	+	+	v	+	v	−	−	−
= " III	+	+	+	+	+	+	+	−	−	v	−	−	−	−
= " IV	+	+	+	−	+	+	+	+	v	+	v	−	−	−
= " miscellaneous	+	+	+	+	+	+	+	+	v	v	−	−	−	−
P. chlororaphis	+	+	+	+	+	+	+	+	+	−	−	−	−	−
P. aureofaciens	+	+	+	+	+	+	+	v	v	−	−	−	−	−
P. putida	+	+	+	+	+	−	+	−	−	v	−	−	−	−
P. aeruginosa	+	+	+	−	−	+	−	+	−	−	+	+	+	−

a   Data from Billing (1970a,b), Brocklehurst & Lund (1981). Doudoroff & Palleroni (1974), Fahy (1981), Hildebrand (1973). Lelliott et al. (1966), Sands et al. (1970, 1980), Stanier et al. (1966). See Doudoroff & Palleroni (1974) for full genus description and major separations.

b   +, >90% strains positive; −, >90% strains negative; v, results variable between strains.

c   KBA, medium B of King et al. (1954); KAA, medium A of King et al. (1954).

d   Less than 20 pathovars studied in detail. Further tests for identification in text. See also tests in Billing (1970a,b), Lelliott et al. (1966), Sands et al. (1970, 1980).

e   Pathovar delphini v; pvs passiflora, savastanoi & tagetis negative. Others tested are positive.

f   Test of value to separate within P. syringae pathovars. See note d for references.

g   Publication error, results transposed in Billing (1970b).

h   Listed as positive in Sands et al. (1980). Other publications list as negative.

i   Listed as variable in Sands et al. (1980). Other publications list as negative.

j   No hypersensitive reaction but atypical greasy lesions then tissue collapse (Fahy 1981).

k   Pathovar savastanoi variable; pv. tagetis negative. Others tested are positive.

l   P. marginalis includes strains other than P. fluorescens biotype II. See text.

(a)   (b)

*FIGURE 8.1.   Bacterial canker caused by P. syringae
pv. syringae or pv. morsprunorum: (a)   stem lesion on
apricot (bark cut away); (b) sunken lesions developing
from leaf scar infections of cherry.*

   Geographical Distribution and Importance.   Bacterial
canker of stone fruit (Prunus spp.) is a serious disease of
cherry trees, but may also cause early death in apricots,
peaches, nectarines, plums and prunes.   In Australia, in
all stone fruit trees except cherry, the disease is
generally of minor importance once healthy trees become
established (Vock, 1978).
   Bacterial canker of stone fruit is usually attributed
to the pathovar P. syringae pv. syringae, a relatively
unspecialized pathogen with a wide host range, both as a
parasite and an epiphyte.   A more specialized pathogen,
P. syringae pv. morsprunorum, is restricted predominantly to
cherry and plum, and differs from pv. syringae not only in
a narrower host range, but also in being able to infect
through leaf scars in autumn without prior wounding

(Crosse, 1966). The pathovar morsprunorum is the major cause of canker in cherry and plum in southern England (Crosse, 1966; Garrett et al., 1966). Both pathovars have been found on cherry and plum in Australia (Foulkes & Lloyd, 1980), but the relative importance of each is unknown.

Isolation and Identification. Pseudomonas syringae pvs syringae and morsprunorum can be readily isolated from leaf surfaces during the growing season (Crosse, 1959; Freigoun & Crosse, 1975). Diluted leaf washings are spread over the surface of KBA supplemented with cycloheximide (10-50 μg/ml) and incubated at 25-28C for 2-3 days. The bacteria can also be isolated from necrotic leaf spots on young leaves by removing plant tissue from the margin of a necrotic spot, macerating it in a drop of sterile water and after about 30 min, streaking the fluid over the surface of KBA.

Isolation of the bacterium from a canker is more difficult. In general, isolation should be attempted from young cankers only, prior to the summer period. Isolations are made from the woody tissue at the advancing edge of the canker, as described above for leaf spots. The wood may be surface sterilized in alcohol and/or 0.1-1.0% sodium hypochlorite prior to maceration (Latorre & Jones, 1979).

On KBA Pseudomonas syringae colonies are white, raised, mucoid and glistening, often with radial streaks through the colonies (Crosse, 1959). Most isolates of pv. syringae produce a blue fluorescent pigment when grown on KBA, but many isolates of pv. morsprunorum do not (Garrett et al., 1966). Phage typing has been used extensively to separate strains of pv. syringae and pv. morsprunorum, including variants within pv. morsprunorum (Crosse & Garrett, 1963; Garrett et al., 1966; Persley & Crosse, 1978). Further differences between the two pathovars are described by Garrett et al. (1966).

Pathogenicity. Host trees should be inoculated when dormant, for during the growing season the plant shows considerable resistance to establishment of the pathogen (Crosse, 1966). Peach trees are preferable hosts for pv. syringae whereas plum trees are often used for pv. morsprunorum. A 24-48 h culture is used to make a suspension of approximately 10^6 cells/ml. The suspension is injected into the stem and leaf scars, using a hypodermic needle (Crosse & Garrett, 1966). An alternative method is to make a small (< 1cm), wedge-shaped cut into the stem

deep enough to reach the hardwood, add 1-2 drops of
inoculum to the wound and then bind with plastic adhesive
tape. If the plants are in the growing phase, a hypodermic
needle is used to prick and innoculate the stems, petioles
and midribs. The inoculated plants are kept in a humid
atmosphere for 2-3 days after inoculation (Luketina &
Young, 1979). Necrotic lesions on woody stems accompanied
by gummosis may take at least a month to develop. In
young, green tissue, the early symptoms are collapse and
necrosis of the tissue.

Excised fruit such as young lemon or cherry fruit can
also be used for pathogenicity tests. Fruit is inoculated
by pricking with a hypodermic needle containing a
suspension of the bacterium (10^6 cells/ml) and then
incubated in a humidity chamber until lesions appear, some
3-6 days later (Garrett et al., 1966).

Bacterial Blossom Blight or Blast of Pear

Symptoms. Bacterial blossom blight or blast of pear
(Pyrus communis), caused by Pseudomonas syringae pv.
syringae, develops when cool, moist weather persists during
flowering or may be associated with late frosts. Typical
symptoms include blossom blight, but the pathogen also
infects shoots, leaves and buds and causes cankers in the
branches. The role of the canker phase in overwintering of
the bacterium is not clearly understood. Compared with
cankers in stone fruit trees, those in pear trees are not
generally responsible for dieback and death of older trees
(Crosse, 1966). The disease may be confused with early
symptoms of fireblight (see Chapter 5).

Geographical Distribution and Importance. The
disease appears occasionally as light infections on some
pear tree varieties in Australia and also in most pear -
growing districts throughout the world.

Isolation and Identification. P. syringae pv.
syringae can be readily isolated from the surface of
leaves, flowers and fruits during summer (Waissbluth &
Latorre, 1978). This epiphytic population is the main
inoculum for blossom infection, which can be serious in
some varieties (Crosse, 1966). Bacterial isolates can be
identified as P. syringae pv. syringae by their colony form
on KBA, reaction in the LOPAT tests (Table 8.1) and
pathogenicity tests on pear or peach trees.

(a)   (b)

FIGURE 8.2. P. syringae pv. syringae: (a) on bean
(brown spot); (b) on navel orange (citrus blast and
black pit)

Brown Spot of Bean

Symptoms. The characteristic symptoms on bean
Phaseolus vulgaris are reddish-brown, circular to angular
lesions, often surrounded by a narrow yellow band on the
leaves (Fig. 8.2a), stems and pods (Harrison & Freeman,
1965; Vock, 1978).

Infested seed is common and can contribute substantially
to early disease development. The bacterium is transmitted
from plant to plant in the field by rain splash. Infection
and spread are favoured by cool, wet and windy weather.

Geographical Distribution and Importance. Brown spot
of bean is an important disease in bean-growing areas of
Australia (Harrison & Freeman, 1965; Wimalajeewa &
Nancarrow, 1978) and the U.S.A. (Hoitink et al., 1967).

Isolation and Identification. The bacterium can be
readily isolated from plant lesions onto KBA. Colonies
which produce a fluorescent pigment should be subject to
LOPAT tests (Table 8.1).

Pathogenicity. Susceptible bean and peach seedlings
are inoculated for pathogenicity tests. The stems are
wounded by light pricking with a sterile hypodermic needle,
inoculated with the bacterial suspension (10^6-10^7 cells/ml)
and then the plants kept in a humid atmosphere for 2-3
days. Necrotic lesions appear around the inoculum sites
after 3-6 days. Pathogenicity to peach distinguishes pv.
syringae from pv. phaseolicola. Inoculation of isolates
into detached lemon fruit or bean pods is also a useful
test.

Citrus Blast and Black Pit.

Symptoms. The pathogen readily invades through injury
sites on young tissue. Rapidly spreading, dark brown
blotches develop on young growth, usually originating at
the base of a leaf blade or an axillary bud. Shoots may
become completely girdled and blighted and leaves die,
often remaining attached to the stem. Black pit, most
common on lemons, is initiated by injury and develops as
round, sunken spots, up to 10mm diameter (Fig. 8.2b).

Geographical Distribution and Importance. Citrus
blast, which occurs on Citrus spp. in most regions of the
world except the hot tropics (Klotz, 1978), is generally a
minor disease. In Australia the disease is uncommon but
may occasionally cause severe damage when associated with
sandblasting or frost.

Bacterial Leaf Spot of Hibiscus spp.

Smith (1943) identified P. syringae pv. syringae as the
cause of a leaf spot of Hibiscus spp. and Goss (1962)
reported P. syringae pv. syringae as the causal agent of a
bacterial leaf spot of Hibiscus rosa-sinensis in Western
Australia. The disease occurred predominantly on the
cultivar Apple-Blossom. P. syringae pv. syringae has also
been confirmed, using bacteriophage typing (Garrett,
unpublished data), as the pathogen in New South Wales.
Moniz (1963) published a brief description of a bacterial
leafspot of the hibiscus cultivar Apple-Blossom in South
Australia, proposing the name P. hibiscicola Moniz 1963 for

a fluorescent pseudomonad. The type strain, so-called, is actually P. maltophilia (Hayward, unpubl.) and P. hibiscicola is therefore not a valid species.

C. *Pseudomonas syringae pv. atrofaciens: Basal Glume Rot of Wheat and Other Cereals.*

Major Synonym. **Pseudomonas atrofaciens** (McCulloch 1920) Stevens 1925.

Symptoms. P. syringae pv. atrofaciens (McCulloch 1920) Young, Dye & Wilkie 1978 infects stalks and leaves but is most readily observed on spikelets. Lesions commence at the base of glumes and may extend over part or all of the glume (Fig. 8.3a). The initially watersoaked, dark green lesions turn brown and, if glumes are removed and held to the light, are translucent with dark brown to black margins. Lesions may also develop on grain and severely infected spikelets may contain shrivelled seed. On stalks, watersoaked lesions develop below the head and may spread laterally to encircle the stalk. Watersoaked leaf lesions are generally small (2-5mm), occurring irregularly over the leaf surface but elongate to 5-10mm and become yellow then brown as the tissue dies (Noble, 1933; Wilkie, 1973).

Geographical Distribution and Importance. Basal glume blotch is generally a minor but common disease of wheat (Triticum aestivum) and barley (Hordeum vulgare) in most regions of the world where excessive moisture is present at heading (Wiese, 1977). The disease may be more prevalent than recognised at present as symptoms are frequently inconspicuous or confused with frost injury or Septoria glume blotch (Noble, 1933).

Isolation and Identification. The pathogen was originally described by McCulloch (1920). A more recent description is provided by Wilkie (1973). The pathogen is readily isolated on KBA.

(a)   (b)

*FIGURE 8.3.   (a) P. syringae pv. atrofaciens causing
basal glume rot of wheat;   (b) P. syringae pv. glycinea
causing bacterial blight of soybean.*

D. *Pseudomonas syringae pv. coronafaciens:*   Halo Blight of
Oats and other Cereals.

Major   Synonym.   Pseudomonas   coronafaciens   (Elliott
1920) Stevens 1925.   Schaad & Cunfer (1979) proposed that
P. coronafaciens pv. zeae Ribeiro, Durbin, Arny & Uchytil
1977, P. coronafaciens subsp. atropurpurea (Reddy & Godkin
1923) Stapp 1928,   (P. coronafaciens pv. atropurpurea (Reddy
& Godkin 1923) Young, Dye & Wilkie 1978) and P. striafaciens
(Elliott 1927) Starr & Burkholder 1942 are   all   synonyms of
P. coronafaciens.

Symptoms.   Halo blight of oats caused by P. syringae
pv. coronafaciens (Elliott 1920) Young, Dye & Wilkie 1978
commences as tan coloured spots (1–2mm diameter) with
greasy looking margins.   Lesions usually occur irregularly
over leaf surfaces but sheaths and glumes are occasionally

affected. Lesions elongate (4-5mm), darken and develop a prominent translucent halo. Lesions may coalesce, particularly at leaf margins, forming a border of brown tissue with a greasy looking margin. In severe infections leaves yellow and dry. Stripe blight of oats differs from halo blight by producing no halos. Clear watersoaked lesions develop with abundant exudate which dries to a white scale (Elliott, 1927; Wilkie, 1972). Similar symptoms develop on other cereals.

Host Range. Economically important hosts are oats (Avena sativa) and maize (Zea mays), but a wider range of cereals and grasses are susceptible (Elliott, 1927; Bradbury, 1970a, b; Schaad & Cunfer, 1979).

Considerable overlap in host range exists in the above listed synonyms. P. coronafaciens pv. zeae was originally described on the basis that strains of P. coronafaciens failed to infect maize and P. coronafaciens pv. zeae failed to infect oats (Ribeiro et al., 1977). However Schaad & Cunfer (1979) found that with the exception of reaction on maize, both strains had the same host range. Similarly they reported that P. coronafaciens subsp. atropurpurea, originally described as the cause of a halo blight of Bromus spp., had a similar host range to P. coronafaciens. Two isolates of P. striafaciens studied by Schaad & Cunfer (1979) infected only oats. These results are similar to those of Elliott (1927) who inoculated a range of Avena spp. and produced a slight reaction on barley with P. striafaciens but not on other cereals and grasses. Tessi (1953) showed that P. striafaciens (stripe blight) is a non-toxin producing variant of the halo blight pathogen.

Geographical Distribution and Importance. Halo blight and stripe blight are common in most oat growing regions of the world, including Australia, but generally cause little yield reduction unless severe infection occurs prior to emergence of the panicle (Dickson, 1956). Chocolate spot of maize described in the United States (Ribeiro et al. 1977) has not been recorded in Australia.

Isolation and Identification. P. syringae pv. coronafaciens may be readily isolated on KBA and can be distinguished as a distinct subgroup of P. syringae on the basis of carbon source spectrum and serological reaction (Ribeiro et al., 1977; Schaad & Cunfer, 1979). Toxin - producing strains produce tabtoxins (Ribeiro et al., 1977) which can be identified by the technique of Gasson (1980).

Because of the variability in virulence of strains of
P. syringae pv. coronafaciens, Schaad & Cunfer (1979)
recommend pathogenicity tests be conducted on a range of
hosts including oats, maize and a Bromus spp., with
confirmatory identification by serology.

E. *Pseudomonas syringae pv. glycinea: Bacterial Blight of Soybean*

Major Synonym. P. glycinea Coerper 1919

Symptoms. Characteristic symptoms of bacterial blight
of soybean (Glycine max) caused by P. syringae pv. glycinea
(Coerper 1919) Young, Dye & Wilkie 1978 include brown,
angular lesions on the leaves and stems which coalesce to
form dark-brown necrotic areas with yellow margins (Vock,
1978). Some strains of the bacterium produce a wide
chlorotic "halo" similar to halo blight of bean, especially
at lower temperatures (Fig. 8.3b) (Moffett, 1976).
Most crop infections originate from contamination of the
seed coat during harvest or through infection of healthy
seedlings from infested debris from a previous crop. There
is some evidence that the bacterium may have an epiphytic
phase on leaves and in buds and this may be a continual
source of inoculum (Leben et al., 1968).

Geographical Distribution and Importance. Bacterial
blight of soybean is a common disease of soybean in
Australia and elsewhere. In Australia it is occasionally
serious in coastal and wetter zones of New South Wales and
Queensland. The bacterium is often active only in early
stages of growth. Xanthomonas campestris pv. glycines is
more prevalent on soybean under warm summer conditions (see
Chapter 9).

Isolation and Identification. The bacterium can be
isolated from leaf and stem lesions onto KBA. The colonies
are recognized by their characteristic fluorescent pigment
and by the LOPAT tests. Confirmatory tests (in addition to
pathogenicity tests) are phage sensitivity and serological
tests (Billing, 1970b; Otta & English, 1971). P. syringae
pv. glycinea may be distinguished from pv. tabaci (which is
also pathogenic to soybean) by the inability of the former
to utilize betaine, sorbitol and erythritol (Sands et al,
1980).

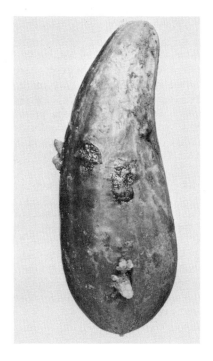 

(a)   (b)

FIGURE 8.4. (a) P. syringae pv. lachrymans causing
angular leaf spot of cucumber (fruit lesions);
(b) P. syringae pv. pisi causing bacterial blight of
pea, typical fan-shaped lesions.

Pathogenicity. Soybean plants at the trifoliate leaf
stage are spray inoculated with a dilute suspension of the
bacterium in sterile water (10^6 cells/ml), kept under
high humidity for 2 days and in a glasshouse 12 days.

F. *Pseudomonas syringae* pv. *lachrymans*: Angular Leaf Spot of Cucurbits

Major Synonym. P. lachrymans (Smith & Bryan 1915)
Carsner 1918.

Symptoms. The most conspicuous symptom of angular
leaf spot of cucurbits, caused by P. syringae pv. lachrymans
(Smith & Bryan 1915) Young, Dye & Wilkie 1978 is the "tear
drop" exudation from active angular leaf lesions. The

"tear drops" dry to an obvious encrustation and lesions
fall out, giving the leaves a ragged appearance. Infection
of young fruit may cause extensive fruit drop. The
pathogen may invade the fruit systemically through the
stem-peduncle junction (Pohronezny et al., 1978) and cause
fruit tissue breakdown with extensive soft rotting. Seed
is readily infected through systemic invasion of the fruit
(Wiles & Walker, 1951). Lesions on fruit often exude
conspicuous drops of fluid which are usually heavily
contaminated with secondary bacteria (Fig. 8.4a).

Geographical Distribution and Importance. Angular
leafspot, predominantly a disease of cucumber, Cucumis
sativus is only a minor disease of most freshmarket
cucumbers in Australia but may be a serious disease of
Lebanese cucumber cultivars under warm humid conditions in
coastal New South Wales. The disease is reported in the
United States as a severe problem on pickling cucumbers
from several regions (Pohronezny et al., 1978). Angular
leafspot occurs on a wide range of cucurbits from most
regions of the world (Bradbury, 1967a).

G. *Pseudomonas syringae* pv. *maculicola*: *Peppery leaf of Crucifers*

Major Synonym. Pseudomonas maculicola (McCulloch 1911)
Stevens 1913.

Symptoms. P. syringae pv. maculicola (McCulloch 1911)
Young, Dye & Wilkie 1978 causes a peppery leafspot on
cauliflower leaves involving a general flecking caused by
numerous, superficial brown to purple spots, often only 1mm
diameter, developing from stomatal infections. Spots may
coalesce to form large necrotic areas. Veinal infection
may occur and cause leaf puckering. Peppery spot symptoms
also occur on rape and mustard but lesions tend to be
larger (2-3mm) and watersoaked spots frequently develop on
stem tissue.

Geographical Distribution and Importance. Peppery
leafspot is a relatively uncommon disease of crucifer
vegetables in Australia but may occasionally cause severe
losses to cauliflower crops following frosting or cold wet
weather. The disease has been reported from most regions
of the world and has been investigated as a severe disease
of cauliflower Brassica oleracea var. botrytis (Goldsworthy,

1926), broccoli <u>Brassica</u> <u>oleracea</u> var. <u>italica</u> (Smith & Ramsey, 1953), radish <u>Raphanus</u> <u>sativus</u> (Williams & Keen, 1966) and cabbage <u>Brassica</u> <u>oleracea</u> var. <u>capitata</u>, associated with freeze injury (Sumner, 1972). Strains of the pathogen also cause severe leaf and pod spotting on Brown Sarson rape (<u>Brassica</u> <u>napus</u> var. <u>napus</u>) and some cultivars of white mustard (<u>B.</u><u>hirta</u>) and Indian mustard (<u>B.</u><u>juncea</u>) (Fahy, unpubl.)

H. Pseudomonas syringae pv. pisi: Bacterial blight of Pea

Major Synonym. <u>Pseudomonas</u> <u>pisi</u> Sackett 1916.

Symptoms. Bacterial blight of pea, caused by P.<u>syringae</u> pv. <u>pisi</u> (Sackett 1916) Young, Dye & Wilkie 1978, usually commences at one or a few loci associated with seed borne infection. All above-ground parts of the pea plant may become infected and this can occur at any stage of growth.

Leaf lesions begin as small, angular, water-soaked spots but soon develop into irregular shaped regions, often with a distinct fan-shaped appearance if infection occurs where the stipule joins the stem or the leaflet joins the midrib (Fig. 8.4b). Lesions are sharply defined, becoming dark brown at the edges with lighter brown centres. Stem lesions may be extensive, often invading stipules and leaflets. Pod lesions develop as sunken, circular to irregular areas about 1-1.5cm diameter, and for several days retain a dark green water- soaked appearance. Infection of the suture may split the pod. Cream coloured ooze may be present on all lesions under favourable conditions. Infected seed may be symptomless (Harrison, 1964; Young & Dye, 1970).

Host Range. Bacterial blight occurs naturally only on field and garden peas (<u>Pisum</u> <u>sativum</u>), although other hosts have been claimed. For example, Ark (1944) reported infection of purple vetch (<u>Vicia</u> <u>benghalensis</u>) in a pasture containing field pea but did not provide evidence that the pathogen was P.<u>syringae</u> pv. <u>pisi</u>.

Geographical Distribution and Importance. Bacterial blight of pea has a worldwide distribution but its spread is restricted by quarantine and seed certification. In the southern states of Australia the disease can on occasions cause severe yield losses. The bacterium is commonly seed-borne in field peas but in garden and processing seed crops disease-free seed schemes and crop rotation appear to control the disease effectively.

Bacterial blight caused by P. syringae pv. pisi may be confused with identical or similar symptoms caused by P. syringae pv. syringae and P. viridiflava (Taylor & Dye, 1972) on peas. These latter two pathogens occur under more restricted environmental conditions and are sometimes associated with frost damage. It is therefore essential to confirm the presence of pv. pisi by isolation and identification.

Isolation and Identification. The pathogen is readily isolated from diseased tissue on KBA but P. syringae pv. syringae, P. viridiflava and other pectolytic pseudomonads may also be present (Taylor & Dye, 1972).

P. syringae pv. pisi may be separated from P. viridiflava on biochemical reactions (Table 8.1). In addition, P. syringae pv. pisi utilises homoserine while P. syringae pv. syringae, and P. viridiflava do not (Hildebrand, 1973; Sands et al., 1980). Symptoms of pathogenicity tests and bacteriophage and serological typing are also used to distinguish the three pea pathogens (Taylor, 1972a).

Pathogenicity. Pathogenicity tests readily separate the three common pathogens of pea (Taylor, 1972b; Taylor & Dye, 1972). Young pea seedlings are wounded by needle prick of unfurling foliage and saturated by spray inoculation with a water suspension (approximately 10^7 cells/ml) of a 24-48 h culture grown on KBA. Plants are held in a humid chamber for 2 days (18-21C) and then returned to the glasshouse bench. Young excised pods may be stab inoculation and held in a humid chamber at 25C.

P. syringae pv. pisi causes small water-soaked lesions at wound sites and possibly stomatal infection of young foliage, clearly visible 4-5 days after inoculation. In contrast, pv. syringae causes water-soaked patches which are clearly visible after 2 days in the humid chamber; on removal from the chamber, lesions rapidly shrivel and dry. P. viridiflava causes severe rotting and complete collapse of foliage after only 2 days in the humid chamber. On young pods, pv. pisi causes extensive water-soaked lesions whilst pv. syringae generally causes dark, sunken lesions.

I. *Pseudomonas syringae* pv. *phaseolicola:* Halo Blight
   of Bean.

Major Synonym. P. phaseolicola (Burkholder 1980) Dowson
1943.

Symptom. Typical halo blight symptoms caused by
P. syringae pv. phaseolicola (Burkholder 1926) Young, Dye &
Wilkie 1978 include small, brown, angular, greasy leaf
lesions surrounded by broad chlorotic halos (Fig. 8.5a).
Some strains of the bacterium can infect leaves without
inducing chlorotic 'halos'. Lesions on stems and pods are
generally greasy, sometimes with cream-coloured exudates
(Fig. 8.5b). Pod lesions eventually become depressed and tan
in colour (Vock, 1978).
   The bacterium is seed-borne, both externally and
internally. Seed-borne infection originates through
movement of the bacterium from an external pod lesion to
the surface of an adjacent underlying seed. If the sutures
of the pod become infected, the bacterium invades the
vascular system and internally infects the seed (Zaumeyer,
1932). Infected seed, particularly those of white-seeded
cultivars, may show distinct yellow patches on the seed
coat, or in severe cases, the whole seed may appear
to be wrinkled. The seed coats often become infested
externally through contact of the seed coat with plant
debris (Grogan & Kimble, 1967).
   Most crop infections originate from infected seed which
show either few or no external symptoms (Taylor et al.,
1979). The bacterium is transmitted in the field by rain
splash. Cool, wet weather favours spread and infection.
   P. syringae pv. phaseolicola has an overlapping host
range with pv. glycinea and is phenotypically closely
related to pv. glycinea and pv. mori (Schroth et al.,
1971). However, pv. phaseolicola is distinct from pv.
glycinea on the basis of identity of their chlorosis -
inducing toxins; the former produces phaseolotoxin and the
latter coronatine (Mitchell, 1982).

Geographical Distribution and Importance. Halo blight
is a potentially serious seed borne disease of French bean
(Phaseolus vulgaris) in Australia (Guy & Wimalajeewa, 1977)
and many bean producing regions if the world. The pathogen
attacks other Phaseolus spp. and related legumes (Hayward &
Waterston, 1965b; Chapter 15).

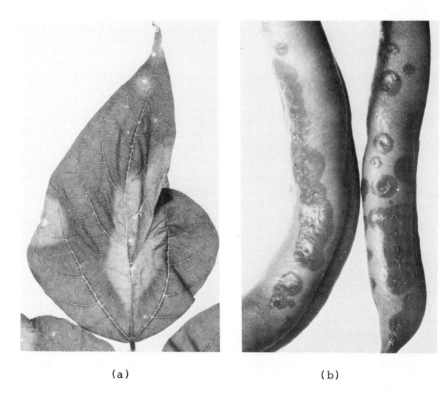

(a)   (b)

FIGURE 8.5.   *P. syringae* pv. *phaseolicola* causing
*halo blight of bean: (a) leaf symptoms,   (b) pod
lesions.*

Infection of pasture species, including siratro (Macroptilium atropurpureum) is a danger to bean seed
certification schemes. Pathovar phaseolicola has recently
been reported on pigeon pea (Cajanus cajan) in Queensland
(Wallis, Teakle & Hayward, unpubl.)

Isolation and Identification. The bacterium can be
isolated from leaf and stem lesions on KBA. P. syringae pv.
phaseolicola colonies produce the characteristic
fluorescent pigment, and these colonies should be subjected
to LOPAT (Table 8.1) and pathogenicity tests. Confirmatory
tests include phage sensitivity and serological tests
(Taylor, 1970a) and production of extra- cellular toxins
(Gasson, 1980). Pathovar phaseolicola may be distinguished
from pv. syringae by the former's inability to utilize
mannitol, inositol, sorbitol and erythritol (Sands et al.,
1980).

Pathogenicity. Inoculum for pathogenicity tests is usually prepared by making a dilute bacterial suspension (10^6 cells/ml) in sterile water and lightly spraying onto the leaves and stems of young bean seedlings. The sprayed plants are kept in a glasshouse in a humid atmosphere for several days. Detached bean pods can also be inoculated with the bacterial suspension and incubated in a humid chamber.

In bean seedlings and bean pods the bacterium induces typical halo blight symptoms. Most isolates produce phaseolotoxin, a non-specific toxin which causes chlorosis on a wide range of plants (Ferguson & Johnston, 1980).

The bacterium can be isolated from internally infected seed by first washing the seed to remove biocides, grinding to flour and then suspending for 2h in sterile water. Dilutions of the supernatant are streaked onto KBA and incubated for 3 days at 25C (Taylor, 1970b).

P. syringae pv. phaseolicola can be further distinguished from pv. syringae by peach seedling inoculation; pv. phaseolicola does not cause lesions when inoculated to peach stem whereas pv. syringae does.

J. *Pseudomonas syringae pv. tabaci: Wildfire of Tobacco and Soybean*

Major Synonyms. Pseudomonas tabaci (Wolf & Foster 1917) Stevens 1925. P. angulata (Fromme & Murray 1919) Stevens 1925.

Symptoms. The initial symptom of wildfire, caused by P. syringae pv. tabaci (Wolf & Foster 1917) Young, Dye & Wilkie 1978, are circular, yellow-green areas 3-6mm diameter on the leaves. Within a day small dead specks appear in the centre of the spots and the yellow-green halo becomes more prominent. Necrotic spots may fuse resulting in irregular dead areas. Severely affected leaves become twisted and distorted. Non-toxin producing variants produce a typical dark angular leaf spot and lesions often coalesce to form larger irregular dead areas sometimes with evidence of dried exudation.

On soybean, wildfire causes a distinct yellow halo with a necrotic centre (Fig. 8.6a) which may be a pustule or blight lesion. Lesions may coalesce to form large necrotic areas and consequent leaf tattering. Premature, severe defoliation may occur (Kennedy & Tachibana, 1973).

(a)   (b)

FIGURE 8.6.(a) *P. syringae* pv. *tabaci causing wild-*
fire on soybean; (b) P. *syringae* pv. *tagetis causing*
apical chlorosis of marigold.

Host Range. The major hosts are tobacco (<u>Nicotiana</u>
spp.) and soybean. <u>P</u>. <u>syringae</u> pv. <u>tabaci</u> is capable of
infecting a wide range of plants (Bradbury, 1967b) and may
be a common rhizoplane organism on a wider range of hosts
(Valleau et al., 1944). Virulent strains of the pathogen,
appear to survive more readily as pathogens of tobacco
rather than as rhizoplane residents (Fulton, 1980).

Geographical Distribution and Importance. <u>P</u>. <u>syringae</u>
pv. <u>tabaci</u> is present throughout the world on tobacco and
soybean. It is rarely a problem on tobacco in Australia
but occasionally occurs as a seedbed disease in coastal New
South Wales and has caused serious quality losses in
Queensland crops. Seedbed hygiene and Bordeaux applications
generally control the disease. Resistant cultivars are
used in some countries but most Australian cultivars are
susceptible.

The pathogen produces a chlorosis inducing toxin (Stewart, 1971) and non toxin producing variants (formerly P. angulata) cause a similar disease termed blackfire of tobacco. Blackfire disease may be initiated by mutation of virulent toxin-producing strains (Fulton, 1980).

Wildfire is generally a minor disease of soybean but may occasionally cause serious losses in regions of the world with high summer rains, including south east Queensland. Varieties susceptible to bacterial pustule (Xanthomonas campestris pv. glycines) are most affected as P. syringae pv. tabaci appears to be a poor primary pathogen of soybean, invading predominantly through pustule lesions and, to a lesser extent, blight (P. syringae pv. glycinea) lesions (Chamberlain, 1956).

Isolation and Identification. P. syringae pv. tabaci is readily isolated on KBA and may be distinguished readily from other P. syringae pathovars by production of a wilt of tobacco leaves instead of the normal hyper-sensitive reaction when injected into the mesophyll layer. Toxin-producing strains are readily detected.

K. *Pseudomonas syringae pv. tagetis: Apical Chlorosis and Leaf Spot of Marigold*

Major Synonym. P. tagetis Hellmers 1955.

Symptoms. An angular leafspot of marigold (Tagetis erecta) caused by P. syringae pv. tagetis (Hellmers 1955) Young, Dye & Wilkie 1978 was first described by Hellmers (1955). Trimboli et al. (1978) described an apical chlorosis of glasshouse marigolds in New South Wales caused by a variant of P. syringae pv. tagetis (Fig. 8.6b) which produced a toxin capable of inhibiting photosynthesis. The toxin, tagetitoxin, has been partially characterised (Mitchell & Durbin, 1981).

An amended description of P. syringae pv. tagetis was presented by Trimboli et al. (1978). The pathogen naturally infects marigolds (Tagetis spp.) and can infect a wider range of Asteraceae following inoculation.

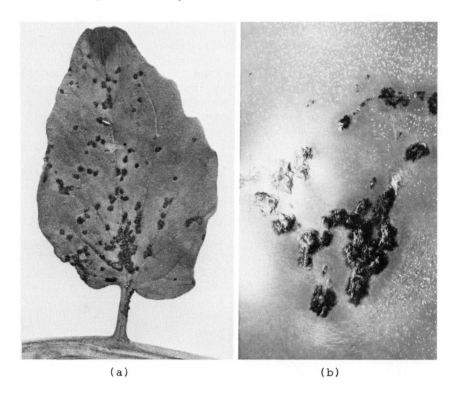

(a)   (b)

FIGURE 8.7.   *P. syringae* pv. *tomato causing
bacterial speck of tomato: (a) leaf lesions, (b) fruit
lesions.*

L. *Pseudomonas syringae* pv. *tomato: Bacterial Speck of
Tomato.*

Major Synonym.   P. tomato Okabe 1933.

Symptoms.   P. syringae pv. tomato (Okabe 1933) Young,
Dye & Wilkie 1978 causes bacterial speck of tomato
(Lycopersicon esculentum).   Typical symptoms include small,
dark brown to black spots with narrow yellow halos (Fig.
8.7a).   Lesions may coalesce to form irregular, dark brown,
necrotic patches.   Fruit lesions are very small, dark,
raised specks (Fig. 8.7b) (Vock, 1978; Wilkie & Dye, 1974).
Crop infection can originate from external seed-borne
contamination or through infection of healthy seedlings
from infested debris of a previous crop.   Warm humid
weather favours infection and spread of the bacterium.

Geographical Distribution and Importance. Bacterial speck can cause widespread leaf damage to crops of commercial tomatoes and is sometimes a problem in tomato seedlings. P. syringae pv. syringae may also cause similar symptoms in seedlings (Jones et al., 1981).

Isolation and Identification. The bacterium can be isolated from leaf and stem lesions onto KBA. P. syringae pv. tomato colonies are recognized by their production of a fluorescent pigment and by the LOPAT tests (Table 8.1).
P. syringae pv. syringae and pv. tomato may cause similar symptoms . Group I isolates pathogenic to tomato should be tested on a range of hosts susceptible to pv. syringae. Syringomycin production, and carbon source utilization of erythritol and L-lactate are also useful in separation of the two pathovars (Jones et al., 1981).

Pathogenicity. Tomato plants at the two to four leaf stage are spray inoculated with a dilute suspension of the bacterium (10^6 cells/ml) in sterile water, kept in a high humidity for 2 days and then in a glasshouse for a further 4-6 days. Stems can also be inoculated by lightly pricking with a hypodermic needle containing the bacterial suspension.

M. Other Pseudomonas syringae Pathovars

The following is a listing of diseases caused by other pathovars of P. syringae which are of minor importance in Australia.

P. syringae pv. antirrhini (Takimoto 1920) Young, Dye & Wilkie 1978: Seedling Blight of Snapdragon (Antirrhinum majus).

Major synonyms. P. antirrhini Takimoto 1920; P. fluorescens var. antirrhinastrini Moffett 1966.
Distribution. Australia, Japan, U.K.
Key references. Simpson et al. (1971).

P. syringae pv. apii (Jagger 1921) Young, Dye & Wilkie 1978: Bacterial Blight of Celery (Apium graveolens).

(a)   (b)

FIGURE 8.8.(a)   *P. syringae* pv. *eriobotryae* causing
stem cankers of loquat;   (b) *P.syringae* pv. *savastoni*
causing galling of oleander flowers, leaves and stem.

Major synonym. P. apii Jagger 1921.
Distribution. Australia, North America, U.S.S.R.

Thayer & Wehlburg (1965) found P. cichorii rather than
P. syringae pv. apii, to be the cause of bacterial blight of
celery in Florida. Thayer (1965) reported P. syringae pv.
apii had a lower optimum temperature for pathogenicity
(20C) than P. cichorii .

P. syringae pv. aptata (Brown & Jamieson 1913) Young,
Dye & Wilkie 1978:   Bacterial Blight of Beet (Beta
vulgaris).

Major synonym.   P. aptata (Brown & Jamieson 1913)
Stevens 1925.

Distribution. Australia, Europe, Japan, U.S.A.

This disease has been recorded on a wide range of beets including sugar beet, fodder beet, silverbeet and chard. Elliott (1951) also lists the disease on several unrelated plants.

Key reference. Elliott (1951).

P. syringae pv. delphinii (Smith 1904) Young, Dye & Wilkie 1978: Black spot of Delphinium spp.

    Major synonym. P. delphinii (Smith 1904) Stapp 1928.
    Distribution. Worldwide.
    Key reference. Smith (1904); Elliott (1951).

P. syringae pv. eriobotryae (Takimoto 1931) Young, Dye & Wilkie 1978: Bud Rot of Loquat (Eriobotrya japonica) (Fig. 8.8a).

    Major synonym. P. eriobotryae (Takimoto 1931) Dowson 1943.
    Distribution. Australia, Japan.
    Key references. Takimoto (1931); Wimalajeewa et al. (1978).

P. syringae pv. helianthi (Kawamura 1934) Young, Dye & Wilkie 1978: Bacterial Leaf Spot of Sunflower (Helianthus annuus).

    Major synonym. P. helianthi (Kawamura 1934), Savulescu 1947.
    Distribution. Australia, Japan, U.S.A.
    Key references. Kawamura (1934); Elliott (1951).

P. syringae pv. mori (Boyer & Lambert 1893) Young, Dye & Wilkie 1978: Bacterial Blight of Mulberry (Morus spp.)

    Major synonym. P. mori Boyer & Lambert 1893) Stevens 1913.
    Distribution. Common disease of mulberry worldwide.
    Key references. Doidge (1915); Adam & Pugsley (1934); Schroth et al. (1971).

P. syringae pv. passiflorae (Reid 1938) Young, Dye & Wilkie 1978: Grease-spot of Passionfruit (Passiflora edulis).

Major synonym. P. passiflorae (Reid 1939) Burkholder 1948.
Distribution. Australia, New Zealand.
Key references. Reid (1938); Doepel (1965).

P. syringae pv. primulae (Ark & Gardner 1936) Young, Dye & Wilkie 1978: Bacterial Leaf Spot of Primula and Polyanthus (Primula spp.).

Major synonym. P. primulae (Ark & Gardner 1936), Starr & Burkholder 1942.
Distribution. Australia; U.S.A.
Key references. Ark & Gardner (1936).

P. syringae pv. savastanoi (Smith 1908) Young, Dye & Wilkie 1978: Galling and Excrescences of Oleaceae and Nerium oleander (Fig. 8.10b).

Major synonyms. P. syringae subsp. savastanoi (Smith 1908) Janse 1982; P. tonelliana (Ferraris 1926) Burkholder 1948; P. savastanoi (Smith 1908) Stevens 1913; P. savastanoi subsp. fraxini (Brown 1932) Dowson 1943; P. savastanoi var. nerii Smith 1928; P. fraxini (Brown 1932) Skoric 1938. Agrobacterium tonellianum (Ferraris 1926) Starr et al. 1943.
Janse (1982) proposed that three sub groups of this pathogen based on taxonomic and pathogenicity studies: P. syringae subsp. savastanoi pv. oleacae, causing parenchymatic galls on some species of Oleaceae, including European olive (Olea europaea); pv. fraxini, causing galls and wartlike excrescences on common ash Fraxinus excelsior; and pv. nerii causing galls on Nerium oleander and various Oleaceae spp.
Distribution. P. s. subsp. savastanoi pv. fraxini is restricted to Europe. P. s. subsp. savastanoi pv. oleacae occurs in Europe and North and South America. It does not occur in Australia. P. s. subsp. savastanoi pv. nerii is widespread throughout the world on Nerium oleander and is common in Australia (Fig. 8.8b).
Key references. Elliott (1951); Wilson & Magie (1963); Janse (1982).

P. syringae strain from Protea cynaroides: Bacterial Leaf
Spot of King Protea (Protea cynaroides).

A strain of P. syringae has been isolated from King
Protea in Australia. Wimalajeewa et al. (1983) suggested
that the strain may be a new pathovar of P. syringae, but
further work is necessary to establish its status.

Some other P. syringae pathovars not recorded in
Australia are listed in Table 8.2. Most are minor
pathogens of restricted host range and distribution.
However, P. syringae pv. persicae causes a highly
destructive disease of peach in France and is a threat to
all other peach growing countries.

IV. Group II Pathogens

A. *Pseudomonas viridiflava*

P. viridiflava (Burkholder 1930) Dowson 1939 appears to
be a common epiphyte and potential pathogen of a diverse
range of plants. It is often a secondary pathogen in
association with P. syringae or Xanthomonas campestris
pathovars and may be isolated instead of the primary
pathogen. It is also a rapid, invasive primary pathogen
under specific conditions such as frost damage. In most
cases it causes a rapid watery rot of leafy or succulent
stem tissue on a wide range of plants including; pea, bean,
cowpea, crucifers, pumpkin, chrysanthemum, grape, tomato,
peach, Lupinus angustifolius,Actinidia chinensis, Delphinium
cultorum, Papaver somniferum and others. A review of host
range and symptoms is provided by Wilkie et al. (1973).

B. *Isolation and Identification*

Most strains of P. viridiflava produce a yellow
diffusible pigment on KBA. The LOPAT tests provide a
satisfactory means of identifying this species. It is
possible this pathogen has been misidentified as P. syringae
in a number of instances (Billing, 1970a; Wilkie et al.
1973).

TABLE 8.2.   *Some Pseudomonas syringae Pathovars Not Recorded in Australia*

Pathovar	Principal hosts	Key references
aceris	maple (Acer spp.)	Ark (1939)
berberidis	barberry (Berberis spp.	Thornberry & Anderson (1931a)
cannabina	hemp (Cannabis sativa)	Sutic & Dowson (1959)
ciccaronei	carob (Ceratonia siliqua)	Ercolani & Caldarola (1972)
dysoxyli	kohekohe (Dysoxylum spectabile	Hutchinson (1949)
garcae	coffee (Coffea arabica)	Amaral et al. (1956)
japonica[a]	barley (Hordeum vulgare) wheat (Triticum aestivum)	Mukoo (1955)
lapsa	maize (Zea mays)	Ark (1940)
mellea	tobacco (Nicotiana) spp.	Johnson (1923); Elliott (1951)
papulans	apple (Malus domestica)	Dhanvantari (1977); Burr & Hurwitz (1979)
persicae[b]	peach (Prunus persica)	Prunier et al. (1970)
porri	leek (Allium ampeloprasum var. porrum)	Samson et al. (1978)
ribicola	Ribes aureum	Bohn & Maloit (1946)
sesami	sesame (Sesamum indicum)	Bradbury (1981)
theae	tea (Camellia sinensis)	Okabe & Goto (1955)
ulmi	elm (Ulmus spp.)	Šutić & Tešić (1958)
viburni	Viburnum spp.	Thornberry & Anderson (1931b)

[a] *synonym P. striafaciens var. japonica*
[b] *synonym P. morsprunorum subsp. persicae.*

V. Group III Pathogens

A. *Pseudomonas cichorii*

Major Synonym. P. endiviae Kotte 1930; P. papaveris Lelliott & Wallace 1955.

Symptoms. P. cichorii (Swingle 1925) Stapp 1928 may be common on lettuce as an epiphyte and may be associated with P. marginalis or X. campestris pv. vitians (Burkholder, 1954). Grogan et al. (1977) reported a destructive disease of lettuce from California caused by P. cichorii. Outside leaves appear healthy but firm necrotic areas develop on the leaf blades and petioles of the second and third outermost leaves. The pathogen was isolated from soil and root samples.

Host Range. This pathogen has been isolated from a diverse range of plants and may also be a common soil organism. Wilkie & Dye (1973) reviewed the natural hosts for P. cichorii which are chicory (Cichorium intybus), endive (C. endiva), head lettuce (Lactuca sativa var. capitata) lettuce (L. sativa), cabbage (Fig. 8.9a), clover (Trifolium repens), chrysanthemum (Chrysanthemum indicum), tobacco, celery, Scindopus spp., cauliflower, gerbera (Gerbera jamesonii) and Shirley poppy (Papaver rhoeas). They also reported tomato as a new host.

Identification. P. cichorii is readily distinguished as a Group III organism by the LOPAT tests and carbon source utilization tests (Table 8.1).

B. *Pseudomonas agarici:* Drippy Gill of Mushroom

Symptoms. P. agarici Young 1970 is the cause of drippy gill of the mushroom (Agaricus bisporus). The characteristic symptom is the formation of droplets of almost pure colonies of mucoid, glistening bacteria (Fig. 8.9b) which develop on the surfaces of gills within a dark brown to black, watersoaked spot about 2 mm in diameter (Young, 1970). The colonies may coalesce with age and gills eventually collapse. Fine longitudinal splits up to 2 cm long may develop in the stipe.

Geographical Distribution and Importance. Drippy gill occurs worldwide but causes little yield loss. It is

(a)   (b)

*FIGURE 8.9 (a) P. cichorii lesion on cabbage.
(b) Young colonies of P. agarici on mushroom gills.*

sometimes associated with poorly grown crops of Agaricus
bisporus and is often found in association with poor
compost pasteurization.

Pathogenicity. P. agarici is a Group III member (Table
8.1) but is distinct from P. cichorii on the basis of carbon
source utilization tests (Fahy, 1981). Identification may
be confirmed by pathogenicity tests. A few drops of a
suspension of the bacterium (10^7 cells/ml) are injected
into the gill region of unopened caps and left overnight at
15-25C. It is preferable to use growing mushrooms but
excised caps will also develop lesions.

VI. Group IV Pathogens

A. *Pseudomonas marginalis*. *Marginal Leaf Spot of Lettuce and Other Diseases*

Nomenclature. The pathovar list (Dye et al. 1980) divides P. marginalis into three pathovars: P. marginalis pv. marginalis (Brown 1918) Stevens 1925, originally described as a cause of marginal leaf spot of lettuce (Brown, 1918); P. marginalis pv. pastinacae (Burkholder 1960, Young, Dye & Wilkie 1978), cause of bacterial rot of parsnip roots (Pastinaca sativa) (Burkholder, 1960) and P. marginalis pv. alfalfae Shinde & Lukezic 1974, cause of a discolouration of lucerne roots (Medicago sativa) (Shinde & Lukezic, 1974). Pathovars pastinacae and alfalfae have not been reported in Australia. Pathovar pastinacae differs from the other pathovars by being arginine dihydrolase negative, and is not a member of Group IV (Table 8.1). Pathovar marginalis is worldwide in distribution.

Identification. There is currently confusion in the naming of P. marginalis and P. marginalis pathovars. It appears that a diverse range of fast growing fluorescent pseudomonads, mostly allied to P. fluorescens have been termed P. marginalis. Stanier et al. (1966), after studying two plant isolates (from lettuce and dahlia) and six soft rotting soil isolates, concluded that P. marginalis was P. fluorescens biotype B (now biotype II). Brocklehurst & Lund (1981) found pectolytic P. fluorescens biotype II caused post harvest breakdown of celery, but two other undescribed P. fluorescens groups were also responsible. There is a tendency to identify as P. marginalis all organisms of the P. fluorescens-P. putida type with the ability to soft rot potato or other vegetable tissue or lyse pectate gels at neutral pH (Sands et al, 1980).

Host Range. Brocklehurst & Lund (1981) reviewed the diseases reported to be caused by P. marginalis on a wide range of vegetables which included lettuce (Lactuca sativa), celery (Apium graveolens) and an association with pink eye of potatoes (Solanum tuberosum). Post harvest breakdown of a range of vegetables is also reported to be associated with P. marginalis.

Marginal Leaf Spot of Lettuce. Marginal leaf spot is normally a minor but common disease of lettuce in Australia, but may become significant in wet seasons. As marginal lesions develop, a distinct darkened brown veinal system is highlighted and is characteristic of this disease. Ooze is abundant and fluorescent pseudomonads are readily isolated on KBA. The disease occurs worldwide. In Japan (Tsuchiya et al, 1979) P. marginalis is prevalent on lettuce grown in plastic tunnel culture. P. cichorii and P. viridiflava are readily isolated in association with P marginalis and all three pathogens cause similar symptoms but prevalence may vary with growing conditions and temperature.

VII.   Group V Pathogens

A. *Pseudomonas tolaasii: Bacterial Blotch of Mushrooms*

Symptoms. P. tolaasii Paine 1919 causes bacterial blotch, a serious disease of cultivated mushrooms Agaricus bisporus and A. bitorquis. Characteristic symptoms are light to dark brown, sunken lesions appearing on caps during all stages of growth or in storage (Fig. 8.10a). Verticillium spp. also cause similar lesions but these are generally not sunken, and mycelium develops after incubation of excised caps in a humid chamber for 24 h.

Identification. P. tolaasii is a member of Group V (Table 8.1). It can be readily identified by inoculating excised mushroom caps with a drop of a bacterial suspension (10^7 cells/ml) and incubating in a humid chamber overnight at 15-25C. Typical brown sunken lesions develop on inoculated areas.

Confirmatory tests. Most strains injected into tobacco produce a distinct greasy lesion in 48 h, quite unlike the usual hypersensitivity reaction. This may be associated with the toxin produced by P. tolaasii. The pathogen is not P. fluorescens biotype II as described in Bergey's Manual but belongs to a distinct group within the P. fluorescens complex containing both saprophytes and pathogens (Fahy, 1981).

Geographical Distribution and Importance. Bacterial blotch is of worldwide distribution. It accounts for a 5% loss pre- and post-harvest in Australia. P. tolaasii is a component of the normal microflora of mushroom tissue (Fahy et al, 1981) and may develop from damaged tissue associated

 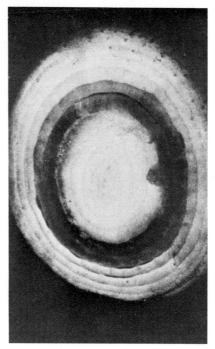

(a)   (b)

FIGURE 8.10. (a) Bacterial blotch of mushroom cap
by P. tolaasii. (b) Internal brown staining of onion
caused by P. aeruginosa.

with insects, mites or Verticillium but is generally
associated with prolonged surface wetness of the cap tissue.

B. *Pseudomonas sp.*: *Mummy Disease of Mushroom*

Mummy disease is a serious disease of the cultivated
mushroom and is common worldwide. Its etiology is poorly
understood but it is believed to be a Group V pseudomonad
carried intracellularly in mushroom tissue (Schisler et al,
1968; van Zaayen & Waterreus, 1974; Fahy, 1981). It
occasionally causes serious losses in Australian crops.

The disease is recognised by the enlarged, bell-shaped
base to the stalks with an associated proliferation of
mycelium. Mushrooms frequently fail to develop perfect
caps and may be distorted (symptoms also common in virus-

infected beds). Unlike virus-infected mushrooms, the stalks can be pulled from the beds readily with a distinct "cracking" sound. Infected beds fail to yield heavily.

The disease is diagnosed by thin sectioning of infected stipes and examination for presence of intracellular rod-shaped bacteria either by Gram stain (Gram negative) or by electron microscopy (van Zaayen & Waterreus, 1974).

C. *Pseudomonas aeruginosa: Internal Browning of Onion*

P. aeruginosa (Schroeter 1872) Migula 1900 is a common soil and plant saprophyte and is of medical importance as a wound pathogen. It is not normally considered to be a plant pathogen. It has been reported as the cause of a disease of lettuce, banana, tobacco and some other crops but generally insufficient work has been carried out to confirm pathogenicity. Dunaway & Mead (1978) have reported an association of P. aeruginosa with a lethal blight of palms in Florida.

In Australia, Cother et al. (1976) reported that P. aeruginosa was associated with a serious post harvest internal brown rot of onion in southern New South Wales. Tesoriero et al. (1982) found P. gladioli pv. alliicola caused internal rot of bulbs in the field but P. aeruginosa, commonly isolated with P. gladioli pv. alliicola, caused internal browning without soft rot (Fig. 8.10b).

VIII. Ungrouped Pathogenic Species

The following valid species were originally described as fluorescent pseudomonads but have not been the subject of recent published taxonomic studies and therefore cannot be placed into any grouping listed in the Determinative Scheme (Table 8.1).

A. *Pseudomonas asplenii: Bacterial Leaf Blight of*
Bird's-Nest Fern

Ark & Tompkins (1946) first described a bacterial leaf blight of bird's-nest fern (Asplenium nidus) caused by P. asplenii (Ark & Tompkins 1946) Savulescu 1947 in California. The disease is characterized as discrete

(a)   (b)

FIGURE 8.11. (a) Angular watersoaked lesion on papaya caused by P. caricapapayae. (b) pod twist of bean, caused by P. flectens.

watersoaked spots which gradually enlarge to invade the whole frond. The pathogen has not been reported elsewhere.

B. *Pseudomonas betle:* Bacterial Leaf Spot of Betel

Bacterial leaf spot of betel (*Piper betle*), caused by P. betle Ragunathan 1928 was first described in Sri Lanka by Ragunathan (1928). The pathogen causes an angular, water soaked leaf spot with a yellow halo, which is particularly damaging under monsoonal conditions. Severely infected vines usually die. The disease is widespread in southern Asia, but is not recorded in Australia.

C. *Pseudomonas caricapapayae:*   *Leaf Spot of Papaya*

P. caricapapayae Robbs 1956, which causes an angular water soaked leaf spot of papaya (Carica papaya), (Fig. 8.11a). It was originally described by Robbs (1956) in Brazil. The disease is generally only a minor problem in Australia.

D. *Pseudomonas flectens:*   *Pod Twist of Bean*

Pod twist caused by P. flectens Johnson 1956 was first described on bean (Phaseolus vulgaris) and siratro (Macroptilium atropurpureum) by Johnson (1956). The disease is common in the summer months in the coastal region of Queensland from Cairns to Brisbane, but is only a minor problem in commercial crops which mature in winter months. The disease is characterised by watersoaked areas on young pods which may wither and fall. Remaining pods develop curls and twists as infected areas fail to enlarge (Fig. 8.11b). Affected areas darken and a shiny encrustation of dried ooze may be obvious. The bean blossom thrip (Taeniothrips nigricornis) may spread the disease.

References

Adam, D.B. & Pugsley, A.T. (1934). Bacterial diseases in Victoria. Journal of Agriculture, Victoria 32, 304-311, 323.

Amaral, J.F.do., Teixeira, C. & Pinheiro, E.D. (1956). O bactério causador da mancha aurcolada do cafeeiro. Arquivos do Instituto Biológico, São Paulo 23, 151-155.

Ark, P.A. (1939). Bacterial leaf spot of maple. Phytopathology 29, 968-970.

Ark, P.A. (1940). Bacterial stalk rot of field corn caused by Phytomonas lapsa n.sp. Phytopathology 30, 1.

Ark, P.A. (1944). Bacterial blight of purple vetch caused by Phytomonas pisi (Abst.) Phytopathology 34, 933.

Ark, P.A. & Gardner, M.W. (1936). Bacterial leaf spot of Primula. Phytopathology 26, 1050-1055.

Ark, P.A. & Tompkins, C.M. (1946). Bacterial leaf blight of Bird's Nest Fern. Phytopathology 36, 758-761.

Arny, P.C., Lindow, S.E. & Upper, C.D. (1976). Frost sensitivity of Zea mays increased by application of Pseudomonas syringae. Nature, London 262, 282-284.

Billing, E. (1970a). Pseudomonas viridiflava (Burkholder, 1930) Clara, 1934. Journal of Applied Bacteriology 33, 492-500.

Billing, E. (1970b). Further studies on the phage sensitivity and the determination of phytopathogenic Pseudomonas spp. Journal of Applied Bacteriology 33, 478-491.

Bohn, G.W. & Maloit, J.C. (1946). Bacterial spot of native golden currant (Ribes aureum). Journal of Agricultural Research 73, 281-290.

Bradbury, J.F. (1967a). Pseudomonas lachrymans. CMI Descriptions of Pathogenic Fungi and Bacteria No.124. Kew: Commonwealth Mycological Institute.

Bradbury, J.F. (1967b). Pseudomonas tabaci. CMI Descriptions of Pathogenic Fungi and Bacteria No.129. Kew: Commonwealth Mycological Institute.

Bradbury, J.F. (1970a). Pseudomonas coronafaciens. CMI Descriptions of Pathogenic Fungi and Bacteria No.235. Kew: Commonwealth Mycological Institute.

Bradbury, J.F. (1970b). Pseudomonas striafaciens. CMI Descriptions of Pathogenic Fungi and Bacteria No.238. Kew: Commonwealth Mycological Institute.

Bradbury, J.F. (1981). Pseudomonas syringae pv. sesami. CMI Descriptions of Pathogenic Fungi and Bacteria No.696. Kew: Commonwealth Mycological Institute.

Brocklehurst, T.F. & Lund, B.M. (1981). Properties of pseudomonads causing spoilage of vegetables stored at low temperature. Journal of Applied Bacteriology 50, 259-266.

Brown, N.A. (1918). Some bacterial diseases of lettuce. Journal of Agricultural Research 13, 367-388.

Burkholder, W.H. (1954). Three bacteria pathogenic on head lettuce in New York State. Phytopathology 44, 592-596.

Burkholder, W.H. (1960). A bacterial brown rot of parsnip roots. Phytopathology 50, 280-282.

Burr, T.J. & Hurwitz, B. (1979). The etiology of blister spot of 'Mitsu' apple in New York State. Plant Disease Reporter 63, 157-160.

Chamberlain, D.W. (1956). Methods of inoculation of wildfire of soybean and the effect of bacterial pustule on wildfire development. Phytopathology 46, 96-98.

Cother, E.J., Darbyshire, B. & Brewer, J. (1976). Pseudomonas aeruginosa: cause of internal rot of onions. Phytopathology 66, 828-834.

Crosse, J.E. (1957). Bacterial canker of stone-fruits. III. Inoculum concentration and time of inoculation in relation to leaf-scar infection of cherry. Annals of Applied Biology 45, 19-35.

Crosse, J.E. (1959). Bacterial canker of stone-fruits. IV. Investigation of a method for measuring the inoculum potential of cherry trees. Annals of Applied Biology 47, 306-317.

Crosse, J.E. (1966). Epidemiological relations of the pseudomonad pathogens of deciduous fruit trees. Annual Review of Phytopathology 4, 291-310.

Crosse, J.E. & Garrett, C.M.E. (1963). Studies on the bacteriophagy of Pseudomonas morsprunorum, Ps.syringae and related organisms. Journal of Applied Bacteriology 26, 159-177.

Crosse, J.E. & Garrett, C.M.E. (1966). Bacterial canker of stone-fruits. VII. Infection experiments with Pseudomonas morsprunorum and P.syringae. Annals of Applied Biology 58, 31-41.

Dhanvantari, B.N. (1977). A taxonomic study of Pseudomonas papulans Rose 1917. New Zealand Journal of Agricultural Research 20, 557-561.

Dickson, J.G. (1956). "Diseases of Field Crops" 2nd edition. New York: McGraw-Hill. 517pp.

Doepel, R.F. (1965). Grease spot of passion fruit. Journal of Agriculture, Western Australia 6, 291.

Doidge, E.M. (1915). The South African mulberry blight. Annals of Applied Biology 2, 115-124.

Doudoroff, M. & Palleroni, N.J. (1974). Genus 1. Pseudomonas Migula 1894. In "Bergey's Manual of Determinative Bacteriology" 8th edition, pp.217-243. (Ed. R.E. Buchanan & N.E. Gibbons). Baltimore: Williams & Wilkins.

Dunaway, J.K. & Mead, D.G. (1978). Preliminary studies on lethal palm blight. Proceedings of the Florida State Horticultural Society 91, 243-245.

Dye, D.W., Bradbury, J.F., Goto, M., Hayward, A.C., Lelliott, R.A. & Schroth, M.N. (1980). International standards for naming pathovars of phytopathogenic bacteria and a list of pathovar names and pathovar strains. Review of Plant Pathology 59, 153-168.

Elliott, C. (1927). Bacterial stripe blight of oats. Journal of Agricultural Research 35, 811-824.

Elliott, C. (1951). "Manual of Bacterial Plant Pathogens" 2nd edition. Waltham, Massachusetts: Chronica Botanica. 186pp.

Ercolani, G.L. & Caldarola, M. (1972). Pseudomonas ciccaronei sp. n., agente di una maculatura fogliare del carrubo in Puglia. Phytopathologia Mediterranea 11, 71-73.

Fahy, P.C. (1981). The taxonomy of the bacterial plant pathogens of mushroom culture. Mushroom Science 11, 293-312.

Fahy, P.C., Nair, N.G. & Bradley, J.K. (1981). Epidemiology and biological control of bacterial blotch caused by Pseudomonas tolaasii. Mushroom Science 11, 343-352.

Ferguson, A.R. & Johnston, J.S. (1980). Phaseolotoxin-induced chlorosis, ornithine accumulation and inhibition of ornithine carbamoyl transferase in different plants. Physiological Plant Pathology 16, 269-276.

Foulkes, J.A. & Lloyd, A.B. (1980). Epiphytic populations of Pseudomonas syringae pv. syringae and P.syringae pv. morsprunorum on cherry leaves. Australasian Plant Pathology 9, 114-116.

Freigoun, S.O. & Crosse, J.E. (1975). Host relations and distribution of a physiological and pathological variant of Pseudomonas morsprunorum. Annals of Applied Biology 81, 317-330.

Fulton, R.W. (1980). Tobacco blackfire disease in Wisconsin. Plant Disease 64, 100.

Garrett, C.M.E., Panagopoulos, C.G. & Crosse, J.E. (1966). Comparison of plant pathogenic pseudomonads from fruit trees. Journal of Applied Bacteriology 29, 342-356.

Gasson, M.J. (1980). Indicator technique for antimetabolite toxin production by phytopathogenic species of Pseudomonas. Applied and Environmental Microbiology 39, 25-29.

Goldsworthy, M.C. (1926). Studies on the spot disease of cauliflower; a use of serum diagnosis. Phytopothology 16, 877-884.

Goss, O.M. (1962). Hibiscus leaf spot. Journal of Agriculture, Western Australia 3, 519.

Grogan, R.G. & Kimble, K.A. (1967). The role of seed contamination in the transmission of Pseudomonas phaseolicola in Phaseolus vulgaris. Phytopathology 57, 28-31.

Grogan, R.G., Misaghi, I.J., Kimble, K.A., Greathead, A.S., Ririe, D. & Bardin, R. (1977). Varnish spot, a destructive disease of lettuce in California caused by Pseudomonas cichorii. Phytopathology 67, 957-960.

Gross, D.C. & De Vay, J.E. (1977a). Population dynamics and pathogenesis of Pseudomonas syringae in maize and cowpea in relation to the in vitro production of syringomycin. Phytopathology 67, 475-483.

Gross, D.C. & De Vay, J.E. (1977b). Production and purification of syringomycin, a phytotoxin produced by Pseudomonas syringae. Physiological Plant Pathology 11, 13-28.

Guy, G. & Wimalajeewa, D.L.S. (1977). Levels of common and halo blight seed infection in an imported variety of French beans. Australian Plant Pathology Society Newsletter 6, 2.

Harrison, D.E. (1964). Bacterial blight of peas. Journal of Agriculture, Victoria 62, 276-282.

Harrison, D.E. & Freeman, H. (1965). Bacterial brownspot (Pseudomonas syringae) of french bean. Journal of Agriculture Victoria 63, 523-526.

Hayward, A.C. & Waterston, J.M. (1965a). Pseudomonas syringae. C.M.I. Descriptions of Pathogenic Fungi and Bacteria No.46. Kew: Commonwealth Mycological Institute.

Hayward, A.C. & Waterston, J.M. (1965b). Pseudomonas phaseolicola. C.M.I. Descriptions of Pathogenic Fungi and Bacteria No.45. Kew: Commonwealth Mycological Institute.

Hellmers, E. (1955). Bacterial leafspot of African marigold (Tagetes erecta) caused by Pseudomonas tagetis sp.n. Acta Agriculturae Scandinavica 5, 185-200.

Hildebrand, D.C. (1973). Tolerance of homoserine by Pseudomonas pisi and implications of homoserine in plant resistance. Phytopathology 63, 301-302.

Hoitink, H.A.J., Hagedorn, D.J. & McCoy, E. (1967). Survival, transmission and taxonomy of Pseudomonas syringae van Hall, the causal organism of bacterial brown spot of bean (Phaseolus vulgaris L.). Canadian Journal of Microbiology 14, 437-441.

Hutchinson, P.B. (1949). A bacterial disease of Dysoxylum spectabile caused by the pathogen Pseudomonas dysoxyli n. sp. New Zealand Journal of Science and Technology B30, 274-286.

Jagger, I.C. (1921). Bacterial leafspot of celery. Journal of Agricultural Research 21, 185-188.

Janse, J.D. (1982). Pseudomonas syringae subsp. savastanoi (ex Smith) subsp. nov., nom. rev., the bacterium causing excrescences on Oleaceae and Nerium oleander L. International Journal of Systematic Bacteriology 32, 166-169.

Johnson, J. (1923). A bacterial leafspot of tobacco. Journal of Agricultural Research 23, 481-483.

Johnson, J.C. (1956). Pod twist: a previously unrecorded bacterial disease of French bean (Phaseolus vulgaris L.). Queensland Journal of Agricultural Science 13, 127-158.

Jones, J.B., McCarter, S.M. & Gitaitis, R.D. (1981). Association of Pseudomonas syringae pv. syringae with a leaf spot disease of tomato transplants in southern Georgia. Phytopathology 71, 1281-1285.

Kawamura, E. (1934). Bacterial leafspot of sunflower. Annals of the Phytopathological Society, Japan 4, 25-28.

Kennedy, B.W. & Tachibana, H. (1973). Bacterial diseases. In "Soybeans: Improvement, Production, and Uses", pp.491-504. (Ed. B.E. Caldwell). Wisconsin: American Society of Agronomy.

King, E.O., Ward, M.K. & Raney, D.E. (1954). Two simple media for the demonstration of pyocyanin and fluorescein. Journal of Laboratory and Clinical Medicine 44, 301-307.

Klement, Z. (1977). Bacterial canker and dieback of apricots (Pseudomonas syringae van Hall). EPPO Bulletin 7, 57-68.

Klotz, L.J. (1978). Fungal, bacterial, and nonparasitic diseases and injuries originating in the seedbed, nursery, and orchard. In "The Citrus Industry" Vol.IV, pp.1-66. (Ed. W. Reuther, E.C. Calavan & G.E. Carman). University of California.

Latorre, B.A. & Jones, A.L. (1979). Pseudomonas morsprunorum, the cause of bacterial canker of sour cherry in Michigan, and its epiphytic association with P.syringae. Phytopathology 69, 335-339.

Leben, C., Rusch, V. & Schmitthenner, A.F. (1968). The colonization of soybean buds by Pseudomonas glycinea and other bacteria. Phytopathology 58, 1677-1681.

Lelliott, R.A., Billing, E. & Hayward, A.C. (1966). A determinative scheme for the fluorescent plant pathogenic pseudomonads. Journal of Applied Bacteriology 29, 470-489.

Lindow, S.E., Arny, D.C. and Upper, C.D. (1978). Erwinia herbicola: a bacterial ice nucleus active in increasing frost injury to corn. Phytopathology 68, 523-527.

Lucas, G.B. (1965). "Diseases of Tobacco". 2nd edition. New York: The Scarecrow Press. 778pp.

Luketina, R.C. & Young, J.M. (1979). Nomenclatural status of *Pseudomonas oryzicola* Klement 1955, *Pseudomonas papaveris* Lelliott and Wallace 1955, and *Pseudomonas syringae* var. *capsici* (Orsini 1942) Klement 1956. New Zealand Journal of Agricultural Research 22, 349-353.

McCulloch, L. (1920). Basal glume rot of wheat. Journal of Agricultural Research 18, 543-552.

Misaghi, I. & Grogan, R.G. (1969). Nutritional and bio-chemical comparisons of plant pathogenic and saprophytic fluorescent pseudomonads. Phytopathology 59, 1436-1450.

Mitchell, R.E. (1982). Coronatine production by some phyto-pathogenic pseudomonads. Physiological Plant Pathology 20, 83-89.

Mitchell, R.E. & Durbin, R.D. (1981). Tagetitoxin, a toxin produced by *Pseudomonas syringae* pv. *tagetis*: purific-ation and partial characterization. Physiological Plant Pathology 18, 157-168.

Moffett, M.L. (1976). A halo-producing strain of *Pseudomonas glycinea* in Australia. Australian Plant Pathology 5, 5-6.

Moniz, L. (1963). Leaf-spot of apple-blossom. Current Science 32, 177.

Mukoo, H. (1955). [On the bacterial blacknode of barley and wheat and its causal bacteria]. "Jubilee Public-ation in Commemoration of the Sixtieth Birthdays of Prof. Yoshihiko Tochinai and Prof. Teikichi Fukushi". Sapporo, Japan. Cited in Dye et al. (1980).

Noble, R.J. (1933). Basal glume rot. Agricultural Gazette of New South Wales 44, 107-109.

Okabe, N. & Goto, M. (1955). [Bacterial plant disease in Japan. IV. Studies on bacterial shoot blight of tea-plant by *Pseudomonas theae* n.sp.]. Report of the Faculty of Agriculture, Shizuoka University 5, 63-71 (English summary).

Otta, J.D. & English, H. (1971). Serology and pathology of *Pseudomonas syringae*. Phytopathology 61, 443-452.

Pohronezny, K., Larsen, P. & Leben, C. (1978). Observations on cucumber fruit invasion by *Pseudomonas lachrymans*. Plant Disease Reporter 62, 306-309.

Palleroni, N.J. & Doudoroff, M. (1972). Some properties and taxonomic subdivisions of the genus *Pseudomonas*. Annual Review of Phytopathology 10, 73-100.

Paulin, J.P. & Luisetti, J. (1978). Ice nucleation activity among phytopathogenic bacteria. In "Proceedings of the IVth International Conference on Plant Pathogenic Bacteria", pp.725-731. (Ed. Station de Pathologie Vegetale et Phytobacteriologie). Angers, France: I.N.R.A.

Persley, G.J. & Crosse, J.E. (1978). A bacteriophage specific to race 2 of the cherry strain of Pseudomonas morsprunorum. Annals of Applied Biology 89, 219-222.

Prunier, J.P., Luisetti, J. & Gardan, L. (1970). Etudes sur les bactérioses des arbres fruitiers. II. Caractérisation d'un Pseudomonas non-fluorescent agent d'une bactériose nouvelle du pecher. Annales de Phytopathologie 2, 181-197.

Ragunathan, C. (1928). Bacterial leaf spot of betel. Annals of the Royal Botanic Gardens of Peradeniya 11, 51-62.

Reid, W.D. (1938). Grease-spot of passion-fruit. New Zealand Journal of Science and Technology A20, 260-265.

Ribeiro, R. de L.D., Durbin, R.D., Arny, D.C. & Uchytil, T.F. (1977). Characterization of the bacterium inciting chocolate spot of corn. Phytopathology 67, 1427-1431.

Robbs, C.F. (1956). Uma nova doenca bacteriana mamoeiro (Carica papaya L.). Revista da Sociedade Brasileira de Agronomica 12, 73-76.

Samson, R., Poutier, F. & Rat, B. (1978). Une nouvelle maladie du poireau: La graisse bactérienne à Pseudomonas syringae. Revue Horticole 219, 20-23.

Sands, D.C., Schroth, M.N. & Hildebrand, D.C. (1970). Taxonomy of phytopathogenic pseudomonads. Journal of Bacteriology 101, 9-23.

Sands, D.C., Schroth, M.N. & Hildebrand, D.C. (1980). Pseudomonas. In "Laboratory Guide for Identification of Plant Pathogenic Bacteria", pp.36-44. (Ed. N.W. Schaad). St Paul, Minnesota: American Phytopathological Society.

Schaad, N.W. & Cunfer, B.M. (1979). Synonomy of Pseudomonas coronafaciens, Pseudomonas coronafaciens pathovar zeae, Pseudomonas coronafaciens subsp. atropurpurea and Pseudomonas striafaciens. International Journal of Systematic Bacteriology 29, 213-221.

Schisler, L.C., Sinden, J.W. & Sigel, E.M. (1968). Etiology of mummy disease of cultivated mushrooms. Phytopathology 58, 944-948.

Schroth, M.N., Vitanza, V.B. & Hildebrand, D.C. (1971). Pathogenic and nutritional variation in the halo blight group of fluorescent pseudomonads of bean. Phytopathology 61, 852-857.

Shinde, P.A. & Lukezic, F.L. (1974). Isolation, pathogenicity and characterisation of fluorescent pseudomonads associated with discoloured alfalfa roots. Phytopathology 64, 857-865.

Simpson, C.J., Jones, G.E. & Taylor, J.D. (1971). Seedling blight of Antirrhinum caused by Pseudomonas antirrhini. Plant Pathology 20, 127-130.

Skerman, V.B.D., McGowan, V., & Sneath, P.H.A. (1980). Approved list of bacterial names. International Journal of Systematic Bacteriology 30, 225-420.

Smith, E.F. (1904). Bacterial leaf spot diseases. Science, Washington N.S. 19, 417-418.

Smith, C.O. (1943). A leaf spot of Hibiscus sp. induced by Pseudomonas syringae. Phytopathology 33, 82-84.

Smith, M.A. & Ramsey, G.B. (1953). Bacterial spot of broccoli. Phytopathology 43, 583-584.

Stanier, R.Y., Palleroni, N.J. & Doudoroff, M. (1966). The aerobic pseudomonads: a taxonomic study. Journal of General Microbiology 53, 159-271.

Stapp, C. (1961). "Bacterial Plant Pathogens". Oxford University Press. 292pp.

Stewart, W.W. (1971). Isolation and proof of structure of wildfire toxin. Nature London 229, 174-178.

Sumner, D.R. (1972). Effect of freezing injury on head rot and spot of cabbage. Phytopathology 62, 322-325.

Šutić, D. & Dowson, W.J. (1959). An investigation of a serious disease of hemp (Cannabis sativa L.) in Yugoslavia. Phytopathologische Zeitschrift 34, 307-314.

Šutić, D. & Tešić, Ž. (1958). Jedna nova bacteriza bresta izazivač Pseudomonas ulmi n.sp. Zastita Bilja 45, 13-25.

Takimoto, S. (1931). [Bacterial bud rot of loquat]. Journal of Plant Protection, Tokyo 13, 728-732.

Taylor, J.D. (1970a). Bacteriophage and serological methods for the identification of Pseudomonas phaseolicola (Burkh.) Dowson. Annals of Applied Biology 66, 387-395.

Taylor, J.D. (1970b). The quantitative estimation of the infection of bean seed with Pseudomonas phaseolicola (Burkh.) Dowson. Annals of Applied Biology 66, 29-36.

Taylor, J.D. (1972a). Specificity of bacteriophages and antiserum for Pseudomonas pisi. New Zealand Journal of Agricultural Research 15, 421-431.

Taylor, J.D. (1972b). Races of Pseudomonas pisi and sources of resistance in field and garden peas. New Zealand Journal of Agricultural Research 15, 441-447.

Taylor, J.D. & Dye, D.W. (1972). A survey of the organisms associated with bacterial blight of peas. New Zealand Journal of Agricultural Research 15, 432-440.

Taylor, J.D., Dudley, C.L. & Presly, L. (1979). Studies of halo-blight seed infection and disease transmission in dwarf beans. Annals of Applied Biology 93, 267-277.

Tesoriero, L.A., Fahy, P.C. & Gunn, L.V. (1982). First record of bacterial rot of onion in Australia caused by Pseudomonas gladioli pv. alliicola and association with internal browning caused by Pseudomonas aeruginosa. Australasian Plant Pathology, 11, 56-57.

Tessi, J.L. (1953). Comparative study of two bacteria pathogenic on oats and detection of a toxin which is the origin of their differences. Revista Investigaciones Agricolas Buenos Aires 7, 131-145.

Thayer, P.L. (1965). Temperature effect on growth and pathogenicity to celery of Pseudomonas apii and P.cichorii. Phytopathology 55, 1365.

Thayer, P.L. & Wehlburg, C. (1965). Pseudomonas cichorii, the cause of bacterial blight of celery in the Everglades. Phytopathology 55, 554-557.

Thornberry, H.H. & Anderson, H.W. (1931a). A bacterial disease of barberry caused by Phytomonas berberidis n.sp. Journal of Agricultural Research 43, 29-36.

Thornberry, H.H. & Anderson, H.W. (1931b). Bacterial leaf-spot of viburnum. Phytopathology 21, 907-912.

Trimboli, D., Fahy, P.C. & Baker, K.F. (1978). Apical chlorosis and leaf spot of Tagetes spp. caused by Pseudomonas tagetis Hellmers. Australian Journal of Agricultural Research 29, 831-839.

Tsuchiya, Y., Ohata, K., Iemura, H., Sanematsue, T., Shirata, A. & Fujii, H. (1979). [Identification of causal bacteria of head rot of lettuce]. Bulletin of the National Institute of Agricultural Sciences C.33, 77-99.

Valleau, W.D., Johnson, E.M. & Diachun, S. (1944). Root infection of crop plants and weeds by tobacco leaf spot bacteria. Phytopathology 34, 163-174.

van Zaayen & Waterreus, H.A.J.I. (1974). Intracellular occurrence of bacteria in mummy-diseased mushrooms. Phytopathology 64, 1474-1475.

Vock, N.T. (1978). "Handbook of Plant Diseases" Vol.1 & 2. Brisbane: Queensland Department of Primary Industries.

Waissbluth, M.E. & Latorre, B.A. (1978). Source and seasonal development of inoculum for pear blast in Chile. Plant Disease Reporter 62, 651-655.

Wiese, M.W. (1977). "Compendium of Wheat Diseases". St Paul Minnesota: American Phytopathological Society. 106pp.

Wiles, A.B. & Walker, J.C. (1951). The relation of Pseudomonas lachrymans to cucumber fruits and seeds. Phytopathology 41, 1059-1064.

Wilkie, J.P. (1972). Halo blight of oats in New Zealand. New Zealand Journal of Agricultural Research 15, 461-468.

Wilkie, J.P. (1973). Basal glume rot of wheat in New Zealand. New Zealand Journal of Agricultural Research 16, 155-160.

Wilkie, J.P. & Dye, D.W. (1973). Pseudomonas cichorii causing tomato and celery diseases in New Zealand. New Zealand Journal of Agricultural Research 17, 123-130.

Wilkie, J.P. & Dye, D.W. (1974). Pseudomonas tomato in New Zealand. New Zealand Journal of Agricultural Research 17, 131-135.

Wilkie, J.P., Dye, D.W. & Watson, D.R.W. (1973). Further hosts of Pseudomonas viridiflava. New Zealand Journal of Agricultural Research 16, 315-323.

Williams, P.H. & Keen, N.T. (1966). Bacterial blight of radish. Plant Disease Reporter 50, 192-195.

Wilson, E.E. & Magie, A.R. (1963). Physiological, serological and pathological evidence that Pseudomonas tonelliana is identical with Pseudomonas savastanoi. Phytopathology 53, 653-659.

Wimalajeewa, D.L.S. & Nancarrow, R.J. (1978). The incidence of bacterial blight of French bean (Phaseolus vulgaris) in East Gippsland, Victoria. Australian Journal of Experimental Agriculture and Animal Husbandry 18, 318-320.

Wimalajeewa, D.L.S., Pascoe, I.G. & Jones, D. (1978). Bacterial stem canker of loquat. Australasian Plant Pathology 7, 33.

Wimalajeewa, D.L.S., Hayward, A.C. & Greenhalgh, F.C. (1983). A bacterial leaf spot of Protea cynaroides (King Protea). Annals of Applied Biology 102 (in press).

Young, J.M. (1970). Drippy gill: a bacterial disease of cultivated mushrooms caused by Pseudomonas agarici n.sp. New Zealand Journal of Agricultural Research 13, 977-990.

Young, J.M. & Dye, D.W. (1970). Bacterial blight of peas caused by Pseudomonas pisi Sackett, 1916 in New Zealand. New Zealand Journal of Agricultural Research 13, 315-324.

Young, J.M., Dye, D.W., Bradbury, J.F., Panagopoulos, C.G. & Robbs, C.F. (1978). A proposed nomenclature and classification for plant pathogenic bacteria. New Zealand Journal of Agricultural Research 21, 153-177.

Zaumeyer, W.J. (1932). Comparative pathological histology of three bacterial diseases of bean. Journal of Agricultural Research 44, 605-632.

9

Xanthomonas

M. L. Moffett and B. J. Croft

I.	Introduction	189
II.	Isolation and Identification	190
III.	*Xanthomonas campestris* Pathovars	192
IV.	*Xanthomonas albilineans*: Leaf Scald of Sugarcane	217
V.	*Xanthomonas ampelina*: Bacterial Blight of Grapevine	220
VI.	*Xanthomonas axonopodis*: Gummosis of Imperial Pasture Grass	220
VII.	*Xanthomonas fragariae*: Angular Leaf Spot of Strawberry	221
VIII.	*Xanthomonas populi* (inv.): Bacterial Canker of Poplar	222
	References	222

I. Introduction

Most members of the genus Xanthomonas are plant pathogens and despite reports of their being isolated from clinical material and water, the source of all confirmed identifications has been living plants or materials of plant origin. Unidentified xanthomonads have been reported to be associated with plants as epiphytes on healthy tissue or more frequently on plants affected by other pathogens. Skerman et al. (1980) list five valid species of Xanthomonas: X. albilineans, X. ampelina, X. axonopodis, X. campestris and X. fragariae.

The causal agent of bacterial canker of poplar (Populus spp.) is considered to be a xanthomonad, X. populi (Ridé & Ridé, 1978). X. populi is not a valid name because it was not included in the Approved Lists by Skerman et al. (1980). However, molecular biological studies have shown that the causal agent of bacterial canker of poplar falls within the Xanthomonas group (De Ley et al., 1978).

X. campestris (Pammel 1895) Dowson 1939 is comprised of 123 pathovars (Dye et al., 1980), of which thirty-two have been recorded in Australia. The valid names of all pathovars are given in Chapter 14 and those which occur in Australia, are listed in Chapter 15, together with their hosts.

The pathovars cannot at present be differentiated on the basis of standard physiological tests although most appear to have narrow host ranges. Starr (1981) reviews various aspects of host specialization and possible synonomy within this group.

Starch hydrolysis differs consistently amongst pathovars. Some pathovars produce a well-defined zone of hydrolysis on starch agar plates. Bacteriophages have been shown to be useful for identification of certain strains of Xanthomonas (see Chapter 12 of this volume).

Brief descriptions of the diseases caused by some of the more important pathovars of X. campestris and the other Xanthomonas spp., and details of their host range and geographical distribution are given below. Details of media and methods referred to are given in Chapter 16.

II.   Isolation and Identification

A. *Isolation Methods*

The methods for the isolation of xanthomonads from infected plant material are similar to those used for the other plant pathogenic bacteria, as described in Chapter I. Any special precautions are noted below.

The preferred medium for isolation is the non-selective medium, sucrose peptone agar (SPA) (Hayward, 1960). Its usefulness lies in the fact that the rate of growth and colony type of xanthomonads on SPA is characteristic of the genus. The colonies are also readily distinguishable from those of other pathogens, such as the fluorescent, levan-producing pseudomonads (Hayward, 1979).

Nutrient agar (eg. Difco or Oxoid) and glucose yeast extract calcium carbonate agar (GYCA) (Dye, 1962) are not as suitable as SPA for general isolation purposes. Most xanthomonads grow poorly on nutrient agar and the colony form is difficult to differentiate from that of other bacteria. Xanthomonads grow well on GYCA but its opacity makes viewing of colonies difficult. However, GYCA is a useful storage medium for xanthomonads.

The SX agar medium of Schaad & White (1974), which is based on soluble starch and cycloheximide, is recommended by Dye (1980) as a selective medium for xanthomonads that hydrolyse starch. The medium is particularly useful in epidemiological studies where the aim is to isolate a starch-hydrolysing xanthomonad from plants, debris or soil. Its dark blue colour makes viewing of individual colonies difficult.

B. Cultural and Physiological Characteristics

Initial diagnosis can be made on a few characteristics. Xanthomonads are rod-shaped, non-sporing, Gram negative rods, motile with a single polar flagellum. They have a slow growth rate on agar medium compared with that of non-pathogens commonly associated with the diseased plant material. Xanthomonads take from 2 days in the case of X. campestris pathovars to between 7 and 14 days for X. albilineans to appear on isolation plates.

On SPA, the colonies are circular, smooth, domed and mucoid, with the exception of X. albilineans, which is butyrous. Most xanthomonads produce yellow-pigmented colonies. These pigments have been called xanthomonadins (Starr et al., 1977). The mucilaginous extracellur slime consists of an unusual hetero-polysaccharide known as xanthan gum. The intensity of the yellow colour varies with the medium and sometimes with the organism. For example, X. campestris, pv. pruni and pv. vitians are frequently paler than pv. campestris. Albino forms also occur, in which colonies are white and mucoid (e.g. X. campestris pv. mangiferaeindicae and pv. manihotis.)

In physiological tests, glucose and other carbohydrates are metabolised oxidatively; nitrite is not produced from nitrate; tests for catalase are positive and oxidase negative; and hydrogen sulphide is produced from cysteine. Although these characteristics are not consider-ed to differentiate members of the genus Xanthomonas from the genus Pseudomonas (Dye & Lelliott, 1974), the mucoid nature of colonies of Xanthomonas on SPA or other media with a high percentage of available carbohydrate, is characteristic of these organisms and differs from colonies of pseudomonads on the same medium.

Confirmatory tests include; inability to use asparagine as sole carbon and nitrogen source; growth factors needed in carbon source tests which include utilization (alkali from) of acetate, citrate, malate, propionate and succinate but usually not benzoate, oxalate or tartrate as a sole carbon source; delayed utilisation of gluconate; hydrolysis of starch and Tween 80 by most members of the genus; inability to produce acid from rhamnose, inulin, adonitol, dulcitol, inositol or salicin and rarely from sorbitol; acid not produced in purple milk; and sodium hippurate is not hydrolysed (Dye & Lelliott, 1974). The five Xanthomonas spp. can be differentiated from one another on the basis of a few physiological tests (Table 9.1).

C. Pathogenicity

Many xanthomonads, particularly the X. campestris pathovars, can only be identified with certainty on the basis of pathogenicity tests. These are usually conducted by inoculating a sterile distilled water suspension of growth from a 24-48 h culture on SPA, containing approximately 10^8 cells/ml, into susceptible host plants. The inoculation methods generally used for leaf stem, pod, and fruit inoculation with suspected bacterial plant pathogens are suitable (see Chapters 1 and 16). Incubation of the plants under conditions of high relative humidity for 18-48h after inoculation is critical for symptom development.

III. *Xanthomonas campestris* Pathovars

Twenty-three pathovars of X. campestris are described below. Reference to the original descriptions of these and other pathovars are given by Dye et al. (1980). Their major hosts are listed by Dye and Lelliott (1974).

A. Xanthomonas campestris pv. alfalfae: Leaf Spot of Lucerne

Major Synonym. X. alfalfae (Riker, Jones & Davis 1935) Dowson 1943.

Symptoms. X. campestris pv. alfalfae (Riker et al. 1935) Dye 1978 causes small, round, watersoaked leaf spots with a light green to yellow marginal areas. The spots enlarge and become brown with a yellow centre. Leaf fall is associated with severe spotting. On stems, watersoaked

TABLE 9.1 *Physiological Tests for the Differentiation of* Xanthomonas *spp.*[a]

Test[b]	Species				
	X. albilineans	X. ampelina	X. axonopodis	X. campestris	X. fragariae
Growth at 36C	+	-	+	+	-
Mucoid growth on SPA	-	-	-	+	+
Milk proteolysis	-	-	-	+	-
Acid production from:					
arabinose	-	+	-	+	-
cellobiose	-	-	-	+	-
trehalose	-	-	+	+	-

a Data from Dye and Lelliott (1974) and Dye (1980).
b The methods of Dye (1962) are recommended. See Chapter 16 for details.

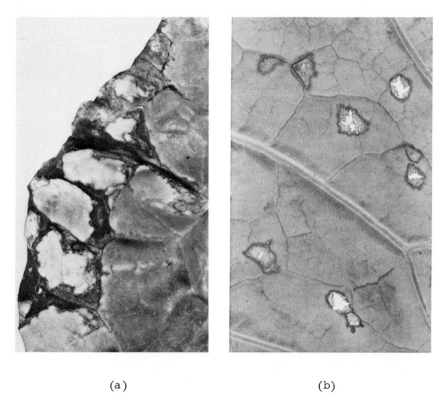

(a)   (b)

*FIGURE 9.1.   Black rot of crucifers caused by X. camp-
estris pv campestris: (a) hydathode infection and
(b) stomatal infection.*

or greasy, circular or elongated lesions with a dark purple
margin appear.   (Brigham, 1957; Moffett & Irwin, 1975;
Vock 1978).

   Host Range.   Occurs naturally on lucerne (Medicago
sativa).   Several other legumes are infected by artificial
inoculation (Moffett & Irwin, 1975).

   Geographical Distribution and Importance.   The disease
is widespread, occurring in Australia (Queensland and
northern New South Wales), Asia (India, Japan), Central
America (Nicaragua), Africa (Sudan), USA, (Iowa, Kansas,
Maryland, Wisconsin); Europe (Romania, USSR) (Bradbury,
1981a).

B. *Xanthomonas campestris pv. begoniae:* *Bacterial Wilt and Leaf Spot of Begonia.*

Major Synonym. X. begoniae (Takimoto 1934) Dowson 1939.

Symptoms. X. campestris pv. begoniae (Takimoto 1934) Dye 1978 causes minute circular to angular watersoaked spots on the leaves. The spots enlarge to dark green lesions up to 5 mm in diameter. As the lesions age, they dry to a brown, papery, angular spot with a greasy margin. The spots are more evident on the undersurface of the leaves. Lesions can also occur around the margins or along the veins resulting in distortion of the leaves. On the stems and petioles, dark green to brown, watersoaked streaks approximately 5 mm long by 1 mm wide appear. These lesions enlarge and become brown, and frequently have a central longitudinal split (Dye, 1963).

Host Range. Begonia spp.

Geographical Distribution and Importance. Widespread occurrence, including Australia, New Zealand, North America (Canada, USA), the West Indies, South America (Brazil), Asia (India, Japan), Middle East (Iran), Western Europe (Taylor et al., 1981).
   The disease can be particularly damaging in nurseries, when plants are grown under high humidity.

C. *Xanthomonas campestris pv. campestris:* *Black Rot of Crucifers.*

Major Synonym. X. campestis (Pammel 1895) Dowson 1939.

Symptoms. The initial symptoms caused by X. campestris pv. campestris (Pammel 1895) Dowson 1939 are yellow, v-shaped areas with dark veins at the margin of infected leaves. Affected areas dry and turn brown. The black veins may extend down the leaf into the petiole and the main stem (Fig. 9.1a). Certain strains, sometimes called X. campestris pv. aberrans (Knosel 1961) Dye 1978, invade via the stomates of the leaf lamina causing necrotic areas limited by the veins (Fig 9.1b). In some cases, the veins of the mid-rib are discoloured black (Moffett et al., 1976).
   In stems, the pathogen invades the vascular tissue. Where seed transmission results in systemic invasion of the vascular tissue, the young plant usually collapses before

reaching maturity. However, vascular invasion frequently follows infection via the hydathodes causing the vascular tissue to darken. A black ring of vascular tissue is apparent when a petiole or stem is cut transversely (Vock, 1978; Walker 1952, 1969).

Host Range. Principally <u>Brassica</u> spp. including broccoli (<u>B.</u> <u>oleracea</u> var. <u>italica</u>), Brussels sprouts (<u>B.</u> <u>oleracea</u> var. <u>gemmifera</u>), cabbage (<u>B.</u> <u>oleracea</u> var. <u>capitata</u>), cauliflower (<u>B.</u> <u>oleracea</u> var. <u>botrytis</u>, turnip (<u>B.</u> <u>rapa</u> var. <u>rapa</u>), radish (<u>Raphanus</u> <u>sativus</u>), shepherd's purse (<u>Capsella</u> <u>bursa-pastoris</u>), and stock (<u>Matthiola</u> <u>incana</u>), <u>Boerhavia</u> <u>erecta</u>, (Hayward & Waterston, 1965a; Simmonds, 1966; Young, 1969).

Geographical Distribution and Importance. Black rot occurs in crucifer growing areas throughout the world. The pathogen is seed borne and this has contributed to its wide distribution. In Australia, although hot water seed treatment at 52C for 30 min or 50C for 20 min (Vock 1978) has reduced the level of seed transmission and subsequently the severity of outbreaks of black rot, it is still an important disease of crucifers.

D. *Xanthomonas* *campestris* pv. *citri*: *Citrus Canker*.

Major Synonym. X. <u>citri</u> (Hasse 1915) Dowson 1939.

Symptoms. Citrus canker, caused by X. <u>campestris</u> pv. <u>citri</u> (Hasse 1915) Dye 1978, attacks all above-ground parts of the trees, particularly the young leaves, twigs, branches and fruit. On leaves, infection appears as small (1-3 mm), watersoaked spots. The spots enlarge and become raised and spongy with crater-like centres. Margins of spots are sharply defined, often with a yellow halo. Leaf spots may reach 6mm in diameter, but the average size is 3-4mm (Fig. 9.2a).
Lesions on shoots are rough, yellow-brown eruptions of the bark. They may merge to form continuous scabbed areas, leading to shoot death. Fruit lesions are firm and woody, often depressed at the centre and split by large cracks and are up to 2cm diameter (Fig. 9.2b). Severely infected fruit is heavily scabbed.

Host Range. Although early records give the pathogen a wide host range, the disease has only been reported on a

(a)   (b)

FIGURE 9.2.   Citrus canker, caused by X. campestris
pv. citri. (a) leaf lesions. (b) fruit lesions.

few genera (Citrus, Poncirus and Fortunella) during the
past 35 years. In Citrus, canker has been found on many
species and in descending order of susceptibility, the
species are grapefruit, lime, orange, lemon, tangerine and
mandarin (Elliott, 1951).

   Geographical Distribution and Importance.   Citrus
canker probably originated in South-East Asia and spread to
elsewhere in Asia, Africa, South America and Oceania
(Hayward & Waterston, 1964a).
   Citrus canker is the most serious disease of citrus in
the tropics and sub-tropics.

   Quarantine Precautions. Citrus canker has been
eradicated from northern Australia, New Zealand, South
Africa and Florida, USA. All citrus-exporting countries
without canker, including Australia, maintain a strict

prohibition on import of citrus plants and fruit unless from canker-free countries.

New citrus species and varieties may be imported into Australia only as seed. In <u>Citrus</u>, the presence of nucellar seedlings allows the propagation of material true to type. Citrus canker may also be seed-borne but application of a seed treatment together with establishment of seedlings in quarantine minimises this risk.

E. *Xanthomonas* *campestris* pv. *corylina:*   Bacterial Blight
   of Hazelnut.

Major Synonym.   X. <u>corylina</u> (Miller, Bollen, Simmons, Gross & Barss 1940) Starr & Burkholder 1942.

Symptoms.   (X. <u>campestris</u> pv. <u>corylina</u> Miller et al. 1940) Dye 1978 causes angular watersoaked spots on the leaves, 2-3 mm diameter, which turn reddish brown. On shoots and twigs, the lesions are slightly sunken, dark brown and oval-shaped (Wimalajeewa & Washington, 1980). Cankers may be formed which may girdle the stem. On the fruit, reddish brown spots (1-3mm diameter) are formed on the husks and superficial dark brown to black spots appear on the fruit.

Host Range.   <u>Corylus</u> <u>avellana</u> (hazelnut, filbert, cob-nut).

Geographical Distribution and Importance.   Reported from U.S.A., U.K., Turkey and France (Locke & Barnes, 1979). In Australia, the disease occurs in Victoria (Wimalajeewa & Washington, 1980) where it is not considered an important disease.

F. *X. campestris* pv. *cucurbitae:*   Bacterial Spot
   of Pumpkin

Major Synonym.   X. <u>cucurbitae</u> (Bryan 1926) Dowson 1939).

Symptoms.   X. <u>campestris</u> pv. <u>cucurbitae</u> (Bryan 1926) Dye 1978 causes small, brown or yellow angular leaf spots, 1-2 mm wide. Where spots occur together segments of the leaf brown and die. Infection frequently occurs at the leaf margin causing necrosis. On fruit, circular, greasy spots form, with a yellow crust of dried ooze over the

(a)   (b)

*FIGURE 9.3.   (a) X. campestris pv. cucurbitae causing
bacterial spot of pumpkin (fruit and seed infection).
(b) X. campestris pv. glycines causing bacterial
pustule of soybean.*

centre of the spot.   Invasion of the fruit flesh extends to
the fruit cavity, resulting in seed contamination (Fig.
9.3a) (McLean, 1958,   Vock, 1978).

Host Range.   Pumpkin (*Cucurbita maxima*);   watermelon
(*Citrullis lanatus* var. *caffer*);   rockmelon (*Cucumis
melo*);   cucumber (*Cucumis sativus*);   zucchini (*Cucurbita
pepo*).

Geographical Distribution and Importance.   Bacterial
spot occurs in Australia (particularly in the Lockyer
Valley of south-east Queensland) and other cucurbit-growing
countries.

G. *Xanthomonas* campestris pv. *glycines:*   Bacterial Pustule
   of Soybean

Major Synonyms.   X. glycines (Nakano 1919) Magrou &
Prevot 1948; X. phaseoli var. sojense   (Hedges 1922) Starr &
Burkholder 1942.

Symptoms.   X. campestris pv. glycines (Nakano 1919) Dye
1978 causes small, yellow leaf spots with light-brown
centres (Fig. 9.3b).   A raised brown pustule develops at
the centre of each spot, especially on the under surface.
Pustules collapse with age.   Tan pustules occur on infected
stems (Hedges, 1924;   Vock, 1978).

Host Range.   Soybean (Glycine max).

Geographical Distribution and Importance.   Bacterial
pustule is widespread in soybean-growing countries,
including Australia.

H. *Xanthomonas* campestris pv. *holcicola:*   Bacterial Streak
   of Sorghum and Maize.

Major Synonyms.   X. holcicola (Elliott 1930) Starr &
Burkholder 1942.

Symptoms.   X. campestris pv. holcicola (Elliott 1930)
Dye 1978 causes long, narrow watersoaked leaf streaks up to
33m wide and 20cm long.   These become reddish brown and are
frequently covered by a creamy scale of dried bacterial
exudate.   Streaks coalesce to form irregular areas, destroying most of the leaf (Fig. 9.4a) (Watson, 1971, Vock, 1978).
Although X. campestris pv. holcicola cross inoculates with
hosts of the X. campestris pv. translucens group, symptoms
are distinct (Moffett & McCarthy, 1973).

Host Range.   Sorghum spp. (cultivated species and weed
hosts) and maize (Zea mays).

Geographical Distribution and Importance.   Prevalent
in most sorghum growing regions of the world including
Australia and New Zealand.   In Queensland the disease is
common on sorghum and maize.

I. <u>Xanthomonas</u> <u>campestris</u> pv. <u>incanae</u>: *Bacterial Blight of Stock.*

Major Synonyms. <u>X</u>.<u>incanae</u> (Kendrick & Baker 1942) Starr & Weiss 1943.

Symptoms. <u>X</u>.<u>campestris</u> pv. <u>incanae</u> (Kendrick & Baker 1942) Dye 1978 affects the vascular system of the main stem of stock. It often extends into the leaf petiole causing the leaves to yellow, followed by a sudden wilt. The vascular tissue becomes black and the discolouration extends into the cortical tissue particularly at the node. Irregular, external, black lesions may extend longitudinally along the stem. The plant wilts and collapses (Kendrick & Baker, 1942). The pathogen is seed borne and the disease commonly occurs in home gardens where seedlings are raised from seed which has not been hot water treated.

Host Range. Stock (<u>Matthiola</u> <u>incana</u>).

Geographical Distribution and Importance. Australia, New Zealand, North America, amongst others. The disease may cause significant losses to flower producers if seed borne infection occurs.

J. <u>Xanthomonas</u> <u>campestris</u> pv. <u>juglandis</u>: *Walnut Bacterial Blight.*

Major Synonym. <u>X</u>.<u>juglandis</u> (Pierce 1901) Dowson 1939.

Symptoms. <u>X</u>.<u>campestris</u> pv. <u>juglandis</u> (Pierce 1901) Dye 1978 attacks young growth of fruit, buds, leaves and twigs but not branches of one or more years of age. Small dark brown or black, round or angular spots are formed on leaves, young nuts and green twigs (Fig. 9.4b) (Miller et al., 1940).

Host Range. Walnut <u>Juglans</u> <u>regia</u>; <u>J</u>.<u>ailantifolia</u>, <u>J</u>.<u>ailantifolia</u> var. <u>cordiformis</u>, <u>J</u>.<u>californica</u>, <u>J</u>.<u>cinerea</u>, <u>J</u>.<u>hindsii</u>, <u>J</u>.<u>nigra</u> (Bradbury, 1967).

Geographical Distribution and Importance. Walnut bacterial blight is widespread, in parts of Australia, New Zealand, Europe, North and South America, Africa and Asia (Bradbury, 1967). In Australia, the disease is of moderate

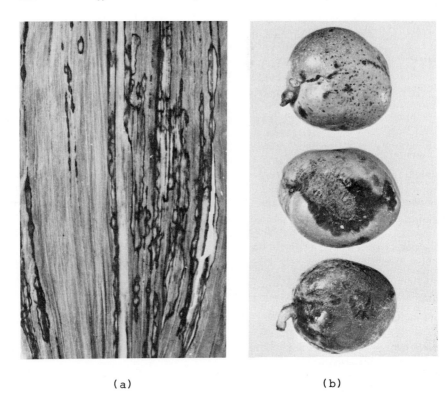

(a)   (b)

FIGURE 9.4.   (a) Bacterial streak of sorghum, caused
by X. campestris pv. holcicola. (b) Fruit symptoms
of walnut bacterial blight (X. campestris pv.
juglandis).

importance   in   New   South   Wales,   Victoria   and   Western
Australia, and is a serious disease in Tasmania.

K. *Xanthomonas campestris* pv. *malvacearum*:   Bacterial
   Blight of Cotton.

   Major Synonym. X. malvacearum (Smith 1901) Dowson 1939.

   Symptoms.   Angular   water   soaked   leaf   spots,   which
become brown, are the most common symptom of bacterial
blight caused by X. campestris pv. malvacearum (Smith 1901)
Dye 1978 (Fig. 9.5a).   Lesions may also extend into veins
which   blacken.   The   leaf   phase   triggers   premature
defoliation.   Boll infections develop as greasy circular

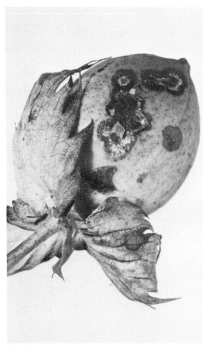

(a)   (b)

*FIGURE 9.5.   Bacterial blight of cotton caused by
X. campestris pv. malvacearum: (a)   leaf symptoms.
(b)   boll and bract symptoms.*

spots on carpels which blacken with age (Fig. 9.5b). Infection at the base of carpels may prevent boll maturation.
Secondary bollrots are commonly associated with blight
lesions.   Severe early phases of the disease may kill
seedlings or result in lesions termed "black arm" which
girdle and blacken the stem.   This often causes extensive
defoliation and boll loss (Davis & Sandridge, 1977; Bird et
al., 1981).

Host Range.   Cotton (Gossypium hirsutum, G. barbadense),
kapok tree (Ceiba pentandra, Hibiscus vitifolius, Thurberia
thespesioides, Jatropha curcas, (Hayward & Waterston 1964b).

Geographical Distribution and Importance.   Bacterial
blight is one of the most serious diseases of cotton
throughout the world in regions with summer rains.   In

Australia, it occurs in all cotton-growing districts. The severity varies from year to year and from planting to planting in a particular district but losses of 10% have been estimated. Acid-delinting of the seed reduces external seed transmission, with significant reduction of seedling blight and "black arm" symptoms, but the organism is also borne internally. The pathogen survives many years in dry cotton debris.

L. *Xanthomonas campestris* pv. *mangiferaeindicae*: Black Spot of Mango.

Major Synonyms.   Pseudomonas mangiferaeindicae Patel, Moniz & Kulkarni 1948.

Symptoms.   X. campestris pv. mangiferaeindicae (Patel, Moniz & Kulkarni 1948) Robbs, Ribeiro & Kimura 1974 causes black, raised angular areas on the leaves. These are restricted by the veins and frequently surrounded by a yellow margin (Fig. 9.6a). The lesions may extend from the mid-rib to the leaf margin. On fruit, black, oval, raised areas with star-shaped cracks appear (Fig. 9.6b). Black stem cankers are filled with gummy exudate (Moffett et al., 1979; Steyn et al., 1974).

Host Range: Mango (Mangifera indica).

Geographical Distribution and Importance.   Australia, South Africa, India, Reunion Is. In Australia, black spot is present in all mango growing areas but is severe only in restricted plantings, on susceptible varieties.

M. *Xanthomonas campestris* pv. *manihotis*: Cassava Bacterial Blight.

Major Synonym.   X. manihotis (Arthaud-Berthet & Bondar 1915) Starr 1946.

Symptoms.   X. campestris pv. manihotis (Arthaud-Berthet & Bondar 1915) Dye 1978 causes angular leaf spots, leaf blight, wilting, defoliation and tip die back of cassava (Fig. 9.7).

Isolation.   Colonies are white, domed and mucoid on SPA and nutrient agar. Yellow-pigmented colonies occur in

(a)   (b)

FIGURE 9.6.   Black spot of mango caused by X. campestris
pv. mangiferaeindicae: a) leaf lesions.   b) fruit
lesions.

a closely-related pathovar, X. campestris pv. cassavae,
which is also isolated from water-soaked, leaf spots on
cassava.   Some evidence suggests that pv. cassavae may be a
yellow variant of pv. manihotis (Persley, 1980).

   Host Range.   Cassava (Manihot esculenta) and other
Manihot spp.

   Geographical Distribution and Importance.   Widespread
and damaging in many countries in South and Central America
and Africa (Lozano, 1975).   It also occurs in Asia, but
appears to be less severe, with the exception of Indonesia.
In Africa, the disease is more damaging in the savanna and
forest-savanna transition zone than in the forest (Persley,
1977, 1980).   This may be related to the fact that the

(a)   (b)

FIGURE 9.7. Cassava bacterial blight caused by X. campestris pv. manihotis showing (a) angular, water-soaked leaf spots and (b) defoliation and tip die-back.

pathogen survives longer in plant debris in the drier zones than in the wet forest environment (Persley, 1980).

Quarantine Precautions. The pathogen is disseminated in vegetative cuttings and the import of vegetative material comes under quarantine control. As the pathogen can also be seed-borne (Persley, 1979), true seed to be imported into Australia is hot water treated (60C/20 min) and grown in an insect-screened greenhouse for observation.

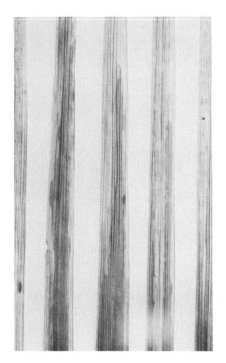 

(a)   (b)

FIGURE 9.8.   (a) Bacterial blight of rice caused
by X. campestris pv. oryzae; (b) Bacterial leaf streak
of rice caused by X. campestris pv. oryzicola.

N. Xanthomonas campestris pv. oryzae: Bacterial Blight
     of Rice.

   Major Synonym.   X. oryzae (Ishiyama 1922) Dowson 1943.

   Symptoms.   X. campestris pv. oryzae (Ishiyama 1922) Dye
1978, commonly causes on leaves of young rice plants
watersoaked streaks at the margins.   These enlarge and
coalesce to give yellowish lesions with wavy edges which
may extend to cover most of the leaf, which turns white or
greyish and dies. These symptoms differ from early symptoms
of bacterial leaf streak of rice,   X. campestris pv.
oryzicola (Fig. 9.8b) (see section S).   Leaf sheaths may
also be affected by bacterial blight. The "kresek" syndrome,
which occurs in tropical regions, is a strong systemic
infection in which leaves of young rice plants wither and

die (Ou, 1972; Aldrick et al., 1973). Advanced infections of leaf streak are difficult to distinguish from blight.

Host Range. Cultivated and wild rice (O. sativa, O. rufipogon, O. australiensis). Natural infection occurs on weeds (Leersia oryzoides, L. oryzoides var. japonica, Zizania latifolia in Japan and Leptochloa spp. and Cyperus spp. in the tropics (Bradbury, 1970a).

Geographical Distribution and Importance. Widespread in Asia, where bacterial blight increased in importance after the widespread cultivation of high-yielding, dwarf varieties of rice in the 1960's. Bacterial blight has been reported recently from South America (Lozano, 1977) and Africa (Buddenhagen, et al., 1979). The disease is of major importance in monsoonal climates.

Bacterial blight occurs on wild and cultivated rice in north-western Australia (Aldrick et al., 1973 but not in the major rice-growing areas in North Queensland and New South Wales. Strict quarantine precautions are maintained on the import of rice seed into Australia and on the movement of seed within the country.

O. *Xanthomonas campestris* pv. *phaseoli: Common Blight of Bean.*

Major Synonyms. X. phaseoli (Smith 1897) Dowson 1939; X. phaseoli var. fuscans (Burkholder 1930) Starr & Burkholder 1942.

Symptoms. X. campestris pv. phaseoli (Smith 1897) Dye 1978 causes small, angular, watersoaked leaf-spots, which coalesce to form large, brown, necrotic areas, frequently with a bright yellow margin (Fig. 9.9a); on stems, dark green, watersoaked streaks become brown; on pods, watersoaked spots appear with a yellow ooze from the centre, later becoming sunken and reddish brown (Fig. 9.9b). The pod lesions on bean are often difficult to distinguish from those of halo blight (Pseudomonas syringae pv. phaseolicola (Walker, 1969; Vock, 1978).

Host Range. French and navy beans (Phaseolus vulgaris); mung bean (Vigna radiata); black gram (Vigna mungo); Phasey bean (Macroptilium lathyroides); Lablab niger.

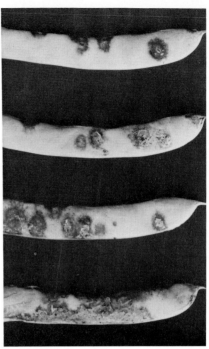

(a)   (b)

FIGURE 9.9. Common blight of bean, caused by
X. campestris *pv.* phaseoli*. (a) leaf symptoms and*
(b) pod symptoms.

Geographical   Distribution   and   Importance.   Common
blight occurs in most countries where beans are grown
commercially.   In Australia, it is widespread (Queensland,
New South Wales, Western Australia, Victoria) and of
moderate importance.   The disease is seed-borne but can be
controlled by the use of disease-free seed (Hayward &
Waterston, 1965b).

P. *Xanthomonas campestris* pv. *pruni*
    Bacterial Spot of Stone Fruit.

Major Synonym. X. *pruni* (Smith 1903) Dowson 1939.

Symptoms.   X. *campestris* pv.   *pruni* (Smith 1903) Dye
1978 causes small, circular to angular, watersoaked leaf
spots, which dry to dark brown to purple spots and separate

(a)   (b)

FIGURE 9.10. *Bacterial spot of stone fruit caused by X. campestris pv. pruni. Lesions on (a) peach fruit; (b) plum fruit.*

from the surrounding tissues, to form a "shot hole" lesion. Where lesions are close together, the surrounding tissue yellows and leaf fall frequently occurs. On twigs, greasy, dark green, elongated areas occur, which develop into sunken, tan cankers. On peach fruit, tan pinpoint spots appear, which crack to form pits on the fruit surface, often with associated gumming (Fig 9.10a). On plum fruit, circular, large, greasy spots occur which darken to black lesions, with central cracking as the fruit enlarges (Fig 9.10b) (Anderson, 1956; Vock, 1978).

Host Range. Prunus spp. including apricot (Prunus armeniaca), cherry (P. avium), almond (P. dulcis), peach and nectarine (P. persica) and Japanese plum (P. salicina) (Hayward & Waterston, 1965c).

Geographical Distribution and Importance. Bacterial spot has been recorded from most countries where stone fruit are grown (Hayward & Waterston, 1965c).

In Australia, bacterial spot is the most important bacterial disease of stone fruit in Queensland, and is also present in Western Australia, New South Wales and Victoria.

Q. Xanthomonas campestris pv. ricini: Bacterial Leaf Spot of Castor.

Major Synonyms. X. ricini (Yoshii & Takimoto 1928) Dowson 1939; X. ricinicola (Elliott 1930) Dowson 1939; X. anandensis Desai & Shah 1963.

Symptoms. X. campestris pv. ricini (Yoshii & Takimoto 1928) Dye 1978 causes angular leaf spots which can lead to premature leaf fall (Sabet, 1959).

Host Range. Castor (Ricinus communis).

Geographical Distribution and Importance. Bacterial leaf spot of castor is widely distributed in Africa, Asia, America and Europe, but has not been recorded in Australia. Most African isolates are white, while those from other areas are yellow (Bradbury, 1973b).

R. Xanthomonas campestris pv. sesami: Bacterial Blight of Sesame.

Major Synonym. X. sesami Sabet & Dowson 1960.

Symptoms. X. campestris pv. sesami (Sabet & Dowson 1960) Dye 1978 causes dark, olive green leaf spots which increase in size to 2-3 mm and become dark red-brown to black. The spots coalesce to cover large portions of a leaf. Stems and capsules may also be affected, with oval, slightly raised, dark red-brown lesions.

Host Range. Sesame (Sesamum indicum)

Geographical Distribution. Sudan, India and Venezuela (Bradbury, 1981b).

Quarantine   Precautions.   Seed   introduced   into Australia is hot water treated and sown in quarantine for observation.

S. *Xanthomonas campestris* pv. *translucens and Related Pathovars: Translucent Leaf Stripe of Cereals and Related Grasses.*

Major   Synonyms   and   Associations.   X. campestris   pv. translucens (Jones, Johnson & Reddy 1917) Dye 1978 (formerly X. translucens (Jones et al. 1917) Dowson 1939) includes a number of races (or special forms), some with overlapping host ranges on artificial inoculation (Dye & Lelliott, 1974).   Six races have been given separate pathovar status (Dye et al., 1980): X. campestris pv. cerealis (Hagborg 1942) Dye 1978 (syn. X. translucens f. sp. cerealis Hagborg 1942) from Agropyron spp., Bromus spp.; X. campestris pv. hordei (Hagborg 1942) Dye 1978 (syn. X. translucens f. sp. hordei Hagborg 1942) from barley (Hordeum spp.); X. campestris pv. oryzicola (Fang et al. 1957) Dye 1978 (syn X. translucens f. sp. oryzicola (Fang et al. 1957) Bradbury 1971, X. oryzicola Fang et al. from rice; X. campestris pv. phleipratensis (Wallin & Reddy 1945) Dye 1978 (syn. X. translucens f.sp. phleipratensis (Wallin & Reddy 1945) from Phleum pratense; X. campestris pv. secalis (Reddy, Godkin & Johnson 1924) Dye 1978 (syn. X. translucens f.sp. secalis (Reddy, Godkin & Johnson 1924) from rye (Secale cereale); X. campestris pv. undulosa (Smith, Jones & Reddy 1919) Dye 1978 (syn. X. translucens f.sp. undulosa (Smith, Jones & Reddy 1919) from wheat (Triticum spp.).

Symptoms.   The disease is characterized on all hosts by the production of water soaked lesions, generally elongated, which remain translucent for a long time before drying and frequently exude small droplets of ooze which dry to a yellow crust (Dowson, 1957; Dye & Lelliott, 1974).   Necrosis follows and lesions usually dry to a brown stripe pattern (Fig. 9.8b).   On wheat, elongated dark brown stripes appear on the glumes ("black chaff").   Similar symptoms, termed "physiological black chaff", occur on some wheat cultivars and superficially resemble the bacterial disease (Fig. 9.11a).

Host Range.   The major natural host range for each pathovar is listed above.   In addition Moffett & McCarthy (1973) have described X. campestris pv. translucens (possibly

 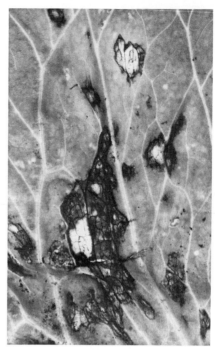

(a)   (b)

FIGURE 9.11. (a) X. campestris pv. translucens
causing bacterial black chaff of wheat; (b) X.
campestris pv. vitians causing dry leaf spot of lettuce.

X. campestris pv, cerealis) on Japanese millet (Echinochloa
utilis).

Identification. It cannot be assumed that isolation of a
xanthomonad exhibiting typical symptoms from one of the
above hosts is sufficient to place an isolate in one of the
above pathovars. Barley in particular may be infected by
more than one pathovar. Dye & Lelliott (1974) describe
host ranges on cross inoculation.

Geographical   Distribution   and   Importance.   Most
pathovars have wide distributions although problems of
identification and nomenclature have confused records.
Formerly most occurences were recorded as X. translucens and
sometimes as special forms ot X. translucens. Identification
to the present pathovar system would require host range

testing in most cases. Bacterial leaf streak of rice
caused by X. campestris pv. oryzicola is widespread in most
rice producing countries. It is generally far less
important than X. campestris pv. oryzae (see Section N).
The disease has been reported in Australia from the
Northern Territory but not from Queensland or New South
Wales.

X. campestris pv. undulosa occurs in most wheat growing
regions of the world and is reported from New South Wales
Resistant cultivars have reduced the importance of this
disease. The disease on Japanese millet in Queensland is
of moderate importance in wet seasons. Other pathovars
have not been confirmed on host range tests as present in
Australia but may occur as minor diseases.

T. *Xanthomonas campestris* pv. *vasculorum:* *Gumming Disease*
   of Sugarcane.

Major Synonym. X. vasculorum (Cobb 1893) Dowson 1939.

Symptoms. X. campestris pv. vasculorum (Cobb 1893) Dye
1978 causes chlorotic leaf stripes which may become
necrotic. The pathogen invades the vascular tissues of the
stem producing dark areas and bacterial slime. In
susceptible varieties, yellow bacterial slime may form
below the terminal bud, leading to the death of the top of
the plant (Hughes, 1961).

Host Range. Sugarcane (Saccharum inter-specific
hybrids); also occurs naturally on maize (Zea mays);
Dictyosperma album, Thysanolaena maxima, Roystonea regia
and Areca catechu (Bradbury, 1973c).

Geographical Distribution and Importance. Gumming
disease is widespread in many sugarcane-growing countries.
The history of gumming disease of sugarcane in Australia
was highlighted by the occurrence of sporadic epidemics
which caused severe losses (Hughes, 1961). Gumming disease
was a serious disease in the early years of the Australian
sugar industry but has not been observed for many years and
is presumed to be eradicated.

Quarantine Precautions. Vegetative material of
sugarcane is grown in quarantine for two years after
introduction to Australia, to avoid the introduction of
gumming and other diseases of sugarcane.

U. **Xanthomonas** **campestris** pv. **vesicatoria**:   Bacterial Spot
of Tomato and Capsicum.

Major Synonym.   X.**vesicatoria** (Doidge 1920) Dowson 1939.

Symptoms.   X.**campestris** pv. **vesicatoria** (Doidge 1920)
Dye 1978 causes irregular greasy spots on leaves and stems,
which become dark tan to black, frequently with yellow
margins (Fig. 9.12a). The leaves yellow and fall.   Fruit
spots are circular, tan, up to 8 mm wide, slightly sunken
with a central scab (Fig. 9.12b). (Mingtan & Watson, 1973,
Vock 1978).

Host   Range.   Wide   host   range,   including   tomato
(**Lycopersicon** **esculentum**), capsicum (**Capsicum** **annuum**), cape
gooseberry (**Physalis** **peruviana**), wild gooseberry (**P** **minima**),
(Hayward & Waterston, 1964c).

Geographical Distribution and Importance.   Widespread
in Australia, Europe, North and South America and Africa
(Hayward & Waterston, 1964c).   In Australia, bacterial spot
is widespread in tomato and capsicum growing areas along
the east coast.   Bacterial spot causes losses on tomatoes
and, more frequently, on capsicum in Queensland.

V. **Xanthomonas** **campestris** pv. **vitians**:   Dry Leaf Spot of
Lettuce.

Major Synonym.   X.**vitians** (Brown 1918) Dowson 1943.

Symptoms.   X.**campestris** pv. **vitians** (Brown 1918) Dye
1978 causes leaf spots which are angular, watersoaked and
dry to become light-brown and papery.   Where large numbers
of spots occur close together, the surrounding tissue
becomes brown and dies (Schroth et al., 1964;   Vock, 1978).

Host Range.   Lettuce (**Lactuca** **sativa**).

Geographical   Distribution   and   Importance.   The
pathogen is widespread in many countries.   In Australia the
disease occurs in most lettuce growing areas of Queensland
and in restricted plantings in other states.   The dry leaf
spot   may   be   prevalent   during   wet   weather   causing
significant market losses. See also the associated diseases,
Pseudomonas **virdiflava**, **P**. **cichorii** and **P**. **marginalis**, which
are described in Chapter 8.

(a)   (b)

FIGURE 9.12.   Bacterial spot of tomato caused by
X. campestris pv. vesicatoria: (a) leaf lesions;
(b) fruit lesions.

W. Xanthomonas campestris pv. zinniae: Bacterial Leaf Spot
of Zinnia.

Major Synonym.   X. nigromaculans f.sp. zinniae Hopkins &
Dowson 1949.

Symptoms.   X. campestris pv. zinniae (Hopkins & Dowson
1949) Dye 1978 causes leaf lesions which are irregularly
angular to circular, reddish to dark brown, 1-4 mm diameter
and surrounded by a prominent yellow halo.   The plant
collapses when the growing tips of seedlings are affected
(Sleesman et al., 1973).   The host range is restricted to
zinnia (Zinnia elegans).

Geographical Distribution and Importance.   The disease
occurs world wide, due to seed borne distribution.   It may
cause extensive damage to nursery plantings.

IV.   *Xanthomonas albilineans*: Leaf Scald of Sugarcane

A. Major Synonym.

<u>Pseudomonas</u> <u>albilineans</u> (Ashby 1929) Krasil'nikov 1949.

B. Symptoms.

<u>X</u>. <u>albilineans</u> (Ashby 1929) Dowson 1943 is the cause of leaf scald of sugarcane. The disease can occur in either a chronic or acute form. In the chronic phase, the characteristic symptoms are narrow, white "pencil-line" stripes on leaf blades and sheaths (Fig. 9.13a); stunted stalks with stiff upward and inward curling leaves, scalded at the tips; chlorosis on some leaves; profuse side-shooting (Fig. 9.13b), which begin from the base of the stalks; and internal reddening of the vascular bundles in the nodal regions of the stalk. The acute phase is characterised by the sudden death of affected cane. This may be followed by extensive formation of side-shoots (Martin & Robinson, 1961).

C. Host Range

Sugarcane (<u>Saccharum</u> interspecific hybrids). <u>X</u>. <u>albilineans</u> has been recorded as a natural infection on grasses in Australia, particularly blady grass (<u>Imperata</u> <u>cylindrica</u> var. <u>major</u>, <u>Brachiaria</u> <u>piligera</u>, <u>Paspalum</u> <u>conjugatum</u> and <u>Paspalum</u> <u>dilatatum</u> (Persley, 1973). Sweet corn (<u>Zea</u> <u>mays</u> convar. <u>saccharata</u>) is particularly susceptible on inoculation, and can be used for rapid pathogenicity tests (Persley, 1972).

D. Geographical Distribution and Importance. Leaf scald is widespread and damaging, in most sugarcane growing countries. In Australia, it occurs in most sugarcane districts in coastal Queensland and northern New South Wales. The disease can be controlled by the use of resistant varieties.

(a)   (b)

FIGURE 9.13. *Leaf scald of sugarcane caused by*
Xanthomonas albilineans: (a) 'pencil-lines' on leaves,
(b) profuse formation of side-shoots.

E. Isolation.

X. albilineans can be isolated from the "pencil-lines"
stripes on the leaves or the internal tissue of infected
stalks.   The recommended isolation medium is SPA plus
100ppm cycloheximide (Persley, 1972).   Minute, circular,
translucent, moist, shining, honey-yellow colonies appear
in 5-7 days.

F. Serological Diagnosis.

Techniques have been developed for serological diagnosis
of X. albilineans, using either a variation of the enzyme-
linked immunosorbent assay (ELISA) of Clark & Adams (1977),
immunofluorescence (Leoville & Coleno, 1975) or micro-
agglutination (Ricaud et al., 1978).

The ELISA method of Clark and Adams (1977) has been modified in Queensland to detect X. albilineans. Specimens are assayed by preparing an exudate of leaf pieces (sections 6 x 1 cm, cut into 2-3 mm x 10 mm pieces) which are incubated for 2 h at 28C in 2-3 ml of PBS-Tween. Alternatively a vascular extract is prepared by drawing 2 ml of PBS-Tween through the vascular cells of an internode of a stalk under vacuum. Extracts from healthy and known diseased plants are prepared in the same way to act as controls. Details of the procedure are given in Table 9.2.

TABLE 9.2   Diagnosis of Xanthomonas albilineans by the ELISA method[a].

---

1. Coat wells of micro-titre plate with 0.2 ml 1/1000 guinea pig antisera to X. albilineans diluted in coating buffer. Incubate overnight at 4-6C.
2. Wash three times with PBS-Tween.
3. Add 0.2 ml of test sample, incubate 4-6h at 37C.
4. Wash three times with PBS-Tween.
5. Add 0.2 ml 1/100 rabbit antisera to X. albilineans diluted in PBS-Tween and incubate overnight at 4-6C.
6. Wash three times in PBS-Tween
7. Add 0.2 ml 1/500 alkaline phosphatase anti-rabbit IgG (goat) diluted in PBS-Tween. Incubate 4-6 h at 37C.
8. Wash three times in PBS-Tween.
9. Add 0.25 ml 1mg/ml 2-nitrophenyl phosphate in buffer. Incubate at room temperature 30 min.
10. Stop reaction by adding 0.05 ml 3M NaOH.
11. A positive reaction can be seen as a dark yellow colour change. The result can be read visually or with a spectrophotometer.

---

[a]   ELISA, enzyme-linked immunosorbent assay. See Clark & Adams (1977) for details of method and composition of recommended buffers.

The threshold of sensitivity of the modified ELISA technique to detect X. albilineans is comparable to the threshold of sensitivity for plant inoculation. However, the ELISA technique had the advantage of giving results in 36 h compared with 3-4 wk for isolation and plant inoculation. The ELISA technique can also be used to diagnose acute-stage infection, where isolation is not possible due to saprophytic contamination.

V. *Xanthomonas ampelina*: Bacterial Blight of Grapevine

A. Symptoms. X. ampelina Panagopoulus 1969 affects buds, spurs, young shoots, petioles, flowers, fruit, stalks and leaves. The most characteristic symptom is the formation of cankers on spurs, young shoots and branches.

B. Host Range. Grapevine (Vitis vinifera).

C. Geographical Distribution and Importance. Bacterial blight is an important disease of grapevines in Greece, France, and South Africa (Bradbury, 1973a). In Australia all introductions of grapevine propagating material are hot water treated and grown in quarantine for inspection, to avoid the inadvertent introduction of the disease.

VI. *Xanthomonas axonopodis*: Gummosis of Imperial Pasture Grass

A. Symptoms.

X. axonopodis Starr & Garces 1950 infects Imperial and Micay pasture grasses. Diseased stems are elongated and partly bare, with a few pale yellow leaves at the top, giving them a characteristic 'flag-like' appearance. Pale stripes run between the main veins on many affected leaves. Diseased stems show internal red-brown vascular discoloration at the nodes, when sliced longitudinally (Bradbury, 1977a).

The host range is restricted to Axonopus scoparius, A. micay, A. compressus and A. affinis.

FIGURE 9.14. *Angular leaf spot of strawberry caused by* Xanthomonas fragariae, *showing leaf symptoms.*

VII. *Xanthomonas fragariae*: Angular Leaf Spot of Strawberry

A. *Symptoms*

X. fragariae Kennedy & King 1962 causes watersoaked, angular spots on the leaf undersurfaces, which coalesce to form irregular, reddish-brown spots observable on the upper surface. These areas dry, giving a ragged appearance to the leaf (Fig. 9.14). Petioles, runners and flowers may also be blighted (Kennedy & King 1962; Dye & Wilkie, 1973). The host range is restricted to strawberry (Fragaria x ananassa).

B. *Geographical Distribution and Importance.*

Restricted to Australia, New Zealand, USA, Venezuela, Sicily (Bradbury, 1977b). In Australia, the disease occurred in 1975 in restricted plantings in New South Wales following release of strawberry runners from quarantine. The disease was eradicated and no outbreaks have been recorded since then (McGechan & Fahy, 1976).

VIII. *Xanthomonas populi* (inv.): Bacterial Canker of Poplar

A. *Major Synonym.* <u>Aplanobacter</u> <u>populi</u> Ridé 1958
(originally <u>Aplanobacterium.</u>)

B. *Symptoms.* <u>X. populi</u> (inv.) Ridé & Ridé 1978 initially
infects young branches as slightly swollen areas with
superficial cracks from which may ooze a dense mucous in
spring. Large cankers may develop at these sites over
several seasons or secondary invasion of cankers may lead
to the death of the affected branch (Ridé & Ridé, 1978).

C. *Host Range.* Poplar (<u>Populus</u> spp.)

D. *Geographical Distribution.* Northern and central
Europe. The disease does not extend to warmer regions of
Europe.

References

Aldrick S., Buddenhagen, I.W. & Reddy, A.P.K. (1973).
    The occurrence of bacterial leaf blight in wild and
    cultivated rice in Northern Australia. <u>Australian</u>
    <u>Journal of Agricultural Research</u> 24, 219-227.
Anderson, H.W. (1956). Disease of drupe or stonefruits.
    In "Diseases of Fruit Crops", pp.189-261. New York:
    McGraw-Hill.
Bird, L.S., Brinkerhoff, L.A. & Davis, R.G. (1981).
    Bacterial blight. In "Compendium of Cotton Diseases",
    pp.25-28. (Ed. G.M. Watkins). St Paul, Minnesota:
    American Phytopathological Society.
Bradbury, J.F. (1967). <u>Xanthomonas juglandis.</u> <u>C.M.I.</u>
    <u>Descriptions of Pathogenic Fungi and Bacteria</u> No.130.
    Kew: Commonwealth Mycological Institute.
Bradbury, J.F. (1970a). <u>Xanthomonas oryzae.</u> <u>C.M.I.</u>
    <u>Descriptions of Pathogenic Fungi and Bacteria</u> No.239.
    Kew: Commonwealth Mycological Institute.
Bradbury, J.F. (1970b). <u>Xanthomonas oryzicola.</u> <u>C.M.I.</u>
    <u>Descriptions of Pathogenic Fungi and Bacteria</u> No.240.
    Kew: Commonwealth Mycological Institute.

Bradbury, J.F. (1973a). Xanthomonas ampelina. CMI
  Descriptions of Pathogenic Fungi and Bacteria No.378.
  Kew: Commonwealth Mycological Institute.
Bradbury, J.F. (1973b). Xanthomonas ricini. CMI
  Descriptions of Pathogenic Fungi and Bacteria No.379.
  Kew: Commonwealth Mycological Institute.
Bradbury, J.F. (1973c). Xanthomonas vasculorum. CMI
  Descriptions of Pathogenic Fungi and Bacteria No.380.
  Kew: Commonwealth Mycological Institute.
Bradbury, J.F. (1977a). Xanthomonas axonopodis. CMI
  Descriptions of Pathogenic Fungi and Bacteria No.557.
  Kew: Commonwealth Mycological Institute.
Bradbury, J.F. (1977b). Xanthomonas fragariae. CMI
  Descriptions of Pathogenic Fungi and Bacteria.
  No.558. Kew: Commonwealth Mycological Institute.
Bradbury, J.F. (1981a). Xanthomonas campestris pv. alfal-
  fae. CMI Descriptions of Pathogenic Fungi and Bacteria
  No.698. Kew: Commonwealth Mycological Institute.
Bradbury, J.F. (1981b). Xanthomonas campestris pv. sesami.
  CMI Descriptions of Pathogenic Fungi and Bacteria
  No.700. Kew: Commonwealth Mycological Institute.
Brigham, R.D. (1957). Stem lesions associated with
  Xanthomonas alfalfae. Phytopathology 47, 309-310.
Buddenhagen, I.W. Buong, H.H. & Ba, D.D. (1979). Bacterial
  leaf blight found in Africa. International Rice
  Research Institute Newsletter 4(1),11.
Clark, M.F. & Adams A.N. (1977). Characteristics of the
  microplate method of enzyme-linked immunosorbent assay
  for the detection of plant viruses. Journal of General
  Virology 34, 475-483.
Davis R.G. & Sandridge, T.L. (1977). Epidemiology of
  bacterial blight of cotton. Mississippi Agricultural
  and Forestry Experiment Station Technical Bulletin 88.
De Ley, J., Segers, P. & Gillis, M. (1978). Intra and
  intergeneric similarities of Chromobacterium and
  Janthinobacterium Ribonucleic Acid Cistrons. International Journal of Systematic Bacteriology 28, 154-168.
Dowson, W.J. (1957). "Plant Diseases Due to Bacteria". 2nd
  edition. Cambridge University Press, 232pp.
Dye, D.W. (1962). The inadequacy of the usual determinative tests for the identification of Xanthomonas
  spp. New Zealand Journal of Science 5, 393-416.
Dye, D.W. (1963). Xanthomonas begoniae (Takimoto 1934)
  Dowson 1939, in New Zealand. New Zealand Journal of
  Science 6, 313-319.

Dye, D.W. (1980). Xanthomonas. In "Laboratory Guide for Identification of Plant Pathogenic Bacteria", pp.45-49. (Ed. N.W. Schaad). St. Paul, Minnesota: American Phytopathological Society.

Dye, D.W. & Lelliott, R.A. (1974). Genus II. Xanthomonas Dowson 1939. In "Bergey's Manual of Determinative Bacteriology", 8th edition, pp.243-249. (Ed. R.E. Buchanan & N.E. Gibbons). Baltimore: Williams & Wilkins.

Dye, D.W., & Wilkie, J.P. (1973). Angular leaf spot of strawberry in New Zealand. New Zealand Journal of Agricultural Research 16, 311-314.

Dye, D.W., Bradbury, J.F., Goto, M., Hayward, A.C., Lelliott, R.A. & Schroth, M.N. (1980). International standards for naming pathovars of phytopathogenic bacteria and a list of pathovar names and pathotype strains. Review of Plant Pathology 59, 153-168.

Elliott, C. (1951). "Manual of Bacterial Plant Pathogens". Massachusetts: Chronica Botanica. 186pp.

Hayward, A.C. (1960). A method for characterizing Pseudomonas solanacearum. Nature, London 186, 405-406.

Hayward, A.C. (1979). Isolation and characterisation of Xanthomonas. In "Identification Methods for Microbiologists", 2nd edition, pp.15-32. (Ed. F.A. Skinner & D.W. Lovelock). London: Academic Press.

Hayward, A.C. & Waterston, J.M. (1964a). Xanthomonas citri. C.M.I. Descriptions of Pathogenic Fungi and Bacteria No.11. Kew: Commonwealth Mycological Institute.

Hayward, A.C. & Waterston, J.M. (1964b). Xanthomonas malvacearum. C.M.I. Descriptions of Pathogenic Fungi and Bacteria No.12. Kew: Commonwealth Mycological Institute.

Hayward, A.C. & Waterston, J.M. (1964c). Xanthomonas vesicatoria. C.M.I. Descriptions of Pathogenic Fungi and Bacteria No.20. Kew: Commonwealth Mycological Institute.

Hayward, A.C. & Waterston, J.M. (1965a). Xanthomonas campestris. C.M.I. Descriptions of Pathogenic Fungi and Bacteria No.47. Kew: Commonwealth Mycological Institute.

Hayward, A.C. & Waterston, J.M. (1965b). Xanthomonas phaseoli. C.M.I. Descriptions of Pathogenic Fungi and Bacteria No.48. Kew: Commonwealth Mycological Institute.

Hayward, A.C. & Waterston, J.M. (1965c). Xanthomonas pruni. C.M.I. Descriptions of Pathogenic Fungi and Bacteria No.50. Kew: Commonwealth Mycological Institute.

Hedges, F. (1924). A study of bacterial pustule of soybean and a comparison of Bact. phaseoli sojense Hedges with §Bact. phaseoli E.F.S. Journal of Agricultural Research 29, 229-251.

Hughes, C.G. (1961). Gumming Disease. In "Sugar-cane Diseases of the World" Vol.I, pp.55-71. (Ed. J.P. Martin, E.V. Abbott & C.G. Hughes). Amsterdam: Elsevier.

Kendrick, J.B. & Baker, K.F. (1942). Bacterial blight of garden stocks and its control by hot-water seed treatment. University of California Agricultural Experiment Station Bulletin 665.

Kennedy, B.W. & King, T.H. (1962). Angular leaf spot of strawberry caused by Xanthomonas fragariae sp. nov. Phytopathology 52, 873-75.

Leoville, F., & Coleno, A. (1975). Detection de Xanthomonas albilineans (Ashby) Dowson, agent de l'echandure de la canne à sucre dans des boutures contaminées. Annales de Phytopathologie 8, 233-236.

Locke, T. & Barnes, D. (1979). Xanthomonas corylina on cob-nuts and filberts. Plant Pathology 28, 53.

Lozano, J.C. (1975). Bacterial blight of cassava. PANS (Pest Articles and News Summaries) 21, 38-43.

Lozano, J.C. (1977). Identification of bacterial leaf blight in rice, caused by Xanthomonas oryzae, in America. Plant Disease Reporter 61, 644-648.

McGechan, J.K., & Fahy, P.C. (1976). Angular leaf spot of strawberry, Xanthomonas fragariae: first record of its occurrence in Australia, and attempts to eradicate the disease. Australian Plant Pathology Society Newsletter 5, 57-59.

McLean, D.M. (1958). A seed-borne bacterial cotyledon spot of squash. Plant Disease Reporter 42, 425-426.

Martin, J.P. & Robinson, P.E. (1961). Leaf scald. In "Sugar-Cane Diseases of the World" Vol.1, pp.78-107. (Ed. J.P. Martin, E.V. Abbott & C.G. Hughes). Amsterdam: Elsevier.

Miller, P.W., Bollen, W.B., Simmons, J.E., Gross, H.N. & Barss, H.P. (1940). The pathogen of filbert bacteriosis compared with Phytomonas juglandis, the cause of walnut blight. Phytopathology 30, 713-733.

Mingtan, L. & Watson, T. (1973). Bacterial spot of tomato and pepper in California. Plant Disease Reporter 57, 258-259.

Moffett, M.L. & Irwin, J.A.G. (1975). Bacterial leaf and stem spot (Xanthomonas alfalfae) of lucerne in Queensland. Australian Journal of Experimental Agriculture and Animal Husbandry 15, 223-226.

Moffett, M.L. & McCarthy, G.J.P. (1973). Xanthomonas translucens on Japanese millet (Echinochloa crusgalli var. frumentacea). Australian Journal of Experimental Agriculture and Animal Husbandry 13, 452-454.

Moffett, M.L., Trimboli, D. & Bonner, I.A. (1976). A bacterial leaf spot disease of several Brassica varieties. Australian Plant Pathology Society Newsletter 5, 30-32.

Moffett, M.L., Peterson, R.A. & Wood, B.A. (1979). Bacterial black spot of mango. Australasian Plant Pathology 8, 54-56.

Ou, S. (1972). "Rice Diseases". Kew: Commonwealth Mycological Institute. 368 pp.

Persley, G.J. (1972). Isolation methods for the causal agent of leaf scald disease. Sugarcane Pathologists Newsletter 8, 24.

Persley, G.J. (1973). Naturally occurring alternative hosts of Xanthomonas albilineans in Queensland. Plant Disease Reporter 57, 1040-42.

Persley, G.J. (1977). Distribution and importance of cassava bacterial blight in Africa. In "Cassava Bacterial Blight, Report of an interdisciplinary workshop held at IITA, Ibadan, Nigeria, 1-4 November, 1976", pp.9-14. (Ed. Gabrielle Persley, Eugene R. Terry & Reginald MacIntyre). Ottawa: International Development Research Centre.

Persley, G.J. (1979). Studies on the survival and transmission of Xanthomonas manihotis on cassava seed. Annals of Applied Biology 93, 159-166.

Persley, G.J. (1980). Studies on cassava bacterial blight in Africa. PhD thesis, University of Queensland, Australia. 182pp.

Ricaud, C., Felix, S. & Ferre, P. (1978). A simple serological technique for the precise diagnosis of leaf scald disease in sugar-cane. In "Proceedings of the IVth International Congress on Plant Pathogenic Bacteria", pp.337-340. (Ed. Station de Pathologie Végétale et Phytobacteriologie). Angers, France: I.N.R.A.

Ridé, M. & Ridé, S. (1978). Xanthomonas populi, (Ridé) Comb. nov. (Syn. Aplanobacter populi Ride), specificite, variabilite et absence de relations avec Erwinia cancerogena European Journal of Forest Pathology 8, 310-333.

Schaad, N.W. & White, W.C. (1974). A selective medium for soil isolation and enumeration of Xanthomonas campestris. Phytopathology 64, 876-880.

Schroth, M.N., Thompson, J.P., Bardin, R. & Greathead, A. (1964). Bacterial spot of lettuce. California Agriculture No.11, 2-3.

Sabet, K.A. (1959). Studies in the bacterial diseases of Sudan crops. II. Bacterial leaf disease of castor (Ricinus communis L.). Annals of Applied Biology 47, 49-56.

Simmonds, J.H. (1966). "Host Index of Plant Diseases in Queensland". Brisbane: Queensland Department of Primary Industries.

Skerman, V.B.D., McGowan, V. & Sneath, P.H.A. (1980). Approved lists of bacterial names. International Journal of Systematic Bacteriology 30, 225-420.

Sleesman, J., White, D.G. & Ellett, C.W. (1973). Bacterial leaf spot of zinnia: A new disease in North America. Plant Disease Reporter 57, 555-557.

Starr, M.P. (1981). The Genus Xanthomonas. In "The Prokaryotes", pp.742-763. (Ed. M.P. Starr, H. Stolp, H.G. Truper, A. Balows & H.G. Schlegel). Berlin: Springer-Verlag.

Starr, M.P., Jenkins, C.L., Bussey, L.B. & Andrews, A.B. (1977). Chemotaxonomic significance of the xanthomonadins, novel brominated aryl-polyene pigments produced by bacteria of the genus Xanthomonas. Archives of Microbiology 113, 1-9.

Steyn, P.L., Viljoen, N.M. & Kotz, J.M. (1974). The causal organism of bacterial black spot of mangoes. Phytopathology 64, 1400-1404.

Taylor, E.H., Bradbury, J.F. & Preece, T.F. (1981). Xanthomonas campestris pv. begoniae. CMI Descriptions of Pathogenic Fungi and Bacteria No.699. Kew: Commonwealth Mycological Institute.

Vock, N.T. (1978). "A Handbook of Plant Diseases", Vol.1&2. Brisbane: Queensland Department of Primary Industries.

Walker, J.C. (1952). Disease of crucifers. In "Diseases of Vegetable Crops", pp.123-172. New York: McGraw-Hill.

Walker, J.C. (1969). Bacterial diseases. In "Plant Pathology" 3rd edition, pp.104-174. New York: McGraw-Hill.

Watson, D.R.W. (1971). A bacterial pathogen of sorghum in New Zealand. New Zealand Journal of Agricultural Research 14, 944-947.

Wimalajeewa, D.L.S. & Washington, W.S. (1980). Bacterial blight of hazelnut. Australasian Plant Pathology 9, 113-114.

Young, J.M. (1969).   An alternative weed host for
   Xanthomonas   campestris.   Plant   Disease   Reporter   53,
   820-821.

Mollicutes and Rickettsia-like Bacteria
in Plants
G. M. Behncken

I.	Introduction	229
II.	Discovery of MLO and RLO as Plant Pathogens	230
III.	Taxonomy of Plant MLO and RLO	231
IV.	Diagnostic Characteristics	232
V.	Control	242
	References	243

I. Introduction

There are many plant diseases which, until 1967, could not be positively associated with any known group of plant pathogens. Because of this, and because they were usually transmitted by leafhoppers, the causal agents were assumed to be viruses and bacteriologists took little interest in them.

Repeated demonstration of the association of prokaryotic micro-organisms with diseases such as aster yellows and Pierce's disease of grapevine (<u>Vitis</u> <u>vinifera</u>) plus recent rapid advances in culturing some of these micro-organisms, should provoke much greater interest in these plant pathogens in the future.

The micro-organisms considered in this chapter are similar to described members of three taxonomic groups, <u>viz</u>. the mycoplasmas, the rickettsiae and the newly designated spiroplasmas, all of which are on the fringes of 'conventional' bacteriology. The terminology used to describe these micro-organisms has become somewhat confused because of our inability to culture many of them <u>in</u> <u>vitro</u> and thus clearly demonstrate pathogenicity and define their cellular and cultural properties. This chapter follows the most common practice and uses the terms 'mycoplasma-like organism (MLO)' and 'rickettsia-like organism (RLO)'. However, within these loosely-defined groups, the spiroplasmas have been more critically characterised and named and it is highly likely that the RLO will soon be subdivided because of differences in their localisation in host plant tissues and in their cultural requirements.

II. Discovery of MLO and RLO as Plant Pathogens

In 1967, Doi et al. first demonstrated that plants affected by several 'yellows-type' diseases contained mycoplasma-like bodies in their phloem cells and that the symptoms of these diseases could be alleviated by treating the plants with tetracycline antibiotics. Since then MLO have been found associated with over 200 different plant diseases in all parts of the world (Maramorosch, 1974; Maramorosch et al., 1970; Nienhaus & Sikora, 1979). In Australia, the diseases legume little leaf, witches'-broom of lucerne (Medicago sativa) and big bud of tomato (Lycopersicon esculentum) were the first to be shown to be associated with MLO (Bowyer et al., 1969). Since then MLO have been associated with green petal of strawberry (Fragaria x ananassa) and strawberry mycoplasma yellows (Gowanlock et al., 1976; Greber & Gowanlock, 1979; Shanmuganathan & Garrett, 1976), yellow crinkle of pawpaw (Carica papaya), bunchy top of peanut (Arachis hypogaea), little leaf of sweet potato (Ipomoea batatas), virescence of choko (Sechium edulc) and sesame (Sesamum indicum) (Gowanlock et al., 1976) and phyllody of foxglove (Digitalis purpurea) (Munro, 1978). Many records of MLO in a range of other crop and weed species with little leaf or phyllody symptoms in Australia remain unpublished.

However, beyond the simple association of MLO with disease symptoms, our understanding of them as plant disease agents and the relationship between different MLO is still sketchy. In fact, because no MLO has yet been successfully isolated, maintained in culture, and reinoculated into a host plant, the final proof of pathogenicity is still lacking.

Two important plant diseases, citrus stubborn and corn stunt were initially considered to be caused by typical MLO. However, in 1971 a micro-organism was isolated from trees affected by citrus stubborn and cultured in vitro (Fudl-Allah et al., 1972; Saglio et al., 1971a, 1971b); by 1973, it had been characterised and described as Spiroplasma

citri, the type species of a new group known as spiroplasmas (Saglio et al., 1973; Cole et al., 1973a, 1973b);
and by 1974 pathogenicity had been confirmed (Markham et
al., 1974). The agent causing corn stunt of maize (Zea
mays) was also shown to be a spiroplasma (Chen & Liao,
1975). Since then, spiroplasmas have been isolated from
several other plant diseases, insects and the surface of
flowers (Davis, 1979). No spiroplasmas have yet been
reported from Australia.

A completely different type of micro-organism with a
morphology similar to rickettsiae in animals and insects
was first seen in dodder (Cuscuta spp.) in 1970 (Giannotti
et al., 1970). These RLO were later found associated with
important plant diseases such as Pierce's disease of
grapevines (Hopkins & Mollenhauer, 1973; Goheen et al.,
1973) and citrus greening (Moll & Martin, 1974). At least
twenty diseases have now been linked with RLO in either
phloem or xylem tissue (Hopkins, 1977; Nienhaus & Sikora,
1979) but only two RLO, both xylem restricted, have been
cultured in vitro (Davis et al., 1978, 1980; Wells et al.,
1981). In Australia, rugose leaf curl of clovers
(Trifolium spp.) and rickettsia yellows of strawberry have
been associated with RLO in phloem tissue (Behncken &
Gowanlock, 1976; Greber & Gowanlock, 1979). Kenaf crinkle
leaf, a new disease of kenaf (Hibiscus cannabinus), is
associated with a xylem-limited RLO (Behncken et al., 1981).

III. Taxonomy of Plant MLO and RLO

The taxonomy of MLO, spiroplasmas and RLO found in
plants is still tentative. Based on the limited amount of
available information, their place in the existing classification scheme for bacteria and similar micro-organisms is
given in Table 10.1.

Two genera, Thermoplasma and Anaeroplasma, have not yet
been classified under this scheme. Although S.citri is the
only plant-infecting micro-organism with a reasonably
secure place in this scheme, three other spiroplasmas from
plants affected with corn stunt, cactus witches'-broom and
lettuce yellows diseases have been suggested as separate
species within this genus (Davis, 1979). The MLO have been
designated largely on their ultrastructural characteristics
which may prove misleading. Similarly, differences between

TABLE 10.1.   *Probable   Classification   of   Mollicutes   and Rickettsia-Like Bacteria in Plants*

Class Bacteria	
Order Rickettsiales	
Family Rickettsiaceae	(Plant RLO?)
Class Mollicutes	
Order Mycoplasmataceae	
Family Mycoplasmataceae	
Genus Mycoplasma	(Plant MLO?)
Genus Ureaplasma	
Family Acholeplasmataceae	
Genus Acholeplasma	
Family Spiroplasmataceae	(spiroplasmas)
Genus Spiroplasma	(e.g. S.citri)

the RLO which infect phloem cells and those isolated from xylem suggest that eventually they may need to be allocated to taxonomically distinct groups.

IV.   Diagnostic Characteristics

A. *Diagnosis*

There are several characteristics of MLO, spiroplasmas and RLO, and the diseases they cause, which have been used in disease diagnosis and identification of the presumed pathogen.   These are the types of symptoms produced and remission of symptoms by antibiotic treatment;   the mode of transmission and vector specificity;   tissue localisation; and morphology and ultrastructure of the micro-organism.   A fifth characteristic, viz. the ability of the micro-organism to multiply in vitro, is of limited usefulness at present but for those groups of organisms to which it does apply, rapid advances in pathogen identification and characterisation are taking place. The properties of existing groups of mollicutes and RLO are summarised in Table 10.2.

B. *Symptoms and Symptom Remission*

Although originally called 'yellows-type' diseases because general or marginal chlorosis of foliage is such a common symptom, the range of symptoms caused by MLO, spiroplasmas and RLO is extremely diverse.   Different organisms can cause almost identical symptoms and the same isolate can produce different symptoms in different plant species.   Apart from chlorosis, symptoms associated with a reduction in growth such as the production of small and/or distorted leaves, internode shortening, proliferation of axillary shoots and stunting of plants have been associated with all three groups of micro-organisms.   Some of these symptoms can also be caused by other pathogens such as viruses and by some insects such as eriophyid mites.   Some organisms, e.g. the Pierce's disease RLO, can also infect many plants without producing symptoms. Thus, symptomatology is generally regarded as an unreliable diagnostic characteristic despite the voluminous and detailed descriptions of symptoms by earlier workers.

However, despite this general caution about the value of symptomatology as a diagnostic aid, there are some types of symptom which are regularly associated with MLO or RLO infections.   For example, phyllody or greening of flowers is usually associated with MLO in the phloem.   Similarly, marginal leaf necrosis or scorching with stunting, decline in vigour or death of plants has been associated with several xylem-borne RLO.

The ability to induce remission of symptoms and resumption of normal growth by drenching or injecting affected plants with antibiotics has been taken as evidence that MLO and RLO seen in diseased plants are the causal agents.   Such an effect is certainly strong evidence that these diseases are not caused by viruses as previously assumed.   Tetracycline antibiotics can induce remission of symptoms associated with all three types of micro-organisms but remission by penicillin, which acts specifically on cell walls, is indicative of involvement of a bacterium or RLO.

TABLE 10.2   Comparative Characteristics of Mollicutes and Rickettsia-Like Organisms Associated With Plant Diseases

Diagnostic characteristic	Micro-organism			
	MLO	Spiroplasma	Phloem RLO	Xylem RLO
Symptoms	chlorosis small leaves proliferation phyllody stunting	chlorosis small leaves stunting	chlorosis small leaves stunting	marginal necrosis general decline stunting
Symptom remission				
(i) chemotherapy				
- tetracyclines	+	+	+	+
- penicillin	-	-	+	-
(ii) temperature sensitivity				
- heat therapy	+			+
- cold therapy	?			+

TABLE 10.2   Continued.   Comparative Characteristics of Mollicutes and Rickettsia-Like Organisms Associated With Plant Diseases

Diagnostic characteristic	Micro-organism			
	MLO	Spiroplasma	Phloem RLO	Xylem RLO
Transmission by insects	leafhoppers, planthoppers, psyllids, cercopids? (circulative)	leafhoppers, (circulative)	leafhoppers, psyllids (circulative)	leafhoppers, cercopids (non-circulative)
Tissue localisation	phloem	phloem	phloem	xylem
Morphology				
- wall structure	single membrane	single membrane	membrane + cell wall	membrane + cell wall
- 'R' layer	not applicable	not applicable	-	+
Culture in vitro	-	+	-	+

C. Mode of Transmission

None of the plant MLO, spiroplasmas, nor RLO is sap-transmissible and therefore early studies were hindered by the need to rely on graft transmission, or the use of dodder or insect vectors.

Natural spread of these micro-organisms is by insects. Various reports (Nienhaus & Sikora, 1979) of seed transmission and nematode transmission have not been confirmed. All the insect vectors known to date are phloem or xylem feeders and most are leafhoppers (Cicadellidae), planthoppers (Fulgoridae), cercopids or spittle bugs (Cercopidae) or psyllids (Psyllidae).

The relationship of insect vectors to MLO and phloem-restricted RLO suggests a circulative form of transmission in which the insect requires a minimum latent period of several days, and often 2-3 weeks or longer. This implies that the organism multiplies in the vector before transmission can occur and electron microscopy of sections of various tissues from infective insects has confirmed this. In contrast, the Pierce's disease organism, a xylem-limited RLO, has a very short latent period of as little as 2h in some vector species; this is probably only the time needed to acquire the RLO from the xylem. It is too short a period for imbibed RLO to passage through the haemocoele and salivary glands, let alone multiply in the insect, and implies a different relationship between vector and RLO. It has also recently been shown that trans-stadial passage does not occur in the principal Pierce's disease vector (Purcell, 1978) suggesting that the RLO is retained anterior to the midgut of the insect.

Vector specificity needs to be used with caution as a diagnostic character. Although some diseases, e.g. rugose leaf curl associated with Austroagallia torrida, have only one known vector, this may only reflect an inadequate search. Other diseases, e.g. Pierce's disease, are transmitted by a large number of vectors. Some vector species are also known to transmit several other diseases, including some virus diseases.

Experimental inoculation of potential vector species and subsequent transmission by such insects has recently been used in the search for natural vectors of S. citri (Kaloostian et al., 1979; Markham & Townsend, 1979). In a search for possible vectors of an MLO or RLO, a knowledge of the feeding preference of candidate insects, i.e. whether they are phloem or xylem feeders, may be of value.

D. *Localisation of Micro-Organisms within Plant Tissue*

MLO and spiroplasmas have been found only in phloem sieve tubes and companion cells of diseased plants. RLO can occur in either phloem cells (Fig. 10.1) or xylem elements (Fig. 10.2). Some studies have reported MLO and RLO in both phloem and xylem and also in parenchyma or mesophyll tissues but these findings appear to be rare occurrences. Infected cells can be detected by direct light microscopy of unfixed or fixed plant sections, particularly if specific staining techniques are used (Deeley et al., 1979; Marwitz & Petzold, 1980). The presence of spiroplasmas and RLO has also been shown by phase contrast microscopy of vascular extracts. Individual MLO or RLO bodies are seen in more structural detail by scanning or transmission electron microscopy.

Rarely are all vascular bundles in one cross-section of tissue, or all phloem/xylem cells within a bundle, found containing MLO or RLO bodies. Infection usually occurs only in random cells along a strand with little or no movement into adjacent strands. The concentration of bodies in infected cells varies from very few to dense aggregations suggesting complete blockage. MLO or RLO bodies may be loosely distributed within the cell or distributed around the periphery of cells embedded in a matrix material. Some infections may be accompanied by densely staining material (Fig. 10.1).

It has been postulated that many of the plant symptoms associated with MLO or RLO are the direct result of interrupted translocation of water and nutrients through the vascular system. Recent work with Pierce's disease (Hopkins, 1981) supports this hypothesis. Although relatively few xylem vessels were blocked with high concentrations of RLO in any one cross-section, serial sectioning over a 5 cm length of vascular tissue showed up to 80% of vessels completely plugged. Both symptoms and rate of vector acquisition were correlated with the amount of xylem plugging.

E. *Morphology and Ultrastructure*

The micro-organisms found in plants have been tentatively allied to existing taxa and referred to as MLO or RLO largely on the similarities seen in the morphology and ultrastructure of the individual cells of the organism.

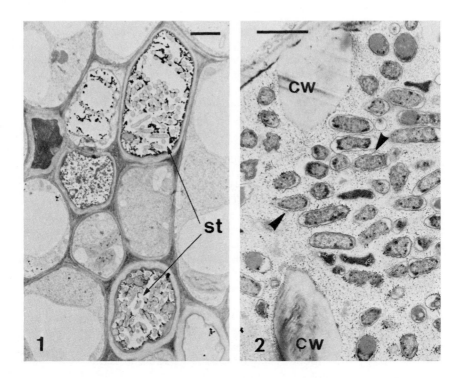

FIGURE 10.1 *RLO in phloem sieve tube cells (st) of red clover affected by rugose leaf curl disease. Bar equals 2* μm.

FIGURE 10.2 *RLO in a xylem cell of kenaf (Hibiscus cannabinus) affected by kenaf crinkle leaf disease. The inner membrane and cellular contents of some of the RLO cells have contracted away from the outer cell walls. Note the ridged wall of RLO cells (arrows) and secondary thickening (cw) characteristic of xylem cell walls. Bar equals 2* μm.

Plant MLO, like existing members of the genus Mycoplasma, are small, highly pleomorphic micro-organisms, bounded by a single, trilaminar membrane (Fig. 10.3). As seen in thin sections of fixed plant material, MLO vary in morphology from very small, round, dense bodies ca. 50-100 nm in diameter to large, globular bodies up to 10 μm in diameter. In loosely packed aggregations, and especially near, or passing through, the sieve pores, many MLO bodies are filamentous. The internal ultrastructure of MLO is not clearly defined apart from structures which resemble ribosomes and fibrillar DNA.

Spiroplasmas have a single membrane similar to mycoplasmas but produce many helical bodies 150-200 nm in diameter and 2-15 μm in length (Fig. 10.4). This helical morphology, which has a regular wavelength and amplitude, was overlooked in many early studies but is easily seen when thicker sections (200 nm instead of 50 nm) are examined. In many sections, small round bodies 40-60 nm in diameter appear to be attached to the helical cells. The motility of these helical bodies can be demonstrated by phase contrast or dark field light microscopy of tissue extracts or preparations from young broth cultures. The helical morphology of spiroplasma cells has also been demonstrated by scanning electron microscopy and freeze etching techniques.

The ability of many spiroplasmas to maintain a helical morphology in the absence of a rigid cell wall has not been fully explained (Davis, 1979). However, it should be noted that some isolates of S. citri and some spiroplasmas in haemolymph and salivary glands of infective leafhoppers or cultured on agar do not produce helical cells. Examination of in vitro cultures has also shown that the morphology of spiroplasmas changes with age and is influenced by several nutritional factors (Davis, 1979). Some surface structure on spiroplasma cells, including the possibility of an external slime layer (Razin et al., 1973), has been shown by freeze etching and electon microscopy.

In contrast to MLO and spiroplasmas, RLO are bounded by a plasma membrane and a cell wall. Both membrane and cell wall are trilaminar but the cell wall is often dense and the individual layers obliterated. In xylem-limited RLO, as in rickettsiae and Gram negative bacteria, the R layer between the plasma membrane and cell wall is densely stained (Fig. 10.5). This dense R layer is absent in phloem-limited RLO such as that associated with rugose leaf curl. Most RLO, especially in young, active host cells, appear as rod-shaped cells 150-500 nm in diameter and usually 1-4 μm in length. The outer cell wall is either undulating or ridged (Fig. 10.2). Some spherical cells are seen in most sections and, in what appear to be degenerating forms, RLO in many older vascular bundles seem to become more pleomorphic and granular with markedly thickened and distorted cell walls (Fig. 10.6).

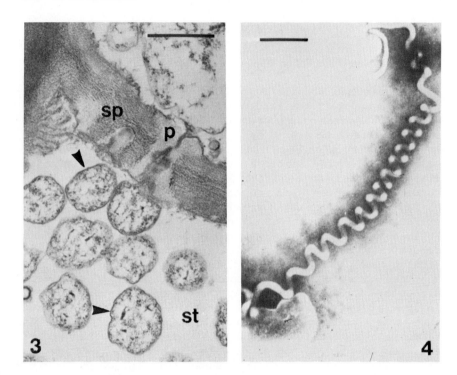

FIGURE 10.3   MLO in phloem sieve tube (st) of bell-
vine (*Ipomoea plebeia*) affected by phyllody and little
leaf symptoms.   One MLO cell is beginning to move into
the pore (p) in the sieve plate (sp).   Note the single
membrane structure of MLO (arrows).   Bar equals 500 nm.

FIGURE 10.4   Helical filaments of *Spiroplasma citri*
growing in culture medium (from Cole et al., 1973).

F. *In vitro* Culture

No culture method is yet available for the isolation
and long term maintenance of MLO or phloem-limited RLO from
plants.   However, recent work (Smith et al., 1981) has
resulted in a medium in which the MLO from aster yellows
could be maintained for up to 72h.

Several spiroplasmas and at least two xylem-limited RLO
have now been successfully cultured in several laboratories
and more detailed studies of their properties and relationships are now possible. Factors which have contributed to
the successful culture of spiroplasmas include the use of

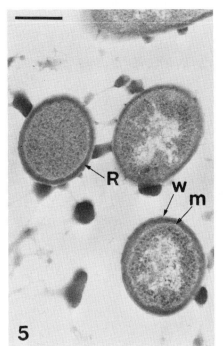
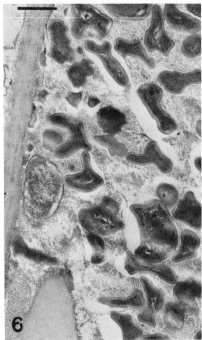

FIGURE 10.5 Cross-sections of RLO associated with
kenaf crinkle leaf disease, showing the dark stained R
layer (R) between the outer cell wall (w) and inner
plasma membrane (m). Bar equals 250 nm.

FIGURE 10.6 Distorted RLO in a xylem cell of kenaf
(Hibiscus cannabinus) affected by kenaf crinkle leaf
disease. Bar equals 500 nm.

sorbitol or sucrose to increase the osmotic pressure of the
culture medium, removal of possible plant inhibitors by
centrifugation, isolation from insect vectors rather than
plants, and the inclusion of specific chemicals such as
α-ketoglutarate. As these key factors have been
progressively identified, media composition has been
greatly simplified (Allen & Donndelinger, 1982; Davis,
1979).

The first RLO to be successfully cultured was the
Pierce's disease organism (Davis et al., 1978) with
isolations made from petiole sap onto PD-2 medium (Davis et
al., 1980) containing the following: pancreatic digest of

casein (4 g/l), papaic digest of soymeal (2 g/l), trisodium citrate (1 g/l), disodium succinate (1 g/l), 10ml hemin chloride stock (0.1% hemin chloride in 0.05N NaOH), magnesium sulphate (1 g/l), dipotassium hydrogen phosphate (1.5 g/l), potassium dihydrogen phosphate (1 g/l), Bacto-agar (15 g/l) and bovine serum albumin (2 g/l).

On PD-2 medium at pH 7.0, small, circular (0.5 - 1.0 mm), white-opalescent colonies form in 7-10 days at 28C. Pathogenicity of the Gram negative bacterium cultured has been proven by inoculating green stem cuttings of grapes with bacterial suspensions under vacuum and reisolating the organism from inoculated plants which develop symptoms. Cultures have retained pathogenicity for up to six months with weekly sub-culturing. To date, further characteris- ation of these RLO has not been published but serological comparisons have confirmed the Pierce's disease RLO as the cause of alfalfa dwarf and almond leaf scorch. Recently, the RLO associated with phony peach and prune scald diseases has also been cultured (Wells et al., 1981).

V. Control

Although some of the diseases associated with, or caused by, MLO, spiroplasmas and RLO may cause considerable economic losses, few practical control measures are available or have been adequately assessed.

Selection of clean planting or propagating material has been the major means of disease avoidance. Where alternative hosts of the micro-organisms or the insect vectors are known, eradication of these hosts from crop margins may reduce the rate of disease spread. Whether removal of diseased plants within a crop is worthwhile will depend on a detailed knowledge of the epidemiology of the disease and vector ecology.

In some crops, varietal differences in susceptibility to these micro-organisms or vector preference have been documented but little attempt seems to have been made to breed for resistance. Direct control measures by antibiotic treatment or indirect measures such as chemical control of vector populations have in the past usually given negative or only transient results. However, more recent attempts to control lethal yellowing of coconut palm (Cocos nucifera), decline of pear (Pyrus communis),

and X-disease of peaches (<u>Prunus</u> <u>persica</u>) in the USA
(McCoy, 1982) and citrus yellow shoot in China by pressure
injection of antibiotics have been more successful.

References

Allen, R.M., & Donndelinger, C.R. (1982). Cultivation <u>in</u>
<u>vitro</u> of spiroplasmas from six plant hosts and two
leafhopper vectors in Arizona. <u>Plant Disease</u> 66,
669-672.

Behncken, G.M. & Gowanlock, D.H. (1976). Association of a
bacterium-like organism with rugose leaf curl disease
of clovers. <u>Australian Journal of Biological Sciences</u>
29, 137-146.

Behncken, G.M., McLean, G.D., & Brook, K.D. (1981). Kenaf
crinkle-leaf - a stunting disease of Kenaf (<u>Hibiscus</u>
<u>cannabinus</u>). In "Proceedings Kenaf Conference May
28-29, 1981," pp. 41-44. Brisbane: CSIRO.

Bowyer, J.W., Atherton, J.G., Teakle, D.S., & Ahern, G.A.
(1969). Mycoplasma-like bodies in plants affected by
legume little leaf, tomato big bud, and lucerne
witches' broom diseases. <u>Australian Journal of
Biological Sciences</u> 22, 271-274.

Chen, T.A., & Liao, G.H. (1975). Corn stunt spiroplasma:
Isolation, cultivation, and proof of pathogenicity.
<u>Science</u> 188, 1015-1017.

Cole, R.M., Tully, J.G., Popkin, T.J., & Bove, J.M.
(1973a). Morphology, ultrastructure and bacteriophage
infection of the helical mycoplasma-like organism
(<u>Spiroplasma</u> <u>citri</u> gen. nov., sp. nov.) cultured from
'stubborn' disease of citrus. <u>Journal of Bacteriology</u>
115, 367-386.

Cole, R.M., Tully, J.G., Popkin, T.J., & Bove, J.M.
(1973b). Ultrastructure of the agent of citrus
'stubborn' disease. <u>Annals New York Academy of Science</u>
225, 471-493.

Davis, R.E. (1979). Spiroplasmas: newly recognised
arthropod-borne pathogens. In "Leafhopper Vectors and
Plant Disease Agents" pp. 451-484. (Ed. K. Maramorosch
& K.F. Harris.) New York : Academic Press.

Davis, M.J., Purcell, A.H., & Thomson, S.V. (1978). Pierce's
disease of grapevines: Isolation of the causal bacterium. <u>Science</u> 199, 75-77.

Davis, M.J., Purcell, A.H., & Thomson, S.V. (1980).
Isolation media for the Pierce's disease bacterium.
Phytopathology 70, 425-429.

Deeley, J., Stevens, W.A., & Fox, R.T.V. (1979). Use of
Dienes' stain to detect plant diseases induced by
mycoplasmalike organisms. Phytopathology 69, 1169-1171.

Doi, Y., Teranaka, M., Yora, K., & Asuyama, H. (1967).
Mycoplasma - or PLT group-like micro-organisms found in
the phloem elements of plants infected with mulberry
dwarf, potato witches' broom, aster yellows, or
paulownia witches' broom. Annals Phytopathological
Society Japan 33, 259-266.

Fudl-Allah, A. E-S.A., Calavan, E.C., & Igwegbe, E.C.K.
(1972). Culture of a mycoplasma-like organism
associated with stubborn disease of citrus. Phytopathology 62, 729-731.

Giannotti, J., Vago, C., Marchoux, G., & Duthoit, J.L.,
(1970). Infection de plante par un type inhabituel de
micro-organisme intracellulaire. Comptes rendus
hebdomadaire des seances de l'Academie des Sciences,
Paris D271, 2118-2119.

Goheen, A.C., Nyland, G., & Lowe, S.J. (1973). Association
of a rickettsia-like organism with Pierce's disease of
grapevines. Phytopathology 63, 341-345.

Gowanlock, D.H., Greber, R.S., Behncken, G.M. & Finlay, J.
(1976). Electron microscopy of mycoplasma-like bodies
in several Queensland crop species. Australian Plant
Pathology Society Newsletter 5 (Suppl.), Abstract 223.

Greber, R.S., & Gowanlock, D.H. (1979). Rickettsia-like
and mycoplasma-like organisms associated with two
yellows-type diseases of strawberries in Queensland.
Australian Journal of Agricultural Research 30,
1101-1109.

Hopkins, D.L. (1977). Diseases caused by leaf-hopper-
borne, rickettsia-like bacteria. Annual Review of
Phytopathology 15, 277-294.

Hopkins, D.L. (1981). Seasonal concentration of the
Pierce's disease bacterium in grapevine stems, petioles
and leaf veins. Phytopathology 71, 415-418.

Hopkins, D.L., & Mollenhauer, H.H. (1973). Rickettsia-like
bacterium associated with Pierce's disease of grapes.
Science 179, 298-300.

Kaloostian, G.H., Oldfield, G.N., Pierce, H.D. & Calavan,
E.C. (1979). Spiroplasma citri and its transmission to
citrus and other plants by leafhoppers. In "Leafhopper
Vectors and Plant Disease Agents", p.447-450. (Ed. K.
Maramorosch & K.F. Harris). New York: Academic Press.

McCoy, R.E. (1982). Use of tetracycline anti-biotics to control yellows diseases. Plant Disease 66, 539-542.

Maramorosch, K. (1974). Mycoplasmas and rickettsiae in relation to plant diseases. Annual Review of Microbiology 28, 301-324.

Maramorosch, K., Granados, R.R., & Hirumi, H. (1970). Mycoplasma diseases of plants and insects. Advances in Virus Research 16, 135-193.

Markham, P.G. & Townsend, R. (1979). Experimental vectors of spiroplasmas. In "Leafhopper Vectors and Plant Disease Agents", pp. 413-445. (Ed. K. Maramorosch & D.F. Harris). New York: Academic Press.

Markham, P.G., Townsend, R., Bar-Joseph, M., Daniels, M.J., Plaskitt, A., & Meddins, B.M. (1974). Spiroplasmas are the causal agents of citrus little-leaf disease. Annals of Applied Biology 78, 49-57.

Marwitz, R. & Petzold, H. (1980). Ein verbesserter fluoreszenzmikroskopischer Nachweis fur mukoplasmaahnlichen Organismem in Pflanzengewebe. Phytopathologische Zeitschrift 97, 327-331.

Moll, J.N., & Martin, M.M. (1974). Comparison of the organism causing greening disease with several plant pathogenic Gram negative, rickettsia-like organisms and mycoplasma-like organisms. INSERM International Congress, Sept. 11-17, 1974. Paris. pp.89-96.

Munro, D. (1978). A mycoplasma in foxglove. Australian Plant Pathology Society Newsletter 7, 10-11.

Nienhaus, F., & Sikora, R.A. (1979). Mycoplasmas, spiroplasmas, and rickettsia-like organisms as plant pathogens. Annual Review of Phytopathology 17, 37-58.

Purcell, A.H. (1978). Lack of transstadial passage by Pierce's disease vector. Phytopathology News 12, 217-218.

Razin, S., Hasin, M., Neeman, Z., & Rottem, S. (1973). Isolation, chemical composition, and ultrastructural features of the cell membrane of the mycoplasma-like organism Spiroplasma citri. Journal of Bacteriology 116, 1421-1435.

Saglio, M.P., Lafleche, D., Bonissol, C., & Bove, J.M. (1971a). Isolement et culture in vitro des mycoplasmes associes au 'stubborn' de agrumes et leur observation au microscope electronique. Comptes rendus hebdomadaire des seances de l'Academie des Sciences, Paris. Series D272, 1387.

Saglio, M.P., Lafleche, D., Bonissol, C. & Bove, J.M. (1971b). Isolement, culture, et observation au microscope electronique des structure de type mycoplasme associes a la maladie du stubborn des agrumes at leur comparison avec les structure observees dans le cas de la maladie du greening des agrumes. Physiologie Vegetale 9, 569-582.

Saglio, P., L'hospital, M., Lafleche, D., Dupont, G., Bove, J.M., Tully, J.G., & Freundt, E.A. (1973). Spiroplasma citri gen. and sp. n.: a mycoplasma-like organism associated with 'Stubborn' disease of citrus. International Journal of Systematic Bacteriology 23, 191-204.

Shanmuganathan, N. & Garrett, R.G. (1976). Little leaf of strawberry. Australian Plant Pathology Society Newsletter 5 (Suppl.), Abstract 83.

Smith, A.J., McCoy, R.E., & Tsai, J.H. (1981). Maintenance in vitro of the aster-yellows mycoplasma-like organism. Phytopathology 71, 819-822.

Wells, J.M., Raju, B.C., Lowe, S.K., Feelay, J.C. & Nyland, G. (1981). Isolation and growth medium for the bacteria associated with phony peach and plum scald diseases. Phytopathology 71, 912.

11

The Sugarcane Ratoon Stunting Disease Bacterium
D. S. Teakle

I.	Introduction	247
II.	Symptoms	248
III.	Host Range	248
IV.	Geographical Distribution and Importance	250
V.	Diagnosis	250
VI.	Isolation	251
VII.	Characteristics of the Bacterium	252
VIII.	Control Measures	254
	References	255

I. Introduction

Ratoon stunting disease of sugarcane was originally
described from Australia by Hughes & Steindl (1955). For
many years, it was thought to be caused by a virus. More
recently, a small coryneform bacterium was associated with
the disease (Fig. 11.1a) (Maramorosch et al., 1973; Teakle
et al., 1973; Gillaspie et al., 1973). This bacterium has
now been cultured in vitro (Davis et al., 1980; Liao &
Chen, 1981) and its pathogenicity confirmed (Davis et al.,
1980; Teakle & Ryan, unpub. data). The bacterium has not
yet been named and its relationships with most other
coryneform bacteria have not been established. The only
similar bacterium known was isolated from green couch grass
or Bermuda grass (Cynodon dactylon) affected by white leaf
(caused by a mycoplasma-like organism) from Taiwan (Davis
et al., 1980, Liao & Chen, 1981).

The study of these bacteria and the diseases they cause
is difficult for several reasons, including the generally
mild symptoms induced in host plants, the restriction of
the bacterium to the xylem of the host, and its small size,
slow growth rate and fastidious nutritional requirements.

PLANT BACTERIAL DISEASES
ISBN 0 12 247660 3
247

A comprehensive review of ratoon stunting disease (RSD) of sugarcane was written by Steindl (1961). A recent review contains new information on etiology (Gillaspie & Teakle, in press).

II. Symptoms

Infected RSD-sensitive varieties, such as Q28, Q94, NCo310 and Trojan show stunting and unthriftiness, especially during drought conditions. However, these symptoms also have other causes and specific diagnosis depends on the presence of internal symptoms which are seen when a diseased stalk is sliced longitudinally with a sharp knife.

Internal symptoms are of two types depending on the age of the tissues. In mature cane the nodes show discoloured (red, orange or yellow) vascular bundles. The discolouration is usually present only in the lower portion of the node. It is rarely longer than 3 mm. (Fig. 11.1b).

In immature cane the nodes and internodes near the growing point may be discoloured pink. This is a less reliable symptom than the vascular discolouration in mature cane but is useful in assays using inoculation of CP44-101 or Q28 setts.

III. Host Range

Although the RSD bacterium has been found to occur naturally only in sugarcane (Saccharum inter-specific hybrids), inoculation experiments have shown that it can infect a large number of other members of the family Poaceae. These susceptible hosts include cultivated species, such as maize (Zea mays), sorghum (Sorghum bicolor) and sweet sudan grass (Sorghum sudanense), and many weed and pasture grasses, including Johnson grass (Sorghum halepense), green couch grass (Cynodon dactylon) and Rhodes grass (Chloris gayana), (Steindl, 1961). Most hosts are infected symptomlessly but vascular necrosis is reported for elephant grass (Pennisetum purpureum) (Matsuoka, 1971), bana grass (Pennisetum purpureum x

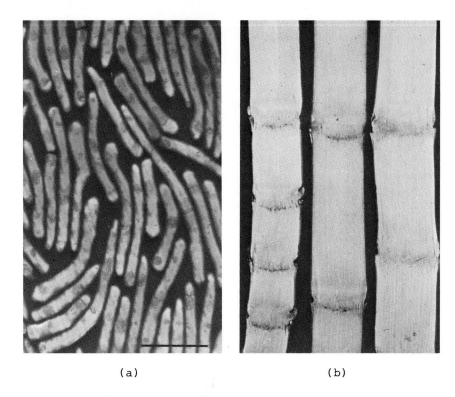

(a)   (b)

FIGURE 11.1   (a) Cells of the ratoon stunting disease bacterium isolated from sugarcane, grown on SC medium and negatively-stained with phosphotungstate for electron microscopy. Note the darkly-staining mesosomes in the cells. bar = 1 μm. (b) Ratoon stunting disease symptoms in mature sugarcane (2 stalks on left) and a healthy stalk (right). Note that the vascular necrosis is confined to a narrow band at the base of each node. (Photo courtesy Queensland Bureau of Sugar Experiment Stations).

<u>americanum</u>) (Steindl & Teakle, 1974), and a sorghum-sudan grass hybrid, which may also show wilting (Benda, 1975).

A bacterium closely related to the RSD bacterium has been found occurring naturally in <u>Cynodon</u> <u>dactylon</u> in Taiwan. This bacterium infected sugarcane following inoculation, but did not cause RSD symptoms (Davis et al., 1980).

IV.   Geographical Distribution and Importance

RSD occurs in most sugarcane growing countries (Ricaud et al., in press).   In Australia RSD is a major disease. It is present and common in all sugarcane-growing districts.   In years with normal or above normal rainfall losses are probably only a few percent overall.   However, in years with substantially below-normal rainfall, greater losses occur.   These losses may reach 30% in individual plantings.

V.   Diagnosis

A.   *Presumptive Diagnosis*

Presumptive diagnosis based on external symptoms is not possible because many other agents are able to cause unthriftiness and stunting in sugarcane. However presumptive diagnosis on the basis of internal symptoms, either in mature or immature stalk tissue, is possible with susceptible varieties.   In mature stalks, which are sliced longitudinally with a sharp knife, the vascular bundles should be discoloured in the lower part of the node.   The discoloured strands are seen as dots, commas, and other straight or curved shapes up to 3 mm in length, depending on the angle at which they are cut.   The discoloured strands should occur at different levels when the one node is repeatedly sliced longitudinally and several adjacent nodes in the one stalk should show typical symptoms (Steindl, 1961).

B.   *Confirmatory Diagnosis*

Confirmatory diagnosis is based on one or more of the following tests:
Transmission to sugarcane indicator plants: Particularly if symptoms in cane are doubtful, transmission to indicator plants is advisable.   The cut ends of single-node cuttings of a susceptible sugarcane variety, such as Q28, are dipped in juice expressed from the cane to be tested, and the cuttings are planted in the glasshouse or field.   Under good growing conditions, the shoots from the cuttings may

show the pink discolouration of immature tissues after 6 wk and discolouration in the vascular bundles of the nodes of mature cane after 2-6 months (Steindl, 1961).

Transmission to elephant grass or bana grass indicator plants: Elephant grass or bana grass "uprights" are plants grown from 2-node cuttings, with the lower, disbudded node producing roots in soil and the upper node producing an aerial shoot. If the shoot is cut horizontally 3 wk after planting and the cut surface covered with drops of RSD inoculum, a brown discolouration develops inside the base of the shoot after 3 wk incubation. This test has the advantage over sugarcane sett inoculation in that symptoms are produced more rapidly (Matsuoka, 1971; Steindl & Teakle, 1974). However, the test has the disadvantage that it is less specific, since Erwinia spp., Pseudomonas cichorii, Xanthomonas albilineans, X. malvacearum X. phaseoli are able to produce similar symptoms (Betti et al., 1976).

Presence of the RSD Bacterium in Expressed Vascular Sap: An internode stalk cutting is fitted with a rubber adapter attached to a source of compressed air (e.g. a vacuum pump). The air is allowed to pass through the stalk cutting and droplets of xylem exudate are sucked up with a pasteur pipette, placed on a slide under a coverslip and examined microscopically (oil immersion phase-contrast, x 1000) for cells of the bacterium (Richardson, 1978).

Presence of the RSD Bacterium in Vascular Washings: An internode stalk cutting is fitted with rubber sleeves and placed in the neck of a vacuum flask. The vacuum pump is operated while at the same time 5 ml sterile water is pipetted onto the top of the cutting and sucked through into the flask. After sieving out any large particles, the vascular washings are centrifuged (e.g. 5000 g for 10 min), and the pellet is resuspended in a small volume of water and examined microscopically for the RSD bacterium (Teakle et al., 1973).

VI. Isolation

A. *Isolation Method*

Isolation is more difficult than for many bacterial pathogens because the RSD bacterium is fastidious in its growth requirements and slow growing, allowing overgrowth by contaminating organisms.

Although the RSD bacterium colonises only the vascular tissue of sugarcane, it is present in stalks, leaves and roots. The immature tissues are less well colonised than more mature tissues. Isolations are usually made from the lower portion of the stalk which contains a relatively high population of the bacterium and can be thoroughly surface-sterilized without destroying the bacteria in the vascular tissues.

A suitable isolation technique is as follows: Strip the leaves from the lower portion of an infected stalk; scrub with soap and water; cut off a piece about 200 mm long; swab one end of the cutting with absolute ethanol and flame off. With a surface-sterilized knife make an oblique cut through the flamed end of the cutting. With surface-sterilized pliers, squeeze a drop of juice from the flamed end onto the surface of SC agar in a petri dish. Streak out with a flamed loop using the 16-streak method. Incubate at 28C for 1-2 wk. Remove contaminants daily.

Contamination can be reduced by isolating from cane free of stalk rots, by first diluting the drop of inoculum 1:10 with sterile water (Davis et al., 1980) and/or by isolating in a laminar flow hood.

B. *Isolation Media*

Early efforts to isolate the RSD organism using standard media commonly used to culture plant pathogenic bacteria and many other media were unsuccessful. Media were later devised which were suitable for the fastidious, slow-growing RSD bacterium. One devised by Liao & Chen (1981) is based on that used for isolation of the Legionnaires disease bacteria (Legionella spp.). The SC medium devised by Davis et al., (1980), has been the medium mainly used in Queensland (Table 11.1). The problem of crystallisation of the cysteine in the medium has been largely solved by halving the amount of cysteine added.

VII.   Characteristics of the Bacterium

A. *Morphology*

Cells are usually straight or slightly curved rods, sometimes inflated at the end or in the middle, usually measuring 0.15 - 0.3 x 1 - 4 μm. Since chains of cells may

TABLE 11.1   Composition of SC Medium

Autoclaved component	Amount in 500 ml
Corn meal agar (Difco or BBL)	8.5 g
Soytone (Difco), Phytone (BBL) or Soy Peptone (Gibco)	4.0 g
Bovine hemin chloride (Sigma Type 1) (0.1% solution in 0.05 $\underline{N}$ NaOH	7.5 ml
$MgSo_4.7H_2O$	0.1 g
K_2HPO_4 (0.1 M)	10 ml
KH_2PO_4 (0.1 M)	40 ml
Distilled water	400 ml
Autoclave for 15 min at 121C.	Adjust to pH 6.6

Filtered component (0.2 μm membrane or Seitz filter)	
Glucose	0.25 g
Cysteine, free base (Sigma)	0.5 g
Bovine serum albumen fraction V (Sigma)	1 g
Distilled water	50 ml
Adjust to pH6.6	

Add 50 ml filtered component to 500 ml
autoclaved component

occur, greater lengths are sometimes recorded (Teakle *et al.*, 1973; Gillaspie *et al.*, 1973). Bacterial cells in the xylem of the vascular bundles of sugarcane are often embedded in an amorphous matrix. If this material is expressed, microcolonies of the bacterium may be seen (Kao & Damann, 1978). In electron micrographs, the cells are seen to divide by the production of a septum, and mesosomes are often present (Fig. 11.1a). Cells negatively-stained with phosphotungstate are often narrower than cells stained with uranyl acetate, and phosphotungstate-stained cells more commonly show mesosomes (Teakle *et al.*, 1979).

B. Colony Characteristics

When grown aerobically on SC medium for 2 wk at 26-30C, the colonies are 0.1 - 0.3 mm in diameter, and are circular with entire margins, convex and non-pigmented (Davis et al., 1980).

C. Physiological Characteristics

The RSD bacterium is aerobic, non-motile, gram-positive, non-spore-forming, non-acid-fast, catalase-positive and oxidase-negative (Davis et al., 1980). The cardinal temperatures are approximately 15, 28 and 31C. The bacterium is sensitive to many antibiotics at 50 µg/ml including kanamycin, streptomycin, erythromycin, chloramphenicol, tetracycline and penicillin, but not actidione. It can utilise glucose, fructose, maltose, mannitol and mannose. The pH range for growth is approximately 5.5 - 9. (Teakle & Van Pham, unpub. data).

D. Serological Properties

The RSD bacterium and the Cynodon dactylon bacterium have been shown to be related but not identical in gel double-diffusion tests (Davis et al., 1980). Antiserum against partially purified preparations of the RSD bacterium from diseased sugarcane has been used in indirect fluorescent-antibody tests to aid in the detections of the bacterium in crude juice samples (Harris & Gillaspie, 1978). Similarly this antiserum has been used in immune electron microscopy to aid in detection (Damann et al., 1978). The RSD bacterium was not shown to be serologically related to some other bacteria including some species of corynebacteria (Davis et al., 1980).

VIII.   Control Measures

Control is difficult because of the ease of mechanical transmission via wounds sustained during planting and harvesting operations. This combined with the difficulties of field diagnosis make efficient control difficult. The main control measures are heat treatment, harvester treatment, and resistant varieties.

The most widely recommended control measure is to plant cane given a heat treatment, e.g. hot water at 50C for 2h, hot air at 58C (inlet temperature) for 8 h, or aerated steam at 52C for 4 h (Steindl, 1961; Mayeux et al., 1979.) When properly applied, the treatments eradicate the disease, but in commercial practice a few escapes may occur due to close packing of the cane.

Harvester treatment involves the decontamination of the cutter bar of harvesting machinery by washing followed by the use of heat or of chemicals, especially those containing 0.1% quaternary ammonium compounds (Steindl, 1961). Alternatively the cutter bar of harvesting equipment may be low-set so that it self cleans as it passes through the surface soil (C.C. Ryan, pers. comm.).

The use of resistant or tolerant varieties is also possible. This has received less attention than it deserves because the search for resistance or tolerance has required field trials. However, more rapid screening methods have recently been proposed. These depend on selecting clones which have either a low flow rate of water through healthy single-node stalk cuttings (Teakle et al., 1975) or a relatively low number of cells of the RSD bacterium in expressed xylem fluid (Gillaspie et al., 1976).

References

Benda, G.T.A. (1975). On the wilting of a sorghum-sudan grass hybrid infected with ratoon stunting disease of sugarcane. Proceedings of the American Phytopathological Society 2, 65.

Betti, J.A., Costa, A.S., Paradela, F.O., Soave, J. & Matsuoka, S. (1980). Vascular discoloration in the nodes of elephant grass, Penisetum purpureum, plants caused by several species of bacteria. Fitopatologia Brasileira 5, 139–148.

Damann, K.E. Jr., Derrick, K.S., Gillaspie, A.G. Jr., Fontenot, D.B. & Kao, J. (1978). Detection of the RSD-associated bacterium by serologically specific electron microscopy. Proceedings of the International Society of Sugarcane Technologists 16, 433–437.

Davis, M.J., Gillaspie, A.G. Jr., Harris, R.W. & Lawson, R.H. (1980). Ratoon stunting disease of sugarcane: Isolation of the causal bacterium. Science 240, 1365–1367.

Gillaspie, A.G. Jr., & Teakle, D.S. (in press). Ratoon stunting disease. In "Diseases of Sugarcane". Vol 1. (Ed. C. Ricaud, B.T. Egan, A.G. Gillaspie, Jr., & C.G. Hughes). Amsterdam: Elsevier.

Gillaspie, A.G. Jr., Davis, R.E. & Worley, J.F. (1973). Diagnosis of ratoon stunting disease based on the presence of a specific micro-organism. Plant Disease Reporter 57, 987-990.

Gillaspie, A.G. Jr., Flax, G. & Koike, H. (1976). Relationship between numbers of diagnostic bacteria and injury by ratoon stunting disease in sugarcane. Plant Disease Reporter 60, 573-575.

Harris, R.W. & Gillaspie, A.G. Jr., (1978). Immunofluorescent diagnosis of ratoon stunting disease. Plant Disease Reporter 62, 193-196.

Hughes, C.G. & Steindl, D.R.L. (1955). Ratoon stunting disease of sugar cane. Queensland Bureau of Sugar Experiment Stations Technical Communication No. 2. 54pp.

Kao, J. & Damann, K.E., Jr. (1978). Microcolonies of the bacterium associated with ratoon stunting disease found in sugarcane xylem matrix. Phytopathology 68, 545-551.

Liao, C.H. & Chen T.A. (1981). Isolation, culture, and pathogenicity to Sudan grass of a corynebacterium associated with ratoon stunting of sugarcane and with Bermuda grass. Phytopathology 1303-1306.

Maramorosch, K., Plavsic-Banjac, B., Bird, J. & Liu, L.J. (1973). Electron microscopy of ratoon stunted sugarcane: microorganisms in zylem. Phytopathologische Zeitschrift 77, 270-273.

Matsuoka, S. (1971). Elephant grass, an indicator plant for ratoon stunting virus of sugarcane. FAO Plant Protection Bulletin 19, 110-115.

Mayeux, M.M., Cochran, B.J. & Steib, R.J. (1979). An aerated steam system for controlling ratoon stunting disease. Transactions American Society of Agricultural Engineering 22, 653-656.

Ricaud, C., Egan, B.T., Gillespie, A.G. Jr., & Hughes, C.G. (Eds.) (in press) "Diseases of Sugarcane". Vol. 1. Amsterdam: Elsevier.

Richardson, S.R. (1978). An improved method of xylem-sap extraction using positive pressure for the rapid diagnosis of ratoon stunting disease. Sugarcane Pathologists Newsletter 21, 17-18.

Steindl, D.R.L. (1961). Ratoon stunting disease. In "Sugarcane Diseases of the World" Vol. 1. (Ed. J.P. Martin, E.V. Abbott & C.G. Hughes). Amsterdam: Elsevier.

Steindl D.R.L. & Teakle, D.S. (1974). Recent developments in the identification of ratoon stunting disease. Proceedings Queensland Society Sugarcane Technologists 41, 101-104.

Teakle, D.S., Smith, P.M. & Steindl, D.R.L. (1973). Association of a small coryneform bacterium with the ratoon stunting disease of sugarcane. Australian Journal of Agricultural Research 24, 869-874.

Teakle, D.S., Smith, P.M. & Steindl, D.R.L. (1975). Ratoon stunting disease of sugarcane: possible correlation of resistance with vascular anatomy. Phytopathology 65, 138-141.

Teakle, D.S., Kontze, D. & Appleton, J.M. (1979). A note on the diagnosis of ratoon stunting disease of sugarcane by negative-stain electron microscopy of the associated bacterium. Journal of Applied Bacteriology 46, 279-284.

12

Bacteriophages for the Identification of Plant Pathogenic Bacteria

G. J. Persley

I.	Introduction	259
II.	Specificity of Bacteriophages	260
III.	Methodology	261
IV.	Diagnostic Use of Bacteriophages	265
V.	Detection of Plant Pathogenic Bacteria	268
VI.	Conclusion	269
	References	270

I. Introduction

The purpose of this chapter is to outline the methods for the isolation and characterisation of bacteriophages and to discuss their use in the identification of plant pathogenic bacteria. The advantages and disadvantages of the technique are discussed, and examples given of its use with various pathogens. For further details, readers are referred to the recent comprehensive review by Billing & Garrett (1981). Earlier reviews by Okabe & Goto (1963) and Vidaver (1976) also discuss the occurrence and potential uses of bacteriophages in plant pathology.

Many plant pathogenic bacteria are difficult to distinguish from closely related pathogens and from associated epiphytic bacteria. Conventional cultural and physiological tests are sometimes sufficient to identify the pathogen. However, such tests are often inadequate to distinguish many pathogens.

Plant inoculation is also valuable in diagnosis, but this is often time consuming. Techniques involving serology (including the recent advent of monoclonal antibodies) and bacteriophages are useful for the rapid identification of pathogens for diagnostic purposes or for the identification of species or strains of epidemiological or ecological significance.

Although phages specific for many plant pathogenic bacteria have been identified, they have not been widely used. However, a few laboratories, (e.g. East Malling Research Station, U.K.) have made extensive use of phages for diagnosis and more specialized ecological and epidemiological studies.

II.   Specificity of Bacteriophages

Some phages have a broad spectrum of activity while others, including many temperate phages, are highly specific. In human and animal pathology, phages have been most useful for distinguishing epidemiological types of a single pathogen (Billing & Garrett, 1981). In plant pathology, the main aim has been to find phages that will aid identification of individual pathogens.

Phages with a high degree of specificity have frequently been found in infected plant material (Hayward, 1964a; Billing 1963, 1970; Taylor, 1970, 1972; Persley, 1980). Highly specific phages have also been obtained from soil beneath infected plants (Crosse & Garrett, 1963; Persley & Crosse, 1978).

The specificity of phages must be established before they can be used for identification purposes. Ideally, the phage should be tested against ten or more authentic cultures of each of the following: cultures of the specific pathogen both from different host plants and different geographic areas; other closely related pathogens; and related epiphytic bacteria commonly associated with the pathogen.

Claims for specificity of phages must be closely examined, as they are often made on inadequate grounds. Absolute specificity is rare. Consequently, reliance on one phage, without supporting tests, for positive identification of a pathogen is not recommended . When relying solely on phages for identification, it is preferable to use several phages and note the pattern of reaction. Phage typing can also be used in association with physiological, serological or pathogenic tests (Taylor, 1972.).

III.   Methodology

The methods for the isolation, growth and preservation of bacteriophages have been described by Billing (1969). The methods of phage typing commonly used for plant bacteriophages are similar to those described by Adams (1959) for medical typing schemes.

A. *Growth Conditions*

A medium which allows rapid growth of the host bacterium will usually be satisfactory for phage multiplication. For plating, 15-20 ml of agar medium per 9 cm plate is often adequate, but the optimum depth of medium will depend on the phage-host system. If the host ceases to multiply, the phage will also cease to grow. This is important in the case of phages which form small plaques, and sufficient media must be available to allow the phages to multiply.

A concentration of 1% agar (lower than that commonly used in isolation media) is recommended to allow larger plaque formation. The optimum temperature of incubation may influence the type of phages selected by isolation procedures. However, it is usual to incubate phages at the optimum temperature for growth of the host bacterium.

B. *Plating Methods*

Three methods are commonly used for plating phages to give isolated plaques: pour plates, surface plating, and the agar layer method.

In the pour plate method, the host suspension is added to the molten agar medium and the mixture poured into a plate. This gives a more even lawn than pouring the medium onto the inoculum in the plate. The phage suspension may also be added to the molten mixture before pouring. However, phage multiplication may be restricted by the depth of the agar. It is preferable to streak the suspension onto the dried surface of the solidified medium using a loop, or to plate serial dilutions of the phage preparation, using a Pasteur pipette or a syringe. After the phage drops have been applied to the surface of the plate, the drops should be allowed to be absorbed before the plates are moved.

In the surface plating method, the surfaces of the agar medium should be thoroughly dried (e.g. by incubating for 2 h open and inverted at 37C). Two ml of bacterial suspension are pipetted on to the surface and the excess rapidly decanted. The liquid should be rapidly absorbed, preferably by inoculating the plates while still warm and leaving the lids tilted until the plates are dry. Dilutions of the phage preparation are then spotted onto the bacterial lawn with a loop or a Pasteur pipette. This inoculum should also be absorbed before the plate is moved.

In the agar layer method, phage and host preparations are incorporated into a thin layer of soft agar which is poured onto the dried surface of a nutrient agar base. The soft agar is usually 0.6% agar, and is dispensed in 3 ml quantities in sterile containers and kept molten at 45C in a water bath. Dilutions of phage suspension are added to the series of tubes. A drop of the host suspension is then added to each tube, and the contents of the tube gently mixed. The contents are poured as quickly as possible over the surface of a nutrient plate, ensuring that the whole surface is covered. Both the base and the soft agar must be poured with the plates resting on a level surface.

Irrespective of the choice of method, the optimum amount of host inoculum is about 10^8 viable cells per 9 cm plate. This should give a confluent lawn of bacterial growth. The cultures should be in their active growth stage, as either broth cultures or suspensions prepared from agar cultures. The volume of inoculum will vary with the cultures but it is usually kept in the range of 0.01-0.05 ml per plate.

The method of plating for plaque detection is a matter of choice. The soft agar layer technique is preferable for showing small plaques. Pour plating is the most convenient in non-specialised laboratories. To avoid the necessity for making dilutions, a loopful of phage suspension can be streaked onto the dried surface of a pour plate seeded with the host, in the same way as a streak plate is made to obtain isolated bacterial colonies.

C. Isolation Methods

Most virulent bacteriophages active against plant pathogenic bacteria have been isolated from either infected plant material or the soil beneath diseased plants. The usual method for the isolation is to add infected plant material or soil to an actively growing broth culture of the host bacterium with incubation for 48 h. For example, in isolating phages against <u>Xanthomonas</u> <u>campestris</u> pv. <u>manihotis</u>, 5g of macerated leaf tissue showing angular leaf spots was added to sterile 250 ml flasks containing 30 ml of a 48 h culture grown in phage broth at 30C (Persley, 1980).

The phage broth of Crosse & Hingorani (1958), containing (in g/l): Bactopeptone 5, yeast extract, 3, glycerol, 20 is recommended. This medium is solidified with 1% agar for plating. The purpose of the enrichment phase is to allow multiplication of the phages and their easier detection on plating.

After incubation, the liquid is decanted and centrifuged at approximately 1000g for 30 min. Five ml of the supernatant is transferred to a sterile 25 ml screw-capped bottle and shaken vigorously with 0.1 ml chloroform.

After the chloroform has settled, the supernatant is tested for the presence of phage by the method of Crosse & Garrett (1963). One ml of the test liquid is mixed in a sterile petri dish with approximately 20 ml of molten, cooled (45C) phage agar and 1 ml of a sterile distilled water suspension of the indicator strain containing approximately 10^8 cells/ml. The plates are dried open and inverted at 37C for 1 h and incubated at 30C. The plates are examined for plaque formation after 24 h.

Chloroform is a convenient agent for sterilising source material or lysates for storage, usually with 0.5 ml chloroform per 10 ml phage suspension. Some phages may be sensitive to chloroform and in these cases the phage must be separated from the contaminating bacteria by filtration, using a filter of 0.45 μm pore size. Some phages may readily absorb to the filter and pre-washing the filter with nutrient broth is advisable.

Host range and plaque mutants can arise during propagation, particularly if the propagating strain is changed. It is therefore desirable to prepare sufficient high-titre stocks for long-term use and to use the same bacterial strain for phage propagation. If several preparations are to be tested for the presence of phage, spotting drops on the surface of a dried, seeded agar plate is a useful preliminary test.

D. *Phage Purification*

Single plaques from isolation plates are suspended in 3 ml phage broth and held at 25°C for 2h. The suspension is then streaked onto dried agar plates sown with the propagating strain, in a manner analagous to streaking bacterial cultures to obtain isolated colonies. The procedure is repeated three times to obtain a single plaque type.

E. *Storage*

Most workers have found storage in nutrient broth (e.g. the phage broth described above) at 0-5C satisfactory. The phage titre may fall with time, but residual phage can survive for several years. Freeze-dried preparations can be used, but survival is often low (Billing & Garrett, 1981). Phages active against X.<u>campestris</u> pv. <u>manihotis</u> have survived in freeze dried preparations for up to 2 yr. (Persley, unpubl. data).

F. *Preparation of High Titre Stocks and Routine Test Dilutions*

High titre (HT) stock suspensions can be prepared by the method described by Billing (1969). Pour plates are prepared containing 30 ml phage agar and 1 ml of a sterile distilled water suspension of the propagating strain from a 24-48 h culture. A single plaque from a purification plate is suspended in 3 ml phage broth. The phage suspension (0.1 ml) is spread over the surface of the pour plates. After incubation at 30C for 24 h the phage is harvested by adding 5 ml phage broth per plate and allowing the plates to stand at 25C for 4 h. The liquid is then pipetted into sterile 25 ml screw-capped bottles and 0.1 ml chloroform added per 5 ml phage broth. The phage suspensions are stored at 4C.

The number of plaque forming units (pfu)/ml is estimated by preparing a ten-fold dilution series in phage broth and spotting 0.02 ml drops onto the dried surfaces of pour plates sown with the propagating strain. Plaques are counted after incubation for 24 h at 30C. The routine test dilution (RTD) is noted for each phage. This is the dilution which gives barely confluent lysis on the propagating strain.

G. Sensitivity Tests

The pour plate method is the most convenient for phage typing. A pour plate containing the test isolate of the bacterium is prepared, as described above. The phage preparations are spotted onto the plate surface with a sterile Pasteur pipette and the drops are allowed to absorb before the plates are incubated at 30C.

Phages are usually tested at both high titre (HT) and routine test dilution (RTD). Reactions at high titre may be due to phage lysis, lethal absorption or bacteriocin activity. For this reason, reactions at RTD or RTD x 10 are normally more useful for typing purposes.

IV. Diagnostic Use of Bacteriophages

A. Pseudomonas

Most of the phage studies with pseudomonads have been with Pseudomonas syringae, since this species contains a group of plant pathogenic and epiphytic bacteria which are difficult to distinguish from one another (see Chapters 7 and 8).

Stolp (1961) made an extensive study of pseudomonad bacteriophages and found many instances where phages lysed both saprophytes and pathogens. Crosse & Garrett (1961) and Billing (1963, 1970) also observed shared phage sensitivities between pathogenic and saprophytic fluorescent pseudomonads (Group I of Lelliott et al., 1966). However, they also isolated phages able to differentiate certain pseudomonad pathovars and pathotypes. Crosse & Garrett (1961), and Garrett et al. (1966) developed a phage-typing system to separate P. syringae pv. syringae on pear from P. syringae pv. syringae on lilac and P. syringae pv. morsprunorum on cherry.

Among stone fruit pathotypes, phages have been of value in distinguishing differences in host specificity and differences between distinct pathogens on a single host. Using three phages (A7, B1, A15), cherry isolates of P. syringae pv. morsprunorum (which are lysed by phage A7), can be distinguished from plum isolates (which are lysed by phage A15) (Crosse & Garrett, 1961; Freigoun & Crosse, 1975). Race 1 cherry isolates can be distinguished from race 2 cherry isolates in that the latter are lysed by phage B1 (Persley & Crosse, 1978).

Some pathogens from different hosts were originally classified as P. syringae pv. syringae because of their similarity in physiological characters (Billing & Garrett, 1981). Phage tests have shown that they can be distinguished from one another on phage reactions, which reflect their host of origin. Pear, citrus and lilac host types can be distinguished from one another on the basis of phage type (Garrett et al., 1966; Billing, 1970).

Amongst non-fluorescent pseudomonads (see Chapter 7) all Japanese isolates of P. caryophylli have been reported to be susceptible to one highly specific phage (Nishimura & Wakimoto, 1971). However, the phage has not been used in dignosis nor epidemiological studies (Billing & Garrett, 1981).

Four biotypes of P. solanacearum have been defined, using physiological tests (Hayward, 1964b). Phages active against biotype 2 have been identified, but they have not proved to be reliable in distinguishing P. solanacearum biotype 2 from Corynebacterium sepedonicum, which produces similar symptoms in potato tubers.

B. *Xanthomonas*

Several studies have shown that phages active against Xanthomonas campestris pathovars have a high degree of specificity (e.g. X. campestris pv. pruni, pv. carotae, pv. vesicatoria) (Eisenstark & Bernstein, 1955; Klement, 1959).

Stolp & Starr (1964) made a major study of the phages of xanthomonads isolated from soil, but the phages did not show a useful degree of specificity. Isolates of X. campestris pv. malvacearum have been divided into two groups on the basis of physiological tests (Hayward, 1964a). These two groups could also be distinguished on the basis of phage tests. Phages were frequently detected on infected cotton leaves and there was some correlation between the presence of X. campestris pv. malvacearum group 1 or 2 and the group specificity of phages isolated from the same material. Phages isolated from 12 other X. campestris pathovars occasionally lysed group 2 isolates of X. campestris pv. malvacearum.

The xanthomonad phages isolated from plant material by Hayward (1964a) were more specific than those isolated from soil by Stolp & Starr (1964). However, the phages have not been widely used in further diagnostic or epidemiological studies of bacterial blight of cotton.

Sutton & Wallen (1967) studied 310 isolates of X. campestris pv. phaseoli and identified 8 phage types. There was some suggestion of a relationship between phage type and geographical origin of isolates and also their virulence.

Fifteen phage types of X. campestris pv. oryzae were identified by Wakimoto (1960) and Goto (1965). However, no correlation was observed between phage type and virulence. Goto & Starr (1972) concluded that phages were of little differential value for this pathogen.

Three bacteriophages isolated from cassava infected with bacterial blight were specific to X. campestris pv. manihotis (Persley, 1980). Furthermore, the phages differentiated between X. campestris pv. manihotis isolated from different geographic areas. At routine test dilution, the African phages lysed only isolates from West, Central and East Africa, while the Asian phage lysed isolates from Asia (Indonesia, Malaysia and the Philippines), South America and Mauritius, but not those from Africa.

The similarity of isolates from many parts of Africa and their difference from South American and Asian isolates suggests that the pathogen may have been present in Africa for many years and has evolved differently there than in South America, its centre of origin. The isolate from Mauritius differed from those from the African mainland, suggesting that Mauritius was not the primary source of infection for the African mainland.

C. *Agrobacterium*

Many phages have been isolated against Agrobacterium spp. (Boyd, et al., 1970; Garrett, 1978), but no correlation has been observed between phage sensitivity and host plant, country of origin, or virulence. However, biovars of Agrobacterium have quite different phage sensitivities (Kerr, pers. comm.). Phages are routinely used in genetic studies usually to distinguish plasmid transconjugants from donors (Van Larebeke et al., 1975).

D. *Erwinia*

Phages lysing the fireblight pathogen, Erwinia amylovora have been studied extensively (e.g. Billing, 1960; Billing et al, 1961; Billing & Baker, 1963; Ritchie & Klos, 1977). There are no reports of these phages lysing other species in the "amylovora" group, but members of the "herbicola" group are commonly sensitive. Some E. amylovora phages are highly specific.

Phages have also been isolated from one walnut pathogen, E. nigrifluens, but not from another, E. quercina pv. rubrifaciens (Zeitoun & Wilson, 1969). The phages have not been used in ecological studies.

E. *Corynebacterium*

Phages with a high degree of specificity have been isolated for Corynebacterium michiganense subsp. nebraskense (Vidaver & Mandel, 1974) and C. michiganense subsp. michiganense (Wakimoto et al., 1969; Echandi & Sun, 1973). These have been used for diagnostic purposes.

A phage isolated against C. flaccumfaciens subsp. flaccumfaciens also lysed strains of C. flaccumfaciens subsp. poinsettiae (Klement & Lovas), 1960, confirming relationships demonstrated between these two species by other methods (see Chapter 4). Phages may be used more extensively in this genus for diagnostic purposes, since conventional physiological tests are often inadequate.

V.   Detection of Plant Pathogenic Bacteria

A. *Epidemiological Studies*

Phages have been used to forecast the outbreak of epidemics of bacterial blight of rice, caused by X. campestris pv. oryzae (Mizukami & Wakimoto, 1969). An increase of phage specific to the bacterial blight pathogen in nursery, paddy field or irrigation water areas was observed prior to an epidemic. Thus, increases in phage populations were used to forecast disease outbreaks. However, there has been some debate as to the reliability of this technique, which has not been extended to other bacterial diseases.

The differentiation of cherry and plum strains of P. syringae pv. morsprunorum by phage typing was used in ecological studies on bacterial blight of stone fruit trees in South-East England. The unique sensitivity of cherry strains to phage A7 and the stability of cherry and phage strains during passage through both hosts (Crosse &

Garrett, 1970) enabled cross inoculation and mixed infection experiments to be monitored (Billing & Garrett, 1981).

Phages have also been used in epidemiological studies with English isolates of P. syringae pv. morsprunorum to show a relationship between host specificity and sensitivity to phage A7 (Crosse & Garrett, 1970).

Phages of E. amylovora distinguished capsulated from non-capsulated strains (Billing, 1960) and, to some extent, virulent from avirulent strains (Bennett, 1978 ; Bennett & Billing, 1978).

B. *Detection of Low Levels of Infection*

Highly specific phages have been used to detect plant pathogenic bacteria in material from which sampling by conventional means would often give false negative results. The presence of the pathogen is presumptively identified when the titre of specific phage increases after its incubation with the test sample for several hours.

The method was first used by Katznelson & Sutton (1951) for the detection of halo blight in bean seed. However, the technique has not been widely adopted by other workers. Some false negative results have been observed when using the technique with P. syringae pv. phaseolicola on bean seed (Billing & Garrett, 1981). These inconsistencies may be due to a deficiency in the phage/bacterium interaction and to the presence of a phage inhibitor in the seed macerates.

VI. Conclusion

Phage sensitivities have had little impact on the classification and identification of plant pathogenic bacteria. The lack of impact on classification is understandable, in that recent taxonomic trends have been towards grouping pathotypes which are similar phenotypically. In contrast, most studies with bacteriophages have concentrated on the identification of phages specific to particular pathovars or strains.

Certain pathovars can in fact be distinguished both by their host specificity and their phage sensitivity, although they are indistinguishable by conventional physiological tests.   This is particularly useful for plant pathologists who are more concerned with pathological differences than taxonomic similarities.

It is more surprising that plant bacteriophages have not been used more extensively in epidemiological studies, particularly since phages and bacteriocins have been major tools in the epidemiological study of human and animal diseases.   Billing & Garrett (1981) have suggested one possible reason for this is that in temperate climates, fungal and viral diseases of plants are more economically important than bacterial diseases and most laboratories are consequently oriented to mycology or virology.   In the tropics, bacterial diseases are more prevalent and severe.   In these areas, specialist bacteriologists are rare and expertise in phage techniques is limited.   More conventional physiological tests are often adequate for diagnostic purposes and there is little incentive to develop phage typing systems.   However, phage techniques are not difficult and are less cumbersome and time-consuming than many physiological tests.   There is considerable scope for the wider use of bacteriophages in epidemiological and ecological studies of bacterial plant diseases.

References

Adams, M.H. (1959). "Bacteriophages". New York: Interscience.

Bennett, R.A. (1978).   Characteristics of the fibreblight pathogen in relation to virulence.   Ph.D Thesis, University of London, U.K.

Bennett, R.A. and Billing, E. (1978). Capsulation and virulence in Erwinia amylovora.   Annals of Applied Biology 89, 41-45.

Billing, E. (1960).   An association between capsulation and phage sensitivity in Erwinia amylovora.   Nature, London 186, 819-820.

Billing, E. (1963).   The value of phage sensitivity tests for the identification of phytopathogenic Pseudomonas spp. Journal of Applied Bacteriology 26, 93-210.

Billing, E. (1969). Isolation, growth and preservation of bacteriophages.   In "Methods in Microbiology" Vol.3B, pp.315-329.   (Ed. J.R. Norris & D.W. Ribbons) London: Academic Press.

Billing, E. (1970). Further studies on the phage sensitivity and the determination of phytopathogenic Pseudomonas spp. Journal of Applied Bacteriology 33, 478-491.

Billing, E. & Baker, L.A.E. (1963). Characteristics of Erwinia-like organisms found in plant material. Journal of Applied Bacteriology 26, 58-65.

Billing, E. & Garrett, C.M.E. (1981). Phages in the identification of plant pathogenic bacteria. In "Microbial Classification and Identification". (Ed. M. Goodfellow & R.G. Board). London: Academic Press.

Billing, E., Baker, L.A.E., Crosse, J.E. & Garrett, C.M.E. (1961). Characteristics of English isolates of Erwinia amylovora (Burrill) Winslow et al. Journal of Applied Bacteriology 24, 195-211.

Boyd, R.J., Hildebrandt, A.C. & Allen, O.N. (1970). Specificity patterns of Agrobacterium tumefaciens phages. Archiv fur Mikrobiologie 73, 324-330.

Crosse, J.E. & Garrett, C.M.E. (1961). Relationship between phage type and host plant in Pseudomonas morsprunorum Wormald. Nature, London 192, 379-380.

Crosse, J.E. & Garrett, C.M.E. (1963). Studies on the bacteriophagy of Pseudomonas mors-prunorum, Ps. syringae and related organisms. Journal of Applied Bacteriology 26, 159-177.

Crosse, J.E. & Garrett, C.M.E. (1970). Pathogenicity of Pseudomonas mors-prunorum in relation to host specificity. Journal of General Microbiology 62, 315-327.

Crosse, J.E. & Hingorani, M.K. (1958). A method for isolating Pseudomonas mors-prunorum phages from the soil. Nature, London 181, 60-61.

Echandi, E. & Sun, M. (1973). Isolation and characterization of a bacteriophage for the identification of Corynebacterium michiganense. Phytopathology 63, 1398-1401.

Eisenstark, A. & Bernstein, L.B. (1955). Specificity of bacteriophages of Xanthomonas pruni. Phytopathology 45, 596-598.

Freigoun, S.O. & Crosse, J.E. (1975). Host relations and distribution of a physiological and pathological variant of Pseudomonas morsprunorum. Annals of Applied Biology 81, 317-330.

Garrett, C.M.E. (1978). The epidemiology and bacteriology of Agrobacterium tumefaciens. Ph.D. Thesis, University of London, U.K.

Garrett, C.M.E., Panagopoulos, C.E. & Crosse, J.E. (1966). Comparison of plant pathogenic pseudomonads from fruit trees. Journal of Applied Bacteriology 29, 342-356.

Goto, M. (1965). Phage-typing of the causal bacteria of bacterial leaf blight (Xanthomonas oryzae) and bacterial leaf streak (X.translucens f. sp. oryzae) or rice in the tropics. Annals of the Phytopathological Society of Japan 30, 253-257.

Goto, M. & Starr, M.P. (1972). Phage-host relationships of Xanthomonas citri compared with those of other xanthomonads. Annals of the Phytopathological Society of Japan 38, 226-248.

Hayward, A.C. (1964a). Bacteriophage sensitivity and biochemical group in Xanthomonas malvacearum. Journal of General Microbiology 35, 387-398.

Hayward, A.C. (1964b). Characteristics of Pseudomonas solanacearum. Journal of Applied Bacteriology 27, 265-277.

Katznelson, H. & Sutton, M.D. (1951). A rapid phage plaque count method for detection of bacteria as applied to the demonstration of internally borne bacterial infections of seed. Journal of Bacteriology 61, 689-701.

Klement, Z. (1959) Some new specific bacteriophages for plant pathogenic Xanthomonas spp. Nature, London 184, 1248-1249.

Klement, Z & Lovas, B. (1960). Biological and morphological characterization of the phage for Xanthomonas phaseoli var. fuscans. Phytopathologische Zeitschrift 37, 321-329.

Lelliott, R.A., Billing, E. & Hayward, A.C. (1966). A determinative scheme for the fluorescent plant pathogenic pseudomonads. Journal of Applied Bacteriology 29, 470-489.

Mizukami, T. & Wakimoto, S. (1969). Epidemiology and control of bacterial leaf blight of rice. Annual Review of Phytopathology 7, 51-72.

Nishimura, J. & Wakimoto, S. (1971). Ecological studies on bacterial wilt disease of carnation. I. Some characteristics and mode of multiplication of Pseudomonas carophylli phage. Annals of the Phytopathological Society of Japan 37, 301-306.

Okabe, N. & Goto, M. (1963). Bacteriophages of plant pathogens. Annual Review of Phytopathology 1, 397-418.

Persley, G.J. (1980). Studies on bacterial blight of cassava in Africa. Ph.D. thesis, University of Queensland, Australia.

Persley, G.J. & Crosse, J.E. (1978). A bacteriophage specific to race 2 of the cherry strain of Pseudomonas morsprunorum. Annals of Applied Biology 89, 219-222.

Ritchie, D.F. & Klos, E.J. (1977). Isolation of Erwinia amylovora bacteriophage from aerial parts of apple trees. Phytopathology 67, 101-104.

Stolp, H. (1961). Neue Erkenntnisse uber phytopathogene Bakterien und die von ihnen verursachten Krankheiten. Phytopathologische Zeitschrift 42, 197-262.

Stolp, H. & Starr, M.P. (1964). Bacteriophage reactions and speciation of phytopathogenic xanthomonads. Phytopathologische Zeitschrift 51, 442-478.

Sutton, M.D. & Wallen, V.R. (1967). Phage types of Xanthomonas phaseoli isolated from beans. Canadian Journal of Botany 45, 267-280.

Taylor, J.D. (1970). Bacteriophage and serological methods for the identification of Pseudomonas phaseolicola (Burkh.) Dowson. Annals of Applied Biology 66, 387-395.

Taylor, J.D. (1972). Specificity of bacteriophages and antiserum for Pseudomonas pisi. New Zealand Journal of Agricultural Research 15, 421-431.

Van Larebeke, N., Genetello, C.H. Schell, J., Schilperoort, R.A., Hermans, A.K., Hernalsteens, J.P., & Van Montagu, M. (1975). Acquisition of tumor-inducing ability by non-oncogenic agrobacteria as a result of plasmid transfer. Nature London 225, 742-743.

Vidaver, A.K. (1976). Prospects for control of phytopathogenic bacteria by bacteriophages and bacteriocins. Annual Review of Phytopathology 14, 451-465.

Vidaver, A.K. & Mandel, M. (1974). Corynebacterium nebraskense, a new orange-pigmented phytopathogenic species. International Journal of Systematic Bacteriology 24, 482-485.

Wakimoto, S. (1960) Classification of strains of Xanthomonas oryzae on the basis of their susceptibility against bacteriophages. Annals of the Phytopathological Society of Japan 25, 193-198.

Wakimoto, S., Uematsu, T. & Mizukami, T. (1969). Bacterial canker disease of tomato in Japan (2) - Properties of bacteriophages specific for Corynebacterium michiganense (Smith) Jensen. Annals of the Phytopathological Society of Japan 35, 168-173.

Zeitoun, F.M. & Wilson, E.E. (1969). The relation of bacteriophage to the walnut tree pathogens, Erwinia nigrifluens and Erwinia rubrifaciens. Phytopathology 59, 756-761.

13

Preservation of Microbial Cultures

L. I. Sly

I.	Introduction	275
II.	Choice of Method	276
III.	Periodic Subculture	277
IV.	Preservation by Freeze-Drying	277
V.	Preservation by Liquid Drying	283
VI.	Cryogenic Storage	284
VII.	Storage under Mineral Oil	287
VIII.	Preservation in Sterile Soil	289
IX.	Storage in Sterile Distilled Water	290
X.	Preservation on Porcelain Beads	291
XI.	Preservation in Gelatin Discs	292
XII.	Preservation over Phosphorus Pentoxide *in vacuo*	293
XIII.	Conclusion: The Role of Culture Collections	294
	References	295

I. Introduction

All microbiologists are concerned at some time with the maintenance and preservation of the cultures with which we work. It is necessary to have convenient methods to keep cultures alive, to keep them in a genetically stable form and to save labour. The choice of method depends on the nature of the microorganism and on the preservation objectives. For example, the method to be used depends on whether the culture is to be preserved for a few days until a positive identification is made, for the duration of a research project or for future long term reference. The choice of method also depends on the nature of the microorganisms and on the facilities available. The preservation method also reflects the difference in the biological properties of the bacteria, viruses, fungi, algae and protozoa and in their ability to survive in natural and artificial environments.

Research on preservation is a long term and often tedious process of changing conditions and monitoring effects. Apart from a few specialist laboratories, most culture collections and microbiologists opt to apply generally accepted methods for the preservation of their strains rather than optimizing the preservation conditions for each. In the event that the common methods are unsuccessful, it is necessary to investigate conditions for the preservation of these more difficult strains.

Preservation methods have a common objective of reducing the organism's metabolic rate as low as possible while still maintaining viability. A high recovery or survival rate with a minimum of damage or change to the surviving organisms is also highly desirable.

This chapter draws attention to the general methods available for the preservation of cultures and indicates areas where conditions might be varied to improve survival. The steps in a number of preservation methods which are suitable for the preservation of plant pathogenic bacteria are also outlined. Where appropriate, the instructions will be presented in a form which has been successfully used in the culture collection of the Department of Microbiology of the University of Queensland for many years. A review of preservation methods has been made by Lapage et al. (1970b) and readers are advised to refer to this paper when seeking more detailed information.

II. Choice of Method

There would be little disagreement that the methods of choice for long term preservation are freeze-drying (lyophilization) and cryogenic storage. There are exceptions, but with developments and minor modifications, these methods have proved to be successful and are able to be applied across a wide variety of microorganisms.

However, not all laboratories have these facilities and there are a number of simple but well proven methods of preservation which are not widely used but are worth consideration. They require little capital expenditure and many are suitable for laboratories with limited resources. They may only be suitable for particular types of microorganisms and although most are not suitable for long term storage, they are useful for short term storage and considerably better than routine subculture. They include storage under mineral oil, preservation in sterile soil, sterile distilled water, on porcelain beads, in gelatin discs, or over phosphorous pentoxide in vacuo.

III. Periodic Subculture

Periodic transfer or subculture is the traditional method used by microbiologists to maintain isolates in the laboratory. Apart for some cultures for which no long term preservation methods are yet available, periodic subculture is not recommended for long term preservation. Genetic change through selection of variants is likely to occur, the chances of contamination and mislabelling are high and the risk of culture loss is greater than in other methods. Nevertheless, although periodic subculture is not the method of choice for long term preservation, there is some evidence that many bacteria and fungi are able to survive for ten or more years on sealed agar slopes or in agar stabs at room temperature or in refrigerators. The longevity of such cultures is influenced by the nature of the organism itself, the composition and pH of the medium, the degree of aeration, and the temperature of storage. Low temperatures are usually preferred but there are exceptions. For example, some strains of Pseudomonas cepacia prefer storage at room temperature. The degree of hydration is also an important factor and slow uncontrolled dehydration often leads to a loss of viability.

IV. Preservation by Freeze-Drying

A. *Principles*

Freeze-drying (lyophilization) has been widely used as the preferred method for long term preservation for many years. The method is suitable for many types of microorganisms including most bacteria, yeasts, sporing fungi and some viruses, but is generally unsuitable for non-sporing fungi, some viruses, algae and protozoa. Freeze-drying is well suited to culture collections especially those which supply cultures on demand, as large numbers of ampoules may be produced and are easily distributed. Many cultures are able to survive for periods of twenty to thirty years but there are exceptions which require special suspending media and others for which suitable conditions have yet to be found.

Freeze-drying combines two of the most successful long term preservation methods, freezing and drying. The overall process involves the removal of water vapour by vacuum sublimation from the frozen state. The method thereby overcomes the problems associated with drying from the liquid state and the dried ampoules may be stored at room temperature in the dark, although long term survival is improved by storage in refrigerators.

Freeze-drying is the most technologically complex of the preservation methods in use, requiring the highest level of technical skill and high capital expenditure for equipment. However, if workshop facilities are available it is possible to manufacture a simple freeze-dryer for little more than the cost of a suitable vacuum pump which may be used for other purposes as well.

Because of the broad range of freeze-drying apparatus available it will not be possible nor necessary in this chapter to give specific procedural instructions for their operation. Technical handbooks should be consulted before any such equipment is operated.

Freeze-dryers use one of two methods for freezing the cell suspension prior to the drying process. In the pre-freezing method the cell suspensions are frozen in the ampoules before being dried under vacuum, freezing being achieved using a mixture such as dry-ice in ethanol. The alternative method is known as centrifugal freeze drying where the cell suspension is frozen by evaporative cooling under vacuum while the ampoules are spun in a low speed centrifuge to minimize foaming.

It is essential to use a suitable preservation suspending medium to protect the living organisms from damage during the freezing and drying stages. The functions of such preservatives include stabilization of protein, prevention of freezing damage and protection against over drying. The choice of the preservative depends on the organism and it must maintain the organism in a viable state and allow good recovery from the dried state.

There is a wide range of preservatives in use. One which has been used successfully in many culture collections is Mist. desiccans (Fry & Greaves, 1951). This is prepared by mixing three parts of sterile horse serum to one part of a filter sterilized solution containing 12 g Difco peptone and 30 g glucose in 100 ml of distilled water.

Although this suspending medium is more expensive than others such as double strength skim milk, it is our experience that Mist. desiccans is an extremely reliable medium and can be used as a suspending medium for a wide range of microorganisms. Further information on the composition of preservation suspending media may be found in papers by Greaves (1964), Lapage et al. (1970a) and Redway & Lapage (1974).

B. Procedures

The freeze-drying process can be conveniently divided into a number of stages. The procedures followed in the culture collection of the University of Queensland are outlined below.

(i) Preparation of the ampoules
1. Type the accession number of the culture on Whatman No. 1 filter paper and the date of freeze drying on the reverse side.
2. Cut the labels to the dimensions of approximately 4 mm x 25 mm.
3. Insert a label into each 0.5 ml freeze-drying ampoule so that the first letter or digit of the accession number is at the bottom of the tube. Allow sufficient space to avoid visual obstruction of the number by the freeze-dried pellet.
4. Using a swab stick, plug the neck of each ampoule with cotton wool to a depth of 12 mm with the cotton wool projecting about the same distance.
5. Pack the ampoules in a brown paper bag and sterilize in a hot air oven at 160C for 1 h.

(ii) Culture purity check and growth of the culture
1. Subculture the organism into 2 ml of the liquid medium optimal for its development and incubate this until growth is visible, or alternatively prepare a suspension from the stock culture.
2. Using this suspension inoculate a sterile agar slope and a sterile plate of the growth medium and incubate both for the desired time until the early stationary phase of population growth is reached at the optimum growth temperature.

3.   Examine the plate culture with a plate microscope for purity of colony form and prepare a smear from an isolated colony, stain by Gram's method and examine to establish that the culture has the correct morphology and stain reaction.

(iii) Suspension of the cells in the preservation medium
1.   Open the brown paper bag containing the sterilized ampoules.
2.   Using a sterile 1 ml pipette transfer 1 ml of Mist. desiccans to the slope culture and discard the pipette into a disinfectant cylinder.
3.   Taking a sterile Pasteur pipette and bulb prepare a dense suspension (approximately 10^8 cells/ml) of the culture in the Mist. desiccans by repeatedly drawing it into the pipette and washing down the growth on the slope. For safety and to avoid cross contamination be careful to avoid producing aerosols.
4.   When the growth is suspended dispense two drops (0.1 ml) of the suspension into the bottom of each ampoule, replace the cotton wool plug and place the completed ampoule into a rack. Take care not to contaminate the inner sides of the ampoules as this suspending medium will char during ampoule sealing.

(iv) Operation of the freeze-dryer

Lapage et al. (1970b) have published detailed procedures for the operation of centrifugal freeze dryers used in the National Collection of Type Cultures. It is not intended to repeat this as the operational procedures depend largely on the type of facilities available. The following remarks are confined to the design and operation of a simple freeze-dryer of the pre-freeze type which has been successfully used in this collection for the last twenty years.

Based on the original design of Greaves (1956) the freeze-dryer was manufactured in the departmental workshop and has been described previously (Skerman, 1973). It is simple to construct and operate and apart from a vacuum pump which is usually available in most laboratories, it is inexpensive to make.

The freeze-dryer consists of an evacuation chamber constructed from a brass anaerobic jar connected via a 2 cm diameter pipe to a water vapour trap immersed in a dry-ice ethanol slurry in a Dewar flask. Ampoules are placed in a solid aluminium freezing block (11.5 cm diameter x 5 cm high) which has been drilled to hold seventy ampoules. The block containing the ampoules is frozen by plunging into a slurry of dry-ice and ethanol. The vacuum is provided by an Edwards Speedivac two stage high vacuum pump (model 25C 20A) and is maintained at 0.01 mm Hg (0.01 Torr) for 6-8h. The vacuum is monitored by a Vacustat (Edwards High Vacuum Company).

Procedure

1. Prepare a slurry of crushed dry ice and 96% ethanol in the Dewar flask surrounding the vapour trap. Continue adding dry ice until the mixture becomes viscous.
2. Prepare a slurry of crushed dry ice and 96% ethanol to a depth of 25 mm in a plastic container (approximate diameter 16 cm). Continue adding dry ice until the mixture becomes viscous.
3. Plunge the aluminium block into the dry ice-ethanol mixture in the plastic container and allow it to cool. Set the block up on an angle of 45° and slip the ampoules into position. Allow 1 min for the contents of the ampoules to freeze and then return the block to the upright position in the dry ice-ethanol bath for a further 5 min.
4. Transfer the aluminium block containing the frozen ampoules to the evacuation chamber.
5. After lightly smearing the seals with high vacuum grease, fit the lid of the evacuation chamber and seal firmly.
6. Close all stop cocks.
7. Switch on the vacuum pump.
8. After 5-10 min check the vacuum indicated on the Vacustat and ensure that the vacuum is increasing satisfactorily and that no leaks are indicated.
9. After 6-8h when the vacuum has reached 0.01 mm Hg, turn the vacuum pump off and immediately fill the evacuation chamber and ampoules with dry high purity nitrogen.
10. Open the evacuation chamber, remove the aluminium freezing block containing the ampoules and place it in a holding chamber such as an anaerobic jar and flush with dry high purity nitrogen.

(v) Sealing of the ampoules under vacuum

1. Use a pair of scissors to trim the cotton wool plugs off at the rim of the ampoules.

2. Using a sterile swab stick push the trimmed cotton wool plug down the ampoule until the bottom of the plug is approximately 5 mm above the top of the label.
3. Constrict the necks of the ampoules using an ampoule constrictor or manually in a bunsen flame.
4. Re-evacuate the ampoules on an ampoule manifold.
5. Commencing at the top, collapse the constriction of each ampoule by means of small opposed gas flames using a micro-cross-fire burner.
6. Ampoules sealed under vacuum must be checked for leaks with a high frequency tester.

(vi) Sealing of the ampoules under nitrogen

1. An alternative to sealing ampoules under vacuum is to fill them with an inert gas such as dry high purity nitrogen before sealing. It is technically easier than sealing under vacuum and there is less chance of releasing fine particles containing microbes when they are opened. On the other hand it is easier to detect faulty seals in vacuum ampoules. In our experience it is possible to take ampoules directly from the ampoule holding chamber and seal them directly in a fine gas-air flame without resorting to the use of an ampoule manifold. A diverse range of bacterial cultures prepared in this way have survived for more than twenty years.

(vii) Ampoule testing and culture recovery

1. With a glass ampoule cutting knife make a score mark on the glass near the centre of the cotton wool plug.
2. Swab the area of the ampoule around the score mark with cotton wool dampened with 70% ethanol.
3. Apply a red-hot glass rod to the score mark to break the ampoule, leaving the cotton wool plug in place.
4. With a sterile Pasteur pipette aseptically transfer 6-8 drops of liquid medium to the freeze-dried material in the ampoule.
5. Resuspend the freeze-dried culture and transfer a few drops to a suitable agar plate and the remainder (including the label) to a tube of suitable liquid medium.
6. Incubate the inoculated broth and agar plate cultures at a suitable temperature.

7. The subsequent plate growth provides a convenient estimate of the survival of the organism by observing if the growth is confluent, individual colonies or no growth at all. This method may be easily quantified to measure the survival.
8. Plate out the subsequent growth in the broth and on the plate and incubate.
9. Check the subsequent colony morphology for purity.
10. Gram stain a smear prepared from a single colony and check the cellular morphology for purity.
11. Test the culture for selected properties that characterise it and especially specific properties such as pathogenicity.
12. Record the ampoules and their preservation date and store in the dark at 4C.
13. Establish a program of viability checking at predetermined intervals such as 1 yr, 5 yr etc. depending on the organism and its survival rate.

V. Preservation by Liquid Drying

Some strains of bacteria which are sensitive to freeze-drying are able to be preserved by drying from the liquid state rather than the frozen state. The method was developed by Annear (1954, 1956, 1962) and has been used successfully to preserve bacteria, yeasts, fungi and viruses. The method used in this collection is similar to the modification of Annear's method published by Banno et al. (1979).

Procedure

1. Prepare ampoules as outlined in the freeze-drying procedure.
2. Prepare a dense suspension of cells in <u>Mist. desiccans</u> and dispense in 0.1 ml quantities into ampoules so that most of the suspension is absorbed into the filter paper label.
3. Trim the cotton wool plug and push the plug down close to the top of the filter paper label with a swab stick.
4. Constrict the ampoules in a fine gas-air flame and attach to an ampoule manifold connected to a vacuum pump.
5. Immerse the lower half of the ampoules into a water bath controlled at 25C.

6. Turn on the vacuum pump. For the first few minutes regulate the vacuum in the ampoules until degassing is complete and then apply a vacuum of 0.01 Torr for 6-8 h.
7. Seal the ampoules under vacuum or fill with dry high purity nitrogen before sealing.
8. Establish a program of viability checks.

VI.   Cryogenic Storage

A. *Principles*

Most microorganisms including bacteria, yeasts, fungi, viruses, bacteriophages and some algae and protozoa can survive long term storage in the frozen state by markedly reducing their metabolic rate. This method is also suitable for the preservation of animal and human cells.

Microorganisms have been stored in freezers at temperatures around -20C and -70C. The lower the temperature the less is the loss of viability of most microorganisms and temperatures higher than -70C should not be used for long term storage but may be satisfactory for periods of up to 1 yr.

The use of ultra-low temperatures obtained by freezing in liquid nitrogen at -196C has provided microbiologists with a simple standardised technique which has been used successfully to preserve a wide range of microorganisms and mammalian cells with a much reduced viability loss and a high degree of genetic stability.

Although many bacteria survive freezing in their growth medium, the addition of cryoprotectants such as 5-10% glycerol or dimethyl-sulphoxide (DMSO) affords some protection from the stresses of freezing. Other cryoprotectants such as methanol, sugars, starch and polyvinyl-pyrrolidone have been used by various workers. Some cryoprotectants at concentrations required to afford protection during freezing and thawing may be toxic and affect the recovery of the organism unless they are diluted out or removed completely.

The rate of cooling should be slow and controlled down to -20C to -40C and then rapid to the final freezing temperature. The rate of thawing should be as rapid as possible. Rapid freezing rates may lead to intracellular ice crystal formation and electrolyte imbalance and cause lethal cell damage.

In general, bacteria, yeasts and fungi are less sensitive to freezing damage than algae, protozoa and tissue cultures where the choice of cryoprotectant and freezing rate are very significant factors.

B. *Procedures*

The following method describes the procedure for cryogenic storage in liquid nitrogen. It is also applicable in principle to storage at other temperatures.

(i) *Preparation of ampoules*

1. Prepare filter paper labels as outlined in Section (i) of the freeze-drying schedule above. As these labels are not clearly visible when the culture is frozen, the ampoules (0.7 ml) are also labelled on the external glass surface with a permanent marking pen.
2. Cap each ampoule with a piece of aluminium foil and place the ampoules in a rack for sterilizing.
3. Sterilize the ampoules in a hot oven at 160C for 1h. During this process the external painted label becomes etched into the glass. Alternatively, presterilized heat-sealable polypropylene ampoules or polypropylene vials with silicon gaskets may be used. These should also be marked on the outside with a suitable permanent marking pen. It is advisable to use an internal label as well in case the outer marking becomes erased.

(ii) *Growth of cultures*

1. Cultures are prepared and checked as outlined in Section (ii) of the freeze-drying schedule.
2. Fungal cultures may be prepared by inoculating 0.3 ml of suitable agar medium in the base of a liquid nitorgen ampoule and incubating until sporulation occurs. Alternatively suspensions of spores or plugs taken from an agar plate may be used.

(iii) *Suspension of cells in preservation medium*

1. Using a sterile 5 ml graduated pipette transfer 5 ml of preservation medium (e.g. suitable liquid growth

medium containing 5-10% glycerol or 5% dimethyl sulphoxide) to the slope culture and discard the pipette.

2. Taking a sterile Pasteur pipette and bulb suspend the culture in the preservation medium by drawing it into the pipette and washing down the growth on the slope to make a dense suspension.

3. When the growth is suspended, aseptically remove the cap of each ampoule and dispense 0.5 ml (10 drops) of the suspension into the ampoule. Replace the cap of each ampoule.

4. Fungal cultures grown in the base of an ampoule or agar plugs are overlayed with 0.4 ml sterile 10% glycerol.

(iv) Sealing of the ampoules

1. Using a micro-bunsen burner with a gas-air flame seal the glass ampoules and check under a stereo-microscope for hairline cracks. Polypropylene ampoules may be heat sealed or closed with its screw cap.

(v) Freezing of ampoules

1. Pack completed ampoules in the holders in use.
2. Place the sealed ampoules in a $-30C$ deep freezer or controlled rate freezer if available.
3. Leave the ampoules in the freezer until they reach $-30C$. Allow approximately 1 h. The rate of cooling will approximate 1C per min. The rate of cooling may be controlled simply by wrapping ampoules in cotton wool or by placing in boxes of carboard or other suitable material. The rate of cooling should be predetermined.
4. Remove the pre-frozen ampoules from the $-30C$ freezer and quickly transfer them to their predetermined position in the liquid nitrogen Dewar flask. Glass ampoules should be stored in the vapour phase.
5. Catalogue the ampoules and make provision for testing an ampoule from each culture for viability, survival rate and purity.

(vi) Ampoule testing and culture recovery

1. After putting on protective clothing and a face shield, remove the test ampoule from the liquid

nitrogen. Any ampoule which has a hairline aperture through defective sealing may explode if liquid nitrogen has penetrated.

2. Thaw the ampoule by immersing it in a 37C waterbath. Thaw the cell suspension until only a small piece of ice remains, so that the remaining ice melts as the ampoule is transferred to the laboratory bench at room temperature.

3. Swab the area of the ampoule around the gold line with cotton wool dampened with 70% ethanol. Hold the cotton wool around the ampoule and apply pressure with the fingers and thumbs to break the ampoule at the gold line. Heat sealed polypropylene ampoules may be cut with sterile scissors.

4. With a sterile Pasteur pipette aseptically transfer a few drops of the suspended culture to the surface of a suitable agar plate and the remainder to a broth medium. If the culture is inhibited by the cryoprotective agent, the cell suspension should be centrifuged and resuspended before being cultured.

5. Incubate the media under suitable conditions.

6. Plate out the subsequent growth and carry out colonial and cellular purity checks.

VII. Storage under Mineral Oil

A. *Principles*

A simple method of preserving cultures of many bacteria, yeasts and fungi is to store them on agar slopes covered by sterile mineral oil. The oil used is medicinal grade liquid paraffin. Protected in this way, principally from uncontrolled drying, the interval between subculturing may often be extended for several years, and up to 20 yr for some fungi. Long term preservation is often further improved if the oil-layered cultures are stored at 4C.

The microorganism to be preserved is simply grown on its usual maintenance medium on a slope, or in an agar deep or broth culture, and then covered with sterile paraffin oil to a depth of approximately 20 mm, or at least 10 mm above the top of the slope. Cultures are routinely grown on slopes but to economise on oil, slope cultures are often grown on "short" slopes.

This technique is simple, but for purposes of transport is not as convenient as the drying methods and for longevity and subsequent ease of handling, not as convenient as freeze-drying or freezing in liquid nitrogen. However, in the absence of these facilities, storage under oil affords protection to many bacterial and fungal cultures for periods of several years. A disadvantage with this method is that there is a slow diffusion of oxygen through the oil which allows growth to continue at a slow rate and therefore genetic stability may be poor.

B. *Procedures*

1. Prepare a short slope of the usual maintenance medium of the culture to be preserved so that the top of the agar is 50 cm below the cap of the McCartney bottle.
2. Sterilize white medicinal grade paraffin oil by autoclaving at 121C for 60 min, and then drive off any entrapped moisture by heating in a drying oven at 110C for approximately 1 h.
3. Inoculate a culture of the microorganism on the short slope and prepare a purity check plate at the same time.
4. After good growth has occurred, check the purity plate and Gram stain a smear prepared from an isolated colony. If the purity check is satisfactory, aseptically pour 10 ml of sterile paraffin oil onto the slope taking care not to disturb the growth on the slope. The oil must cover the top of the agar slope to prevent the culture drying. To avoid cross contamination, the sterile paraffin is either stored in individual layering quantities and poured onto the culture, or transferred by means of a sterile 10 ml pipette from a bulk supply, discarding the pipette after each transfer is made.
5. Store the oil-layered slope at the same temperature as the agar slope is normally kept.
6. Establish a program of viability checks and routine stock maintenance.
7. To recover cells from a culture which has been covered with oil, tilt the bottle with the slope uppermost, and then harvest some growth and transfer it to a liquid medium. The little oil so transferred with the inoculum will float on the top and the culture subsequently recovered from under the oil layer with a Pasteur pipette.

VIII. Preservation in Sterile Soil

A. *Principles*

Many bacteria and fungi survive well in dried soil for long periods of time (20 yr or more) when stored at room temperature. The method is particularly useful for fungi, Streptomyces and for spore-forming bacteria such as Bacillus and Clostridium. Excellent survival has also been experienced with Rhizobium (Jensen, 1961). Advantages of the method are its low material cost, room temperature storage and genetic stability, which would be expected to be much improved when compared with storage under sterile mineral oil.

B. *Procedures*

1. Select suitable loamy soil, pulverize it and then screen to remove plant debris and large particles.
2. Dispense soil samples to a depth of approximately 1 cm in cotton wool plugged test tubes or screw-capped 25 ml bottles.
3. Add distilled water to the soil to bring it to approximately 60% of its maximum water holding capacity (the soil should be damp).
4. Autoclave the soil at 121C for 1 h on 3 successive days.
5. Test the soil for sterility before use.
6. Heat the soil to dryness in an oven at 105C and then store the soil samples in a desiccator until required.
7. Prepare a suspension of cells in 2% sterile peptone water from a slope culture.
8. Using a sterile pipette or syringe place 0.1 ml portions of cell suspension on each soil sample and allow the moisture to absorb into the soil.
9. Return the soil samples to the desiccator where they may be stored or removed when dried and tightly capped.
10. Establish a programme of viability checks and routine stock maintenance.
11. To recover the culture aseptically transfer a small sample of soil to a suitable broth medium or make a suspension of soil in broth medium and use this to inoculate an agar plate.

IX.   Storage in Sterile Distilled Water

A. Principles

Some bacteria, particularly the Gram-negative rods such as Pseudomonas may be preserved for considerable periods of time when stored as a dense suspension in sterile distilled water. Storage may be at room temperature or slightly reduced to 10-15C if facilities are available. The method is applicable to a narrow-range of bacteria (e.g. Pseudomonas, Agrobacterium and Corynebacterium) and fungi, and as slow growth may continue, genetic stability would not be expected in the long term. As storage is in liquid, contamination is often a problem and one which is compounded when working with a range of similar strains. This method is best used as a source of working stock cultures in conjunction with stocks preserved by other more stable methods where contamination is less likely. For further information refer to papers by De Vay & Schnathorst (1963) and McGinnis et al. (1974).

B. Procedures

1. Dispense distilled water in screw-capped 25 ml bottles and sterilize by autoclaving at 121C for 15 min.
2. Transfer an aliquot of sterile distilled water with a Pasteur pipette to a slope culture and prepare a dense suspension of cells.
3. Transfer the cell suspension to the remaining distilled water. Use a few drops to perform a purity check and then tightly cap the bottles.
4. Store the bottles at room temperature or preferably at 10-15C.
5. Establish a program of viability checks and routine stock maintenance.
6. To recover the culture aseptically transfer a few drops to a fresh agar plate or broth medium and incubate.

X. Preservation on Porcelain Beads

A. *Principles*

A simple method of preserving many microorganisms is to dry a suspension of cells on porcelain beads, using silica gel as the drying agent (Norris, 1963). A layer of silica gel is placed in the bottom of a screw capped bottle. The silica gel is covered by a layer of "slag wool" and porcelain beads are mixed with a dense suspension of cells and placed on top of the slag wool. The bottle is tightly capped and the moisture is removed from the beads by the silica gel. Excess silica gel maintains the beads in a dried state. The method is suitable for the long term preservation of many bacteria and fungi. Perforated glass beads may be used in place of porcelain beads. The culture may be absorbed directly onto silica gel without indicator (Perkins, 1962) but as heat is produced when water is added to silica gel, care should be taken to keep the silica gel cool while the suspension is being absorbed to avoid damage to the cells.

B. *Procedures*

1. Add 3-4 g of "impregnated" silica gel (blue when dry, pink when moist) to a 25 ml McCartney bottle fitted with a rubber-lined metal screw cap.
2. Hold the silica gel in position with a 10 mm layer of commercial "slag wool" (used for insulation purposes) which should be firm but porous.
3. Place 20-30 unglazed porcelain fish spine beads (No. 2) on top of the "slag wool".
4. Sterilize the bottles in a hot air oven at 160C for 1-2 h. The rubber-lined caps must be sterilized separately by autoclaving face down on petri dishes at 121C for 15 min and then dried in a hot air oven at a maximum temperature of 100C before being screwed onto the cooled bottles aseptically.
5. Grow the culture in a cotton wool plugged 150 mm x 12 mm test tube containing 1 ml of suitable medium.
6. When the growth is densely turbid, aseptically tip the procelain beads into the 1 ml of bacterial growth, replace the cotton wool plug and agitate the beads in the medium.

7. Carefully remove all excess culture fluid with a fine-tipped pipette.
8. Tip the moist beads back into the bottle and screw the cap down firmly.
9. The silica gel turns pink as it removes moisture from the beads. The bottle is satisfactory, provided some of the silica gel remains blue. If all the silica gel turns pink due to too much liquid or a faulty seal, the bottle should be discarded.
10. Store the bottles at room temperature or in a refrigerator.
11. Establish a program of viability checks and routine stock maintenance.
12. To recover the organism remove a bead with a sterile wire and transfer it to a tube or plate of a suitable medium and incubate.

XI. Preservation in Gelatin Discs

A. *Principles*

A simple but very effective method for the preservation of bacteria is to store them in dried gelatin discs (Stamp, 1947). The method involves preparing single drops of a dense suspension of cells in nutrient gelatin supplemented with ascorbic acid, and drying these by evacuation over phosphorus pentoxide. The method is suitable for the long term preservation of bacteria but little data is available on survival rates.

B. *Procedures*

1. Sterilize 10 ml of paraffin wax and allow to set as a layer in a sterile glass petri dish. Alternatively a circle of waxed paper (Lapage et al., 1970b) or silicon fluid (Collins, 1967) may be used in the base of the petri dish.
2. Prepare a dense suspension of cells from an agar slope in 10% nutrient gelatin containing 0.25% (w/v) ascorbic acid.
3. Using a sterile Pasteur pipette prepare single drops of the gelatin cell suspension on the sterile paraffin surface. Replace the petri dish lid and allow the drops to set.

4. Transfer the petri dish with the gelatin drops to a vacuum desiccator containing phosphorus pentoxide and evacuate until the drops form dry discs.
5. Transfer the discs aseptically with sterile forceps to sterile tubes and store over phosphorus pentoxide at 4C.
6. Establish a program of viability checks and routine stock maintenance.
7. To recover a culture, remove a disc using sterile forceps and transfer to a suitable broth medium or agar plate.

XII. Preservation over Phosphorus Pentoxide *in vacuo*

A. *Principles*

This method (Sordelli's method) has been successfully used in the National Collection of Type Cultures to preserve a wide variety of bacteria (Lapage et al., 1970b). The culture is preserved by preparing a suspension in horse serum which is deposited in a small glass tube. This tube is then placed in an outer tube containing a small quantity of phosphorus pentoxide in the bottom. The top of the outer tube is constricted and then evacuated and sealed. The ampoules are stored at room temperature or in a refrigerator. The method is suitable for the long term preservation of bacteria, yeasts and fungi and good survival has been observed for periods of 5-28 yr for some strains (Rhodes, 1950; Soriano, 1970).

B. *Procedures*

1. Prepare a dense suspension in sterile horse serum of cells from an agar slope.
2. Transfer a loopful of cell suspension to the inner surface of a sterile small glass tube.
3. Using a glass funnel and rod place a small amount of phosphorus pentoxide into the bottom of another glass tube sufficiently larger in diameter and length to contain the small glass tube.
4. Insert the smaller tube containing the cell suspension into the larger tube containing the phosphorus pentoxide.
5. Constrict the neck of the outer tube using a fine gas-air flame.

6. Attach the constricted tube to a manifold and using a vacuum pump evacuate for 5 min.
7. Seal the outer tube with a fine gas-air flame.
8. Store the sealed ampoules at room temperature or in a refrigerator.
9. Establish a program of viability checks and routine stock maintenance.
10. To recover the culture break open the outer tube by making a score mark with a glass knife and apply a red hot glass rod to crack the glass. Remove the inner tube, resuspend the contents in suitable broth or transfer to an agar plate, and incubate.

XIII.   Conclusion: The Role of Culture Collections

Culture collections occupy a central and essential position in microbiology because effective identification, research and training demand reliable sources of microorganisms. Culture collections have played a fundamental role in the development of microbiology by ensuring that most of the types of microbes that have been described have been safely maintained for the present and future generations. Culture collections thus provide permanent laboratories where strains can be preserved and made available to scientists who wish to repeat, compare or extend work described in the literature.

Culture collections consist of three main types: service collections whose function and organization is chiefly for the preservation and supply of cultures on demand; institutional collections whose supply is mainly for internal use in the institution concerned; and private collections chiefly for personal research purposes. These private collections may be highly specialized and important to other scientists, and often are the only available source of particular strains or kinds of microorganisms.

However, culture collections are more than repositories since they also serve as centres of information on microorganisms and their preservation, and are centres of active research and training on microbial systematics and identification.

Microbiological nomenclature and classification depend on the maintenance of type cultures for later taxonomic studies or identification of newly-discovered organisms.

Culture collections have helped to provide a solid base for microbiological endeavour and to bring stability to nomenclature and classification.

Important isolates should be deposited in one or more recognized culture collections to ensure that strains that are well studied or have unusual properties are preserved in unchanged form for further reference and study. This is particularly important for type material. However, experience shows that the full significance of unusual or unidentifiable strains may only be fully appreciated in the light of new information which may come many years later.

Further information on the location of cultures of microorganisms and the culture collections in which they are held may be obtained from the World Data Center for Microorganisms housed in the Department of Microbiology, University of Queensland, Australia or from the major national culture collections throughout the world.

References

Literature cited and other selected reference literature are listed below.

Annear, D.I. (1954). Preservation of bacteria. Nature, London 174, 359.

Annear, D.I. (1956). The preservation of bacteria by drying in peptone plugs. Journal of Hygiene, Cambridge 54, 487.

Annear, D.I. (1958). Observations on drying bacteria from the frozen and from the liquid state. Australian Journal of Experimental Biology and Medical Science 36, 211-222

Annear, D.I. (1962). Recoveries of bacteria after drying on cellulose fibers (A method for the routine preservation of bacteria). Australian Journal of Experimental Biology and Medical Science 40, 1-8.

Ashwood-Smith, M.J. & Farrant, J. (1980). "Low temperature preservation in medicine and biology". Tunbridge Wells, U.K.: Pitman.

Banno, I. & Sakane, T. (1979). Viability of various bacteria after L-drying. Institute for Fermentation (Osaka) Research Communication 9, 35-45.

Banno, I., Mikata, K. & Sakane, T. (1979). Viability of various yeasts after L-drying. Institute for Fermentation (Osaka) Research Communication 9, 27-34.

Bridges, B.A. (1966). Preservation of microorganisms at low temperature. Laboratory Practice 15, 418.

Clark, W.A. (1976). Selected bibliography of literature on preservation of microorganisms, blood, tissues, and vaccines with emphasis on freezing and freeze-drying (1968-1976). U.S. Department of Health, Education and Welfare, Center for Disease Control, Atlanta.

Clark, W.A. & Sly, L.I. (1975). Liquid nitrogen preservation of fungi in culture collections. Proceedings of First Intersectional Congress of International Association of Microbiological Societies 5, 616-631.

Collins, C.H (1967). "Microbiological Methods", 2nd edition. London: Butterworths.

De Vay, J.E. & Schnathorst, W.C. (1963). Single-cell isolation and preservation of bacterial cultures. Nature, London 199, 775-777.

Elliott, R.F. (1975). Method for preserving mini-cultures of fungi under mineral oil. Laboratory Practice 24, 751.

Elliott, R.F. (1975). Viability of fungous cultures dried and stored over silica gel. New Zealand Journal Science 18, 577-583.

Fry, R.M. & Greaves, R.I.N. (1951). The survival of bacteria during and after drying. Journal of Hygiene, Cambridge 49, 220.

Greaves, R.I.N. (1956). The preservation of bacteria. Canadian Journal of Microbiology 2, 364-371.

Greaves, R.I.N. (1964). Fundamental aspects of freeze-drying bacteria and living cells. In "Aspects Theoretiques et Industriels de la Lyophilisation", pp. 407-410 (Ed. L. Rey). Paris: Hermann.

Hollings, M. & Lelliott, R.A. (1960). Preservation of some plant viruses by freeze-drying. Plant Pathology 9, 63-66.

Hollings, M. & Stone, O.M. (1970). The long term survival of some plant viruses preserved by lyophilization. Annals of Applied Biology 65, 411-418.

Iijuma, R. & Sakane, T. (1973). A method for preservation of bacteria and bacteriophages by drying in vacuo. Cryobiology 10, 379-385.

Jensen, H.L. (1961). The viability of lucerne rhizobia in soil culture. Nature, London 192, 682.

Lapage, S.P. & Redway, K.F. (1974). "Preservation of Bacteria with Notes on other Micro-organisms". Public Health Laboratory Service Monograph No. 7. London: H.M.S.O.

Lapage, S.P., Shelton, J.E. & Mitchell, T.G. (1970a).
Media for the maintenance and preservation of bacteria.
In "Methods in Microbiology" Vol. 3A, pp.2-133. (Ed.
J.R. Norris & D.W. Ribbons). Academic Press: London.

Lapage, S.P., Shelton, J.E., Mitchell, T.G. & Mackenzie,
A.R. (1970b). Culture collections and preservation of
bacteria. In "Methods in Microbiology" Vol. 3A,
pp.135-227. (Ed. J.R. Norris & D.W. Ribbons). London:
Academic Press.

Leben, C. & Sleesman, J.P. (1982). Preservation
of plant pathogen bacteria on silica gel. Plant Disease
66, 327.

McGinnis, M.R., Padhye, A.A. & Ajello, L. (1974). Storage
of stock cultures of filamentous fungi, yeasts, and some
aerobic actinomycetes in sterile distilled water.
Applied Microbiology 28, 218-222.

Moore, L.W. & Carlson, R.V. (1975). Liquid nitrogen
storage of phytopathogenic bacteria. Phytopathology 65,
246-250.

Morris, G.J. & Canning, C.E. (1978). The cryopreservation
of Euglena gracilis. Journal of General Microbiology
108, 27-31.

Morris, G.J. & Clarke, K.J. (1976). Cryopreservation of
Chlorella. Les Colloques de l'Institute National de la
Sante et de la Recherche Medicale 62, 361-366.

Nei, Tokio. (1968). Freezing and drying of micro-
organisms. In "Papers Presented at the Conference on
"Mechanisms of Cellular Injury by Freezing and Drying in
Microorganisms (2-3 October 1968, Sapporo, Japan)".
Tokyo: University of Tokyo Press.

Norris, D.O. (1963). A porcelain bead method for storing
Rhizobium. Empire Journal of Experimental Agriculture
31, 255-258.

Perkins, D.D. (1962). Preservation of Neurospora stock
cultures with anhydrous silica gel. Canadian Journal of
Microbiology 8, 591-594.

Redway, K.F. & Lapage, S.P. (1974). Effect of carbohydrates and related compounds on the long-term preservation
of freeze-dried bacteria, Cryobiology 11, 73-79.

Rhodes, M. (1950). Viability of dried bacterial cultures.
Journal of General Microbiology 4, 450.

Rhodes, M. (1950). Preservation of yeasts and fungi by
desiccation. Transactions of the British Mycological
Society 33, 35.

Skerman, V.B.D.   (1973).   The organization of a small
general culture collection. In "Proceedings of the Second
International Conference on Culture Collections". (Ed.
A.F. Pestana de Castro, E.J. Da Silva, V.B.D. Skerman &
W.W. Leveritt).   Brisbane: Unesco/UNEP/ICRO/ WFCC/World
Data Center for Microorganisms.

Soriano, S.   (1970).   Sordelli's method for preservation of
microbial cultures by desiccation in vacuum.   In "Proceedings of the First International Conference on Culture
Collections",   p.269.   (Ed.   H. Iizuka & T. Hasegawa).
Tokyo: University of Tokyo Press.

Stamp, L.   (1947).   The preservation of bacteria by
drying. Journal of General Microbiology 1, 251-265.

Vincent, J.M. (1970). "A Manual for Practical Study of Root-
Nodule Bacteria" IBP. Handbook No. 15. Oxford: Blackwell
Scientific Publications.

14

Valid Names of Plant Pathogenic Bacteria
Compiled by
M. L. Moffett and D. W. Dye

I.	Introduction	299
II.	*Agrobacterium*	301
III.	*Corynebacterium*	301
IV.	*Erwinia*	302
V.	*Pseudomonas*	302
VI.	*Xanthomonas*	302
	References	314

I. Introduction

At a meeting of the Judicial Commission of the International Committee of Systematic Bacteriology (ICSB) held in Jerusalem in 1973, steps were initiated for a review of all currently valid names of bacteria with the aim of publishing Approved Lists of Bacterial Names. The names retained in these lists were to be valid names of taxa which were adequately described and, if cultivable, for which there was a type, neotype or authentic reference strain available.

The International Code of Nomenclature of Bacteria (1975) Rule 24a provided that after 1 January 1980, priority of publication would date from 1 January 1980. On that date all names published prior to 1 January 1980 and included in the Approved Lists of Bacterial Names of the ICSB would be treated for all nomenclatural purposes as though they had been validly published for the first time on that date. It also provided that those names validly published prior to 1 January 1980 but not included in the Approved Lists would have no further standing in nomenclature and would be available for reuse with new taxa. The names to be included in the Approved Lists would be only those covered by the aegis of the Code.

A committee on Taxonomy of Phytopathogenic Bacteria was established by the International Society for Plant Pathology (ISPP) to examine the consequences of the latest Bacteriological Code (1975 Revision) and to make recommendations on names and type strains to be included in the Approved Lists. Several recommendations were submitted to the ICSB including a list of approved species for retention. However, a number of nomenspecies essential for naming bacteria that cause different and differentiable diseases of plants, were not acceptable because they could not be defined as species. The Taxonomy Committee decided that these nomenspecies were best classified as pathovars. Therefore the Executive Committee of the ISPP and its Committee on Taxonomy of Phytopathogenic Bacteria prepared lists of pathovar names and type strains and "International Standards for Naming Pathovars of Phytopathogenic Bacteria".

The Approved Lists of Bacterial Names were published in the International Journal of Systematic Bacteriology (IJSB) (Skerman et al., 1980) and the ISPP Pathovar Lists and Standards in Review of Plant Pathology (Dye et al., 1980). Certain validly published species names were inadvertently omitted from the Approved Lists as published. These included Pseudomonas cepacia and P. corrugata, both of which have since been revived by publication in IJSB e.g. P. cepacia (Palleroni & Holmes 1981).

The following lists (Table 14.1) include the names of plant pathogenic bacteria extracted from the Approved Lists (1980), the ISPP Lists (1980) and other names proposed up to 31 December, 1982. In the Approved Lists all neotype and proposed neotype strains were designated as type strains whereas in the ISPP Lists all type strains became pathotype strains and all neotype strains became neopathotype strains. All neopathotype strains proposed in 1980 have now become established neopathotype strains in accordance with Standard 9(4) of the Pathovar Standards (Dye et al., 1980). A neopathotype strain is one proposed by valid publication to represent a pathovar where none of the strains upon which the original description was based can be located. Authorities for the neopathotype strains are given by Dye et al., (1980). Orthographic errors have been corrected where noticed.

II. *Agrobacterium*

The Approved Lists of Bacterial Names (1980) list four species of Agrobacterium Conn 1942. However, because some determinative and pathogenicity related characters have been shown to be transmissible on one or more plasmids, some plant pathologists consider that this classification does not accurately reflect the taxonomic relationships of these organisms. Kerr et al. (1978) proposed a complete reorganization of the genus with a different type species having three pathovars.

Holmes & Roberts (1981) proposed an alternative classification based on numerical taxonomic analysis which is largely in agreement with the proposals of Kerr et al. (1978). Agrobacterium is divided into four groups independent of pathogenic state (as discussed in Chapter 3). Neither system of nomenclature is given below because neither is currently valid. A change of this nature requires the approval of the ICSB Judicial Commission, which is not yet available. The currently valid names of Agrobacterium as given in the Approved Lists (1980) are listed below. The type species is A. tumefaciens (Smith & Townsend 1907) Conn 1942.

III. *Corynebacterium*

Nomenspecies of the genus Corynebacterium Lehmann & Neumann 1896 are given in the Approved Lists (1980). The proposals of Dye & Kemp (1977) to classify most of the plant pathogenic coryneform organisms as pathovars is consistent with the specific epithets in the Approved Lists. Recently, Carlson & Vidaver (1982) have proposed another system in which pathovar is replaced by subspecies. All three classifications are validly published and legitimate. Common useage will decide which version is preferred. Also it is likely that these organisms will be reclassified in one or more other genera in the near future since they are not closely related to the type species of the genus, C. diphtheriae (Kruse 1886) Lehmann & Neumann 1896.

IV. *Erwinia*

Nomenspecies of the genus <u>Erwinia</u> Winslow, Broadhurst, Buchanan, Krumwiede, Rogers & Smith 1920 are given in the Approved Lists (1980). Dye (1978a, 1981) proposed an alternative classification based on numerical taxonomic studies which indicate that some organisms are better classified as pathovars. Both names for each organism are given here and both names in each instance are equally valid. The type species is E. <u>amylovora</u> (Burrill 1882) Winslow, Broadhurst, Buchanan, Krumwiede, Rogers & Smith 1920.

V. *Pseudomonas*

Twenty nomenspecies of plant pathogens within the genus <u>Pseudomonas</u> Migula 1894 appear in the Approved Lists (1980). Two species, P. <u>cepacia</u> and P. <u>corrugata</u> were accidentally omitted and have been revived subsequently. Because many strains within the species P. <u>gladioli</u>, P. <u>marginalis</u> and P. <u>syringae</u> can be differentiated principally on the basis of pathogenicity to one or more plant hosts, Young et al. (1978) proposed that they be differentiated as pathovars within these species. The species together with their pathovars are listed below. The type species is P. <u>aeruginosa</u> (Schroeter 1872) Migula 1900.

VI. *Xanthomonas*

Five nomenspecies of the genus <u>Xanthomonas</u> Dowson 1939 appear in the Approved Lists (1980). A sixth, X. <u>populi</u> (Ridé & Ridé, 1978) is not listed and is therefore not a valid name at present. Dye (1978b) proposed pathovars for strains of X. <u>campestris</u> in accord with their ability to be differentiated on the basis of their pathogenicity to specific plant hosts. The species together with their pathovars are listed below. The type species is X. <u>campestris</u> (Pammel 1895) Dowson 1939.

TABLE 14.1   VALID NAMES OF PLANT PATHOGENIC BACTERIA

Species/pathovar/subspecies and authorities	Type/pathotype strain[a]		
	ATCC	PDDCC	NCPPB
AGROBACTERIUM			
A. radiobacter (Beijerinck & van Delden 1902) Conn 1942	19358	5785	3001
A. rhizogenes (Riker, Banfield, Wright, Keitt & Sagen 1930) Conn 1942	11325	5794	2991
A. rubi (Hildebrand 1940) Starr & Weiss 1943	13335	6428	1854
A. tumefaciens (Smith & Townsend 1907) Conn 1942	23308	5856	2437
CORYNEBACTERIUM			
C. betae Keyworth, Howell & Dowson 1956	–	2594	374
C. fascians (Tilford 1936) Dowson 1942	12974	5833	3067
C. flaccumfaciens (Hedges 1922) Dowson 1942	–	2584	1446
pv. flaccumfaciens (Hedges 1922) Dowson 1942	–	2584	1446
subsp. flaccumfaciens (Hedges 1922) Dowson 1942	–	2584	1446
pv. betae (Keyworth, Howell & Dowson 1956) Dye & Kemp 1977	–	2594	374
subsp. betae (Keyworth, Howell & Dowson 1956) Carlson & Vidaver 1982	–	2594	374
pv. oortii (Saaltink & Maas Geesteranus 1969) Dye & Kemp 1977	25283	2632	2113
subsp. oortii (Saaltink & Maas Geesteranus 1969) Carlson & Vidaver 1982	25283	2632	2113
pv. poinsettiae (Starr & Pirone 1942) Dye & Kemp 1977	9682	2566	854
subsp. poinsettiae (Starr & Pirone 1942) Carlson & Vidaver	9682	2566	854
C. ilicis Mandel, Guba & Litsky 1961	14264	2607	1228
C. insidiosum (McCulloch 1925) Jensen 1934	–	2621	1109
C. iranicum (ex Scharif 1961) Carlson & Vidaver 1982	–	3496	2253
C. michiganense (Smith 1910) Jensen 1934	–	2550	2979
pv. michiganense (Smith 1910) Jensen 1934	–	2550	2979
subsp. michiganense (Smith 1910) Jensen 1934	–	2550	2979

Species/pathovar/subspecies and authorities	Type/pathotype strain[a]		
	ATCC	PDDCC	NCPPB
pv. insidiosum (McCulloch 1925) Dye & Kemp 1977	–	2621	1109
subsp. insidiosum (McCulloch 1925) Carlson & Vidaver 1982	–	2621	1109
pv. iranicum (Scharif 1961) Dye & Kemp 1977	–	3496	2253
pv. nebraskense (Schuster, Hoff, Mandel & Lazar 1973) Dye & Kemp 1977	–	3298	2581
subsp. nebraskense (Schuster, Hoff, Mandel & Lazar 1973) Carlson & Vidaver 1982	–	3298	2581
pv. rathayi (Smith 1913) Dye & Kemp 1977	–	2574	2980
pv. sepedonicum (Spieckermann & Kotthoff 1914) Dye & Kemp 1977	33113	2535	2137
subsp. sepedonicum (Spieckermann & Kotthoff 1914) Carlson & Vidaver 1982	33113	2535	2137
subsp. tessellarius Carlson & Vidaver 1982	33566	7221	–
pv. tritici (Hutchinson 1917) Dye & Kemp 1977	11403	2626	1857
C. nebraskense (Schuster, Hoff, Mandel & Lazar 1973) emend. Vidaver & Mandel 1974	–	3298	2581
C. oortii Saaltink & Maas Geesteranus 1969	25283	2632	2113
C. poinsettiae (Starr & Pirone 1942) Burkholder 1948	9682	2566	854
C. rathayi (Smith 1913) Dowson 1942	–	2574	2980
C. sepedonicum (Spieckermann & Kotthoff 1914) Skaptason & Burkholder 1942	33113	2535	2137
ERWINIA			
E. amylovora (Burrill 1882) Winslow, Broadhurst, Buchanan, Krumwiede, Rogers & Smith 1920	15580	1540	683
E. ananas			
pv. ananas Serrano 1928	–	1850	1846
pv. uredovora (Pon, Townsend, Wessman, Schmitt & Kingsolver 1954) Dye 1978	19321	351	800
E. beticola (Abdou 1969) Collins & Jones 1982	–	2256	3494
E. carnegieana Standring 1942	–	5701	439

Species/pathovar/subspecies and authorities	Type/pathotype strain[a]		
	ATCC	PDDCC	NCPPB
E. carotovora (Jones 1901) Bergey, Harrison, Breed, Hammer & Huntoon 1923	15713	5702	312
E. carotovora			
pv. carotovora (Jones 1901) Bergey Harrison, Breed, Hammer & Huntoon 1923	15713	5702	312
pv. atroseptica (van Hall 1902) Dye 1978	–	1526	549
subsp. atroseptica (van Hall 1902) Dye 1969	–	1526	549
E. chrysanthemi Burkholder, McFadden & Dimock 1953	11663	5703	402
E. chrysanthemi			
pv. chrysanthemi Burkholder, McFadden & Dimock 1953	11663	5703	402
pv. dianthicola (Hellmers 1958) Dickey 1979	–	6427	453
pv. dieffenbachiae (McFadden 1961) Dye 1978	–	1568	2976
pv. paradisiaca (Victoria & Barros 1969) Dickey & Victoria 1979	–	2349	EC227
pv. parthenii (Starr 1947) Dye 1978	–	1547	516
pv. zeae (Sabet 1954) Victoria, Arboleda & Muñoz 1975	–	5704	2538
E. cypripedii (Hori 1911) Bergey, Harrison, Breed, Hammer & Huntoon 1923	29267	1591	3004
E. herbicola (Löhnis 1911) Dye 1964	–	272	2971
E. herbicola			
pv. herbicola (Löhnis 1911) Dye 1964		272	2971
pv. milletiae (Kawakami & Yoshida 1920) Goto, Takahashi & Okajima 1980	–	6772	2519
E. mallotivora Goto 1976	29573	5705	2851
E. nigrifluens Wilson, Starr & Berger 1957	13028	1578	564
E. quercina Hildebrand & Schroth 1967	29281	1845	1852
E. quercina			
pv. quercina Hildebrand & Schroth 1967	29281	1845	1852
pv. rubrifaciens (Wilson, Zeitoun & Fredrickson 1967) Dye 1978	29291	1915	2020
E. rhapontici (Millard 1924) Burkholder 1948	29283	1582	1578
E. rubrifaciens Wilson, Zeitoun & Fredrickson 1967	29291	1915	2020
E. salicis (Day 1924) Chester 1939	15712	1587	447
E. stewartii (Smith 1898) Dye 1963	8199	257	2295
E. tracheiphila (Smith 1895) Bergey, Harrison, Breed, Hammer & Huntoon 1923	–	5845	2452
E. uredovora (Pon, Townsend, Wessman, Schmitt & Kingsolver 1954) Dye 1963	19321	351	800

Species/pathovar/subspecies and authorities	Type/pathotype strain[a]		
	ATCC	PDDCC	NCPPB

PSEUDOMONAS

P. agarici Young 1970	25941	2656	2289
P. amygdali Psallidas & Panagopoulos 1975	–	3918	2607
P. andropogonis (Smith 1911) Stapp 1928	23061	2807	934
P. asplenii (Ark & Tompkins 1946) Savulescu 1947	23835	3944	1947
P. avenae Manns 1909	19860	1011	3183
P. betle (Ragunathan 1928) Savulescu 1947	19861	2820	323
P. caricapapayae Robbs 1956	–	2855	1873
P. caryophylli (Burkholder 1942) Starr & Burkholder 1942	25418	512	2151
P. cattleyae (Pavarino 1911) Savulescu 1947	–	2826	961
P. cepacia Palleroni & Holmes 1981	25416	5796	–
P. cichorii (Swingle 1925) Stapp 1928	10857	5707	943
P. cissicola (Takimoto 1939) Burkholder 1948	–	4289	2982
P. corrugata Roberts & Scarlett 1981	–	5819	2445
P. flectens Johnson 1956	12775	3656	539
P. gladioli Severini 1913	10248	3950	1891
P. gladioli			
pv. gladioli Severini 1913	10248	3950	1891
pv. alliicola (Burkholder 1942) Young, Dye & Wilkie 1978	19302	2804	947
P. glumae Kurita & Tabei 1967	–	3655	2981
P. hibiscicola Moniz 1963	19867	3945	1683
P. marginalis (Brown 1918) Stevens 1925	10844	3553	667
P. marginalis			
pv. marginalis (Brown 1918) Stevens 1925	10844	3553	667
pv. alfalfae Shinde & Lukezic 1974	–	5708	2644
pv. pastinacae (Burkholder 1960) Young, Dye & Wilkie 1978	13889	5709	806
P. pseudoalcaligenes subsp. citrulli Schaad, Sowell, Goth, Colwell & Webb 1978	29625	6521	–
P. rubrilineans (Lee, Purdy, Barnum & Martin 1925) Stapp 1928	19307	254	920
P. rubrisubalbicans (Christopher & Edgerton 1930) Krasil'nikov 1949	19308	5777	1027
P. solanacearum (Smith 1896) Smith 1914	11696	5712	325
P. syringae van Hall 1902	19310	3023	281
P. syringae			
pv. syringae van Hall 1902	19310	3023	281

Species/pathovar/subspecies and authorities	Type/pathotype strain[a]		
	ATCC	PDDCC	NCPPB
pv. aceris (Ark 1939) Young, Dye & Wilkie 1978	10853	2802	958
pv. antirrhini (Takimoto 1920) Young, Dye & Wilkie 1978	–	4303	1817
pv. apii (Jagger 1921) Young, Dye & Wilkie 1978	9654	2814	1626
pv. aptata (Brown & Jamieson 1913) Young, Dye & Wilkie 1978	–	459	871
pv. atrofaciens (McCulloch 1920) Young Dye & Wilkie 1978	–	4394	2612
pv. atropurpurea (Reddy & Godkin 1923) Young, Dye & Wilkie 1978	–	4457	2397
pv. berberidis (Thornberry & Anderson 1931) Young, Dye & Wilkie 1978	–	4116	2724
pv. cannabina (Šutić & Dowson 1959) Young, Dye & Wilkie 1978	–	2823	1437
pv. ciccaronei (Ercolani & Caldarola 1972) Young, Dye & Wilkie 1978	–	5710	2355
pv. coronafaciens (Elliott 1920) Young, Dye & Wilkie 1978	–	3113	600
pv. delphinii (Smith 1904) Young, Dye & Wilkie 1978	–	529	1879
pv. dysoxyli (Hutchinson 1949) Young, Dye & Wilkie 1978	19863	545	225
pv. eriobotryae (Takimoto 1931) Young, Dye & Wilkie 1978	–	4455	2331
pv. garcae (Amaral, Teixeira & Pinheiro 1956) Young, Dye & Wilkie 1978	19864	4323	588
pv. glycinea (Coerper 1919) Young, Dye & Wilkie 1978	–	2189	2411
pv. helianthi (Kawamura 1934) Young, Dye & Wilkie 1978	–	4531	2640
pv. japonica (Mukoo 1955) Dye, Bradbury, Goto, Hayward, Lelliott & Schroth 1980 (syn. P.striafaciens var. japonica)	–	6305	3093
pv. lachrymans (Smith & Bryan 1915) Young, Dye & Wilkie 1978	7386	3988	537
pv. lapsa (Ark 1940) Young, Dye & Wilkie 1978	–	3947	2096
pv. maculicola (McCulloch 1911) Young Dye & Wilkie 1978	–	3935	2039
pv. mellea (Johnson 1923) Young, Dye & Wilkie 1978	–	5711	2356
pv. mori (Boyer & Lambert 1893) Young, Dye & Wilkie 1978	19873	4331	1034

Species/pathovar/subspecies and authorities	Type/pathotype strain[a]		
	ATCC	PDDCC	NCPPB
pv. morsprunorum (Wormald 1931) Young Dye & Wilkie 1978	19322	5795	2995
pv. myricae Ogimi & Higuchi 1981	–	7118	–
pv. panici (Elliott 1923) Young, Dye & Wilkie 1978	19875	3955	1498
pv. papulans (Rose 1917) Dhanvantari 1977	–	4048	2848
pv. passiflorae (Reid 1938) Young, Dye & Wilkie 1978	–	129	1387
pv. persicae (Prunier, Luisetti & Gardan 1970) Young, Dye & Wilkie 1978	–	5846	2761
pv. phaseolicola (Burkholder 1926) Young, Dye & Wilkie 1978	19304	2740	52
pv. pisi (Sackett 1916) Young, Dye & Wilkie 1978	–	2452	2585
pv. primulae (Ark & Gardner 1936) Young, Dye & Wilkie 1978	19306	3956	133
pv. ribicola (Bohn & Maloit 1946) Young, Dye & Wilkie 1978	13456	3882	963
pv. savastanoi (Smith 1908) Young, Dye & Wilkie 1978	13522	4352	639
pv. sesami (Malkoff 1906) Young, Dye & Wilkie 1978	19879	763	1016
pv. striafaciens (Elliott 1927) Young, Dye & Wilkie 1978	10730[b]	3961	1898
pv. tabaci (Wolf & Foster 1917) Young, Dye & Wilkie 1978	–	2835	1427
pv. tagetis (Hellmers 1955) Young, Dye & Wilkie 1978	–	4091	2488
pv. theae (Hori 1915) Young, Dye & Wilkie 1978	–	3923	2598
pv. tomato (Okabe 1933) Young, Dye & Wilkie 1978	–	2844	1106
pv. ulmi (Šutić & Tešić 1958) Young, Dye & Wilkie 1978	19883	3962	632
pv. viburni (Thornberry & Anderson 1931) Young, Dye & Wilkie 1978	13458	3963	1921
P. tolaasii Paine 1919	–	2192	2290
P. viridiflava (Burkholder 1930) Dowson 1939	13223	2848	635
P. woodsii (Smith 1911) Stevens 1925[e]	19311	3967	968

Species/pathovar/subspecies and authorities	Type/pathotype strain[a]		
	ATCC	PDDCC	NCPPB

XANTHOMONAS

	ATCC	PDDCC	NCPPB
X. albilineans (Ashby 1929) Dowson 1943	—	196	2969
X. ampelina Panagopoulos 1969	—	4298	2217
X. axonopodis Starr & Garces 1950	19312	50	457
X. campestris (Pammel 1895) Dowson 1939	—	13	528
X. campestris			
pv. campestris (Pammel 1895) Dowson 1939	—	13	528
pv. aberrans (Knösel 1961) Dye 1978	—	4805	2986
pv. alangii (Padhya & Patel 1962) Dye 1978	—	5717	1336
pv. alfalfae (Riker, Jones & Davis 1935) Dye 1978	—	5718	2062
pv. amaranthicola (Patel, Wankar & Kulkarni 1952) Dye 1978	11645	441	570
pv. amorphophalli (Jindal, Patel & Singh 1972) Dye 1978	—	3033	2371
pv. aracearum (Berniac 1974) Dye 1978	—	5381	2832
pv. arecae (Rao & Mohan 1970) Dye 1978	—	5719	2649
pv. argemones (Srinivasan, Patel & Thirumalachar 1961) Dye 1978	—	1617	1593
pv. armoraciae (McCulloch 1929) Dye 1978	—	7	347
pv. arracaciae (Pereira, Paradella & Zagatto 1971) Dye 1978	—	3158	2436
pv. azadirachtae (Desai, Gandhi, Patel & Kotasthane 1966) Dye 1978		3102[c]	2388[c]
pv. badrii (Patel, Kulkarni & Dhande 1950) Dye 1978	11672	571	571
pv. barbareae (Burkholder 1941) Dye 1978	13460	438	983
pv. bauhiniae (Padhya, Patel & Kotasthane 1965) Dye 1978	—	5720	1335
pv. begoniae (Takimoto 1934) Dye 1978	—	194	1926
pv. betlicola (Patel, Kulkarni & Dhande 1951) Dye 1978	11677	312	2972
pv. biophyti (Patel, Chauhan, Kotasthane & Desai 1969) Dye 1978	—	2780	2228
pv. blepharidis (Srinivasan & Patel 1956) Dye 1978	17995	5722	1757
pv. cajani (Kulkarni, Patel & Abhyankar 1950) Dye 1978	11639	444	573
pv. cannabis Severin 1978	—	6570	2877
pv. carissae (Moniz, Sabley & More 1964) Dye 1978	—	3034	2373
pv. carotae (Kendrick 1934) Dye 1978	—	5723	1422

Species/pathovar/subspecies and authorities	Type/pathotype strain[a]		
	ATCC	PDDCC	NCPPB
pv. cassavae (Wiehe & Dowson 1953) Maraite & Weyns 1979	−	204	101
pv. cassiae (Kulkarni, Patel & Dhande 1951) Dye 1978	11638	358	2973
pv. celebensis (Gäumann 1923) Dye 1978	19045	1488	1832
pv. cerealis (Hagborg 1942) Dye 1978	−	1409	1944
pv. citri (Hasse 1915) Dye 1978	−	24	409
pv. clerondendri (Patel, Kulkarni & Dhande 1952) Dye 1978	11676	445	575
pv. clitoriae Pandit & Kulkarni 1979	−	6574	3092
pv. convolvuli (Nagarkoti, Banerjee & Swarup 1973) Dye 1978	−	5380	2498
pv. coracanae (Desai, Thirumalachar & Patel 1965) Dye 1978	−	5724	1786
pv. coriandri (Srinivasan, Patel & Thirumalachar 1961) Dye 1978	17996	5725	1758
pv. corylina (Miller, Bollen, Simmons, Gross & Barss 1940) Dye 1978	19313	5726	935
pv. cucurbitae (Bryan 1926) Dye 1978	−	2299	2597
pv. cyamopsidis (Patel, Dhande & Kulkarni 1953) Dye 1978	−	616	637
pv. desmodii (Patel 1949) Dye 1978	11640	315	481
pv. desmodiigangetici (Patel & Moniz 1948) Dye 1978	11671	577	577
pv. desmodiilaxifloris Pant & Kulkarni 1976	29	6502	3086
pv. desmodiirotundifolii (Desai & Shah 1960) Dye 1978	−	168	885
pv. dieffenbachiae (McCulloch & Pirone 1939) Dye 1978	−	5727	1833
pv. durantae (Srinivasan & Patel 1957) Dye 1978	−	5728	1456
pv. erythrinae (Patel, Kulkarni & Dhande 1952) Dye 1978	11679	446	578
pv. esculenti (Rangaswami & Easwaran 1962) Dye 1978	−	5729	2190
pv. eucalypti (Truman 1974) Dye 1978	−	5382	2337
pv. euphorbiae (Sabet, Ishag & Khalil 1969) Dye 1978	−	5730	1828
pv. fascicularis (Patel & Kotasthane 1969) Dye 1978	−	5731	2230
pv. fici (Cavara 1905) Dye 1978	−	3036	2372
pv. glycines (Nakano 1919) Dye 1978 (syn. X. phaseoli var. sojense)	−	5732	554

Species/pathovar/subspecies and authorities	Type/pathotype strain[a]		
	ATCC	PDDCC	NCPPB
pv. graminis (Egli, Goto & Schmidt 1975) Dye 1978	–	5733	2700
pv. guizotiae (Yirgou 1964) Dye 1978	–	5734	1932
pv. gummisudans (McCulloch 1924) Dye 1978	–	5780	2182
pv. hederae (Arnaud 1920) Dye 1978	–	453	939
pv. heliotropii (Sabet, Ishaq & Khalil 1969) Dye 1978	–	5778	2057
pv. holcicola (Elliott 1930) Dye 1978	–	3103	2417
pv. hordei (Hagborg 1942) Dye 1978	–	5735	2389
pv. hyacinthi (Wakker 1883) Dye 1978	19314	189	599
pv. incanae (Kendrick & Baker 1942) Dye 1978	13462	574	937
pv. ionidii (Padhya & Patel 1963) Dye 1978	–	5736	1334
pv. juglandis (Pierce 1901) Dye 1978	–	35	411
pv. khayae (Sabet 1959) Dye 1978	–	671	536
pv. lantanae (Srinivasan & Patel 1957) Dye 1978	–	5737	1455
pv. laureliae (Dye 1963) Dye 1978	–	84	1155
pv. lawsoniae (Patel, Bhatt & Kulkarni 1951) Dye 1978	11674	319	579
pv. leeana (Patel & Kotasthane 1969) Dye 1978	–	5738	2229
pv. lespedezae (Ayres, Lefebvre & Johnson 1939) Dye 1978	13463	439	993
pv. maculifoliigardeniae (Ark & Barrett 1946) Dye 1978	–	318	971
pv. malvacearum (Smith 1901) Dye 1978	–	5739	633
pv. mangiferaeindicae (Patel, Moniz & Kulkarni 1948) Robbs, Ribeiro & Kimura 1974	11637	5740	490
pv. manihotis (Berthet & Bondar 1915) Dye 1978	–	5741	1834
pv. martyniicola (Moniz & Patel 1958) Dye 1978	–	82	1148
pv. melhusii (Patel, Kulkarni & Dhande 1952) Dye 1978	11644	619	994
pv. merremiae Pant & Kulkarni 1976	30	6747	3114
pv. musacearum (Yirgou & Bradbury 1968) Dye 1978	–	2870	2005
pv. nakataecorchori (Padhya & Patel 1963) Dye 1978	–	5742	1337
pv. nigromaculans (Takimoto 1927) Dye 1978	23390	80	1935
pv. olitorii (Sabet 1957) Dye 1978	–	359	464

Species/pathovar/subspecies and authorities	Type/pathotype strain[a]		
	ATCC	PDDCC	NCPPB
pv. oryzae (Ishiyama 1922) Dye 1978	–	3125	3002
pv. oryzicola (Fang, Ren, Chen, Chu, Faan & Wu 1957) Dye 1978	–	5743	1585
pv. papavericola (Bryan & McWhorter 1930) Dye 1978	14179	220	2970
pv. passiflorae (Pereira 1969) Dye 1978	–	3151	2346
pv. patelii (Desai & Shah 1959) Dye 1978	–	167	840
pv. pedalii (Patel & Jindal 1972) Dye 1978	–	3030	2368
pv. pelargonii (Brown 1923) Dye 1978	–	4321	2985
pv. phaseoli (Smith 1897) Dye 1978	9563	5834	3035
pv. phleipratensis (Wallin & Reddy 1945) Dye 1978	–	5744	1837
pv. phormiicola (Takimoto 1933) Dye 1978	–	4294	2983
pv. phyllanthi (Sabet, Ishag & Khalil 1969) Dye 1978	–	5745	2066
pv. physalidicola (Goto & Okabe 1958) Dye 1978	–	586	761
pv. physalidis (Srinivasan, Patel & Thirumalachar 1962) Dye 1978	17994	5746	1756
pv. pisi (Goto & Okabe 1958) Dye 1978	–	570	762
pv. plantaginis (Thornberry & Anderson 1937) Dye 1978	23382	1028	1061
pv. poinsettiicola (Patel, Bhatt & Kulkarni 1951) Dye 1978	11643	5779	581
pv. pruni (Smith 1903) Dye 1978	19316	51	416
pv. punicae (Hingorani & Singh 1959) Dye 1978	–	360	466
pv. raphani (White 1930) Dye 1978	–	1404	1946
pv. ricini (Yoshii & Takimoto 1928) Dye 1978	19317[d]	5747[d]	1063[d]
pv. rhynchosiae (Sabet, Ishag & Khalil 1969) Dye 1978	–	5748	1827
pv. secalis (Reddy, Godkin & Johnson 1924) Dye 1978	–	5749	2822
pv. sesami (Sabet & Dowson 1960) Dye 1978	–	621	631
pv. sesbaniae (Patel, Kulkarni & Dhande 1952) Dye 1978	11675	367	582
pv. spermacoces (Srinivasan & Patel 1956) Dye 1978	17998	5751	1760
pv. tamarindi (Patel, Bhatt & Kulkarni 1951) Dye 1978	11673	572	584
pv. taraxaci (Niederhauser 1943) Dye 1978	19318	579	940

Species/pathovar/subspecies and authorities	Type/pathotype strain[a]		
	ATCC	PDDCC	NCPPB
pv. tardicrescens (McCulloch 1937) Dye 1978	–	4295	2984
pv. theaecola Uehara, Arai, Nonaka & Sano 1980	–	6774	–
pv. thirumalacharii (Padhya & Patel 1964) Dye 1978	–	5852	1452
pv. translucens (Jones, Johnson & Reddy 1917) Dye 1978	19319	5752	973
pv. tribuli (Srinivasan & Patel 1956) Dye 1978	–	5753	1454
pv. trichodesmae (Patel, Kulkarni & Dhande 1952) Dye 1978	11678	5754	585
pv. undulosa (Smith, Jones & Reddy 1919) Dye 1978	–	5755	2821
pv. uppalii (Patel 1948) Dye 1978	11641	5756	586
pv. vasculorum (Cobb 1893) Dye 1978	–	5757	796
pv. vernoniae (Patel, Desai & Patel 1968) Dye 1978	–	5758	1787
pv. vesicatoria (Doidge 1920) Dye 1978	–	63	422
pv. vignaeradiatae (Sabet, Ishag & Khalil 1969) Dye 1978	–	5759	2058
pv. vignicola (Burkholder 1944) Dye 1978	11648	333	1838
pv. vitians (Brown 1918) Dye 1978	19320	336	976
pv. viticola (Nayudu 1972) Dye 1978	–	3867[c]	2475[c]
pv. vitiscarnosae (Moniz & Patel 1958) Dye 1978	–	90	1149
pv. vitistrifoliae (Padhya, Patel & Kotasthane 1965) Dye 1978	–	5761	1451
pv. vitiswoodrowii (Patel & Kulkarni 1951) Dye 1978	11636	3965[c]	1014
pv. zantedeschiae (Joubert & Truter 1972) Dye 1978	–	2372	2978
pv. zinniae (Hopkins & Dowson 1949) Dye 1978	–	5762	2439
X. fragariae Kennedy & King 1962	–	5715	1469

References

Carlson, R.R. & Vidaver, A.K. (1982). Taxonomy of Coryne-bacterium plant pathogens, including a new pathogen of wheat, based on polyacrylamide gel electrophoresis of cellular proteins. International Journal of Systematic Bacteriology 32, 315-326.

Collins, M.D. & Jones, D. (1982). Taxonomic studies on Corynebacterium beticola Abdou. Journal of Applied Bacteriology 52, 229-233.

Dye, D.W. (1978a). Genus V. Erwinia Winslow, Broadhurst, Buchanan, Krumwiede, Rogers & Smith 1920. In Young, J.M., Dye, D.W. Bradbury, J.F. Panagopoulos, C.G. & Robbs, C.F. (1978). A proposed nomenclature and classification for plant pathogenic bacteria. New Zealand Journal of Agricultural Research 21, 153-177.

Dye, D.W. (1978b). Genus IX Xanthomonas Dowson 1939. In Young, J.M., Dye, D.W., Bradbury, J.F. Panagopoulos, C.G. & Robbs, C.F. (1978). A proposed nomenclature and classification for plant pathogenic bacteria. New Zealand Journal of Agricultural Research 21, 153-177.

Dye, D.W. (1981). A numerical taxonomic study of the genus Erwinia. New Zealand Journal of Agricultural Research 24, 223-231.

Dye, D.W., Bradbury, J.F., Goto, M., Hayward, A.C., Lelliott, R.A. & Schroth, M.N. (1980). International standards for naming pathovars of phytopathogenic bacteria and a list of pathovar names and pathotype strains. Review of Plant Pathology 59, 153-168.

Footnote to Table 14.1

[a]ATCC, American Type Culture Collection, Rockville, Maryland, USA. PDDCC, DSIR Mount Albert Research Centre, Private Bag, Auckland, New Zealand. NCPPB, National Collection of Plant Pathogenic Bacteria, Harpenden, U.K.

[b]P. syringae pv. striafaciens pathotype strain ATCC 10730 reported to be non-pathogenic by Lelliott (unpubl.). Pathogenic reference strains are PDDCC 4483, NCPPB 2394.

[c]non-pigmented strain.

[d]non-pathogenic strain.

[e]P. woodsii is possibly a synonym of P. andropogonis (Nishiyama et al., 1979). See also Chapter 7.

Dye, D.W. & Kemp, W.J. (1977). A taxonomic study of plant pathogenic Corynebacterium species. New Zealand Journal of Agricultural Research 20, 563-582.

Holmes, B. & Roberts, P. (1981). The classification, identification and nomenclature of agrobacteria. Journal of Applied Bacteriology 50, 443-467.

Kerr, A., Young, J.M. & Panagopoulos, C.G. (1978). Genus II Agrobacterium Conn 1942. In Young, J.M., Dye, D.W., Bradbury, J.F. Panagopoulos, C.G. & Robbs, C.F. (1978). A proposed nomenclature and classification for plant pathogenic bacteria. New Zealand Journal of Agricultural Research 21, 153-177.

Nishiyama, K., Kusaba, T., Ohta, K., Nahata, K. & Ezuka, A. (1979). Bacterial black rot of tulip caused by Pseudomonas andropogonis. Annals of the Phytopathological Society of Japan 45, 668-674.

Ogimi, C. & Higuchi, H. (1981). [Bacterial gall of Yamamomo (Myrica rubra S. et Z.) caused by Pseudomonas syringae pv. myricae pv. nov.] Annals of the Phytopathological Society of Japan 47, 443-448.

Palleroni, N.J. & Holmes, B. (1981). "Pseudomonas cepacia sp. nov., nom. rev." International Journal of Systematic Bacteriology 31, 479-481.

Ridé, M. (1958) Sur l'etiologie du chancre suintant du peuplier. Comptes Rendus Hebdomadaires des Seances de l'Academic des Sciences 246, 2795-2798.

Ridé, M. & Ridé, S. (1978). "Xanthomonas populi" (Ridé) Comb. nov. (Syn. Aplanobacter populi Ridé), specificite, varibilité et absence de relations avec Erwinia cancerogena Ù. European Journal of Forest Pathology 8, 310-333.

Schaad, N.W. Sowell, G. Jr, Goth, R.W., Colwell, R.R. & Webb, R.E. (1978). Pseudomonas pseudoalcaligenes subsp. citrulli subsp. nov. International Journal of Systematic Bacteriology 28, 117-125.

Skerman, V.B.D., McGowan, V. & Sneath, P.H.A. (1980). Approved lists of bacterial names. International Journal of Systematic Bacteriology 30, 225-420.

Uehara, K., Arai, K., Nonaka, T., & Sano, I. (1980). [Canker of tea, a new disease and its causal bacterium Xanthomonas campestris pv. theaecola Uehara et Arai pv. nov.] Bulletin of the Faculty of Agriculture, Kagoshima University 30, 17-21.

Young, J.M., Dye, D.W. & Wilkie, J.P. (1978). Genus VII Pseudomonas Migula 1894. In Young, J.M., Dye, D.W., Bradbury, J.F., Panagopoulos, C.G. & Robbs, C.F. (1978). A proposed nomenclature and classification for plant pathogenic bacteria. New Zealand Journal of Agricultural Research 21, 153-177.

15

Bacterial Plant Pathogens Recorded
in Australia
Compiled by
M. L. Moffett

I.	Introduction	317
II.	Explanation of Text Symbols	318
III.	*Agrobacterium*	319
IV.	*Corynebacterium*	320
V.	*Erwinia*	321
VI.	*Pseudomonas*	323
VII.	*Streptomyces*	330
VIII.	*Xanthomonas*	330
IX.	Undetermined Bacterial Pathogens	334
X.	Organisms Currently Unnamed	334
	References	336

I. Introduction

This host/pathogen list was compiled from records provided by plant pathologists from each State in Australia. Records either published, in preparation or on file as well as disease herbaria and culture collections were searched by the various plant pathologists who assisted in preparation of this list (see acknowledgements). This list should serve as a useful guide to the current state of knowledge of bacterial disease records in Australia.

Users should be aware that the accuracy of records in this and any host/pathogen list are dependent upon accurate diagnosis. Where cultures and herbarium specimens are kept it is possible to verify the accuracy of earlier diagnoses. Where no permanent physical records are kept this can never be done. For this reason the

status of each record is listed to assist future veri-
fication. Some records which have been published but
which are now known to be incorrect, or suspected of being
inaccurate, are included with explanations.

II. Explanation of Text Symbols

C　Living culture kept in a State culture collection,
　　the National Collection of Plant Pathogenic Bacteria,
　　Harpenden, U.K. (NCPPB) or the Plant Diseases
　　Division Culture Collection (PDDCC) D.S.I.R.,
　　Auckland, New Zealand. Cultures C(T) are mostly held
　　at the Department of Microbiology, University of
　　Queensland, St. Lucia. 4067.

H　Herbarium specimen available

D　Pathogen isolated, identified but culture not kept

S　Diagnosed on symptoms only

(N)　New South Wales.

(Nt)　Northern Territory.

(Q)　Queensland.

(S)　South Australia.

(T)　Tasmania.

(V)　Victoria.

(W)　Western Australia.

　　Botanical names are taken from Hartley (1978) and Hortus
Third (Anon., 1976).

Host	Occurrence

III. *Agrobacterium*

Agrobacterium - tumourigenic state[1]

Host	Occurrence
Anemone sp.	D(W)
Beta pendula Roth (white birch)	H(N)
Beta vulgaris L. ssp. vulgaris (beetroot, sugar beet)	D(V); S(Q,T)
Betula sp.	D(W)
Brassica napus var. napobrassica (L.) Reichb. (swede turnip)	S(T)
Brassica rapa L. var. rapa (turnip)	S(Q)
Calendula officinalis L. (garden marigold)	S(T)
Chamelaucium uncinatum Schauer. (geraldton wax)	D(W)
Chrysanthemum x morifolium Ramat (chrysanthemum)	H(N): D(V): S(Q)
Citrus sinensis (L.) Osb. (sweet orange)	S(Q)
Codiaeum variegatum (L.) Blume var. pictum (Lodd.) Mull (croton)	S(Q)
Conium maculatum L. (hemlock)	S(N)
Cupressus sp. (cyprus)	H(V)
Cydonia oblonga Miller (quince)	D(W)
Dahlia sp. (dahlia)	H(N); D(W); S(V)
Daucus carota L. (carrot)	S(V)
Diospyros kaki L.f. (persimmon)	D(W)
Eriobotrya japonica (Thunb.) Lindl. (loquat)	D(W)
Eucalyptus maculata Hook. (spotted gum)	D(W)
Ficus carica L. (fig)	D(W)
Fuschsia sp.	C(N); H(N)
Genista monosperma (L.) Lam.	D(W)
Gladiolus tristis L. (gladiolus)	S(V)
Humulus lupulus L. (hop)	S(T)
Jacaranda mimosifolia D. Don	D(W)
Juglans regia L. (walnut)	D(W); S(T)
Lactuca sativa L. (lettuce)	S(V)
Lycopersicon esculentum Miller (tomato)	S(V)
Malus domestica Borkh. (apple)	H(W); D(V); S(Q,T,S)
Morus nigra L. (mulberry)	S(S)
Myoporum sp.	D(W)
Pastinaca sativa L. (parsnip)	S(V)
Phaseolus vulgaris L. (French bean)	S(V)
Prunus armeniaca L. (apricot)	D(W); S(N,V)
Prunus avium (L.) L. (cherry)	H(N); S(T,V); D(S,W)
Prunus cerasus L. (sour cherry)	S(V)

[1] *See Chapter 3 for explanation of nomenclature for Agrobacterium.*

Host	Occurrence
Prunus <u>domestica</u> L. (plum)	H(N); S(T,V): D(S,W)
Prunus <u>dulcis</u> (Miller) D.A. Webb (almond)	C(S); H(Nt); D(S); S(Nt,T,V)
Prunus <u>persica</u> (L.) Batsch (peach)	C(Q,S); H(N,W); D(V); S(T)
Prunus <u>persica</u> var. <u>nectrina</u> (Ait.f.) Maxim (nectarine)	H(N,W)
Prunus <u>salicina</u> Lindl. (Japanese plum)	S(Q); D(S,W)
Prunus sp. (ornamental cherry)	H(N)
Prunus sp.	D(W)
Pyrus <u>communis</u> L. (pear)	D(W); S(N,S,V)
Rheum <u>rhabarbarum</u> L. (rhubarb)	S(N,S)
Ribes <u>uva-crispa</u> L. (gooseberry)	S(T)
Rosa sp. (rose)	C(Q); H(Q); D(N,S,W); S(T,V)
Rubus <u>idaeus</u> L. (raspberry)	S(T,V)
Rubus <u>loganobaccus</u> L.H. Bailey (loganberry)	H(N); S(T)
Sorbus <u>aucuparia</u> L. (rowan)	H(N)
Teline <u>monosperma</u> (L.) Lam.	D(W)
Vitis <u>vinifera</u> L. (grape)	C(S); H(N); S(Q); D(S,W); S(V)

<u>Agrobacterium</u> - rhizogenic state

None of the records for the rhizogenic state (hairy root) have been confirmed. Recent surveys (see Chapter 3) have not detected hairy root in Australia.

Host	Occurrence
Brassica <u>oleracea</u> var. <u>capitata</u> (L.) Alef. (cabbage)	S(V)
Brassica <u>rapa</u> L. var. <u>rapa</u> (turnip)	H(T)
Malus <u>domestica</u> Borkh. (apple)	D(W)
Rosa sp. (rose)	S(Q)
Solanum <u>tuberosum</u> L. (potato)	S(V)

IV.   *Corynebacterium*

<u>C</u>. <u>flaccumfaciens</u> subsp. <u>flaccumfaciens</u>[1] (Hedges 1922) Dowson 1942

    Phaseolus <u>vulgaris</u> L. (French and navy bean)   C(V); D(N,S)

<u>C</u>. <u>michiganense</u> subsp. <u>insidiosum</u> (McCulloch 1925) Carlson & Vidaver 1982

    Medicago <u>sativa</u> L. (lucerne)   C(N); H(N,T); D(S,T,V)

<u>C</u>. <u>michiganense</u> subsp. <u>michiganense</u> (Smith 1910) Jensen 1934

    Capsicum <u>annuum</u> L. (capsicum)   C(Q); H(Q)

---

[1] *Not recorded in Australia since 1969. Use of certified seed appears to have eradicated this disease.*

Host	Occurrence
Lycopersicon esculentum Miller (tomato)	C(N,Q,W); H(N,Q); D(S,V); S(T)
Solanum nigrum L. (black berry nightshade)	D(W)
Corynebacterium sp.	
Lolium rigidum Gaudin (annual ryegrass)[1]	H(W); D(S)
Triticum aestivum L. (wheat)	C(W); H(W)
(originally identified as C. tritici (inv.))	

V. *Erwinia*

E. carotovora (Jones 1901) Bergey, Harrison, Breed, Hammer & Huntoon 1923

E. carotovora pv. atroseptica (van Hall 1902) Dye 1969

Brassica oleracea var. botrytis (L.) Alef. (cauliflower)	C(W)
Solanum tuberosum L. (potato)	C(N,Q); H(N,T); D(T,V)

E. carotovora pv. carotovora (Jones 1901) Bergey, Harrison, Breed, Hammer & Huntoon 1923

Allium cepa var. aggregatum G. Don (shallot)	D(W); S(Q)
Allium cepa L. var. cepa (onion)	D(T); (S,V)
Apium graveolens L. (celery)	C(Q); H(N); D(V); S(S)
Begonia x tuberhybrida Voss (hybrid tuberous begonia)	S(N)
Beta vulgaris ssp. cicla (L.) Koch (silver beet)	S(N,T,V)
Bletia striata (Thunb.) Racshb f. (terrestrial orchid)	S(T)
Brassica chinensis L. (Chinese cabbage)	C(Q); S(Nt)
Brassica oleracea var. botrytis (L.) Alef. (cauliflower)	C(Q); D(V,W); S(N,S)
Brassica oleracea var. capitata (L.) Alef. (cabbage)	C(Q); D(V); S(N,Nt)
Brassica oleracea var. gemmifera DC. (Brussels sprouts)	D(T,W); S(N,S,V)
Brassica oleracea var. italica Plenck (broccoli)	S(V)
Brassica rapa L. var. rapa (turnip)	S(T,V)
Canna sp. (garden canna)	D(V)
Capsicum annuum L. (capsicum)	C(Q); D(W)
Cheiranthus cheiri L. (wall flower)	D(V)
Chrysanthemum x morifolium Ramat (chrysanthemum)	H(N)
Crassula sp.	D(W)
Cucurbita maxima Duch. (pumpkin)	D(V)
Cucurbita pepo L. s. lat. (marrow)	D(Q)
Cyclamen persicum Mill. (cyclamen)	S(N)
Cynara scolymus L. (globe artichoke)	S(V)

---

[1] *Sometimes reported as Corynebacterium rathayi but insufficient evidence from comparative work exists to confirm this identity.*

Host	Occurrence
<u>Dahlia</u> sp. (dahlia) (isolate originally designated E.aroideae)	D(Q)
<u>Daucus</u> <u>carota</u> L. (carrot)	D(Q,V); S(N,S,T)
<u>Eucharis</u> sp.	S(N)
<u>Helianthus</u> <u>tuberosus</u> L. (Jerusalem artichoke)	S(N,V)
<u>Hyacinthus</u> <u>orientalis</u> L. (hyacinth)	S(N,T)
<u>Iris</u> sp.	H(N,V)
<u>Ixia</u> sp. (iscia)	D(V)
<u>Lactuca</u> <u>sativa</u> L. (lettuce)	D(Q,T): S(N,Nt,S,V)
<u>Lilium</u> <u>lancifolium</u> Thunb. (tiger lily)	S(N)
<u>Lilium</u> sp. (lily)	D(V)
<u>Lycaste</u> sp.	D(W)
<u>Lycopersicon</u> <u>esculentum</u> Miller (tomato)	D(Q)
<u>Matthiola</u> <u>incana</u> (L.) R.Br. (stock)	S(V)
<u>Musa</u> <u>acuminata</u> Colla. (cavendish banana)	S(Q)
<u>Narcissus</u> sp. (daffodil)	S(V)
<u>Nicotiana</u> <u>tabacum</u> L. (tobacco)	C(Q)
<u>Pastinaca</u> <u>sativa</u> L. (parsnip)	S(N,V)
<u>Phalaenopsis</u> sp. (Phalaenopsis orchid)	D(Q)
<u>Pisum</u> <u>sativum</u> L. s. lat. (pea)	C(N); H(N)
<u>Rheum</u> <u>rhabarbarum</u> L. (rhubarb)	D(W); S(V)
<u>Sansevieria</u> <u>trifasciata</u> Prain (mother-in-law's tongue)	D(V,W)
<u>Solanum</u> <u>melongena</u> L. (eggplant)	D(W)
<u>Solanum</u> <u>tuberosum</u> L. (potato) C(N,T,W); H(N,T); D(T,V); S(S)	
<u>Spinacia</u> <u>oleracea</u> L. (spinach)	S(V)
<u>Tulipa</u> sp. (tulip)	D(V)
<u>Vallota</u> <u>speciosa</u> (L. f.) T. Durand & Schinz (Scarborough lily)	S(V)
<u>Vanda</u> sp. (Vanda orchid)	C(N); H(N)
<u>Vigna</u> <u>unguiculata</u> ssp. <u>sesquipedalis</u> (L.) Verdc. (snake bean)	H(N)
<u>Zantedeschia</u> <u>aethiopica</u> (L.) K. Spreng (calla lily)	D(V); S(N)
<u>Zea</u> <u>mays</u> L. (maize)	C(N); H(N); S(Nt)
<u>Zea</u> <u>mays</u> convar. <u>saccharata</u> Koern. (sweetcorn)	S(Nt,V)
<u>E</u>. chrysanthemi[1] Burkholder, McFadden & Dimock 1953	
<u>Philodendron</u> <u>selloum</u> C. Koch	S(N)
<u>Saccharum</u> interspecific hybrids (sugar cane)	C(Q)
<u>Solanum</u> <u>tuberosum</u> L. (potato)	C(N,W)
<u>E</u>. cypripedii (Hori 1911) Bergey, Harrison, Breed, Hammer & Huntoon 1923	
<u>Cypripedium</u> sp. (orchid)	S(S)
<u>Paphiopedilum</u> sp. (orchid)	S(S)

[1] *A number of pathovars of <u>Erwinia</u> <u>chrysanthemi</u> have been designated but pathovar designations have not been given in this list because of lack of information.*

Host	Occurrence

E. tracheiphila (Smith 1895) Bergey, Harrison,
      Breed, Hammer & Huntoon 1923
      Citrullus lanatus var. caffer (Schrad.) Mansf.   S(S)
        (watermelon)

Erwinia sp.
    Persea americana Miller (avocado)   S(N)
    Solanum tuberosum L. (potato)   C(N)
    Zantedeschia aethiopica (L.) K. Spreng. (calla lily)   S(S)
    Zea mays L. (maize)   S(N,Q)

VI. *Pseudomonas*

P. aeruginosa (Shroeter 1872) Migula 1900
    Allium cepa L. var. cepa (onion)   C(N); H(N)
    Nicotiana tabacum L. (tobacco)   C(N); H(N)

P. agarici Young 1970
    Agaricus bisporus (Lange) Sing. (mushroom)   C(N)

P. andropogonis (Smith 1911) Stapp 1928
    Bougainvillea spectabilis Willd.   C(N,Q); H(N,Q); D(W)
      (bougainvillea)
    Ceratonia siliqua L. (carob)   C(Q); H(Q)
    Cicer arietinum L. (chick pea)   C(Q)
    Dianthus caryophyllus L. (carnation) C(N,Q); H(N); D(V)
    Mucuna deeringiana (Bort) Merr. (velvet bean) C(Q); H(N)
    Sorghum bicolor (L.) Moench s. lat. (broom   C(Q); H(N,Q)
      millet, sorghum)
    Sorghum sudanense (Piper) Stapf (Sudan grass) H(N); S(Q)
    Trifolium pratense L. (red clover)   C(Q)
    Trifolium repens L. (white clover)   C(Q); H(N)
    Vicia benghalensis L. (purple vetch)   H(N)
    Vicia sativa ssp. nigra (L.) Ehrh. (narrow   H(N)
      leaf vetch)
    Vicia sativa L. ssp. sativa (common vetch)   C(Q); H(N)
    Vicia villosa ssp. dasycarpa (Ten.) Cav.   H(N)
      (woollypod vetch)

P. caricapapayae Robbs 1956
    Carica papaya L. (pawpaw)   C(Q)

P. cattleyae (Pavarino 1911) Savulescu 1947
    Cattleya sp. (Cattleya orchid)   D(Q)
    Phalaenopsis sp. (Phalaenopsis orchid)   D(Q)

P. cepacia Burkholder 1950
    Allium cepa L. var. cepa (onion)   S(S)
    Lycopersicon esculentum Miller (tomato)   C(N)

Host	Occurrence

P. cichorii (Swingle 1925) Stapp 1928
   Brassica oleracea var. capitata (L.) Alef.   C(Q)
     (cabbage)
   Lactuca sativa L. (lettuce)   C(N)
   Papaver nudicaule L. (Iceland poppy)   C(N)
P. flectens Johnson 1956
   Macroptilium atropurpureum (DC.) Urban (siratro)   C(Q); H(N)
   Phaseolus vulgaris L. (French bean)   C(Q); H(N,Q)

Pathovars of P.gladioli Severini 1913

P. gladioli pv. alliicola (Burkholder 1942)
       Young, Dye & Wilkie 1978
   Allium cepa L. var. cepa (onion)   C(N,T); H(N); D(T)
   (originally identified as P.putida)
P. gladioli pv. gladioli Severini 1913
   Freesia hybrida (freezia)   H(N); S(T)
   Gladiolus x hortulanus L.H. Bailey   H(N,T); D(Q,W); S(S)
     (gladiolus)
   Iris sp. (iris)   S(N)

Pathovars of P.marginalis (Brown 1918) Stevens 1925

P. marginalis pv. marginalis (Brown 1918) Stevens 1925
   Allium cepa L. var. cepa[1] (onion)   S(T)
   Beta vulgaris ssp. cicla (L.) Koch (silver beet)   C(N)
   Brassica oleracea var. botrytis (L.) Alef.   C(N)
    (cauliflower)
   Brassica oleracea var. italica Plenck   C(N); H(T); D(T)
    (broccoli)
   Lactuca sativa L. (lettuce)   C(N,Q); H(N,T); D(Q,T)
   Lycopersicon esculentum Miller (tomato)   D(T)
   Philodendron selloum C. Koch   C(N)
   Solanum tuberosum L. (potato)   C(T); D(T)
P. rubrilineans (Lee, Purdy, Barnum & Martin 1925) Stapp 1928
   Saccharum interspecific hybrids (sugar cane)   C(Q,W); D(N)
   Sorghum stipoideum (Ewart & White)   C(W)
    C.A. Gardn. & C.E. Hubbard (annual native sorghum)
P. rubrisubalbicans (Christopher & Edgerton 1930)
       Krasil'nikov 1949
   Saccharum interspecific hybrids (sugar cane)   C(Q); S(N)
P. solanacearum (Smith 1896) Smith 1914
   Acacia difficilis Maiden   D(Nt)
   Acacia mountfordiae Specht   C(Nt)
   Arachis hypogaea L. (peanut)   D(Nt)
   Beta vulgaris ssp. cicla (L.) Koch (silverbeet)   D(Q)

---

[1] *Tasmanian isolate originally identified as P.fluorescens.*

Host	Occurrence
Bidens pilosa L. (cobbler's peg)	D(Q)
Brassica chinensis L. (Chinese cabbage)	D(Nt)
Canavalia ensiformis (L.) DC. (Jack bean)	D(Nt)
Canavalia gladiata (Jacq.) DC. (sword bean)	D(Nt)
Capsicum annuum L. (capsicum)	C(N,Nt,Q)
Capsicum annuum L. (chili)	C(Nt); S(N)
Cassia spectabilis DC.	S(Nt)
Catharanthus roseus (L.) G. Don (pink periwinkle)	H(Nt); S(Nt)
Codiaeum variegatum (L.) Blume var. pictum (Lodd) Mull. Arg. (croton)	D(Nt)
Crassocephalum crepidioides (Benth.) S. Moore (thickhead)	C(Q)
Crotalaria linifolia L.f.	S(Nt)
Cucurbita moschata (Duch.) Poir. (butternut pumpkin)	C(Nt)
Cucurbita pepo L. s. lat. (zucchini)	C(Nt)
Dahlia sp. (dahlia)	D(Q)
Dodonaea lanceolata F. Muell	D(Q)
Gaillardia sp. (a daisy)	S(Nt)
Galphimia glauca Cav.	C(Nt)
Glycine max (L.) Merr. (soybean)	S(Nt)
Helianthus annuus L. (sunflower)	D(Q)
Lycopersicon esculentum Miller (tomato)	C(N,Nt,Q,W); D(V)
Nicotiana tabacum L. (tobacco)	C(Q); S(N)
Phaseolus vulgaris L. (French bean)	D(Q)
Pongamia pinnata (L.) Pierre	D(Nt)
Pultenaea villosa Willd.	D(Q)
Rapistrum rugosum (L.) All. (turnip weed)	D(Q)
Salpiglossis sinuata Ruiz & Pav.	S(V)
Salvia reflexa Hornem (mintweed)	C(Q)
Saritaea magnifica (T. Sprague ex Steenis) Dug.	D(Nt)
Schizanthus sp. (poor man's orchid)	S(V)
Senecio x hybridus (Willd.) Regel	D(V)
Sida rhombifolia L. (common sida)	D(Q)
Sida spinosa L. (spiny sida)	D(Q)
Solanum melongena L. (egg fruit)	C(Nt); D(Q)
Solanum tuberosum L. (potato)	C(N,Q,W); H(N,Q); D(S,V); S(Nt)
Solanum seaforthianum Andr. (Brazilian nightshade)	D(Nt)
Strelitzia reginae Ait. (strelitzia)	C(Q)
Stylosanthes humilis Kunth (Townsville stylo)	C(Nt); H(Nt)
Stylosanthes mucronata Willd.	D(Nt)
Symphytum L. x uplandicum Nym. (Russian comfrey)	D(Q)
Tagetes patula L. (French marigold)	D(Nt,Q)
Trichosanthes anguina L. (snake gourd)	D(Nt)
Tropaeolum majus L. (nasturtium)	D(Q)
Zingiber officinale Rosc. (ginger)	C(Q)
Zinnia elegans Jacq. (zinnia)	C(Nt,Q)

Host	Occurrence

Pathovars of P.syringae van Hall 1902

P. syringae pv. antirrhini (Takimoto 1920) Young, Dye
      & Wilkie 1978

Antirrhinum majus L. (snap dragon)	C(N,Q); H(N,T)

P. syringae pv. apii (Jagger 1921) Young, Dye & Wilkie 1978

Apium graveolens L. (celery)	C(Q)

P. syringae pv. aptata (Brown & Jamieson 1913) Young,
      Dye & Wilkie 1978

Beta vulgaris ssp. cicla (L.) Koch (silver beet)	H(N)
(fodder beet)	S(N)

P. syringae pv. atrofaciens (McCulloch 1920) Young,
      Dye & Wilkie 1978

Avena sativa L. (oats)	C(Q); S(T)
Hordeum vulgare L. (barley)	S(N)
Triticum aestivum L. (wheat)	H(N); D(W); S(V)

P. syringae pv. coronafaciens (Elliott 1920)
      Young, Dye & Wilkie 1978

Avena byzantina C. Koch (Algerian oats)	H(N)
Avena sativa L. (oats)	H(N,W); D(S)

P. syringae pv. delphinii (Smith 1904) Young,
      Dye & Wilkie 1978

Delphinium sp.	H(N); S(T)

P. syringae pv. eriobotryae (Takimoto 1931)
      Young, Dye & Wilkie 1978

Eriobotrya japonica (Thunb.) Lindl. (loquat)	C(V), H(V)

P. syringae pv. glycinea (Coerper 1919) Young,
      Dye & Wilkie 1978

Glycine max (L.) Merr. (soybean)	C(N,Q); H(N,Nt); D(V); S(Nt,S)

P. syringae pv. helianthi (Kawamura 1934) Young,
      Dye & Wilkie 1978

Helianthus annuus L. (sunflower)	C(N); H(N); D(Q)

P. syringae pv. lachrymans (Smith and Bryan 1915)
      Young, Dye & Wilkie 1978

Cucumis melo L. s. lat. (rockmelon)	S(S)
Cucumis sativus L. (cucumber)	C(N); H(N,T); D(W,V,W)
Cucurbita maxima Duch. (pumpkin)	D(V)
Cucurbita pepo L. s. lat. (marrow)	D(V)

P. syringae pv. maculicola (McCulloch 1911)
      Young, Dye & Wilkie 1978

Brassica hirta Moench (white mustard)	C(N); H(N)
Brassica juncea (L.) Czern. & Coss. (Indian mustard)	C(N); H(N)
Brassica napus L. var. napus (rape)	C(N); H(N,T)
Brassica nigra (L.) W. Koch (black mustard)	C(N); H(N)
Brassica oleracea var. botrytis (L.) Alef. (cauliflower)	C(N,Q); H(T); D(V,W); S(S)
Brassica oleracea var. capitata (L.) Alef. (cabbage)	C(Q,N); H(T); D(V,W)

Host	Occurrence
Brassica oleracea var. *gemmifera* DC. (Brussels sprouts)	H(T); D(V)
Brassica rapa L. (Indian rape)	C(N); H(N)
P. syringae pv. *mori* (Boyer & Lambert 1893) Young, Dye & Wilkie 1978	
Morus nigra L. (mulberry)	C(Q); H(N,T,W); D(V,W); S(S)
P. syringae pv. *morsprunorum* (Wormald 1931) Young, Dye & Wilkie 1978	
Prunus avium (L.) L. (cherry)	C(N)
Prunus sp. (stone fruit)	C(N)
P. syringae pv. *passiflorae* (Reid 1938) Young, Dye & Wilkie 1978	
Passiflora edulis Sims (passionfruit)	D(Q,V,W)
P. syringae pv. *phaseolicola* (Burkholder 1926) Young, Dye & Wilkie 1978	
Cajanus cajan (L.) Millsp. (pigeon pea)	C(Q)
Glycine max (L.) Merr. (soybean)	D(W)
Macroptilium atropurpureum (DC.) Urban (siratro)	C(Q)
Neonotonia wightii (Arn.) Lackey (glycine)	C(N,Q); H(N)
Neonotonia sp.	C(N)
Phaseolus coccineus L. (runner bean)	D(T)
Phaseolus lunatus L. (lima bean)	C(N)
Phaseolus vulgaris L. (French bean)	C(N,Q); H(N,T); D(S,T,V,W)
Pueraria lobata (Willd.) Ohwi (kudzu)	D(Q); S(N)
Vigna radiata (L.) Wilczek (mung bean)	C(N); H(N)
P. syringae pv. *pisi* (Sackett 1916) Young, Dye & Wilkie 1978	
Pisum sativum L. s. lat. (pea)	C(N,Q); H(N,T,W); D(T,V)
P. syringae pv. *primulae* (Ark & Gardner 1936) Young, Dye & Wilkie 1978	
Primula sp. (primula & primrose)	S(T,V)
P. syringae pv. *proteae* pv. nov. (proposed by Wimalajeewa, Hayward & Greenhalgh)	
Protea cynaroides L. (king protea)	C(N); H(V)
P. syringae pv. *savastanoi* (Smith 1908) Young, Dye & Wilkie 1978	
Nerium oleander L. (oleander)	H(N,W); D(S); S(T,V)
P. syringae pv. *striafaciens* (Elliott 1927) Young, Dye & Wilkie 1978	
Avena sativa L. (oats)	H(N)
P. syringae pv. *syringae* van Hall 1902	
Aconitum sp. (monk's hood)	D(V)
Aralia sp.	C(N); H(N)
Capsicum annuum L. (capsicum)	C(N)
Carthamus tinctorius L. (safflower)	D(V)
Celosia cristata L. (cockscomb)	C(N); H(N)

Host	Occurrence
Cinnamomum camphora (L.) J.S. Presl (camphor laurel)	D(V)
Citrus aurantium L. sour orange	D(V)
Citrus limon (L.) Burm. f. (lemon)	C(N); H(N,T,W); D(S,V)
Citrus paradisi Macfad.	D(V)
Citrus reticulata Blanco (mandarin)	H(W); S(N)
Citrus sinensis (L.) Osb. (sweet orange)	H(N,W); D(V)
Citrus sinensis var. valencia (L.) Osb. (Valencia orange)	C(N); H(N)
Cyamopsis tetragonoloba (L.) Taub. (guar)	D(Q)
Cydonia oblonga Miller (quince)	H(T)
Delphinium sp. (delphinium)	D(V)
Hibiscus rosa-sinensis L. (Chinese hibiscus)	C(N); H(N); D(W)
Ligustrum ovalifolium Hassk. (privet)	S(T)
Liquidambar styraciflua L. (liquidamber)	H(N)
Macroptilium atropurpureum (DC.) Urban (siratro)	H(N)
Magnolia grandiflora L. (southern magnolia)	D(V)
Magnolia x soulangiana Soul.-Bod. cv. Alexandrina	C(V); H(V)
Magnolia x soulangiana Soul.-Bod. cv. Lennei	C(N); H(N)
Malus domestica Borkh. (apple)	D(W); S(S)
Matthiola incana (L.) R.Br. (stock)	S(N)
Medicago sativa L. (lucerne)	S(N)
Nerium oleander L. (oleander)	S(N)
Panicum miliaceum L. (French millet)	C(A)[1]
Papaver rhoeas L. (shirley poppy)	C(N); H(N,:T)
Pennisetum glaucum (L.) R.Br. (pearl millet)	H(N); D(Q)
Persea americana Miller (avocado)	C(N)
Phaseolus lunatus L. (Lima bean)	S(N)
Phaseolus vulgaris L. (French bean)	C(Q,V); H(N,Q); D(N,T)
Photinia sp.	S(T)
Pisum sativum L. s. lat. (pea)	D(S,V)
Populus trichocarpa Torr. & A. Gray (western balsam)	H(N)
Prunus armeniaca L. (apricot)	C(N,Q); H(N); D(V,W); S(S,T)
Prunus avium (L.) L. (cherry)	C(N,W); H(N,T); D(V); S(S)
Prunus cerasus L. (sour cherry)	D(V)
Prunus domestica L. (plum)	C(N,W); H(T); D(V); S(S)
Prunus dulcis (Miller) D.A. Webb (almond)	S(S)
Prunus mume Siebold & Zucc. (flowering apricot)	D(V)
Prunus persica var. nectrina (Ait. f.) Maxim (nectarine)	D(W,N); S(S)
Prunus persica (L.) Batsch (peach)	C(N); H(N); D(V)
Prunus salicina Lindl. (Japanese plum)	C(Q); D(V)
Prunus serrulata Lindl. (Japanese flowering cherry)	H(N,T)
Pyrus communis L. (pear)	C(N,Q); H(N,Q,T); D(T,V); S(S)
Rosa sp. (rose)	D(W); S(S,T)
Sorghum bicolor (L.) Moench s. lat. (sorghum)	H(Q); S(Q); D(W)

[1] *Culture in NCPPB. State of origin unknown.*

Host	Occurrence

Sorghum sudanense (Piper) Stapf (Sudan grass)   S(Q)
Syringa sp. (lilac)   C(N); H(N); D(V,W); S(T)
Vigna unguiculata (L.) Walp. ssp. unguiculata   C(N,Q); H(N)
  (cowpea)
Vicia faba var. major Harz. (broad bean)   S(S)
Zea mays L. (maize)   C(N); H(N)
P. syringae pv. tabaci (Wolf and Foster 1917) Young,
  Dye & Wilkie 1978
  Glycine max (L.) Merr. (soybean)   C(N,Q); H(N)
  Nicotiana tabacum L. (tobacco)   C(N,Q); H(N); D(V)
P. syringae pv. tagetis (Hellmers 1955) Young,
  Dye & Wilkie 1978
  Tagetes erecta L. (African marigold)   C(N); H(N)
  Tagetes minuta L. (stinking roger)   C(Q); H(Q)
  Tagetes patula L. (French marigold)   C(N); H(N)
P. syringae pv. tomato (Okabe 1933) Young, Dye
  & Wilkie 1978
  Lycopersicon esculentum Miller   C(N,Q,W); H(Q,T,V); D(N,S,T)
  (tomato)
P. tolaasii Paine 1919
  Agaricus bisporus (Lange) Sing. (a cultivated   C(N,Q); S(T,V)
  mushroom)
  Agaricus bitorquis (Quel) Sacc (a cultivated   S(N)
  mushroom)
P. viridiflava (Burkholder 1930) Dowson 1939
  Apium graveolens L. (celery)   C(Q)
  Brassica oleracea var. italica Plenck (broccoli)   C(N)
  Brassica napus L. var. napus (rape)   C(N)
  Carthamus tinctorius L. (safflower)   S(N)
  Lactuca sativa L. (lettuce)   C(N)
  Prunus armeniaca L. (apricot)   C(N)
  Prunus avium (L.) L. (cherry)   C(N); H(N)
  Vitis vinifera L. (grape)   C(N,Q); H(Q)

Unidentified green fluorescent Pseudomonas spp.
  Agaricus bisporus (Lange) Sing. (mushroom) (mummy disease)   C(N)
  Antirrhinum majus L. (snapdragon)   C(Q)
  Asplenium nidus L. (bird's nest fern)   H(T)
  Begonia sp. (begonia)   H(T)
  Beta vulgaris ssp. cicla (L.) Koch (silver beet)   C(N,Q); H(N)
  (fluorescent and non-fluorescent isolates not
  P. syringae pv. aptata)
  Capsicum annuum L. (capsicum)   H(T)
  Chrysanthemum x morifolium Ramat   C(N); H(N)
  (related to P.viridiflava)
  Dactylis glomerata L. (cocksfoot)   H(T)
  Dieffenbachia sp. (dieffenbachia)   H(T)

Host	Occurrence

Mentha spicata L. (spearmint) — H(T); D(T)
Persea americana Miller (avocado) — C(N); H(N)
(related to P. viridiflava)
Tanacetum cinerariifolium (Trev.) Sch.-Bip. (pyrethrum) — H(T)

Pathogens with invalid names
Pseudomonas sp. (P. aleuritidis inv.)
   Aleurites fordii Hemsl. (tung-oil tree) — H(N)
Pseudomonas sp. (P. erodii inv.)
   Pelargonium x hortorum L.H. Bailey — S(N)
Pseudomonas sp. (P. viridilivida inv.)
   Lactuca sativa L. (lettuce) — S(N)

VII.   *Streptomyces*

Streptomyces sp. (identified originally as S scabies inv.)
   Solanum tuberosum L. (potato) — H(N); S(Q,S)
Streptomyces sp.
   Beta vulgaris L. ssp. vulgaris (beetroot) — S(S)

VIII.   *Xanthomonas*

X. albilineans (Ashby 1929) Dowson 1943
   Brachiaria piligera (Benth.) Hughes (hairy armgrass) — C(Q)
   Imperata cylindrica (L.) Beauv. var. major (Nees)
     (C.E. Hubbard (blady grass) — C(Q)
   Paspalum conjugatum Bergius (sourgrass) — C(Q)
   Paspalum dilatatum Poir (paspalum) — C(Q)
   Saccharum interspecific hybrids (sugar cane) — C(Q); S(N)
X. campestris pv. alfalfae (Riker, Jones & Davis 1935) Dye 1978
   Medicago sativa L. (lucerne) — C(N,Q); H(N)
X. campestris pv. bauhiniae (Padhya, Patel &
    Kotasthane 1965) Dye 1978
   Bauhinia galpinii N.E. Br. — C(Q); H(Q)
X. campestris pv. begoniae (Takimoto 1934) Dye 1978
   Begonia rex Putz. (rex begonia) — C(Q); H(N,T); D(W); S(S)
   Begonia x tuberhybrida Voss (tuberous begonia) — C(N); H(N); D(V)
X. campestris pv. campestris (Pammel 1895) Dowson 1939
   Brassica oleracea L. var. acephala (DC.) Alef. (kale) — S(N)
   Brassica chinensis L. (Chinese cabbage) — D(Q)
   Brassica napus var. napobrassica (L.) Reichb. (swede) — D(W)
   Brassica napus L. var. napus (rape) — C(N); H(T); D(T,W)

Host	Occurrence

Brassica <u>oleracea</u> var. <u>botrytis</u> C(N,Q,W); H(Q,T,W) D(V); S(S)
  (L.) Alef. (cauliflower)
Brassica <u>oleracea</u> var. <u>capitata</u>§ C(N,Q,W); H(C,N,Nt)
  (L.) Alef. (cabbage) (Q,T,W); D(V); S(Nt,S)
Brassica <u>oleracea</u> var. <u>gemmifera</u> DC. C(Q); H(N,T); D(N,V,W)
  (Brussels sprouts)
Brassica <u>oleracea</u> var. <u>gongylodes</u> L. (Kohlrabi) C(Q)
Brassica <u>oleracea</u> var. <u>italica</u> Plenck C(N,Q); D(V); S(S)
  (green broccoli)
Brassica <u>oleracea</u> var. <u>ramosa</u> (chou moellier) S(T)
Brassica <u>rapa</u> L. var. <u>rapa</u> (turnip) H(N); D(N,Q,V,W); S(T)
Brassica <u>rapa</u> var. <u>silvestris</u> (Lam.) C(N); H(N); D(V)
  Briggs (oilseed rape)
Capsella <u>bursa-pastoris</u> (L.) Medic (shepherd's purse) D(Q)
Raphanus <u>raphanistrum</u> L. (wild radish) H(T); D(N,Q,W)
Raphanus <u>sativus</u> L. (radish) D(N,Q)
Rapistrum <u>rugosum</u> (L.) All. (turnip weed) D(N,Q)
<u>X</u>. <u>campestris</u> pv. <u>carotae</u> (Kendrick 1934) Dye 1978
  Daucus <u>carota</u> L. (carrot) S(N,S)
<u>X</u>. <u>campestris</u> pv. <u>corylina</u> (Miller, Bollen, Simmons,
  Gross & Barss 1940) Dye 1978
  Corylus <u>avellana</u> L. (hazelnut) C(V); H(V)
<u>X</u>. <u>campestris</u> pv. <u>cucurbitae</u> (Bryan 1926) Dye 1978
  Citrullus <u>lanatus</u> var. <u>caffer</u> (Schrad.) D(Q)
    Mansf. (watermelon)
  Cucumis <u>melo</u> L. s. lat. (rockmelon) D(Q)
  Cucumis <u>sativus</u> L. (cucumber) D(Q)
  Cucurbita <u>maxima</u> Duch. (pumpkin) C(Q); H(Q)
  Cucurbita <u>pepo</u> L. s. lat. (zucchini) C(N,Q); H(N)
<u>X</u>. <u>campestris</u> pv. <u>dieffenbachiae</u> (McCulloch &
  Pirone 1939) Dye 1978
  Anthurium <u>andraenum</u> Linden (flaming lily) C(N,Q)
  Dieffenbachia <u>maculata</u> (Lodd.) G. Don (dieffenbachia) C(Q)
  Dieffenbachia sp. C(N); H(N)
<u>X</u>. <u>campestris</u> pv. <u>eucalypti</u> (Truman 1974) Dye 1978
  Eucalyptus <u>citriodora</u> Hook. (lemon scented C(N)
    spotted gum)
<u>X</u>. <u>campestris</u> pv. <u>glycines</u> (Nakano 1919) Dye 1978
  Glycine <u>max</u> (L.) Merr. (soybean) C(N,Q); H(N,Nt); S(Nt)
<u>X</u>. <u>campestris</u> pv. <u>gummisudans</u> (McCulloch 1924) Dye 1978
  Gladiolus x <u>hortulanus</u> L.H. Bailey (gladiolus) S(N,V)
<u>X</u>. <u>campestris</u> pv. <u>hederae</u> (Arnaud 1920) Dye 1978
  Hedera <u>helix</u> L. (English ivy) H(N); D(N,Q)
<u>X</u>. <u>campestris</u> pv. <u>holcicola</u> (Elliott 1930) Dye 1978
  Sorghum <u>bicolor</u> (L.) Moench s. lat. (sorghum) C(N,Q); H(N,Q)
  Zea <u>mays</u> L. (maize) C(Q)

Host	Occurrence

X. campestris pv. hyacinthi (Wakker 1883) Dye 1978
  Hyacinthus orientalis L. (hyacinth)   D(V); S(N,T)
X. campestris pv. incanae (Kendrick & Baker 1942) Dye 1978
  Cheiranthus sp. (wallflower)   S(N)
  Matthiola incana (L.)   C(N,V); H(N,V); D(Q,W); S(S,T)
    R.Br. (stock)
X. campestris pv. juglandis (Pierce 1901) Dye 1978
  Juglans regia L. (walnut)   C(N,Q); H(N,Q,T); D(S,T,V,W)
X. campestris pv. malvacearum (Smith 1901) Dye 1978
  Gossypium hirsutum L. (cotton) C(N,Nt,Q,W); H(N,NT,Q); D(V); S(Nt)
  Gossypium populifolium F. Muell. (wild cotton)   H(Nt); S(Nt)
  Gossypium sp.   H(Nt); S(Nt)
X. campestris pv. mangiferaeindicae (Patel, Moniz &
      Kulkarni 1948) Robbs, Ribeiro and Kimura 1974
  Mangifera indica L. (mango)   C(N,Q); H(N); S(Nt)
X. campestris pv. oryzae (Ishiyama 1922) Dye 1978
  Oryza australiensis Domin (Australian rice)   D(Nt)
  Oryza rufipogon Griff. (wild rice)   D(Nt)
  Oryza sativa L. (rice)   D(Nt)
X. campestris pv. oryzicola[1] (Fang, Ren, Chen, Chu, Faan
      & Wu 1957) Dye 1978
  Oryza sativa L. (rice)   H(Nt); S(Nt)
  Oryza australiensis Domin (Australian rice)   H(Nt)
X. campestris pv. papavericola (Bryan & McWhorter 1930)
      Dye 1978
  Papaver nudicaule L. (Iceland poppy)   D(W)
  Papaver somniferum L. (opium poppy)   S(T,V)
X. campestris pv. passiflorae (Pereira 1969) Dye 1978
  Passiflora edulis Sims (passionfruit)   D(Q)
X. campestris pv. pelargonii (Brown 1923) Dye 1978
  Pelargonium x hortorum L.H. Bailey (geranium)   D(Q); S(N,V)
  Pelargonium peltatum (L.) L'Her (ivy leaf geranium)   H(N)
  Pelargonium zonale (L.) L'Her (zonal geranium)   H(N); D(W)
  Pelargonium sp.   S(S)
X. campestris pv. phaseoli (Smith 1897) Dye 1978
  Macroptilium lathyroides (L.) Urban (phasey bean)   C(Q)
  Phaseolus vulgaris L. (French &   C(Q); H(N); D(V,W); S(T)
    navy bean)
  Vigna mungo (L.) Hepper (black gram)   D(Q)
  Vigna radiata (L.) Wilczek (mung bean)   H(N); D(Q); S(Nt)
X. campestris pv. plantaginis (Thornberry &
      Anderson 1937) Dye 1978
  Plantago lanceolata L.   C(A)[2]

---

[1] *See chapter 9 for explanation of related pathovars.*

[2] *Culture in NCPPB. State of origin unknown.*

Host	Occurrence

X. campestris pv. poinsettiicola (Patel, Bhatt &
      Kulkarni 1951) Dye 1978

    Euphorbia pulcherrima Willd. ex Klotzsch (poinsettia)   C(Q)

X. campestris pv. pruni (Smith 1903) Dye 1978

Prunus armeniaca L. (apricot)	C(Q)
Prunus avium (L.) L. (sweet cherry)	C(Q); H(N)
Prunus x blineiana Andrew (flowering plum)	H(N)
Prunus domestica L. (plum)	H(N); D(W)
Prunus dulcis (Miller) D.A. Webb (almond)	D(Q)
Prunus persica (L.) Batsch (peach)	C(N,Q); H(N,Q,W); D(V)
Prunus persica var. nectrina (Ait. f.) Maxim (nectarine)	C(N); H(N); D(Q)
Prunus salicina Lindl. (Japanese plum)	C(N,Q); D(V)

X. campestris pv. translucens[1] (Jones, Johnson &
      Reddy 1917) Dye 1978

Echinochloa utilis Ohwi & Yabuno (Japanese millet)	C(N,Q); H(N)
Hordeum vulgare L. (barley)	S(N)
Secale cereale L. (rye)	S(N)
Triticum aestivum[2] L. (wheat)	C(N); H(N)

X. campestris pv. vasculorum (Cobb 1893) Dye 1978

    Saccharum interspecific hybrids (sugar cane)   C(Q); H(N)

X. campestris pv. vesicatoria (Doidge 1920) Dye 1978

Capsicum annuum L. (capsicum)	C(N,Q); H(N)
Datura ferox L. (datura)	C(N)
Lycopersicon esculentum Miller (tomato)	C(N,Q); H(N,Q); D(V,W); S(T)
Lycopersicon peruvianum L. Mill. (wild tomato)	C(Q)
Physalis peruviana L. (cape gooseberry)	D(Q)
Physalis minima L. (wild gooseberry)	D(Q)
Physalis virginiana Miller (gooseberry)	D(Q)

X. campestris pv. vitians (Brown 1918) Dye 1978

    Lactuca sativa L. (lettuce)   C(N,Q); H(N); D(V); S(T)

X. campestris pv. zinniae (Hopkins & Dowson 1949) Dye 1978

    Zinnia elegans Jacq. (zinnia)   C(N,Q); H(N,Nt); S(Nt)

X. fragariae Kennedy & King 1962

    Fragaria x ananassa Duch.[3] (strawberry)   C(N); H(N)

Xanthomonas sp.

Antirrhinum majus L. (snapdragon)	C(Q)
Impatiens sp.	S(S)

---

[1] See chapter 9 for explanation of related pathovars.

[2] A pathovar on this host is also called X. campestris pv. undulosa
(Smith, Jones & Reddy 1919) Dye 1978.

[3] Eradicated; no outbreaks since 1976.

Host	Occurrence

IX.   Undetermined Bacterial Pathogens

Cayratia clematidea (F. Muell.) Domin (leaf spot)   H(N)
Iris sp. (leaf spot)   H(N)
Lychnis coronaria (L.) Desr. (leaf spot)   H(N)
Musa sp. (banana) (from corm)   S(N)
Peperomia sp. (leaf spot)   C(N)
Primula x polyantha Hort. (seedling blight)   C(N); H(N)

X.   Organisms Currently Unnamed

A. Coryneform bacterium (xylem limited):
     ratoon stunting disease
    Saccharum interspecific hybrids (sugar cane)   D(N,Q)

B. Mycoplasma-Like Organisms (MLO).

    The following diseases have been the subject of published reports:
         tomato big bud   )
         lucerne witch's broom   )
         legume little leaf   )
         lettuce green flower   ) MLO or symptoms in plants
         strawberry green petal   ) produced by MLO have been
         strawberry mycoplasma yellows) reported on a wide range of
         pawpaw yellow crinkle   ) hosts in several families in
         clover phyllody   ) all states.
         potato purple top wilt   )

    The relationship between MLO causing these diseases is not
    known.

C. Rickettsia-Like Organism (Phloem Limited):

    rugose leaf curl
         Trifolium spp. (clover)   D(Q)
         Arachis hypogaea L. (peanut)   D(Q)
         Medicago sativa L. (lucerne)   D(Q,W)

    strawberry rickettsia yellows
         Fragariae x ananassa Duch. (strawberry)   D(Q)

Host	Occurrence

D. Rickettsia-Like Organism (xylem limited):

   kenaf crinkle leaf
     Hibiscus cannabinus L. (kenaf)   D(Q,W)

References

Anon. (1976). "Hortus Third". Revised and expanded by the staff of the L.H. Bailey Hortorium. New York. MacMillan.

Dye, D.W., Bradbury, J.F., Goto, M., Hayward, A.C., Lelliott, R.A. & Schroth, M.N. (1980). International standards for naming pathovars of phytopathogenic bacteria and a list of pathovar names and pathovar strains. Review of Plant Pathology 59, 153-168.

Hartley, W. (1979). "A Checklist of Economic Plants in Australia". Melbourne, Australia: C.S.I.R.O. 214pp.

Skerman, V.B.D., McGowan, V. & Sneath, P.H.A. (1980). Approved lists of bacterial names. International Journal of Systematic Bacteriology 30, 225-420.

Acknowledgements

I thank the following for providing the host/pathogen records compiled in this document; P. Fahy, R. Cother, A.B. Lloyd (New South Wales), S. Wimalajeewa (Victoria), P. Sampson (Tasmania), A. Kerr and D. Cartwright (South Australia), K. Sivasithamparam (Western Australia), R. Pitkethley (Northern Territory), C. Ryan, B. Croft, G. Behncken and D. Teakle (Queensland), G.J. Persley and S. Navaratnam (Australian Capital Territory). I thank also A.C. Hayward for his help and advice in compiling this pathogen list and H. Kleinschmidt, Botany Branch, Queensland Department of Primary Industries, Indooroopilly, for checking botanical names and the authorities.

16

Media and Methods for Isolation
and Diagnostic Tests

Compiled by
P. C. Fahy and A. C. Hayward

I.	Introduction	337
II.	General Test Procedures	338
III.	Morphological Features	338
IV.	The Gram Reaction	341
V.	Non-selective Isolation Media	344
VI.	General Growth and Maintenance Media	345
VII.	Selective Isolation Media	347
VIII.	Utilization and Decomposition of Carbon Compounds	350
IX.	Decomposition of Nitrogenous Compounds	355
X.	Decomposition of Macromolecules	358
XI.	Other Physiological and Biochemical Tests	360
XII.	Toxin Bioassays	363
XIII.	Hypersensitivity in Tobacco	366
XIV.	Diagnostic Tests Using Excised Plant Tissues	368
XV.	Pathogenicity Tests	371
	References	374

I. Introduction

This chapter includes methods for describing the morphological features of a bacterium and its Gram stain reaction. Commonly-used, non-selective isolation and maintenance media are given as well as selective isolation media for various genera. Procedures for physiological tests useful for the identification at the generic and species level are described. The tests recommended for the identification of particular pathogens are discussed in Chapters 1-9. More specialized techniques such as toxin bioassay, tobacco hypersensitivity and innoculation of excised plant tissue are also of value. Confirmation of the identity of many plant pathogenic bacteria is dependent on pathogenicity testing and various testing procedures are described. This chapter is a compilation of techniques referred to in Chapters 1 to 9 and should be used in conjunction with these chapters.

Use of this text assumes a basic knowledge of microbiology and reference to one of the numerous publications on general methodology should be made by those unfamiliar with procedures discussed. The American Society for Microbiology Publication "Manual of Methods for General Bacteriology" (Gerhardt, 1981), is recommended for general methodology.

II. General Test Procedures

Unless otherwise stated, autoclaving of all media is performed at 121 C for 15 min sterilization time. The composition of the media is given in g/l distilled water, unless otherwise noted. Tests should be conducted only with actively growing bacteria from a suitable medium i.e. overnight cultures of rapidly growing strains or 2-3 day cultures of most pathogens. Bacteria may be suspended in sterile water to give a suspension which is just turbid and dispensed to all test media by adding 2-3 drops from a sterile Pasteur pipette or inoculating plates with a wire loop. Incubation between 25 and 27 C is recommended for all tests. Incubation temperatures should be less than 30 C. Some <u>Corynebacterium</u> spp. fail to grow at 30 C and many pathogens will not grow above 37 C.

It is recommended to use reference cultures with known reactions to all diagnostic tests. For biochemical tests, strains with known positive and negative reactions should be included.

III. Morphological Features

A. *General Morphology*

The Gram stain (see section IV) usually allows observation of cell size, shape and arrangement. Phase contrast microscopy of fresh cultures is frequently sufficient for observing cell shape, size, motility and refractile polymer inclusions (discussed below). Refractile spores are observed in older cultures.

B. *Motility*

Where motility is not obvious it may be enhanced by transferring actively growing cultures to moistened agar slopes of a suitable growth medium (select a range) or onto "sloppy" agar plates at optimal growth temperatures (generally 25-27 C for most pathogens). Examine slopes daily by gently removing a loopful of growth from the water at the base of the slope. "Sloppy" agar plates may be prepared by melting the appropriate agar medium (0.3%) agar) and pouring into Petri dish. On cooling, inoculate the centre and incubate (24h or longer) until obvious spreading of culture occurs. Transfer a loop of motile inoculum from the colony edge to a moistened agar slope and incubate until turbid, then examine.

C. *Flagella Stain*

Electron microscope negative staining (phosphotungstate or uranyl acetate) of actively motile cells (see above) is easier than light microscope staining procedures. For light microscopy the Leifson (1951) technique is recommended. The procedure must be followed carefully.

Reagents. (a) 1.5% distilled water solution of NaCl (stores indefinitely if tightly capped), (b) 3.0% distilled water solution of BDH reagent grade tannic acid (must be prepared fresh), (c) 1.2% solution of basic fuchsin (certified for flagella stain, in 95% ethanol, stable if capped). Prepare 24 h before mixing ingredients, shake occasionally to dissolve. To prepare Leifson stain mix solutions a, b and c at 1:1:1 v/v and dispense in 25ml McCartney bottles. The stain may be stored indefinitely in a deep freeze (-20C). It is stable for 2 wk at 4C and for 48 h at room temperature.

Slide Preparation. Use new slides and soak for 5 days in chromic acid, keeping separated in Coplin jars. Rinse thoroughly in tap water (10 times) and twice in distilled water. Flame side to be used; when cool, ring an area 2/3 of the side flamed with a grease pencil, for the stain.

Stain Procedure.   Use only highly motile suspension (see IIIB). Dilute until barely turbid. Place a drop on one edge of greased ring and tilt to allow drop to glide down slide; air dry without heat (drop will not glide down a dirty slide - discard). Add exactly 1ml of Leifson stain (at room temperature) to within the waxed ring and stain for exactly 14 min, then wash with running tap water. Air dry. Examine under oil immersion. Stain intensity may be varied by altering staining time.

B. *Determination of the Presence of Poly-β-hydroxybutyrate Inclusions*

Many aerobic, Gram-negative bacteria produce inclusions of poly-β-hydroxybutyrate (PHB) (Hayward, 1960). The presence of PHB inclusions has a number of effects. When heat-fixed smears are stained with a dilute basic fuchsin or safranin solution, the stain tends to be concentrated at the poles (bipolar staining) and the rest of the cell is unstained. These unstained areas are refractile under phase microscopy and show a strong affinity for the lipid stain Sudan black B. Since Sudan black B is a lipid stain of general use not specific for PHB, it cannot be assumed that sudanophilic inclusions invariably consist of this substance. However, experience has shown that where sudanophilia is a gross property of bacterial cells, these inclusions are present. Confirmation of the identity of the inclusions can be obtained by extraction of dried cells with chloroform followed by precipitation in diethyl ether (Hayward, 1960), or by extraction with an alkaline solution of sodium hypochlorite (Williamson & Wilkinson, 1958). PBHA yields crotonic acid on destructive distillation.

PHB inclusions are most prominent on media of high carbon/nitrogen ratio. The tetrazolium chloride medium of Kelman (1954) is suitable, or sucrose peptone agar (SPA) (Hayward, 1960) for those pseudomonads such as P. solanacearum which utilize sucrose as a carbon and energy source. Inclusions can be stained with Sudan black B using the method of Burdon (1946).

Procedure.   The recommended method is that of Burdon (1946) with the modification that a tap water rinse is used after staining with Sudan black B instead of treatment with xylol. The procedure is as follows:

Prepare stain containing Sudan black B powder 0.3g, 70% ethanol 100ml. Shake thoroughly at intervals and stand overnight before use. Keep in a well stoppered bottle. Make a film either of the expressed ooze from a wilted plant or from a culture, dry in air and fix by flaming; cover the entire slide with Sudan black B stain and leave at room temperature for 15 min.; drain off excess stain and dry in air; rinse thoroughly under the tap and again blot dry; counterstain lightly by covering with 0.5% aqueous safranin or dilute carbol fuchsin for 5-10 sec; rinse with tap water, blot and dry. Lipid inclusions are stained blue-black or blue-grey, while the rest of the cell is stained light pink.

IV. The Gram Reaction

A. *Techniques*

Gram reaction is essential for primary division of the bacteria. Gram staining generally gives satisfactory results for the plant pathogens although older cultures of coryneform bacteria may stain Gram negative (see Chapter 4). Two alternatives to the Gram stain, the determination of solubility in 3% KOH solution and aminopeptidase activity are included. These may be used as supplementary tests where results are doubtful. Cultures tested should always be as young as possible and those of less than 24h are recommended.

B. *Gram Stain*

Numerous modifications are available. The following, based on Skerman (1967), gives satisfactory results, using the reagents listed below. Prepare a smear from a young culture (ca.24h), air dry and gently heat fix by light flaming on underside of slide. Flood slide with crystal violet for 1 min. Wash for 3-4 s in a gentle stream of tap water. Flood with iodine solution for 1 min. Wash again with tap water. Decolourize by applying 95% ethanol drop-wise to smear held at an angle against a white background until no more colour runs from lower edge (usually 10-20 s). Wash and counterstain with safranin.

Observe well separated cells under oil immersion without a coloured filter. Microscope condenser must be correctly focused. A blue colour indicates Gram positive; red, Gram negative. Mature spores are unstained. The presence of red cells in a Gram positive organism usually indicates dead cells. Old cultures of Gram positive organisms may frequently stain Gram variable or negative. Check doubtful results with fresh cultures and confirm with one or both of the tests described below.

Reagents. (a) Crystal violet: crystal violet 2.0g, ammonium oxalate 1.0g, distilled water 100ml. (b) Iodine solution: iodine 1.0g, potassium iodide 2.0g, distilled water 100ml. Grind dry in a mortar and dissolve by slowly adding water. Store in a dark bottle. (c) Aqueous safranin: Safranin 0, 2.5% solution in 95% ethanol (stock solution). Dilute 1 in 10 with distilled water.

C. KOH Solubility Test

One or two drops of 3% potassium hydroxide (KOH) are placed on a glass slide. A colony, or a few colonies if they are very small, are picked from the surface of a solid medium with an inoculating loop. The material is stirred in the KOH for 5-10s and the inoculating loop is then raised from the drop. If the KOH solution has become viscous, a thread of slime follows the loop for 0.5-2cm or more. This is a positive reaction and is seen in Gram-negative bacteria. If there is no slime, but a watery suspension that does not follow the loop, the reaction is negative and this is seen in Gram-positive bacteria.

The production of the slimy substance after treatment of Gram-negative bacteria with KOH is probably due to destruction of the cell wall and liberation of the DNA, which is a very viscid compound.

The KOH solubility test was first described in Japan by Ryu (1938, 1940) but has been little used until recently in Europe and the United States. Gregersen (1978) has made a detailed evaluation of the method in routine bacterialogical work, particularly in cases where the interpretation of Gram-stained smears gives cause for doubt. He was particularly interested in the application of the method to Gram-negative and Gram-variable *Bacillus* spp.

All 55 isolates, from numerous genera of Gram negative bacteria gave a Gram negative reaction after 20 h and 72 h incubation. Of 71 isolates of Gram positive bacteria, 70 gave Gram positive reactions by the KOH test after 20 h and 4 days even though 13 of 38 *Bacillus* stained Gram negative after 4 days. One *B. macerans* isolate gave a consistent, false Gram negative reaction to the KOH test.

Suslow et al. (1982) applied the test to a range of plant pathogens and obtained consistent results with 24-48 h cultures. Some strains of Agrobacterium gave inconsistent results if cultures were older than 32 h.

D. *Aminopeptidase Activity*

The procedure of Cerny (1976, 1978) is recommended for the determination of aminopeptidase activity.

The test solution contains 4.0 g of L-alanine-4-nitro-anilidehydrochloride dissolved in 100 ml of 50 mM Tris-maleate buffer (pH 7.0). Distilled water may be used instead of the buffer if the pH is between 6 and 7.5.

A round white cellulose filter paper (Whatman no.1) with a diameter exactly fitting into a Petri dish is impregnated with the freshly prepared test solution described above. This may be done best by spraying the test solution onto the filter paper through a spraying nozzle similar to that used for ninhydrin spraying on chromatography plates. The test solution should be sprayed in such a way that the filter paper becomes moist without becoming wet.

The filter paper prepared in such a way is laid upon the nutrient agar surface. Care must be taken that the impregnated paper comes into contact with the surface colonies without air bubbles. After 5 min at room temperature the amino-peptidase reaction can be observed by holding the petri dishes against a white light source. If colonies of Gram-negative bacteria are present a yellow colour reaction, imparted by the p-nitroaniline is produced. This method is applicable only to surface colonies.

Direct spraying of the test solution on the bacterial colonies is not recommended, because the bacterial colonies may be dispersed. In addition the contrast between the yellow colour reaction and the brownish colour of most agar media is too low to be easily detected.

Alternatively it is possible to use test solution-impregnated filter papers (or other materials) of smaller diameter if the selective distinction of single colonies on agar media is required. The impregnated materials (e.g. filter papers) can be stored under dry conditions. Cerny (1976, 1978) should be consulted for further uses and modifications of this technique.

Cerny (1976, 1978) found that no aminopeptidase activity was detectable in most of the Gram-positive bacteria which he examined, even after prolonged incubation with the substrate. Age of culture affected the rapidity of the reaction with some cultures which had been stored at room temperature for 3 wk showing a considerable loss of amino- peptidase activity. For this reason, only fresh-grown cultures should be used in performing the aminopeptidase test. The correlation between negative Gram stain and aminopeptidase activity is not understood, but may indicate an involvement of the aminopeptidase in cell wall bio- chemistry.

V. Non-selective Isolation Media

A. *Sucrose Peptone Agar (SPA)*

SPA (Hayward, 1960) is suitable for general isolation and for determination of distinctive colony formation of Xanthomonas and levan positive Pseudomonas spp. It is not recommended for Agrobacterium.

SPA contains (in g/l): sucrose 20, peptone 5g, K_2HPO_4 0.5, $MgSO_4.7H_2O$ 0.25, agar 15. pH is adjust- ed to 7.2-7.4 using 40% NaOH.

B. *King's Medium B (KBA)*

KBA is suitable for general isolation and growth of Pseudomonas but most pathogens will grow on it. The medium was initially devised for observation of fluorescein pigments (King et al., 1954) (see Chapter 8).

KBA contains (in g/l): Difco proteose peptone No.3 20, K_2HPO_4 1.5, $MgSO_4.7H_2O$ 1.5, and glycerol 10ml. pH 7.2. See also section XI,C for further details.

C. *Glucose Yeast Extract Calcium Carbonate Agar (GYCA)*

GYCA (Dye, 1962) is suitable for isolation of most bacterial pathogens and is a useful general growth and maintenance medium.

GYCA contains (in g/l): glucose 5, yeast extract (Difco) 5, finely ground $CaCO_3$ 40, agar 15. The $CaCO_3$ must be dispersed throughout the medium immediately before pouring to ensure close contact with the agar surface. A vortex mixer provides good dispersal; quick setting in a shallow bath of chilled water ensures the $CaCO_3$ does not settle. Commercial grades of $CaCO_3$ are suitable if

finely ground but colloidal particles are usually removed
from refined grades, making them unsuitable. The $CaCO_3$
enhances growth of some more fastidious pathogens and
reduces death rate of cells.

D. *Nutrient Agar (NA)*

Various formulae for nutrient agars exist, all containing beef extract and peptone. Many plant pathogens do not
grow readily on these media unless supplemented with yeast
extract at 0.2 to 0.5%. The following formulation (available
from Oxoid) is recommended (in g/l): beef extract powder
(Lab-Lemco) 1, yeast extract 2, peptone 5, NaCl 5, agar
15. pH 7.4. Other commercially available nutrient agars
containing yeast extract may be suitable.

E. *Sucrose Casein Hydrolysate Agar (Medium 523)*

This medium was developed by Price (1973) for isolation
of the annual ryegrass pathogen (see Chapter 4). This medium
is non selective but was derived from the selective medium
of Kado & Heskett (1970) for Corynebacterium.
   Medium 523 contains (in g/l): sucrose 10, casein hydrolysate 8, yeast extract 4, K_2HPO_4 2, $MgSO_4 \cdot 7H_2O$ 0.3 agar 15.

VI.   General Growth and Maintenance Media

A. *Range of Media*

Media containing high levels of carbohydrates are
generally unsuitable for storage of cultures unless well
buffered. GYCA and nutrient agar supplemented with 0.2%
yeast extract are suitable for most organisms.
   Media which are commonly used for the growth and storage
of plant pathogenic bacteria are given below. For
insurance against loss of viability or pathogenicity,
cultures should be stored on more than one maintenance
medium at 4C and room temperature. While most plant
pathogenic bacteria keep better at 4C than room
temperature, there are exceptions (e.g. P. solanacearum, P.
andropogonis.) Preservation methods are discussed in more
detail in Chapter 13.

B. Peptone Yeast Extract Agar (PYEA)

PYEA is particularly suitable for most pseudomonads, except P. solanacearum, which is better stored on SPA slopes.

PYEA contains (in g/l) peptone 10, yeast extract 5g, NaCl 5, agar 15, pH 7.2.

C. Tryptone Glucose Beef Extract Agar (TGEA)

TGEA is a useful growth and storage medium for Erwinia and most other groups.

TGEA (Difco) contains (in g/l) tryptone 5, glucose 1, beef extract powder 3, agar 15.

D. Tetrazolium Chloride Agar (TZCA)

TZC agar (Kelman, 1954) is used as a general growth and isolation medium for P. solanacearum. It is suitable for differentiating wild colony types (white with pink centres) from low virulence mutants which may occur on subculturing. Mutant colonies generally take up the formazen produced on reduction of tetrazolium chloride to form deep red colonies.

TZC agar contains (in g/l): peptone 10, casein hydrolysate (Difco) 1, glucose 5, agar 15, 2,3,5-triphenyl tetrazolium chloride 0.05. The TZC is added as 1 ml of a filter-sterilized 0.5% solution per 100 ml of molten (60C), sterilized medium before pouring plates.

E. Modified Yeast Extract Dextrose Agar (YDCA)

A similar medium to GYCA, YDC is useful for good growth of erwinias and is suitable for short term storage and development of pink and blue pigments (Dye, 1968). The medium contains (in g/l) yeast extract 10, dextrose 5, $CaCO_3$ 20, agar 15. See GYCA for plate preparation.

F. Yeast Salts (YS) Agar and Broth

The yeast salts (in g/l) $NH_4H_2PO_4$ 0.5, K_2HPO_4 0.5, $MgSO_4.7H_2O$ 0.2, NaCl 5, yeast extract (Difco) 5, may serve as the basal medium for most biochemical tests. When solidified with 15 g/l agar, YSA is a general purpose growth medium suitable for most pathogens (Dye, 1962).

VII. Selective Isolation Media

A. *Scope of Selective Media*

A wide range of selective media are described by Schaad (1980) and Starr et al. (1981). The following media have been found useful by authors of this publication. Great care should be taken in the use and interpretation of results of selective media. A number of selective media become more toxic on storage as components react or concentrations increase with dehydration. Some media may be too selective for routine diagnosis. For diagnosis, these media should be used in conjunction with non selective isolation media. Always obtain pure cultures by restreaking onto non selective media to avoid carryover of suppressed bacteria. Further precautions are disucssed in chapters 1 and 6. Selective media for Agrobacterium are given in Chapter 3.

B. *Crystal Violet Pectate (CVP) Medium*

The semi-solid pectate-agar of Cuppels & Kelman (1974) is suitable for partially selective isolation of pectolytic erwinias or pseudomonads. O'Neill & Logan (1975) examined several similar media and recommended CVP with slight modifications. The modifications of Kelman (pers. comm., 1980) are included in the following procedure:

To 500ml of boiling distilled water in a preheated 21 capacity blender add in sequence (beginning at a low blending speed): 1.0ml of 0.075% w/v aqueous crystal violet, 4.5ml 1M NaOH, 3ml 10% $CaCl_2.2H_2O$ (not more than 2 wk old), 2g Difco agar, 1g $NaNO_3$. Blend at high speed for 15 s. Slowly add 9g sodium polypectate (Kluft) while blending to prevent clumping and blend for a further 15 s. Place medium in a 21 flask (add 0.5ml 10% sodium lauryl sulphate if increased selectivity for Erwinia is required), cap with aluminium foil and autoclave. Ensure autoclave pressure drops slowly to prevent frothing. Pour plates as soon as possible and dry 48 h at room temperature before use. Plate surface must be dry when inoculated. Plates keep refrigerated for several weeks.

The quality of polypectate is critical to success of this medium. Some commercial preparations will not gel satisfactorily. R.L. Kluft and Co. Ltd., 5832 Farmwood Heights, Oconomowoc, Wisconsin 53066, USA, markets a product especially prepared for this use. Cother et al. (1980) describe a suitable laboratory technique for preparation of sodium polypectate which should be used at 15g/500ml of medium.

Pectolytic *Erwinia* produce deep cup-like pits while other pectolytic bacteria generally produce shallower, wider pits. Addition of $MnSO_4.4H_2O$ at 2g/500ml of medium (O'Neill & Logan, 1975) is reported to suppress pectolytic pseudomonads. The optional addition of 0.9ml of 1% thallium nitrate (filter sterilized) to the hot medium (500ml) will reduce background growth with a slight reduction in recovery of *Erwinia*. Medium containing thallium nitrate must be used immediately as toxicity increases with time.

C. PT Medium

A selective-differential medium was developed by Burr & Schroth (1977) for detection of soft rot *Erwinia*. Efficiency of isolation from plant debris or rhizosphere soil is enhanced by anaerobic enrichment in the liquid medium prior to plating. Incubate broth for 48 h in an anaerobic jar then plate onto CVP medium or PT medium.

PT medium contains (in g/l): polygalacturonic acid (Sunkist, Corana, California) 5 (other brands may be suitable), $NaNO_3$ 1, K_2HPO_4 4, $MgSO_4.7H_2O$ 0.2, sodium heptadecyl sulphate 0.05 (or use Tergitol[R] anionic 7 (Sigma) 0.1ml), agar 9, and 1M NaOH 17 ml. Autoclave and dispense as plates. The medium will keep refrigerated for one month, but deteriorates slowly after this time.

Incubate 2-3 days then flood with 1% solution of cetrimide (cetyltrimethyl ammonium bromide). Clear zones develop around colonies of *Erwinia* within 30 s and although cetrimide is toxic, colonies may be subcultured within 5 min of flooding. Clear zones only appear around heavy growth and if isolating from soil or debris this may be unlikely to occur and prior enrichment is advised.

D. D3 Medium

D3 medium (in g/l): sucrose 10, arabinose 10, casein hydrolysate 5, LiCl 7, glycine 3, NaCl 5, $MgSO_4.7H_2O$ 0.3, sodium dodecyl sulphate 0.05, bromthymol blue 0.06, acid fuchsin 0.1, agar 15. Adjust to pH 8.2 with NaOH before autoclaving.

D3 medium is a partially selective medium devised by Kado & Heskett (1970) for erwinias, colonies of which are distinguished by a burnt-orange colony with a blue-green to light orange halo in the medium.

E. *Logan's Differential Medium for* Erwinia

The medium contains (in g/l): nutrient agar (Oxoid CM3) 28, yeast extract (Difco) 5, glucose 5. After autoclaving, the medium is cooled to 60C and 10ml of filter-sterilized 0.5% solution of 2,3,5-triphenyl tetrazolium chloride added.

The medium was developed by Logan (1966) to distinguish Erwinia carotovora pv. atroseptica from pv. carotovora. Cultures are streaked on dried plates to obtain single well separated colonies and incubated for 24h at 27C. E. carotovora pv. carotovora reduces the tetrazolium to insoluble red formazan and colonies (about 1.5mm diameter) develop a pink to red/purple centre. Single colonies of pv. atroseptica remain colourless and less than 0.5mm diameter. After 48h the pv. atroseptica colonies reduce the tetrazolium but remain smaller than pv. carotovora. Those of E. chrysanthemi are larger than pv. carotovora (about 2mm) and completely dark red/purple.

F. *SX Agar*

The medium was developed by Schaad & White (1974) for isolation of Xanthomonas campestris pv. campestris from soil and plant debris and selectivity depends on starch utilization. All pv. campestris isolates tested utilized starch but few soil organisms did. Methyl violet B and methyl green were added to increase selectivity and improve colony differentiation.

SX agar contains (in g/l): soluble potato starch 10, beef extract (Difco) 1, ammonium chloride 5, KH_2PO_4 2, agar 15, and methyl violet B 1ml of a 1% solution in 20% ethanol, methyl green 2ml of a 1% solution, cycloheximide (Upjohn) 250mg. The pH (6.8) is unadjusted. Pathovar campestris develops as small translucent colonies surrounded by a clear 4-5mm zone of starch digestion in 3 days (25-30C). By 5 days colonies are 3mm in diameter, mucoid, glistening, convex, circular with entire margins and translucent with purple centres. Starch digestion zones are 8-10mm. Several workers have found the medium useful for other pathovars of X. campestris.

VIII.   Utilization and Decomposition of Carbon Compounds

A. *Oxidative/Fermentative Metabolism of Carbohydrates*

The medium used by Hugh & Leifson (1953) for determination of the oxidative or fermentative utilization of glucose by bacteria may not be suitable for oxidative organisms which produce much ammonia from peptone. The following medium has been devised (Hayward, 1964) for plant pathogenic bacteria and is suitable for determination of biovars in P. solanacearum. The medium is that of Ayers et al. (1919) supplemented with 0.1% peptone and sufficient agar to make semi-solid.

The basal medium for oxidation/fermentation tests contains (in g/l): peptone 1.0, $NH_4H_2PO_4$ 1.0, KCl 0.2, $MgSO_4.7H_2O$ 0.2, Bromthymol blue powder 0.08, agar 3.0. The pH is adjusted to 7.0-7.1 (an olivaceous green colour) by dropwise addition of 40% NaOH solution. The medium is then steamed to melt the agar and dispensed as 90 ml or 18 ml per flask or bottle as preferred and autoclaved. 10 ml or 2 ml volumes of 10% (w/v) glucose solution in distilled water are autoclaved separately and added to either 90 or 18 ml of molten sterile basal medium. The medium is dispensed as 3-4 ml in sterile 150 x 13 mm test tubes.

Duplicate tubes of medium are stabbed to the base with inoculum on a straight inoculating wire; one of the two tubes is then sealed with about 3 ml of molten 3% agar. The tubes are incubated at 28C and examined daily for up to 14 days for evidence of acid production. A change to yellow in the medium (acid pH, less than pH 6.0) indicates acid production from glucose; organisms with an oxidative (respiratory) metabolism of glucose produce acid only at the top 1-2 cm of the open tube where conditions are aerobic; in a fermentative reaction acid is produced under aerobic and anaerobic conditions, i.e., throughout the depth of both open and sealed tubes. Gas production is indicated by disruption of the semi-solid medium and/or by displacement of the agar seal up the tube. The inoculated tubes should be matched with the control tube in order to observe pH changes; in some cases there may be a slight change to alkaline pH in the open tube, indicating that the bacterium does not metabolize glucose.

B. *Acid Production from Carbohydrates*

Hayward's medium (above) or Dye's medium C (below) are suitable for determining acid production from sugars other than glucose for all the bacterial pathogens. Unfortunately taxonomic studies have been conducted without standardization and variations in the medium may yield variations in results, especially with erwinias.

Great care must be taken in comparing results with published works to ensure the medium and incubation temperature and time are the same. These are specified in the appropriate chapters of this volume. It is always advisable to use standard reference cultures.

The following three media, in addition to that of Hayward (1964) (above), are commonly used:

Medium A (Ayers et al., 1919) (in g/l): $NH_4H_2PO_4$ 1.0, KCl 0.2, $MgSO_4.7H_2O$ 0.2, bromthymol blue powder 0.08. Adjust to pH 7.0 before autoclaving. Filter sterilize carbon sources as 10% w/v solutions and add to basal medium to a 1% final concentration.

Medium B (Dye, 1968): 1% peptone water containing bromcresol purple (0.7 ml of 1.5% ethanol solution per l). Filtered carbon source is added aseptically to 1% final concentration after autoclaving.

Medium C (Dye, 1968) (in g/l): $NH_4H_2PO_4$ 0.5, K_2HPO_4 0.5, $MgSO_4.7H_2O$ 0.2, NaCl 5, yeast extract (Difco) 1, agar 12, and bromcresol purple (0.7ml of 1.5% ethanol solution), pH to 6.8, autoclave. Add carbon source (0.5% final concentration) to molten medium and slope.

C. *Carbon Source Utilization Tests*

The utilization of a diverse range of carbon compounds as sole sources of carbon and energy is particularly useful in the identification of pseudomonads. In addition, utilization of some organic acids is frequently used in a number of genera. Breakdown of the acid causes a rise in pH detected by an appropriate indicator (discussed below as alkali production from organic acids).

Successful repeatable carbon source utilization tests require scrupulous attention to detail to avoid chemical contamination of the medium. All chemicals used must be AR grade and all glassware rinsed at leat five times in distilled water before use. Only washed high quality agar should be used. Plastic petri dishes and even laboratory air may introduce inconsistencies into results (Fahy, 1981).

The recommended standard mineral base (SMB) medium (Palleroni & Doudoroff, 1972) is: $Na_2HPO_4.2H_2O$ 4.75g, KH_2PO_4 4.53g, NH_4Cl 1.0g, $MgSO_4.7H_2O$ 0.5g, 5% w/v ferric ammonium citrate solution 1.0 ml, 0.5% w/v $CaCl_2$ solution 1.0ml, washed agar 15g, distilled water 900 ml. Dissolved by steaming for 30 min, then auto- clave as either 90 ml lots or in 2ml lots in 13 x 100 mm screw cap tubes. Filter sterilized, neutralized, carbon sources are added to a final concentration of 0.3% w/v of the active carbon radical to molten agar before pouring plates or sloping tubes. Basal medium will store for 1 yr at 4C and may be remelted for addition of carbon sources. Most filtered carbon sources may be stored as 3% solutions at 4C for 1 yr.

Replica plating procedures are generally used for taxo- nomic studies but individual tubes may be used for diagnostic work. Test isolates must be transferred at least 3 times on a defined medium containing a single utilizable carbon source (usually glucose) before commencing tests. This avoids carry over of complex nutrients and ensures growth factors are not required. A Xanthomonas campestris pathovar may be used as a test strain to check purity and freedom from common growth factors. The use of known reference strains and duplication of results at a different time are strongly recommended.

Test strains are suspended as a non turbid suspension (10^6 cells/ml) and 1-2 drops placed on a slope or replica plate. Visible growth is recorded up to 14 days at 25C. SMB without carbon source should be similarly inoculated and incubated as controls for each strain tested.

Some carbon sources are potentially toxic to the test bacteria and require special handling. Geraniol is added as 1 drop to the lid of an inverted Petri dish and the test strains utilize the vapour. For full details of procedures consult Palleroni & Doudoroff (1972).

D. *Alkali Production from Organic Acids*

Utilization of organic acids may be tested using the OY medium of Dye (1968) for Xanthomonas and Erwinia (in g/l): $NH_4H_2PO_4$ 0.5, K_2HPO_4 0.5, $MgSO_4.7H_2O$ 0.2, NaCl 5, yeast extract (Difco) 0.8, organic acid 2, agar 12, bromthymol blue 0.02, pH to 6.8 before auto - claving. Incubate for up to 21 days at 27C.

For Agrobacterium Kerr & Panagopoulos (1977) used a modified Leifson's medium for malonate utilization containing (in g/l): $(NH_4)_2SO_4$ 2, NaCl 0.6, K_2HPO_4 0.4, KH_2PO_4 0.1, yeast extract 0.1, sodium malonate 3, bromthymol blue 0.025. Tartrate and propionate were tested using the medium of Ayers et al. (1919) (see medium A above). Incubate for 7 days at 25C.

E. Levan Formation

Levan, or poly-fructose, is an extracellular capsular substance produced through the action of the enzyme levan sucrase. Most fluorescent pseudomonads which utilize sucrose as a carbon source produce this enzyme. The colonies formed on a 5% sucrose agar medium are translucent to opaque, shining, mucoid, with a distinctive raised convex (domed) appearance in young cultures. In aged cultures the colonies often lose their domed appearance due to the collapse and liquefaction of the colony. Isolated colonies are usually 3-5 mm in diameter after 2 days incubation and 5-7 mm after 3 days incubation. Colonies typical of levan-producing Pseudomonas may be observed on 2% sucrose peptone agar (SPA) or on nutrient agar to which 5% sucrose has been added.

F. Voges-Proskauer and Methyl Red Tests

Enterobacteriaceae sub groups are routinely different-iated by these tests. They are usually performed on a glucose phosphate peptone broth (0.5% glucose, 0.5% K_2HPO_4, 0.5% peptone) but Dye (1968) found addition of yeast extract necessary for satisfactory growth of some Erwinia. The medium recommended contains (in g/l): glucose 5, $NH_4H_2PO_4$ 0.5, K_2HPO_4 0.5, $MgSO_4.7H_2O$ 0.2, NaCl 5, yeast extract (Difco) 5.

The Voges-Proskauer (VP) reaction depends on the ability of an organism to first produce acid from glucose and subsequently convert the acid end products to neutral end products, acetoin (acetylmethylcarbinol) or 2,3 butanediol which react with the medium on addition of alkali to impart a pink colour (enhanced by the addition of -napthol or creatine).

Cultures are shaker incubated at 27C and tested after 2 and 5 days. One ml samples of culture are added to a tube with 0.6 ml of napthol (5% w/v in absolute ethanol) and

0.2 ml of 40% KOH and shaken vigorously for up to 2 h. Optional addition of a few grains of solid creatine may accelerate the reaction.

Methyl red (MR) indicator (0.1g methyl red dissolved in 300 ml of 95% ethanol and made up to 50 ml with distilled water) added to samples of culture will turn red if pH is at or below 4.2. VP+ cultures may be MR+ in early stages of incubation but become MR- as the acid is converted to neutral end products. True MR+ strains remain MR+ and VP-.

G. *3-Ketolactose Production*

Agrobacterium tumefaciens oxidizes lactose to 3-ketolactose. The method of Bernaerts & De Ley (1963) is used. Bacteria are grown on lactose agar (in g/l lactose 10, yeast extract 1, agar 15), for 2 days then plates are flooded with Benedict's reagent. A bright yellow-orange precipitate of Cu_2O forms around colonies within 1 h if 3-ketolactose is present. Various formulae for Benedict's reagent exist but not all are satisfactory. Benedict's reagent: Solution A - 173g sodium citrate, 100g sodium carbonate dissolved in 600 ml water by heating and made up to 850 ml. Solution B - 18g copper sulphate dissolved in 100ml water, made up to 150 ml then slowly added to solution A.

H. *Reducing Compounds from Sucrose*

This test is of differential value for Erwinia (Dye, 1968). Cultures are shaker-incubated (48h, 27C) in sucrose broth, containing (in g/l): peptone (Difco) 10, beef extract (Difco) 5, sucrose 40. An equal volume of Benedict's reagent (see G. above) is added and tubes held in a boiling waterbath for 10 min. A yellow-orange colour change is positive. The same technique may be employed to detect 2-ketogluconate production from potassium gluconate (used in identification of pseudomonads and some Erwinia.) Potassium gluconate, 40g/l is substituted for sucrose in the above medium or other recommended media.

IX.   Decomposition of Nitrogenous Compounds

A. *Nitrate Reduction*

Plant pathogens differ in their effect on nitrate; some produce nitrite from nitrate and others such as <u>Xanthomonas</u> do not reduce nitrate; others produce gas from nitrate, i.e., they denitrify. The reaction given by those which denitrify is not strong, and may not be evident on all media and may require incubation for periods up to 7 days. Media must not be shaken as dissolved oxygen inhibits the reactions. Check for good growth in the medium employed.

The following semi-solid medium is recommended (in g/l): peptone 10.0, NaCl 5.0, KNO_3 2.0, agar 3.0. Adjust to pH 7.0 with 40% NaOH; steam to dissolve the agar, dispense in 5-10ml quantities in test tubes and autoclave. Inoculate duplicate tubes when molten or remelted and cooled to 40C. Add a heavy loopful of growth to each tube and mix by rotation between palms before the agar sets. One of the two tubes is sealed with 3-5ml of 3% agar. Incubate at 27C for 3-7 days, then test the unsealed tube for the presence of nitrite by addition of starch-iodide reagents (Skerman, 1967) or sulphanilic acid -α napthylamine reagents.

Starch iodide solution contains starch, 0.4g; $ZnCl_2$ 2.0g; water 100ml. Dissolve the zinc chloride in 10ml water. Boil and add the starch. Dilute to 100ml, allow to stand 1wk and filter. Add an equal volume of a 0.2% solution of KI.

Hydrochloric acid solution contains 16ml concentrated HCl and 84ml water. Using clean glass dropping pipettes, place 3-4 drops of each reagent in each tube. A blue colour indicates the presence of nitrite. The test depends on the formation of nitrous acid and its subsequent reaction with potassium iodide with the liberation of iodine, which turns the starch blue. The test is not entirely specific. Control tests should be made on a non-inoculated medium. Metal implements should be avoided.

A negative reaction for nitrite may indicate either that the nitrate has not been reduced, or that the nitrate has been reduced beyond nitrite. In order to differentiate between these possibilities a speck of zinc dust is added to tubes in which no reaction for nitrite, or a weak reaction, has occurred. If the nitrate has not been reduced by the bacterium, there is a reaction after addition of the zinc dust; if there is a weak reaction which does not intensify after addition of the zinc dust, this indicates that most of the nitrate has been reduced beyond nitrite. The occurrence of a weak reaction which intensifies after the addition of zinc dust indicates that a little of the nitrate has been reduced to nitrite.

The tube sealed with agar or vaspar should be observed for the presence of gas bubbles trapped in the medium or beneath the seal each day for 14 days. The reaction is sometimes weak and slow to appear. A stronger reaction may be obtained if the isolates are subcultured several times through a medium containing nitrate in order to enhance the activity of the enzyme nitrate reductase (Stanier et al., 1966). False positives may sometimes be obtained if the medium is stab inoculated when solid as bubbles may appear along the stab marks in the agar. A more subtle cause of error may arise when medium is stored at 4C. Gases, more soluble at 4C, are released into the medium when subsequently incubated at 27C. This effect can be avoided if the medium is re-melted before use.

Nitrate may also be detected by adding 0.5ml of 1.0% sulphanilic acid in 5N acetic acid followed by 0.5ml of 0.6% dimethyl-α-napthylamine (carcinogenic) in 5N acetic acid. A red colour indicates presence of nitrite. Residual nitrate may be detected with zinc dust as described.

Dye (1968) recommends a broth medium for detection of nitrate reduction in Erwinia containing (in g/l): KH_2PO_4 0.5, K_2HPO_4 0.5, $MgSO_4.7H_2O$ 0.2, NaCl 5, yeast extract powder 5, sodium succinate 2, KNO_3 1. Cultures are incubated at 27C and samples tested up to 5 days.

B. Arginine Dihydrolase

The test is of differential value for Pseudomonas. Ammonia is produced from arginine under anaerobic conditions involving an alkaline change in the medium. The test medium (Thornley, 1960) contains (in g/l): Bacto peptone (Difco) 1, NaCl 5, K_2HPO_4 0.3, agar 3, phenol red 0.01, L-arginine HCl 10, pH 7.2. Dispense 3-4ml quantities in 13 x 150mm screw cap tubes and autoclave.

Stab inoculate to base of medium, seal each tube with 3 ml of molten 3% agar and incubate 7 days at 27C. A positive alkaline reaction is indicated by a deep red colour change compared with orange-pink by controls.

C. Hydrogen Sulphide Production

Hydrogen sulphide production from organic sulphur compounds is of differential value for <u>Xanthomonas</u> and <u>Erwinia</u>. H_2S production from peptone is frequently used but cysteine gives more consistent results.

The medium recommended is that of Dye (1968) (in g/l): $NH_4H_2PO_4$ 0.5, K_2HPO_4 0.5, $MgSO_4.7H_2O$ 0.2, NaCl 5, yeast extract (Difco) 5, cysteine hydrochloride 0.1, dispensed in 5ml lots in tubes and autoclaved. A lead acetate strip is suspended over the medium after inoculation and held by a bung or screw cap.

Tubes are examined up to 14 days. Hydrogen sulphide reacts forming a black lead sulphide discolouration of the paper strip. Lead acetate strips may be purchased or prepared by immersing cut filter paper strips in 5% lead acetate, air drying and autoclaving.

D. Phenylalanine Deaminase

The enzyme converts phenylalanine to phenylpyruvic acid, detected by reduction of ferric chloride. The standard medium is (in g/l): yeast extract 3, DL phenylalanine 2, Na_2HPO_4 1, NaCl 5, agar 12. Autoclave in 5ml lots and slope.

A few drops of 10% ferric chloride solution are added to slopes after 3 days incubation at 27C. A green colour indicates a positive reaction. A weak reaction is produced by a few erwinias compared with the strong reaction of <u>Proteus</u>.

E. Urease Production

Hydrolysis of urea to ammonia yields an alkaline reaction, detected by change in pH indicator. The medium of Dye (1968) is recommended: $NH_4H_2PO_4$ 0.5g, K_2HPO_4 0.5g, $MgSO_4.7H_2O$ 0.2g, NaCl 5g, yeast extract (Difco) 1.0g, cresol red ·016g, water 800ml, autoclave in flasks. Filter sterilize 10% urea soln. and add to a final concentration of 2% (200 ml/l); dispense in 5ml quantities. As yeast extract is present in the medium inoculate duplicate tubes, one with and one without urea. A marked increase in alkalinity is regarded as positive for urease production.

F. Indole Production

Cultures are shaker incubated (27C) in a tryptone (1.0%), yeast extract (0.5%) broth. Indole is produced by decomposition of tryptophan present in the medium and is tested for by adding Kovacs' reagent to 1ml samples of broth after 2 and 5 days incubation and shaking. Indole is extracted by amyl alcohol present in the reagent and reacts with the reagent giving a cherry red colour which fades after 15 min.

Kovacs' reagent: dissolve 5g p-dimethylamino-benzaldehyde in 75ml amyl alcohol by gently warming in a water bath (50-55C). Cool and add 25 ml concentrated HCl. Protect from light and store refrigerated. Reagent should be bright yellow to light brown.

X.   Decomposition of Macromolecules

A. Gelatin Hydrolysis (Liquefaction)

Proteolytic bacteria decompose gelatin with loss of gelling properties. Bacteriological grade gelatin should be used as a 12% solution to gel a suitable nutrient medium for growth of the test organism. Lower grades of gelatin will lose gelling ability if autoclaved at 121C for 15 min and will require clearing. Dehydrated nutrient gelatins containing (in g/l) beef extract 3, peptone 5, and gelatin 120 are suitable for most bacteria, but check that good growth occurs. Steam to dissolve media and dispense at 5-10ml per tube, autoclave at 121C for 15 min maximum. Stab inoculate and incubate at 20C for 7-14 days or at optimal growth temperature, then cool at ca. 4C to determine if liquefaction has occurred. Alternatively, prepared gelatin-charcoal tablets may be added to an appropriate growth medium.

B. Action in Milk

Milk proteolysis is a useful diagnostic characteristic for most xanthomonads. Dye (1962) recommends milk agar plates: thin (15ml per 10cm plate) nutrient agar (Difco) plates are prepared; over this agar pour a layer of yeast extract nutrient agar (nutrient agar + 0.5% yeast extract) to which 15% (w/v) sterile skim milk has been added. The skim milk is sterilized by steaming for 1 h on three successive days. The medium is held between 22C and 37C between steamings. Cultures are incubated for 7 days and proteolysis is observed as a clear zone surrounding colonies. Unused plates may be stored at 4C for 2 months.

Acid production may be determined in purple milk which is more sensitive than litmus milk. Skim milk (10% w/v) with 0.4g/l bromocresol purple is dispensed in 5ml quantities in tubes (pH 7.0 with 1M NaOH). The medium is sterilized as described above. A purple to yellow colour change in incubated cultures indicates acid production.

C. Starch Hydrolysis

Soluble starch (0.2%) should be added to a suitable nutrient medium such as YNA (Dye, 1962) (in g/l): yeast extract 5, peptone 5, beef extract powder 5, pH to 6.8 and autoclave.

Starch plates are streaked and incubated for 2-7 days depending on growth, then flooded with iodine solution (see Gram stain). Starch stains blue-black; a clear zone is present where amylase activity (starch hydrolysis) has occurred.

D. Lecithinase (Phospholipase) Activity

The phospholipid emulsion of egg yolk may be broken down by lecithinase, liberating a turbid zone of free fats around a positive lecithinase colony on egg yolk nutrient agar medium. The test is of value in differentiation of erwinias. Incubate at 27C for 7 days.

Egg yolk emulsion is prepared from a fresh hen egg, washed well in soap solution, rinsed and surface sterilized in 70% ethanol for 5 min. The egg is flamed, broken aseptically, and the yolk separated into a sterile measuring cylinder and diluted to 40% v/v with sterile water. The egg yolk is incorporated into molten nutrient agar (cooled to 55C) just before plates are poured at the rate of 10ml/100ml of medium. Plates will keep refrigerated for 2 months.

E. Tween 80 Hydrolysis (Esterase Activity)

Opaque zones develop on a nutrient media containing $CaCl_2$ and Tween 80, a water soluble long chain fatty acid ester. The opaque zones are crystals of the calcium soap.

The medium of Sierra (1957) is recommended (in g/l): peptone (Difco) 10, NaCl 5, $CaCl_2.2H_2O$ 0.1, agar 15; adjust pH to 7.4. Tween 80 is autoclaved separately in 10ml quantities added to 1l of medium, mixed well and plates poured. Test organisms may require incubation for 7 days (25-27C).

XI.   Other Physiological and Biochemical Tests

A. *Kovacs' Oxidase Test*

There are various methods for conducting the oxidase test. Oxidase strips are available commercially which should be used according to the manufacturer's instructions. The following method follows closely that originally described by Kovacs (1956).

Place a Whatman No.1 filter paper in a petri dish and add 3-4 drops of a freshly prepared 1% aqueous solution of tetramethylparaphenylenediamine dihydrochloride on the centre of the paper. A platinum loop heavily charged with growth from a 24-48 h culture of the test organism on nutrient agar is rubbed in a band about 1cm long across the reagent-impregnated paper. With many pseudomonads the change to a purple colour is usually instantaneous. Any change within 10 s of application of the culture may be regarded as a positive result. The reagent solution should be made up weekly or fortnightly and stored in a stoppered dark glass bottle at 4C.

CAUTION. The reagent is an aromatic amine and a highly toxic substance; skin contact with the powder or solution should be avoided!

Choice of medium may be important for the proper execution of this test. False positive reactions may occur where nitrite present in the medium reacts at once with the reagent to give a purple colour. If, therefore, the medium contains nitrite or, more probably, if the medium contains nitrate and the species in question (e.g. some pseudomonads) is able to reduce it to nitrite, an apparently "positive" reaction is likely to ensue.

There is evidence that the N, N-dimethyl-p-phenylenediamine reagent is to be preferred to the tetramethyl form as it is less sensitive to nitrites which may be formed in the culture medium (Hildebrand & Schroth, 1972).

The mechanism of this test is not fully understood. There is evidence that the presence of cytochrome c is correlated with a positive reaction. Examination of the absorption spectrum of several oxidase negative bacteria has shown that they possess cytochromes of type b, and not cytochrome c which is invariably present in oxidase-positive bacteria (Sands et al., 1967).

The oxidase reaction is negative in the Enterobacteriaceae and positive in many pseudomonads and related bacteria. The test is of differential value amongst the pseudomonads (see Chapters 7 and 8).

The presence of a high concentration of a utilizable carbohydrate in the medium on which P. solanacearum is grown for the oxidase test does not appear to affect the result. With other oxidase-positive species, however, false negative results may occur in agar media containing a concentration of glucose greater than 0.5%. Inhibition of the reaction has been observed on media containing 2% glucose; this is believed to be a pH effect resulting when the pH of the medium falls to 5.5-5.0 or below.

The false negative reaction is useful in distinguishing amongst agrobacteria (see Chapter 3). Test isolates are incubated on nutrient agar + 1% glucose for 24h. Fresh reagent is recommended for this test as prepared test strips may not give the false negative reaction.

B. Ice Nucleation Activity (INA)

P. syringae pv. syringae cells were examined by Paulin & Luisetti (1978) for the property, reported by Arny et al. (1976), to act as ice nuclei. They developed a simple laboratory test which is a useful aid in distinguishing between some Group 1 pseudomonads (see Chapter 8). Eighty seven per cent of pathovar syringae isolates from fruit trees were INA positive. All Group 3, 4 and 5 strains tested were negative.

Two day cultures grown on a medium containing (in g/l) yeast extract 5, peptone 5, glucose 5, agar 15, were suspended in 5ml double distilled water in capped test tubes (16mm diameter) and placed in a water bath held at -4C (112g NaCl per litre distilled water or suitable anti-freeze). Positive results were recorded if the suspension froze within 5 min. Distilled water blanks served as controls.

Young (pers. comm.) has found all pathovar syringae isolates from stone fruit tested are INA positive, whereas all of pathovar <u>morsprunorum</u> are INA negative. Young places 1-2 drops of suspension (10^8cells/ml) into 5ml of cooled distilled water in a test tube held in a bath at -8 or -9C. The water will crystallize almost as soon as an INA positive bacterium is added. A mix of saturated saline and crushed ice gives a temperature of -9C.

C. Pigment Production by Fluorescent Pseudomonads

Two media developed by King et al. (1954) have subsequently been found useful (Stanier et al., 1966) for distinguishing a number of species of fluorescent pseudomonads. Almost all fluorescent strains will produce diffusible fluorescent pigments on KBA (section V) which fluoresce blue or green under long wave ultraviolet light (see Chapter 8). A number of these species produce phenazine pigments, enhanced by King's medium A (KAA), which also suppresses fluorescent pigment production. <u>Pseudomonas chlororaphis</u> produces a green crystallizing pigment (chlororaphin); <u>P. aureofaciens</u> a diffusible orange-yellow pigment (phenazine-1-carboxylic acid); <u>P. aeruginosa</u> a deep blue to green pigment (pyocyanin) and rarely a red pigment (pyorubin); <u>P. viridiflava</u> a yellow diffusible pigment.

KAA contains (in g/l): Bacto peptone (Difco) 20, glycerol 10, K_2SO_4 (anhyd.) 10, $MgCl_2$ (anhyd.) 1.4, agar 15 pH 7.2. Dispense as slopes. Pigments may take 1 to 7 days to develop. Difco <u>Pseudomonas</u> Agar P and F are modified formulations of KAA and KBA respectively. They are reported to be superior by some workers.

D. Salt Tolerance

Salt tolerance, generally 2% and 5% NaCl may be determined by visible turbidity after incubation (14 days, 25C) of cultures in YS broth containing the required final concentration of NaCl.

E. Growth Temperature Maxima

Incubate in tubes in a water bath with an accuracy of ±0.25 degrees or better for 7 days and observe for turbidity. YS broth is a suitable medium for most pathogens. To determine growth minima or for slow growing organisms 14 days incubation may be necessary to observe turbidity.

F. Erythromycin Sensitivity

This is a diagnostic test for erwinias (see Chapter 6). Pour and dry plates of Oxoid Diagnostic Sensitivity Test Agar (CM 261). Inoculate plates by the spread plate technique using an L-shaped glass rod and allow to dry. Place an anti-biotic disc (Oxoid or similar) of 15 g erythromycin in centre of dish and incubate. Sensitivity is expressed as a zone around disc free of bacterial growth.

G. Phosphatase Activity

This is a diagnostic test for Erwinia (see Chapter 6). Nutrient agar, containing (in g/l) Lab-Lemco powder 10, bacteriological peptone 10, NaCl 5, agar 15) or Oxoid Blood Agar Base (CM55) is autoclaved in 100ml quantities and cooled to about 50C. Add aseptically 1 ampoule (1ml) of Oxoid phenol- phthalein phosphate 1%. Mix well and pour plates. Inoculate to obtain discrete colonies and incubate 24 h. Add a few drops of ammonia solution to lid of inverted plate. Phosphatase positive colonies become bright pink, usually in under 30 min.

XII. Toxin Bioassays

A. Escherichia coli Indicator Technique for the Detection of Antimetabolite Toxins

P. syringae pathovars produce antimetabolite toxins which can be detected by a simple technique described by Gasson (1980). A modification of this technique is described below by which any newly isolated plant pathogen may be screened for production of a toxin with antibacterial activity. The method is mainly applicable to Group 1 fluorescent pseudomonads (see Chapter 8). However the method could also be applied to pathogens in a search for new unidentified toxins.

Five pathovars of P. syringae have been described which produce extracellular toxins; these toxins cause chlorosis in affected plant tissues by mechanisms which are at present poorly understood. P. syringae pathovars tabaci and coronafaciens produce an antimetabolite named tabtoxin (Stewart, 1971). Induction of chlorosis by this toxin is inhibited by L-glutamine; this and other evidence suggests that the mode of action of the toxin involves inhibition of the biosynthetic enzyme glutamine synthetase.

P. syringae pv. phaseolicola produces a toxin, which has been called phaseolotoxin, and identified as ([N -δ-phosphosulphamyl] ornithylalanylhomoarginine) by Mitchell (1976). Phaseolotoxin has been shown to induce chlorosis on infiltration into leaves, and in vitro to be an inhibitor of the arginine biosynthetic enzyme, ornithine carbamyl transferase (Mitchell, 1979). The effect of the toxin in vitro and in planta can be reversed by addition of either arginine or citrulline. Production of the toxin in infected bean plants results in the accumulation of ornithine (Patel & Walker, 1963).

Gasson (1980) and Staskawicz & Panopoulos (1979) have described rapid and simple bioassays for phaseolotoxin activity. Apparently phaseolotoxin arrests the growth of Escherichia coli in a minimal-glucose medium by inhibiting L-ornithine carbamyltransferase thereby creating a phenotypic requirement for arginine. Inhibition is reversed by citrulline and arginine, but not by ornithine. The method is an elegant and convenient alternative to the usual method of toxin assay involving an appropriate host plant, and opens up the possibility of genetic study of the basis of toxin production.

E. coli is a suitable indicator bacterium for the detection of antimetabolite toxin production for a number of reasons: it is sufficiently distinct taxonomically from pseudomonads to eliminate interference from lysogenic bacteriophages, bacteriocins, or naturally occurring phytotoxin resistance, and it grows well on the minimal salts medium routinely used in studies of plant pathogenic pseudomonads. Its higher optimum growth temperature facilitates the preferential growth of test organisms or indicator when both are present on the same plate.

In the following procedure two effects are demonstrated: inhibition of the growth of E coli B in a defined medium by toxigenic pseudomonad pathvars; reversal of the inhibitory effects with appropriate amino acids.

Bioassay technique: two ml of a distilled water suspension of E. coli B (10^8-10^9 cells/ml) is added to 18 ml of molten (40-45C) Pseudomonas mineral medium (in g/l): ($NH_4H_2PO_4$ 1, KCl 0.2, $MgSO_4.7H_2O$ 0.2, agar 15, pH 7.0, and glucose 0.2% (sterilized separately at 2%). Rotate media bottle to mix bacterium and pour immediately. When agar is set, open and dry inverted plates in an incubator (37-40C, 10-20 min).

Immediately after drying, stab inoculate test isolates to a maximum of eight spaced inoculations per plate. It is advisable to test a number of single colonies from each test strain as the toxin producing character may be lost readily in culture. Incubate (25C, 24h) and observe for presence of inhibition zones in the growth of the indicator bacterium surrounding stab marks, indicating presence of toxins.

In order to show specific reversal of inhibition of growth of the indicator bacterium, prepare pour plates as described above, divide into quarter sectors and stab inoculate with the test isolates. Prior to stab inoculation, place sterile filter paper discs (6-7 mm diameter) in each sector of the plate, the centre of each disc being not more than 2 cm from the edge of the plate. To three of the discs, add 5μl of the following sterile aqueous solutions: L-glutamine, L-arginine, and L-citrulline (each containing 2mg/ml) and to the fourth disc add sterile distilled water as a control. Stab inoculate test isolates not more than 1 cm from the margin of each filter paper disc. Incubate (25C, 24h) and observe for reversal of the inhibitory effect at a position where the zone of diffusion of the amino acid intersects with the zone of diffusion of the toxin. If there is no reversal, the identity of the toxin remains unknown; if the effect is reversed by arginine and citrulline, but not by glutamine then the toxin is phaseolotoxin or a related toxin; if the effect is reversed by glutamine but not by citrulline or arginine then the toxin is tabtoxin or a related toxin.

Gasson (1980) used the test on a wide selection of Group I pseudomonad pathovars. Unidentified toxins were found in isolates of P. syringae pv. syringae and pv. maculicola. The technique did not detect toxins in isolates of pathovars lachrymans, morsprunorum or pisi.

B. Syringomycin Bioassay

Most Pseudomonas syringae pv. syringae isolates, regardless of host of origin, produce syringomycin, a low molecular weight non-specific toxin (Gross & DeVay, 1977). Isolates from citrus produce a similar non-specific toxin, syringotoxin (De Vay et al., 1978).

The test bacterium is point inoculated onto a suitable medium (potato dextrose agar or similar) and grown for 2 days at 25-28C. The surface of the medium is then sprayed with a suspension of indicator organism. The fungus Geotrichum candidum is suitable although other species may be more sensitive (De Vay et al., 1978). After additional incubation (1-2 days) clear inhibition zones are observed around bacterial colonies. The bioassay does not distinguish between syringomycin and syringotoxin.

G. candidum is a far more sensitive organism for syringomycin and syringotoxin bioassay than E. coli (De Vay et al., 1978), but other bacteria such as Bacillus subtilis may be suitable.

XIII. Hypersensitivity in Tobacco

This is a key test of the LOPAT groupings for fluorescent pseudomonads (see Chapter 8) and a general screening procedure for most potential pathogens although some pathogens do not give positive reactions. Hildebrand & Riddle (1971), using controlled temperature glasshouses, found that variations in tobacco host species, growth temperature prior to and after inoculation and light influence the hypersensitivity reaction (HR) in different ways for different groups of pathogens. Standardization of the procedure is therefore necessary if wide use of this diagnostic aid is to be made. Erwinia amylovora and most pathogenic pseudomonads will give a positive HR over a relatively wide range of conditions but xanthomonads and agrobacteria produce reactions only under a restricted range of temperature and light conditions. The procedure below is suitable only for the first group, although some xanthomonads may give a positive HR.

Prepare suspensions of the test organism in 20 ml distilled water and obtain a uniform suspension with the aid of a vortex homogeniser. The suspensions should be clearly opaque and contain 10^8-10^9 cells/ml. Use 1 ml volume disposable plastic 25 gauge syringes to infiltrate leaves of tobacco (Nicotiana tabacum cv. White Burley or Hicks) which are well-developed but which have not yet reached flowering stage. Infiltrate the undersurface of leaves with a suspension of the test organism which has been heat-killed in an autoclave; this serves as one kind of control inoculation. Infiltrate the live test suspension into another leaf, and a suspension of either Escherichia coli B or

<u>Pseudomonas</u> <u>fluorescens</u> as live control suspensions which will give a negative reaction on infiltration. Positive controls are also recommended. When experienced in inoculation, it is possible to inoculate several test strains on the one leaf. Infiltrated leaves should be appropriately identified with labels tied around the petioles. There is some indication that best results are obtained if inoculations are carried out either before 10.00 a.m. or after 3.00 p.m. The test is less sensitive for some pathogens when glasshouse temperatures are less than 20C and is inhibited at temperatures greater than 36C. Examine the plants as early as possible on the day following infiltration and again 24 h later. In the case of most Group I pseudomonads there should be a dry necrotic area throughout the infiltrated area and no effect with the live or killed control suspensions. The rapid onset of necrosis which is characteristic of the HR should be apparent within 8-24 h. Saprophytes may induce a chlorosis of the inoculated region after 3 days.

Hypersensitivity may be regarded as a defense mechanism which results in the inhibition of invading microorganisms. Characteristically, increased permeability, drying and death of host cells occur in the neighbourhood of the invasion, thus isolating the microorganism from living host tissues by a barrier of dead cells and confining them to a restricted area. Klement (1968) has shown that the concentration of bacteria in the infiltrating suspension is critical for the induction of a macroscopic HR. In the case of Group 1 pseudomonads it has been established that a suspension of 5×10^6 cells/ml is the minimum required.

A pathogen of tobacco such as P. syringae pv. tabaci will produce typical symptoms of wildfire on tobacco following infiltration at high concentration of inoculum. The symptoms will take 3-7 days to appear. Avirulent strains of the pathogen produce HR in tobacco and even virulent strains will do so when a line of tobacco resistant to wildfire is challenged. Susceptible host plants inoculated with pseudomonads or xanthomonads pathogenic to that host plant will exhibit typical disease symptoms which are not rapid in onset but take several days or more than a week to appear depending on the environmental conditions. Most work on hypersensitivity has made use of tobacco or pepper as host plant for the induction of HR.

XIV.   Diagnostic Tests Using Excised Plant Tissues

A. *Application*

Although not strictly pathogenicity tests, use of detached organs and segments is a convenient and valuable means of screening likely pathogens and confirming some diagnoses. Some highly specific diagnostic symptoms occur but saprophytes may also produce various reactions and results must be interpreted with care. Commonly used tests are described below but some specific plant reactions are described where appropriate in earlier chapters.

B. *Detached Fruit Inoculations*

Never use mature, ripe fruit. Select immature healthy fruit, preferably from the susceptible host. Avoid bruising, wash well in tap water, swab with 70% ethanol and allow to dry. Inoculate at several points by pricking with a sterilized needle charged with inoculum or through a drop of turbid suspension placed on the fruit surface. Incubate in a closed container (25-27C) lined with damp filter paper. Include cultures with a known reaction as positive controls whenever possible. Also include uninoculated needle punctures as controls. A non pathogenic species may be used for inoculated control punctures. Always replicate.

An optional refinement is to seal needle puncture holes with vaseline to prevent drying. Warm a metal spatula in a flame, dip into vaseline and quickly smear over puncture holes. Flame sterilize between treatments. If performed correctly, a thin smear of vaseline will set over the hole and the fruit will not be damaged.

Peach, plum, apricot and cherry are suitable for screening Xanthomonas campestris pv. pruni which produces typical water-soaked lesions. Lemon fruit can be used for Pseudomonas syringae pv. syringae isolated from most hosts, but bean pods (see below) should also be inoculated as not all isolates are positive for both hosts. Pathovar syringae induces black sunken lesions on lemon, typical of citrus blast, which readily distinguishes it from other P. syringae pathovars.

Whole pears or pear slices are of considerable value in diagnosis of fireblight (Erwinia amylovora). The method of Billing et al. (1960) is recommended: the cut surface of transverse slices of immature pear fruits, placed on damp filter paper in petri dishes, are stabbed six times with a needle charged with culture growth or with bacterial suspension from a lesion. The dishes should be enclosed in polythene bags and incubated at 27C. Drops of milky bacterial exudate appear on the cut surface in 1-3 days if the result is positive. Fruits can be stored at 2C in polythene bags for many months; some cultivars e.g., Conference, can be stored from one season to the next in this way. Immature whole fruits can be used instead of slices and have the advantage that P. syringae pv. syringae, also a cause of blossom blight of pear, will produce localised dry, black lesions on them in 1-7 days. Unlike E. amylovora, P. syringae pv. syringae does not produce ooze.

C. *Bean Pod Inoculations*

Mature fresh garden beans (Phaseolus vulgaris) are readily purchased and suitable. Some canning bean cultivars are resistant to the halo blight pathogen Pseudomonas syringae pv. phaseolicola, and are unsuitable. Pods should be prepared, inoculated and incubated as described for detached fruit.

Virulent strains of the halo blight bacterium will produce a "water soaked" lesion under the vaseline seal, which is very similar to the naturally occurring "grease spot" symptom observed on infected bean plants in the field without wounding. Lesions appear after 48 h and remain water soaked without necrosis for several days. Avirulent organisms, or pathogens, not capable of causing disease in bean produce an effect no different from the control punctures or a pinpoint necrotic spot. Lesions produced by P. syringae pv. syringae are distinguished by having red-brown necrotic margins with a depressed centre which become apparent after 3-5 days. Neither feature is usual with P. syringae pv. phaseolicola. X. campestris pv. phaseoli produces water soaked lesions with a yellow ooze.

D. *Soft Rot of Potato Slices*

This is a crude test for macerating and pectolytic activity of certain bacteria. It is one of the 'LOPAT' tests (see Chapter 8). The following procedure is recommended:

Scrub a fresh, firm, healthy potato tuber with soap and water to remove adhering soil. Flame a peeler or scalpel after dipping in alcohol and peel the tuber; cut off and discard the end pieces and slice the remainder of the tuber transversely into portions 7-8mm thick. Two portions of the tuber from opposite ends should be placed into sterile Petri dishes containing 10-15 ml sterile tap water to serve as controls in order to determine the effect of the endogenous flora on soft rot production. The endogenous flora will vary from tuber to tuber. Cut a V-shaped groove of 3-4 mm depth down the centre of each potato slice including the control slices, using an alcohol-flamed scalpel. Add a heavy loopful of inoculum evenly as a paste down the centre of potato slices in separate Petri dishes for each test isolate; add sterile tap water as for the control slices and incubate at 25-30C for 24-48 h. Replicate test strains in slices from different tubers.

Examine the control and inoculated slices for evidence of soft rot by probing the groove with a sterile straight inoculating wire. The rot may be slight and confined to the groove (as with some xanthomonads) or extensive throughout the slice as in Erwinia carotovora. The control slices should be firm at 24 and 48 h unless the endogenous flora is large.

It should be noted that this is not a sterile technique and not a valid test on incubation beyond 48 h because of the presence of endogenous pectolytic bacteria. Healthy potato tubers contain various bacteria, particularly Bacillus spp., which produce no damage in unwounded tubers. However, they are able to proliferate in cut slices. Similarly there are pectolytic bacteria including pseudomonads in the soil which adhere to tubers; some of these may contaminate the cut slice and produce a soft rot of the slice on prolonged incubation.

E. *Carrot Disc Test for* Agrobacterium *spp.*

The procedure is based on the techniques of Ark & Schroth (1958) and Lippincott & Lippincott (1969). Select healthy undamaged carrots and wash well with soap and water. Rinse, wash with 70% ethanol and allow to dry. Cut transverse slices (10-20 mm) and place in a sterile covered container on sterilized, moist filter paper. It is important to invert slices so that discs are upside down to the way they grow, i.e. the face normally distal from the shoot is turned uppermost and is the one inoculated as some agrobacteria do not induce symptoms on the proximal face.

Inoculate cut surface with a turbid suspension (10^8 - 10^9 cells/ml) using a cotton wool swab or several drops from a Pasteur pipette. Use a known positive control and a distilled water negative control and replicate. Incubate at 25C. Symptoms develop within 10-14 days. Hairy root symptoms develop more rapidly on turnip.

XV. Pathogenicity Tests

A. Special Precautions

Some specific pathogenicity tests are included in earlier chapters. The following special precautions and general procedures are satisfactory for most pathogens.

Plant pathogens may cause a variety of reactions in non hosts when spray inoculated or injected at a high dosage (more than 10^7 cells/ml); for example local necrotic lesions, hypersensitive reactions and toxin reactions may occur. Water soaked invasion of new tissue is rare but may occur with forced infiltration, wounding, prolonged leaf wetness and abnormal growth conditions. Non pathogens may also induce a variety of host reactions. Some workers prefer to use low inoculum levels (less than 10^6 cells/ml) to minimize most of these artificial reactions. For routine screening, however, doses between 10^7 and 10^8 cells/ml are generally used to increase the chance of success and hasten onset of visible symptoms, but the precautions above should be considered.

Reference cultures with known reactions should be used whenever possible. Include plant cultivars that are known to be susceptible to the suspect pathogens. Conduct tests under similar temperature conditions to those in the field at time of infection.

B. Inoculum Preparation

Suspend fresh growth from a suitable agar culture in distilled water to give a concentration between 10^7 - 10^8 cells/ml. A broth culture is not recommended as contamination easily occurs and may go undetected. Plate cultures also eliminate the need for centrifuging and washing of cells.

C. Pre and Post Inoculation Conditions

Incubation at high relative humidity prior to inoculation has not been found to be necessary for successful pathogenicity testing. Selection of plant tissue at the correct stage of development and high relative humidity following inoculation appear to be more important for infection.

Immediately following inoculation, the plants or inoculated tissue must be incubated for 18-48 h at a high relative humidity. They should be placed in a cabinet with 100% r.h. or covered with a moistened plastic bag. In the latter case, they should not be exposed to direct sunlight. The longer the time of incubation, the more rapidly symptoms develop and often the greater the severity of the symptoms.

D. Plant Inoculations with Pathogens Affecting Foliage and Stems

Inoculations should be made on immature, rapidly developing plant tissue e.g. partially expanded leaves, emerging shoots, immature pods or other fruit. Plant tissue usually becomes resistant to infection by bacterial plant pathogens as the tissue reaches maturity. Plant pathologists use various methods of inoculation. The methods described below have given reliable results and the symptoms produced resemble those observed from natural infection.

Leaf inoculation. Spray inoculum over both surfaces of a turgid leaf to run off, without infiltration, using a hand atomiser. A pump maintained at 30-40 kilopascals is suitable. An inexpensive atomiser may be improvised by bending the tip of a disposable syringe needle at an angle to provide a fine mist spray under syringe pressure.

Damage to tissue at inoculation is rarely required for leaf pathogens but a few pricks through drops of the inoculum can be made following spraying if there is concern that the pathogen may only enter through wounds. Grasses and some other monocots are inoculated by spraying the leaves and pricking a drop of inoculum into the leaf whorl. Emerging young shoots such as those on stone fruit trees can be spray-inoculated as described for leaf inoculation.

Infiltration of inoculum under the epidermis of the leaf is not recommended for routine inoculation. Although discrete lesions develop at the margin of the infiltrated tissue, damage occurs over most of the infiltrated area.

Stem Inoculation. A drop of inoculum is placed at the junction of a leaf petiole and the stem. The inoculum is pricked into the stem.

Pod and Other Fruit Inoculation. An immature pod or fruit is wiped with cotton wool soaked in 70% ethyl alcohol. When dry, a drop of inoculum is placed on the surface of the pod or fruit and pricked into the tissue.

E. *Inoculation of Vascular Pathogens*

Vascular pathogens should be prepared as described above and may be inoculated by stem wounding (as described) or by inoculation of the root system, generally with some wounding. Young seedlings may be washed free of soil or potting mix, dipped in a suspension of inoculum and the roots lightly trimmed before repotting. Roots of seedlings in pots may be inoculated in situ by cutting into the soil with a scalpel, then pouring inoculum over the soil. The various inoculation methods described below may be adapted for other vascular pathogens besides P. solanacearum.

F. *Inoculation Tests with Pseudomonas solanacearum*

Tomato plants for greenhouse inoculation are prepared in the following manner. Sow seed in peat/sand potting mix. When germinated and about 4 cm high, with well-developed cotyledonary leaves, transplant to flats. Plants to be inoculated should be transplanted 2 wk prior to inoculation.

The following procedure described by Winstead & Kelman (1952) is recommended for the inoculation of tobacco and tomato plants (see also Moore et al., 1963). Use plants 2 wk-old from transplanting (10-15 cm high). Rutgers tomato and Hicks tobacco are good susceptible plants. Prepare turbid, sterile distilled water suspensions (more than 10^8 cells/ml) of each isolate to be tested. Place 1 drop of inoculum in the leaf axil (about the 3rd mature leaf from top) with a sterile Pasteur pipette. Flame a needle, allow to cool for a few seconds, and then insert through centre of drop down into centre of stem about 1-2 cm. Do not go through to opposite side. Stem inoculations give most rapid and thorough infection. However, root inoculations may be made by cutting roots and pouring a bacterial suspension on soil. Amounts depend on container, etc. Tomato plants should wilt in 5-14 days, and tobacco plants in less than 20 days after stem inoculations.

For root inoculations prepare a turbid suspension (more than 10^8 cells/ml) in 20 ml quantities of sterile distilled water contained in a 25 ml screw-capped bottle. Wound roots by cutting into the soil with a scalpel at several points about 2 cm from either side of the stem of individual plants. Pour sterile water around the base of the stem of control plants and pour 20 ml of inoculum around test plants. Potting mix is not suitable for root inoculation of plants, for which purpose plants should be grown in a soil mix, e.g. a sandy loam.

References

Ark, P.A. & Schroth, M.N. (1958). Use of slices of carrot and other fleshy roots to detect crown gall bacteria in soil. Plant Disease Reporter 42, 1279-1281

Arny, D.C., Lindow, S.E. & Upper, C.D. (1976). Frost sensitivity of Zea mays increased by application of Pseudomonas syringae. Nature, London 262, 282-284.

Ayers S.H., Rupp, P. & Johnson, W.T. (1919). A study of the alkali-forming bacteria in milk. United States Department of Agriculture Bulletin 782.

Bernaerts, M.J. & De Ley, J. (1963). A biochemical test for crown gall bacteria. Nature, London 197, 406-407.

Billing, E., Crosse, J.E. & Garrett, C.M.E. (1960). Laboratory diagnosis of fireblight and bacterial blossom blight of pear. Plant Pathology 9, 19-25.

Burdon, K.J. (1946). Fatty material in bacteria and fungi revealed by staining · dried, fixed slide preparations. Journal of Bacteriology 52, 665-678.

Burr, T.J. & Schroth, M.N. (1977). Occurrence of soft-rot Erwinia spp. in soil and plant material. Phytopathology 67, 1382-1387.

Cerny, G. (1976). Method for the distinction of Gram-negative from Gram-positive bacteria. European Journal of Applied Microbiology 3, 223-225.

Cerny, G. (1978). Studies on the aminopeptidase test for the distinction of Gram-negative and Gram-positive bacteria. European Journal of Applied Microbiology and Biotechnology 5, 113-122.

Cother, E.J. , Blakeney, A.B. & Lamb, S. (1980). Laboratory - scale preparation of sodium polypectate for use in selective media for pectolytic Erwinia spp. Plant Disease 64, 1086-1087.

Cuppels, D. & Kelman, A. (1974). Evaluation of selective media for isolation of soft-rot bacteria from soil and plant tissue. Phytopathology 64, 468-475.

De Vay, J.E. , Gonzalez, C.F. & Wakeman, R.J. (1978). Comparison of the biocidal activities of syringomycin and syringotoxin and the characterization of isolates of Pseudomonas syringae from citrus hosts. In "Proceedings of the IVth International Conference on Plant Pathogenic Bacteria", pp. 643-650. (Ed. Station de Pathologie Végétales et Phytobactériologie). Angers, France: I.N.R.A.

Dye, D.W. (1962). The inadequacy of the usual determinative tests for the identification of Xanthomonas spp. New Zealand Journal of Science 5, 393-416.

Dye, D.W. (1968). A taxonomic study of the genus Erwinia. 1. The "amylovora" group. New Zealand Journal of Science 11, 590-607.

Fahy, P.C. (1981). The taxonomy of the bacterial plant pathogens of mushroom culture. Mushroom Science 11, 293-312.

Gasson, M.J. (1980). Indicator technique for antimetabolite toxin production by phytopathgenic species of Pseudomonas. Applied and Environmental Microbiology 39, 25-29.

Gerhardt, P. (1981). "Manual of Methods for General Bacteriology". Washington: American Society for Microbiology.

Gregersen, T. (1978). Rapid method for distinction of Gram-negative from Gram-positive bacteria. European Journal of Applied Microbiology and Biotechnology 5, 123-127.

Gross, D.C. & De Vay, J.E. (1977). Production and purification of syringomycin, a phytotoxin produced by Pseudomonas syringae. Physiological Plant Pathology 11, 13-28.

Hayward, A.C. (1960). A method for characterizing Pseudomonas solanacearum. Nature, London 186, 405-406.

Hayward, A.C. (1964). Characteristics of Pseudomonas solanacearum. Journal of Applied Bacteriology 27, 265-277.

Hildebrand, D.C. & Riddle, B. (1971). Influence of environmental conditions on reactions induced by infiltration of bacteria into plant leaves. Hilgardia 41, 33-43.

Hildebrand, D.C. & Schroth, M.N. (1972). Identification of the fluorescent pseudomonads. In "Proceedings of the Third International Conference on Plant Pathogenic Bacteria", pp.281-287. (Ed. H.P. Maas Geesteranus.) Wageningen: The Netherlands: Pudoc.

Hugh, R. & Leifson, E. (1953). The taxonomic significance of fermentative versus oxidative metabolism of carbohydrates by various Gram-negative bacteria. Journal of Bacteriology 66, 24-26.

Kado, C.I. & Heskett, M.G. (1970). Selective media for isolation of Agrobacterium, Corynebacterium, Erwinia, Pseudomonas and Xanthomonas. Phytopathology 60, 969-976.

Kelman, A. (1954). The relationship of pathogenicity in Pseudomonas solanacearum to colony appearance on a tetrazolium medium. Phytopathology 44, 693-695.

Kerr, A. & Panagopoulos, C.G. (1977). Biotypes of Agrobacterium radiobacter var. tumefaciens and their biological control. Phytopathologische Zeitschrift 90, 172-179.

King, E.O., Ward, M.K. & Raney, D.E. (1954). Two simple media for the demonstration of pyocyanin and fluorescein. Journal of Laboratory and Clinical Medicine 44, 301-307.

Klement, Z. (1968). Pathogenicity factors in regard to relationships to phytopathogenic bacteria. Phytopathology 58, 1218-1221.

Kovacs, N. (1956). Identification of Pseudomonas pyocyanea by the oxidase reaction. Nature, London 178, 703.

Leifson, E. (1951). Staining, shape and arrangement of bacterial flagella. Journal of Bacteriology 62, 377-389.

Lippincott, J.A. & Lippincott, B.B. (1969). Tumour-initiating ability and nutrition in the genus Agrobacterium. Journal of General Microbiology 59, 57-75.

Logan, C. (1966). Simple method of differentiating Erwinia carotovora variety 'atroseptica' from Erwinia carotovora variety 'aroideae'. Nature, London, 212, 1584-1585.

Mitchell, R.E. (1976). Isolation and structure of a chlorosis-inducing toxin of Pseudomonas phaseolicola. Phytochemistry 15, 1941-1947.

Mitchell, R.E. (1979). Bean halo blight: comparison of Phaseolotoxin and N-phosphoglutamate. Physiological Plant Pathology 14, 119-128.

Moore, E.L., Kelman, A., Powell, N.T. & Bunn, B.H. (1963). Inoculation procedures for detecting resistance of tobacco to Pseudomonas solanacearum in the field. Tobacco Science 7, 17-20.

O'Neill, R. & Logan, C. (1975). A comparison of various selective media for their efficiency in the diagnosis and enumeration of soft-rot coliform bacteria. Journal of Applied Bacteriology 39, 139-146.

Palleroni, N.J. & Doudoroff, M. (1972). Some properties and taxonomic subdivision of the genus Pseudomonas. Annual Review of Phytopathology 10, 73-100.

Patel, P.N. & Walker, J.C. (1963). Changes in free amino acid and amide content of resistant and susceptible beans after infection with the halo blight organism. Phytopathology 53, 522-528.

Paulin, J.P. & Luisetti, J. (1978). Ice nucleation among phytopathogenic bacteria. In "Proceedings of the IVth International Conference on Plant Pathogenic Bacteria", pp. 725-731. (Ed. Station de Pathologie Vegetale et Phytobacteriologie). Angers, France: I.N.R.A.

Ryu, E. (1938). On the Gram-differentiation of bacteria by the simplest method. Journal of the Japanese Society for Veterinary Science 17, 31.

Ryu, E. (1940). A simple method of differentiation between Gram-positive and Gram-negative organisms without staining. Kitasato Archives of Experimental Medicine 17, 58-63.

Sands, D.C., Gleason, F.H. & Hildebrand, D.C. (1967). Cytochromes of Pseudomonas syringae. Journal of Bacteriology 94, 1785-1786.

Schaad, N.W. (Ed). (1980). "Laboratory Guide for Identification of Plant Pathogenic Bacteria". St. Paul, Minnesota: American Phytopathological Society. 72pp.

Schaad, N.W. & White, W.C. (1974). A selective medium for soil isolation and enumeration of Xanthomonas campestris. Phytopathology 64, 876-880.

Sierra, G. (1957). A simple method for the detection of lipolytic acitivity of micro-organisms and some observations on the influence of the contact between cells and fatty substrates. Antonie van Leeuwenhoek 23, 15-22.

Skerman, V.B.D. (1967). "A Guide to the Identification of the Genera of Bacteria" 2nd edition. Baltimore, Maryland: Williams & Wilkins.

Stanier, R.Y., Palleroni, N.J. & Doudoroff, M. (1966). The aerobic pseudomonads: a taxonomic study. Journal of General Microbiology 43, 159-271.

Starr, M.P., Stolp, H., Truper, H.G., Balows, A. & Schlegel, H.G. (Eds.) (1981). "The Prokaryotes" Vol. 1&2. Berlin: Springer-Verlag. 2284pp.

Staskawicz, B.J. & Panopoulos, N.J. (1979). A rapid and sensitive microbiological assay for phaseolotoxin. Phytopathology 69, 663-666.

Stewart, W.W. (1971). Isolation and proof of structure of wildfire toxin. Nature, London 229, 174-178.

Suslow, T.V., Schroth, M.N. & Isaka, M. (1982). Application of a rapid method for Gram differentiation of plant pathogenic and saprophytic bacteria without staining. Phytopathology 72, 917-918.

Thornley, M.J. (1960). The differentiation of Pseudomonas from other Gram-negative bacteria on the basis of arginine metabolism. Journal of Applied Bacteriology 23, 37-52.

Williamson, D.H. & Wilkinson, J.F. (1958). Isolation and estimation of the poly-β-hydroxybutyrate inclusions of Bacillus species. Journal of General Microbiology 19, 198-209.

Winstead, N.N. & Kelman, A. (1952). Inoculation techniques for evaluating resistance to Pseudomonas solanacearum. Phytopathology 42, 628-634.

Index of Bacteria

Agrobacterium, 16, 27–41, 301, 303,
  319–320, 370–371
  gysophilae, 81
  radiobacter, 303
  rhizogenes, 27–28, 303
  rubi, 27–28, 303
  tonellianum, 168
  tumefaciens, 27–28, 303
Aplanobacterium, 222
Aplanobacter populi, 222

Bacillus spp., 21, 24, 101
Bacterium typhi flavum, 81–82

Clostridium spp., 21, 24, 101
Corynebacterium, 16, 45–61, 301,
  303–304, 320–321
  betae, 303
  fascians, 49, 303
  flaccumfaciens, 303
    pv. *betae*, 303
    subsp. *betae*, 48, 303
    pv. *flaccumfaciens*, 303
    subsp. *flaccumfaciens*, 55–57,
      303, 320
    pv. *oortii*, 303
    subsp. *oortii*, 49, 303
    pv. *poinsettiae*, 303
    subsp. *poinsettiae*, 49, 303
  ilicis, 49, 303
  insidiosum, 14, 303
  iranicum, 49, 60, 303
  michiganense, 303
    pv. *insidiosum*, 304
    subsp. *insidiosum*, 51–54, 304,
      320
    pv. *iranicum*, 304
    pv. *michiganense*, 303
    subsp. *michiganense,* 46–51, 303,
      320–321

  pv. *nebraskense*, 304
  subsp. *nebraskense*, 48, 304
  pv. *rathayi*, 304
  pv. *sepedonicum*, 304
  subsp. *sepedonicum*, 48, 304
  subsp. *tessellarius*, 48, 304
  pv. *tritici*, 304
  nebraskense, 304
  oortii, 304
  poinsettiae, 304
  rathayi, 49, 60, 304
  sepedonicum, 304
  sp., on ryegrass, 57–61, 321
  tritici, 49, 60
Cytophaga spp., 20

Erwinia, 16, 67–83, 87–101, 302,
  304–305, 321–323
  amylovora, 9, 68, 70–77, 304, 368
    var. *nigrifluens*, 78
    var. *quercina*, 78
    var. *rubrifaciens*, 79
    var. *salicis*, 79–80
    var. *tracheiphila*, 80
  ananas
    pv. *ananas*, 70–74, 80–81, 304
    pv. *uredovora*, 67, 70–74, 81,
      304
  beticola, 304
  carnegieana, 304
  carotovora, 69, 305, 321
    pv. *atroseptica*, 21, 87–101, 305,
      321
    subsp. *atroseptica*, 305
    pv. *carotovora*, 21, 87–101, 305,
      321–322
  cassavae, 81
  chrysanthemi, 14, 21, 69, 87–101,
    305, 322
    pv. *chrysanthemi*, 305

Erwinia chrysanthemi—continued
  pv. *diathicola*, 305
  pv. *dieffenbachiae*, 305
  pv. *paradisiaca*, 305
  pv. *parthenii*, 305
  pv. *zeae*, 305
  citrimaculans, 81
  cypripedii, 89, 100, 305, 322
  herbicola, 6, 14, 20, 305
    var. *ananas*, 80
    pv. *herbicola*, 70–74, 81–82, 305
    pv. *milletiae*, 70–74, 82, 305
  lathyri, 81
  mallotivora, 70–74, 77–78, 305
  milletiae, 82
  nigrifluens, 70–74, 78, 305
  quercina, 305
    pv. *quercina*, 70–74, 78, 305
    pv. *rubrifaciens*, 70–74, 79, 305
  rhapontici, 14, 89, 100, 305
  rubrifaciens, 14, 305
  salicis, 70–74, 79–80, 305
  sp., on various hosts, 323
  stewartii, 70–74, 82–83, 305
  tracheiphila, 70–74, 80, 305, 323
  uredovora, 67, 81, 305
  vitivora, 81

Flavobacterium rhenanum, 81
Flavobacterium spp., 20, 101

Mycoplasma, 229–243, 334

Pseudomonas, 16, 101, 107–135,
  141–178, 302, 306–308, 323–330,
  362, 363–366
  acidivorans, 108
  aeruginosa, 144, 176, 323, 362
  agarici, 144, 171–172, 306, 323
  albilineans, 217
  alboprecipitans, 118
  aleuritidis, 330
  alliicola, 118
  amygdali, 108, 109–112, 306
  andropogonis, 110–117, 306, 314,
  323
  angulata, 161
  antirrhini, 165
  apii, 166
  aptata, 166
  asplenii, 176–177, 306
  aureofaciens, 144, 362
  avenae, 110–112, 118, 306
  betle, 177, 306

caricapapayae, 178, 306, 323
caryophylli, 110–112, 119, 306
cattleyae, 110–112, 119–120, 306,
  323
cepacia, 110–112, 120, 306, 323
chlororaphis, 144, 362
cichorii, 144, 171–172, 215, 306,
  324
cissicola, 110–112, 121, 306
coronafaciens, 152
  subsp. *atropurpurea*, 152
corrugata, 110–112, 121–122, 306
delphinii, 167
endiviae, 171
eriobotryae, 167
erodii, 330
flectens, 178, 306, 324
fluorescens, 174
  var. *antirrhinastrini,* 165
  biotypes, 144
fraxini, 168
gladioli, 110–112, 122–123, 306,
  324
  pv. *alliicola*, 122–123, 176, 306,
  324
  pv. *gladioli*, 122–123, 306, 324
glumae, 306
glycinea, 154
helianthi, 167
hibiscicola, 150–151, 306
lachrymans, 155
maculicola, 156
mallei, 108
maltophilia, 20, 108, 110–112, 123
mangiferaeindicae, 204
marginalis, 21, 144, 173–174, 215,
  324
  pv. *alfalfae*, 173, 306
  pv. *marginalis*, 173, 306, 324
  pv. *pastinacae*, 173, 306
marginata, 120
mesophilia, 108, 110–112, 123
mori, 167
morsprunorum subsp. *persicae*, 170
multivorans, 120
papaveris, 171
passiflorae, 168
paucimobilis, 108, 110–112, 124
phaseolicola, 159
pisi, 157
primulae, 168
pseudoalcaligenes subsp. *citrulli*,
  110–112, 124, 306
pseudomallei, 108

putida, 144, 173
rubrilineans, 110–112, 124–127, 306, 324
rubrisubalbicans, 110–112, 127–128, 306, 324
savastanoi, 168
  subsp. *fraxini*, 168
  var. *nerii*, 168
setariae, 128
solanacearum, 8, 110–112, 129–135, 306, 324–325, 373–374
spp., on various hosts, 175–176, 329–330
stewarti, 82
stizolobii, 113
striafaciens, 152
  var. *japonica*, 170, 307
stutzeri, 108
syringae, 141–147, 161, 306, 326
  pv. *aceris*, 170, 307
  pv. *antirrhini*, 165, 307, 326
  pv. *apii*, 165–166, 307, 326
  pv. *aptata*, 307, 326
  pv. *atrofaciens*, 151, 307, 326
  pv. *atropurpurea*, 307
  pv. *berberidis*, 170, 307
  pv. *cannabina*, 170, 307
  pv. *ciccaronei*, 170, 307
  pv. *coronafaciens*, 152–154, 307, 326, 364
  pv. *delphinii*, 167, 307, 326
  pv. *dysoxyli*, 170, 307
  pv. *eriobotryae*, 167, 307, 326
  pv. *garcae*, 170, 307
  pv. *glycinea*, 154–155, 159, 307, 326
  pv. *helianthi*, 167, 307, 326
  pv. *japonica*, 170, 307
  pv. *lachrymans*, 155–156, 307, 326
  pv. *lapsa*, 170, 307
  pv. *maculicola*, 156–157, 307, 326
  pv. *mellea*, 170, 307
  pv. *mori*, 159, 167, 307, 327
  pv. *morsprunorum*, 308, 327
  pv. *myricae*, 308
  pv. *panici*, 308
  pv. *papulans*, 170, 308
  pv. *passiflorae*, 168, 308, 327
  pv. *persicae*, 169–170, 308
  pv. *phaseolicola*, 159–161, 208, 308, 327, 364, 369
  pv. *pisi*, 157–158, 308, 327

  pv. *porri*, 170
  pv. *primulae*, 168, 308, 327
  pv. *proteae*, 327
  pv. *ribicola*, 170, 308
  pv. *savastanoi*, 168–169, 308, 327
  subsp. *savastanoi*, 168
  pv. *sesami*, 170, 308
  pv. *striafaciens*, 308, 327
  pv. *syringae*, 143–150, 158, 165, 306, 327–329, 361, 365, 368–369
  pv. *tabaci*, 154, 161–163, 308, 329, 364
  pv. *tagetis*, 163, 308, 329
  pv. *theae*, 170, 308
  pv. *tomato*, 164–165, 308, 329
  pv. *ulmi*, 170, 308
  pv. *viburni*, 170, 308
tabaci, 161
tagetis, 163
testosteroni, 108
tolaasii, 144, 174–175, 308, 329
tomato, 164
tonelliana, 168
viridiflava, 144, 158, 169, 174, 215, 308, 329, 362
viridilivida, 330
woodsii, 113, 117, 308
Pectobacterium, see Erwinia

Rickettsiaceae, 229–243, 334–335

Spiroplasma, 229–243
Streptomyces spp., 9, 25, 330

Xanthomonas, 16, 189–222, 302, 309–313, 330–333
  albilineans, 8–9, 189, 193, 217–220, 309, 330
  alfalfae, 192
  ampelina, 189, 193, 220, 309
  andrandensis, 211
  axonopodis, 189, 193, 220, 309
  begoniae, 195
  campestris, 189–193, 195, 309
    pv. *aberrans*, 309
    pv. *alangii*, 309
    pv. *alfalfae*, 192, 194, 309, 330
    pv. *amaranthicola*, 309
    pv. *amorphophalli*, 309
    pv. *aracearum*, 309
    pv. *arecue*, 309
    pv. *argemones*, 309
    pv. *armoraciae*, 309

Xanthomonas campestris—continued
    pv. *arracaciae*, 309
    pv. *azadirachtae*, 309
    pv. *badrii*, 309
    pv. *barbareae*, 309
    pv. *bauhiniae*, 309, 330
    pv. *begoniae*, 197, 309, 330
    pv. *betlicola*, 309
    pv. *biophyti*, 309
    pv. *blepharidis*, 309
    pv. *cajani*, 309
    pv. *campestris*, 195–196, 309,
        330–331
    pv. *cannabis*, 309
    pv. *carissae*, 309
    pv. *carotae*, 309, 331
    pv. *cassavae*, 205, 310
    pv. *cassiae*, 310
    pv. *celebensis*, 310
    pv. *cerealis*, 212, 310
    pv. *citri*, 196–198, 310
    pv. *clerondendri*, 310
    pv. *clitoriae*, 310
    pv. *convolvuli*, 310
    pv. *coracanae*, 310
    pv. *coriandri*, 310
    pv. *corylina*, 198, 310, 331
    pv. *cucurbitae*, 198–199, 310, 331
    pv. *cyamopsidis*, 310
    pv. *desmodii*, 310
    pv. *desmodiigangetici*, 310
    pv. *desmodiilaxifloris*, 310
    pv. *desmodiirotundifolii*, 310
    pv. *dieffenbachiae*, 310, 331
    pv. *durantae*, 310
    pv. *erythrinae*, 310
    pv. *esculenti*, 310
    pv. *eucalypti*, 310, 331
    pv. *euphorbiae*, 310
    pv. *fascicularis*, 310
    pv. *fici*, 310
    pv. *glycines*, 200, 310, 331
    pv. *graminis*, 311
    pv. *guizotiae*, 311
    pv. *gummisudans*, 311, 331
    pv. *hederae*, 311, 331
    pv. *heliotropii*, 311
    pv. *holcicola*, 200, 311, 331
    pv. *hordei*, 212, 311
    pv. *hyacinthi*, 311, 332
    pv. *incanae*, 201, 311, 332
    pv. *ionidii*, 311

    pv. *juglandis*, 201–202, 311, 332
    pv. *khayae*, 311
    pv. *lantanae*, 311
    pv. *laureliae*, 311
    pv. *lawsoniae*, 311
    pv. *leeana*, 311
    pv. *lespedezae*, 311
    pv. *maculifoliigardeniae*, 311
    pv. *malvacearum*, 202–204, 311,
        332
    pv. *mangiferaeindicae*, 204, 311,
        332
    pv. *manihotis*, 204–206, 311
    pv. *martyniicola*, 311
    pv. *melhusii*, 311
    pv. *merremiae*, 311
    pv. *musacearum*, 311
    pv. *nakataecorchori*, 311
    pv. *nigromaculans*, 311
    pv. *olitorii*, 311
    pv. *oryzae*, 207–208, 214, 312,
        332
    pv. *oryzicola*, 212–214, 312, 332
    pv. *papavericola*, 312, 332
    pv. *passiflorae*, 312, 332
    pv. *patelii*, 312
    pv. *pedalii*, 312
    pv. *pelargonii*, 312, 332
    pv. *phaseoli*, 208–209, 312, 332
    pv. *phleipratensis*, 212, 312
    pv. *phormiicola*, 312
    pv. *phyllanthi*, 312
    pv. *physalidicola*, 312
    pv. *physalidis*, 312
    pv. *pisi*, 312
    pv. *plantaginis*, 312, 332
    pv. *poinsettiicola*, 312, 333
    pv. *pruni*, 209–211, 312, 333,
        368
    pv. *punicae*, 312
    pv. *raphani*, 312
    pv. *ricini*, 211, 312
    pv. *rhynchosiae*, 312
    pv. *secalis*, 212, 312
    pv. *sesami*, 211–212, 312
    pv. *sesbaniae*, 312
    pv. *spermacoces*, 312
    pv. *tamarindi*, 312
    pv. *taraxaci*, 312
    pv. *tardicrescens*, 313
    pv. *theicola*, 313
    pv. *thirumalacharii*, 313

pv. *translucens*, 212–214, 313, 333
pv. *tribuli*, 313
pv. *trichodesmae*, 313
pv. *undulosa*, 212–214, 313, 333
pv. *uppalii*, 313
pv. *vasculorum*, 214, 313, 333
pv. *vernoniae*, 313
pv. *vesicatoria*, 215, 313, 333
pv. *vignaeradiatae*, 313
pv. *vignicola*, 313
pv. *vitians*, 217, 313, 333
pv. *viticola*, 313
pv. *vitiscarnosae*, 313
pv. *vitistrifoliae*, 313
pv. *vitiswoodrowii*, 313
pv. *zantedeschiae*, 313
pv. *zinniae*, 216, 313, 333
citri, 196
corylina, 198
cucurbitae, 198
fragariae, 8, 189, 194, 221, 313, 333
glycines, 200
holcicola, 200
incanae, 201
juglandis, 201

malvacearum, 202
manihotis, 204
nigromaculans f. sp. *zinniae*, 216
oryzae, 207
phaseoli, 208
phaseoli var. *fuscans*, 208
phaseoli var. *sojense*, 200, 310
populi, 8, 189, 222
pruni, 209
ricini, 211
ricinicola, 211
rubrilineans, 124
rubrisubalbicans, 127
sesami, 211
spp., on various hosts, 333
stewarti, 82
translucens, 212–213
   f. sp. *cerealis*, 212
   f. sp. *hordei*, 212
   f. sp. *phleipratensis*, 212
   f. sp. *secalis*, 212
   f. sp. *undulosa*, 212
trifolii, 81
uredovora, 81
vasculorum, 214
vesicatoria, 215
vitians, 215

Subject Index

Acacia spp., 324
Acer spp., 170
Acetoin production, 353–354
Acid production from carbohydrates, 351
Aconitum spp., 327
Actinidia chinensis, 169
Agaricus spp. (cultivated mushroom)
  blotch, 174–175, 329
  drippy gill, 171–172, 323
  mummy, 175–176, 329
Agrobacterium
  bioassay and pathogenicity tests, 33–34, 370–371
  biological control, 37–39
  crown gall, 28–31
  false oxidase reaction, 29, 361
  hairy root, 39–41
  hosts, 29–30, 40–41, 319–320
  isolation, 32–33
  nomenclature and classification, 27–28, 301
  plasmids, 27, 28, 34, 40
  selective media, 32–33
Agrobacterium phages for diagnosis, 267
Agrocin 84, 35, 39
Agropyron spp., 128, 212
Aleurites fordii, 330
Alfalfa, *see Medicago sativa*
Alkali production from organic acids, 352–353
Allium
  ampeloprasum var. *porrum* (leek), 170
  cepa var. *aggregatum* (shallot), 321
  cepa var. *cepa* (onion)
    internal browning, 176
    soft rots, 120, 122–123, 321, 323–324

Almond, *see Prunus* spp.
Alopecurus spp., 118
American holly, *see Ilex opaca*
Aminopeptidase activity, 343–344
Ananas comosus (pineapple), 80–81, 88
Anemone sp., 319
Anguina, 57–61
Annual ryegrass, *see Lolium rigidum*
Anthurium andraeanum, 331
Antirrhinum majus (snapdragon), 165, 326, 329, 333
Apium graveolens (celery)
  blight, 165–166, 171, 326
  soft rot, 88, 90, 169, 173, 321, 329
Apple, *see Malus* spp.
Arachis hypogaea (peanut)
  bunchy top, 320, 334
  wilt, 324
Aralia sp., 327
Areca catechu, 214
Arginine dihydrolase, 356
Asplenium nidus (bird's-nest fern), 176, 329
Austroagallia torrida, 236
Avena spp., (oat)
  basal glume rot, 326
  halo blight, 152–154, 326
  head gummosis, 58
  leaf blight, 118
  stripe blight, 153, 327
Axonopus spp. (imperial pasture grass), 220

Bacterial ooze, 4–5
Bacteriophage methodology
  detecting low levels of pathogens, 269
  epidemiological studies, 268–269
  establishing specificity, 260

Bacteriophage—*continued*
  growth conditions, 261
  high titre stock and routine
    dilutions, 264
  isolation, 262–263
  phage purification, 264
  plating methods, 261–262
  sensitivity tests, 265
  storage, 264
Banana, *see Musa* spp.
Barley, *see Hordeum* spp.
Bauhinia galpinii, 330
Bean, *see Phaseolus* spp.
Beet, *see Beta vulgaris* ssp. *vulgaris*
Begonia spp., 195, 321, 329, 330
Berberis spp., 170
Beta
  pendula (white birch), 319
  vulgaris ssp. *cicla* (silverbeet)
    blight, 166, 326, 329
    leaf spot, 324
    soft rot, 321
    wilt, 324
  vulgaris ssp. *vulgaris* (beetroot,
    sugar beet), 330
    blight, 166
    crown gall, 29, 319
    root rot, 88
    wilt and leaf spot, 48
Betel, *see Piper betle*
Betula sp., 319
Bidens pilosa, 325
Bird's-nest fern, *see Asplenium nidus*
Bletia striata, 321
Boerhavia erecta, 196
Bougainvillea spp., 115–117, 323
Brachiaria piligera, 217, 330
Brassica spp. (crucifer)
  black rot, 195–196, 330–331
  crown gall, 319
  firm rot, 171
  hairy root, 320
  peppery leaf spot, 156–157,
    326–327
  soft rot, 88, 90, 169, 321, 324, 329
  wilt, 315
Bromus spp., 128, 153, 212

Cactus witches'-broom, 231
Cajanus cajan, 160, 327
Calendula officinalis, 319
Camellia sinensis, 170

Canavalia spp., 325
Canna sp., 321
Cannabis sativa, 170
Capsella bursa-pastoris, 196, 331
Capsicum annuum (capsicum), 329
  canker, 46–51, 320
  soft rot, 321
  spot, 215, 327, 333
  wilt, 325
Carbon compounds, utilization and
    decomposition, 350–354
  acid production from carbohydrates,
    351
  alkali production from organic
    acids, 352–353
  carbon source utilization tests,
    351–352
  2-ketogluconate production, 354
  3-ketolactose production, 354
  levan formation, 353
  methyl red test, 353–354
  oxidative/fermentative, 350
  reducing compounds from sucrose,
    354
  Voges–Proskauer reaction, 353–354
Carica papaya, (papaya, pawpaw),
    178, 230, 323
Carnation, *see Dianthus caryophyllus*
Carthamus tinctorius, 327, 329
Cassava, *see Manihot* spp.
Cassia spectabilis, 325
Castanea sativa, 30
Catharanthus roseus, 325
Cattleya spp., 119, 323
Cayratia clematidea, 334
Cayratia japonica, 121
Ceiba pentandra, 203
Celery, *see Apium graveolens*
Celosia cristata, 327
Ceratonia siliqua, 170, 323
Chamelaucium uncinatum, 319
Cheiranthus spp., 321, 332
Chloris gayana, 248
Choko, *see Sechium edule*
Chrysanthemum spp., 30, 169, 171,
    319, 321, 329
Cicer arietinum, 116, 117, 323
Cichorium spp., 171
Cinnamomum camphora, 328
Citrillus spp., (cucurbit)
  spot, 124, 198–199, 331
  wilt, 80, 323

Citrus spp., (citrus)
  blast, 150, 328
  canker, 196–198
  crown gall, 319
  greening, 231
  stubborn, 230
  yellow shoot, 243
Clover, *see Trifolium* spp.
Cocksfoot, *see Dactylis glomerata*
Cocos nucifera, 242
Codiaeum variegatum var. *pictum,*
  319, 325
Coffea arabica, 116, 170
Conium maculatum, 319
Corn, *see Zea mays*
Corylus avellana (hazelnut), 198, 331
Corynebacterium, 45–61
  diagnosis, 46
  nomenclature, 301
Corynebacterium phages for diagnosis,
  268
Cotoneaster spp., 75
Cotton, *see Gossypium* spp.
Couch grass, *see Cynodon dactylon*
Cowpea, *see Vigna unguiculata* ssp.
  unguiculata
Crassocephalum crepidioides, 325
Crassula sp., 321
Crataegus spp., 75
Crocus spp., 123
Crotalaria linifolia, 325
Crown gall, 28–39
  see also Agrobacterium
Crucifer, *see Brassica* spp.
Crystal violet pectate (CVP) medium,
  92, 347–348
Cucumber, *see Cucumis* spp.
Cucumis spp., (cucurbit)
  angular leaf spot, 155–156, 326
  hairy root, 40
  spot, 124, 198–199, 331
  wilt, 80
Cucurbita spp. (cucurbit)
  angular leaf spot, 155–156, 326
  rot, 169, 321
  spot, 124, 198–199, 331
  wilt, 80, 325
Culture collections, 294–295
Cupressus sp., 319
Cuscuta spp., 231
Cyamopsis tetragonoloba, 328
Cyclamen persicum, 321

Cydonia oblonga, 319, 328
Cynara scolymus, 321
Cynodon dactylon (couch grass),
  247–249, 254
Cyperus spp., 208
Cypripedium spp., 89, 322

Dactylis glomerata (cocksfoot), 49,
  329
Dahlia spp., 319, 322, 325
Datura ferox, 333
Daucus carota, 319, 322, 331
Delphinium spp., 167, 169, 326, 328
Denitrification, 355–356
Diagnosis concepts, 1–3
Dianthus caryophyllus (carnation)
  leaf spot, 113–116, 323
  wilt, 119
Dictyosperma album, 214
Dieffenbachia spp., 329, 331
Digitalis purpurea, 230
Diospyros kaki, 319
Diseased plant, *see* Specimen
Dodonaea lanceolata, 325
Dysoxylum spectabile, 170

Echinochloa utilis, 213, 333
Egg yolk reaction, 359
ELISA assay for *Xanthomonas*
  albilineans, 218–220
Eriobotrya japonica (loquat), 167,
  319, 326
Erwinia
  "amylovora" group, 67–80
    isolation media, 70–71
  "carotovora" group, 68, 87–101
  "herbicola" group, 67–74, 80–83
  nomenclature, 302
  soft rots, 21, 87–101
Erwinia phages for diagnosis, 267–268
Erythromycin sensitivity, 363
Esterase activity, 359
Eucalyptus citriodora, 331
Eucalyptus maculata, 319
Eucharis spp., 322
Euchlaena mexicana, 83, 118
Euonymus spp., 30
Euphorbia pulcherrima (poinsettia),
  49, 333

Fasciation, 49
Ficus carica, 319

Fireblight, 68, 75–77
Flagella
  diagnostic value, 18
  stain, 339–340
Fluorescent pigments, 108, 362
Fortunella spp., 197
Fragaria × *ananassa* (strawberry), 221, 230, 333, 334
Fraxinus excelsior, 168
Freesia hybrida, 123, 324
Freeze drying, 277–283
Fuchsia sp., 319

Gaillardia spp., 325
Galphimia glauca, 325
Gasson's toxin bioassay, 363–365
Gelatin hydrolysis, 358
Genista monosperma, 319
Gerbera jamesonii, 171
Ginger, *see Zingiber officinale*
Gladiolus spp. (gladioli), 122–123, 319, 324, 331
Glucose yeast extract calcium carbonate agar (GYCA), 344–345
Glycine max (soybean)
  blight, 154–155, 326, 327
  pustule, 200, 331
  wildfire, 161–163, 329
  wilt, 56, 325
Gossypium spp. (cotton), 202–204, 332
Gram reaction, 15–18
  aminopeptidase activity, 343–344
  gram stain, 341–342
  KOH solubility, 342–343
Grape, *see Vitis vinifera*
Growth temperature maxima, 362–363
Gypsophila paniculata, 81

Hairy root, 39–41
  see also Agrobacterium
Hazelnut, *see Corylus avellana*
Hedera helix, 331
Helianthus
  annuus (sunflower), 167, 325, 326
  tuberosus, 322
Heliconia spp., 133
Hibiscus spp., 150–151
  cannabinus, 231, 335
  rosa-sinensis, 150, 328
  vitifolius, 203

Hordeum spp. (barley)
  basal glume rot, 151, 326
  black node, 170
  leaf blight, 118
  stripe, 128
  stripe blight, 153
  translucent leaf stripe, 212–214, 333
Hugh and Leifson's medium, 350
Humulus lupulus, 319
Hyacinthus orientalis, 322, 332
Hydrogen sulphide production, 357
Hypersensitivity in tobacco, 366–367

Ice nucleation activity, 361–362
Identification
  genus differentiation, 13–25
  preliminary diagnosis, 14
Ilex opaca (American holly), 49
Impatiens spp., 333
Imperata cylindrica var. *major,* 217, 330
Imperial pasture grass, *see Axonopus* spp.
Incubation of cultures, 5–6, 338
Indole production, 358
Inoculation, *see* Plant inoculations
Ipomoea batatas (sweet potato), 25, 230
Iridaceae, 123
Iris sp., 322, 324, 334
Isolation of bacteria
  precautions, 13–14
  procedures, 5–7
Ixia sp., 322

Jacaranda mimosifolia, 319
Jatropha curcas, 203
Juglans regia (walnut)
  bark canker, 78
  blight, 201, 332
  crown gall, 30, 319
  phloem canker, 79
Juglans spp., 201

Kenaf crinkle leaf, 231, 335
2-Ketogluconate production, 354
3-Ketolactose production, 354
King's medium B agar (KBA), 344
KOH solubility test, 342–343
Kovacs oxidase test, 360–361

Lablab niger, 208

Lactuca sativa (lettuce)
  crown gall, 319
  dry leaf spot, 215, 333
  green flower, 334
  leaf spot, 329, 330
  marginal leaf spot, 173–174, 324
  soft rot, 322
  varnish spot, 171
  yellows, 231
Lecithinase activity, 359
Leek, *see Allium ampeloprasum* var.
    porrum
Leersia oryzoides, 208
Legume little leaf, 230, 334
Leptochloa spp., 208
Lethal yellows, 242
Lettuce, *see Lactuca sativa*
Levan formation, 353
Ligustrum ovalifolium, 328
Lilium spp., 322
Lipid stain, 108, 340–341
Liquidambar styraciflua, 328
Lolium spp., 58
  perenne, 123
  rigidum (annual ryegrass), 57–61,
    321
LOPAT, 141
Loquat, *see Eriobotrya japonica*
Lucerne, *see Medicago sativa*
Lupinus angustifolius, 169
Lycaste sp., 322
Lychnis coronaria, 334
Lycopersicon esculentum (tomato)
  big bud, 230, 334
  canker, 46–51, 321
  crown gall, 319
  internal stem rot, 169, 323
  pith necrosis, 121
  soft rot, 322, 324
  speck, 164–165, 329
  spot, 215, 333
  stem bacteriosis, 171
  wilt, 129–134, 325
Lycopersicon peruvianum, 333
Lyophilization, 277

Macroptilium
  atropurpureum, 160, 178, 324, 327,
    328
  lathyroides, 208, 332
Magnolia spp., 328
Maize, *see Zea mays*

Mallotus japonicus, 77–78
Malonate utilization, 352–353
Malus spp., (apple), 328
  blister spot, 170
  crown gall, 30, 319
  fireblight, 75–77
  hairy root, 40, 320
Mangifera indica (mango), 204, 332
Mango, *see Mangifera indica*
Manihot spp. (cassava), 204–206
Marigold, *see Tagetes* spp.
Matthiola incana (stock), 196, 201,
    322, 328, 332
Media
  general, growth and maintenance,
    345–346
  isolation, non-selective, 8, 253,
    344–345
  precautions and uses, 7–10, 92, 347
  selective, 7–10, 32–33, 70–71, 92–93,
    347–349
Medicago sativa (lucerne)
  leaf spot, 192–194, 328, 330
  root discolouration, 173
  tomato pith necrosis pathogen, 121
  wilt, 51–54, 320
  witch's broom, 230, 334
Medicago spp., 52
Melilotus alba, 52
Mentha spicata, 330
Methyl red, 353–354
Milk agar, 358
Milk proteolysis, 358–359
Milletia japonica, 82
MLO, *see Mycoplasma*
Moko disease, 129–131
Mollicutes, *see Mycoplasma*
Morphological features of bacteria,
    338–341
Morus spp. (mulberry), 167
  nigra, 319, 327
Motility, 18–20, 339
Mucuna deeringiana, 113–114, 323
Mulberry, *see Morus* spp.
Musa spp. (banana), 334
  soft rot, 322
  wilt, 129–134
Mushroom. *see Agaricus* spp.
Mycoplasma, 229–243
  control, 242–243
  culture, 240–242
  diagnostic characteristics, 232–242
  taxonomy, 231–232

Myoporum sp., 319

Narcissus sp., 322
Neonotonia spp., 327
Nerium oleander, 168, 327, 328
Nicotiana tabacum (tobacco)
   barn rot, 88, 91
   hypersensitivity, 366–367
   leaf spot, 170, 323
   soft rot, 322
   wildfire and blackfire, 161–163, 329
   wilt, 129–131, 325
Nicotiana spp., 162
Nitrate reduction, 355–356
Nutrient agar (NA), 345

Oak, *see Quercus* spp.
Oat, *see Avena* spp.
Olea europea (olive), 168
Oleraceae, 168
Olive, *see Olea europea*
Onion, *see Allium cepa* var. *cepa*
Opines
   catabolis, 34–35
   identification, 35–38
Orchid brown spot, 119–120
Oryza spp. (rice)
   blight, 207–208
   foot rot, 88
   streak, 207, 212–214, 332
   stripe, 128
Oxidase test, 360–361
Oxidative/fermentative metabolism, 350

Palm
   lethal blight, 176
   lethal yellows, 242
Panicum miliaceum, 128, 328
Papaver spp., 169, 171, 324, 328, 332
Papaya, *see Carica papaya*
Paphiopedilum sp., 322
Parsnip, *see Pastinaca sativa*
Parthenocissus tricuspidata, 121
Paspalum spp., 217, 330
Passiflora edulis (passionfruit), 168, 169, 327, 332
Passionfruit, *see Passiflora edulis*
Pastinaca sativa (parsnip), 173, 319, 322
Pathogenicity tests, *see* Plant inoculations

Pathovar, 141, 300
Pawpaw, *see Carica papaya*
Pea, *see Pisum sativum*
Peach, *see Prunus* spp.
Peanut, *see Arachis hypogaea*
Pear, *see Pyrus communis*
Pectate media, 92–93, 347–349
Pectolytic activity, *see* Soft rot
Pelargonium spp., 330, 332
Pennisetum spp., 248–249, 328
Peperomia sp., 334
Peptone yeast extract agar (PYEA), 341
Persea americana, 323, 328, 330
Phalaenopsis spp., 119–120, 322, 323
Phalaris spp., 58
Phaseolotoxin, 364
Phaseolus spp. (bean), 116, 118
   brown spot, 149–150, 328
   common blight, 208–209, 332
   crown gall, 319
   halo blight, 159–161, 327
   pod twist, 178, 324
   rot, 169
   wilt, 55–57, 320, 325
PHB, *see* Poly-β-hydroxybutrate
Phenylalanine deaminase, 357
Philodendron selloum, 322, 324
Phleum pratense, 212
Phosphatase activity, 363
Phospholipase activity, 359
Photinia sp., 328
Phyllody, 230, 233, 234
Physalis spp., 215, 333
Pigments, bacterial
   diagnostic, 14–15, 362
   screening yellow colonies, 20, 22–23
Pineapple, *see Ananas comosus*
Piper betle (betel), 177
Pisum sativum (pea)
   blight, 157–158, 169, 327, 328
   soft rot, 322
Plantago lanceolata, 332
Plant inoculations, 10, 366–374
   bean pod inoculations, 369
   carrot disc test for *Agrobacterium* spp., 370–371
   detached fruit inoculations, 368–369
   foliage and stem inoculations, 51, 372–373
   hypersensitivity in tobacco, 366–367

inoculum preparation and
conditions, 371
pathogenicity test, special
precautions, 371
vascular pathogens, 53, 373–374
Plasmids (R, and T,), 27, 28, 34, 40
Poinsettia, *see Euphorbia pulcherrima*
Poly-β-hydroxybutyrate (polymer
granules), 108, 340–341
Pomoideae, 75
Poncirus spp., 197
Pongamia pinnata, 325
Poplar, *see Populus* spp.
Populus spp. (poplar), 189, 222, 328
Post harvest rots, 173
see also Soft rot
Potato, *see Solanum tuberosum*
Preservation of microorganisms,
275–295
cryogenic storage, 284–287
in distilled water, 290
freeze drying, 277–283
in gelatin discs, 292–293
liquid drying, 283–284
under mineral oil, 287–288
periodic subculture, 277
over phosphorus pentoxide,
293–294
on porcelian beads, 291–292
short term storage, 276–277
in sterile soil, 289
Primula spp., 168, 327, 334
Protea cynariodes, 327
Prunus spp. (stonefruit)
canker, 143–148, 328, 329
crown gall, 29, 320
hyperplastic canker (almond), 109
spot, 209–211, 333
x-disease (peach), 243
Pseudomonas
differentiation, 16, 24, 108,
110–112, 142, 144–145
fluorescent group, 141–178
nomenclature, 141, 302
non-fluorescent group, 107–135
pigments, 362
toxins, 163, 363–366
Pseudomonas phages for diagnosis,
265–266
Puccinia spp., 81
Pueraria lobata, 327
Pultenaea villosa, 325

Pumpkin, *see Cucurbita* spp.
Purple milk broth, 359
Pyracantha spp., 75
Pyrus communis (pear)
blight, 148, 328
crown gall, 320
decline, 242
fireblight, 75–77

Quercus spp. (oak), 78

Raphanus
raphanistrum, 331
sativus, 157, 196, 331
Rapistrum rugosum, 325, 331
Ratoon stunt bacterium, *see* RSD
bacterium
Reducing compounds from sucrose,
354
Refractile bodies, 108
Rheum rhabarbarum, 89, 320, 322
Rhizoctonia, 89
Ribes spp., 170, 320
Rice, *see Oryza* spp.
Ricinus communis, 211
Rickettsia-like bacteria (RLO),
229–243
control, 242–243
culture, 240–242
diagnostic characteristics, 232–242
taxonomy, 231–232
Rosa spp., 29, 40, 320, 328
Rosaceae, 75
Roystonea regia, 214
RSD bacterium, 247–255
characteristics, 252–254
control, 254–255
diagnosis, 250–251
distribution, 250, 334
host range, 248–249
isolation medium, 251–252
symptoms, 248
Rubus spp., 30, 75, 320
Rye, *see Secale cereale*
Ryegrass toxicity, 57–61

Saccharum interspecific hydrids
(sugarcane), 81
gumming, 214, 333
leaf scald, 217–220, 330
mottle, 88, 91, 322
mottled stripe, 127–128, 324

Saccharum—continued
  red stripe and top rot, 124–127, 324
  ratoon stunt, 247–255, 334
    see also RSD bacterium
Salix spp. (willow), 79–80
Salpiglossis sinuata, 325
Salt tolerance, 362
Salvia reflexa, 325
Sansevieria trifasciata, 322
Saritaea magnifica, 325
Schizanthus sp., 325
Scindopus sp., 171
Sclerotinia, 89
Secale cereale (rye), 118, 212, 333
Sechium edule (choko), 230
Selective media, see Media, selective
Senecio × *hybridus*, 325
Sesamum indicum, 170, 211, 330
Setaria spp., 118
  italica, 118, 128
Shallot, *see Allium cepa* var.
    aggregatum
Sida spp., 325
Snapdragon, *see Antirrhinum majus*
Soft rot
  differentiation of genera, 21
  types of, 21, 87–101, 173–174
Solanum
  melongena, 322, 325
  nigrum, 50, 321
  seaforthianum, 325
Solanum tuberosum (potato)
  black-leg, 95, 98–99, 321
  brown rot, 129–135
  common scab, 25, 330
  hairy root, 320
  pink eye, 173
  purple top wilt, 334
  ring rot, 54–55
  soft rot, 87, 89–101, 321–324
  wilt, 129–135, 324
Sorbus acuparia, 320
Sorghum spp., (sorghum), 248,
    328–329
  red spot, 118
  streak, 200, 331
  stripe, 113–115, 117, 127–128, 323
Soybean, *see Glycine max*
Soytone cornmeal (SC) medium, 253
Specimen, collection and examination,
    3–5
Spinacia oleracea, 322

Spiraea spp., 40
Spiroplasma, 230, 242
  control, 242
  culture, 240–242
  diagnostic characteristics, 232–239
  taxonomy, 231–232
Starch hydrolysis, 359
Stewart's disease, 82–83
Stock, *see Matthiola incana*
Stonefruit, *see Prunus* spp.
Storage of cultures, *see* Preservation
    of microorganisms
Strawberry, *see Fragaria* × *ananassa*
Strelitzia reginae, 325
Stylosanthes spp., 325
Sucrose peptone agar (SPA), 344
Sudan Black B stain, 108, 340–341
Sugar beet, *see Beta vulgaris* ssp.
    vulgaris
Sugarcane, *see Saccharum*
    interspecific hybrids
Sunflower, *see Helianthus annuus*
Sweet corn, *see Zea mays*
Sweet potato, *see Ipomoea batatas*
Symphytum × *uplandicum*, 325
Syringa sp., 329
Syringomycin bioassay, 365–366

Tabtoxin, 364
Tagetes spp. (marigold), 163, 325, 329
Tagetitoxin, 163
Tanacetum cinerariifolium, 330
Teline monosperma, 320
Terete vanda orchid, *see Vanda* spp.
Tetrazolium chloride agar (TZCA),
    346
Thurberia thespesioides, 203
Thysanolaena maxima, 214
Tobacco, *see Nicotiana tabacum*
Tomato, *see Lycopersicon esculentum*
Toxin bioassays
  Escherichia coli indicator, 363–365
  Gasson's, 363–365
  syringomycin, 365–366
Trichosanthes anguina, 325
Trifolium spp. (clover)
  leaf spot, 113–117, 171, 323
  phyllody, 334
  rugose leaf curl, 231, 236, 334
Triplaris filipensis, 116
Tripsacum dactyloides, 83

Triticum spp. (wheat)
  basal glume rot, 151
  black node, 170
  gummosis, 49, 321
  leaf blight, 118
  mosaic, 48
  rust parasitism, 81
  translucent leaf stripe, 212–214, 333
  yellow slime, 49, 321
Tropaeolum majus, 325
Tryptone glucose beef extract agar
    (TGEA), 346
Tulip, *see Tulipa* spp.
Tulipa spp. (tulip), 49, 116, 322
Tween 80 hydrolysis, 359–360

Ulmus spp., 170
Urease production, 357

Vallota speciosa, 322
Vanda spp. (terete vanda orchid),
    116–117, 322
Velvet bean, *see Mucuna deeringiana*
Viburnum spp., 170
Vicia
  benghalensis, 157, 323
  faba var. *major*, 81, 329
  sativa ssp. *nigra*, 323
  sativa ssp. *sativa*, 116, 117, 323
  villosa ssp. *dasycarpa*, 323
Vigna
  mungo, 208, 332
  radiata, 56, 208, 327, 332
  unguiculata ssp. *sesquipedalis*, 322
  unguiculata ssp. *unguiculata*
    (cowpea), 169, 329
Vitis vinifera (grape)
  blight, 220
  crown gall, 30, 320
  leaf spot, 121
  panicle rot, 169, 329

Pierce's disease, 231–233, 236
Voges–Proskauer reaction, 353–354

Walnut, *see Juglans regia*
Watermelon, *see Citrillus* spp.
Wetwood of timber, 24
Wheat, *see Triticum* spp.
Willow, *see Salix* spp.
Wisteria spp., 82

Xanthomonas, 189–222
  isolation, 190
  differentiation, 190–192
  nomenclature, 302
  pathogenicity, 192
Xanthomonas phages for diagnosis,
    266–267

Yeast extract dextrose agar (YDCA),
    346
Yeast salts (YS) medium, 346
Yellow-pigmented bacteria, initial
    screening, 20, 22–23

Zantedeschia aethiopica, 322, 323
Zea mays (corn, maize, sweet corn),
    214, 217, 248, 329
  chocolate spot, 153
  corn stunt, 231
  halo blight, 152–154
  leaf blight, 118
  stalk rot, 88, 118, 170, 322, 323
  streak, 200, 331
  stripe and leaf spot, 113–117
  stripe blight, 153
  wilt, 48, 82–83
Zingiber officinale (ginger), 129, 134,
    325
Zinnia elegans, 216, 325, 333
Zizania latifolia, 208